T0186134

Lecture Notes in Computer Science   13266

More information about this series at https://link.springer.com/bookseries/558

Pascal Caron · Ludovic Mignot (Eds.)

Implementation and Application of Automata

26th International Conference, CIAA 2022
Rouen, France, June 28 – July 1, 2022
Proceedings

 Springer

Editors
Pascal Caron
UFR. des Sciences et Techniques
University of Rouen
Saint-Étienne du Rouvray Cedex, France

Ludovic Mignot
UFR. des Sciences et Techniques
University of Rouen
Saint-Étienne du Rouvray Cedex, France

ISSN 0302-9743   ISSN 1611-3349 (electronic)
Lecture Notes in Computer Science
ISBN 978-3-031-07468-4   ISBN 978-3-031-07469-1 (eBook)
https://doi.org/10.1007/978-3-031-07469-1

This Springer imprint is published by the registered company Springer Nature Switzerland AG
The registered company address is: Gewerbestrasse 11, 6330 Cham, Switzerland

Preface

The 26th International Conference on Implementation and Application of Automata (CIAA 2022) was organized by the Groupe de Recherche Rouennais en Informatique Fondamentale (GR^{2}IF) and the Laboratoire d'Informatique, de Traitement de l'Information et des Systèmes (LITIS) of the Université de Rouen Normandie. The conference took place during June 28 to July 1, 2022.

The CIAA conference series brings together researchers in the field of automata theory and implementation and allows the dissemination of results in these research areas.

This volume of Lecture Notes in Computer Science contains the scientific papers presented at CIAA 2022. The volume also includes extended abstracts of the three invited talks presented by Markus Holzer, Nelma Moreira and Yo-Sub Han, we wish to warmly thank.

The 16 regular papers were selected from 26 submissions covering various fields in the application, implementation, and theory of automata and related structures. Each paper was reviewed by three Program Committee members with the assistance of external referees and thoroughly discussed by the Program Committee.

Papers were submitted by authors from the following countries: Canada, France, Germany, Israel, Japan, Poland, Russia, Slovakia, South Africa, South Korea, Sweden, Taiwan, Turkey, United Kingdom, United States of America.

We wish to thank everybody who contributed to the success of this conference: the authors for submitting their carefully prepared manuscripts, the Program Committee members and external referees for their valuable judgment of the submitted manuscripts, and the invited speakers for their excellent presentations of topics related to the theme of the conference. Last but not least, we would like to express our sincere thanks to the local organizers Solène Guérin, Jean-Gabriel Luque, Florent Nicart and Bruno Patrou.

April 2022

Pascal Caron
Ludovic Mignot

Organization

Organization Committee

Pascal Caron (Chair)   Université de Rouen Normandie, France
Jean-Gabriel Luque   Université de Rouen Normandie, France
Ludovic Mignot   Université de Rouen Normandie, France
Florent Nicart   Université de Rouen Normandie, France
Bruno Patrou   Université de Rouen Normandie, France

Program Committee Chairs

Pascal Caron   Université de Rouen Normandie, France
Ludovic Mignot   Université de Rouen Normandie, France

Steering Committee

Markus Holzer (Chair)   Justus Liebig University Giessen, Germany
Oscar Ibarra   University of California, USA
Sylvain Lombardy   Institut Polytechnique de Bordeaux, France
Nelma Moreira   University of Porto, Portugal
Kai T. Salomaa (Vice-chair)   Queen's University, Canada
Hsu-Chun Yen   National Taiwan University, Taiwan

Program Committee

Marie-Pierre Béal   Université Paris-Est Marne-la-Vallée, France
Francine Blanchet-Sadri   University of North Carolina, USA
Cezar Câmpeanu   University of Prince Edward Island, Canada
Pascal Caron   Université de Rouen Normandie, France
Jan Daciuk   Gdańsk University of Technology, Poland
Mike Domaratzki   University of Manitoba, Canada
Emmanuel Filiot   Université Libre de Bruxelles, Belgium
Yo-Sub Han   Yonsei University, South-Korea
Jan Holub   Czech Technical University in Prague, Czech Republic
Markus Holzer   University of Giessen, Germany
Jarkko Kari   University of Turku, Finland
Galina Jiraskova   Slovak Academy of Sciences, Slovakia

Markus Lohrey	University of Siegen, Germany
Sylvain Lombardy	Institut Polytechnique de Bordeaux, France
Andreas Maletti	University of Leipzig, Germany
Sebastian Maneth	University of Bremen, Germany
Ludovic Mignot	Université de Rouen Normandie, France
Dirk Nowotka	University of Kiel, Germany
Alexander Okhotin	St. Petersburg State University, Russia
Giovanni Pighizzini	University of Milan, Italy
Daniel Reidenbach	Loughborough University, UK
Rogério Reis	University of Porto, Portugal
Michel Rigo	University of Liege, Belgium
Kai Salomaa	Queen's University, Canada
Shinnosuke Seki	University of Electro-Communications, Japan
Jeffrey Shallit	University of Waterloo, Canada
Bruce Watson	Stellenbosch University, South Africa
Hsu-Chun Yen	National Taiwan University, Taiwan

Additional Reviewers

Fan Feng
Pamela Fleischmann
Hermann Gruber
Sang-Ki Ko
Florent Koechlin
Dominik Köppl
Martin Kutrib
Thierry Lecroq
Jean-Gabriel Luque
Nelma Moreira
Štěpán Plachý

Luca Prigioniero
Gabriele Puppis
Narad Rampersad
Andrew Ryzhikov
Lena Katharina Schiffer
Hiroyuki Seki
Kevin Stier
Marek Szykuła
Matthias Wendlandt
Sarah Winter

Contents

Invited Lectures

On 25 Years of CIAA Through the Lens of Data Science

Hermann Gruber[1], Markus Holzer[2(✉)], and Christian Rauch[2]

[1] Knowledgepark GmbH, Leonrodstr. 68, 80636 München, Germany
hermann.gruber@kpark.de
[2] Institut für Informatik, Universität Giessen, Arndtstr. 2, 35392 Giessen, Germany
{holzer,christian.rauch}@informatik.uni-giessen.de

Abstract. We investigate the structure of the co-authorship graph for the *Conference on Implementation and Application of Automata* (CIAA) with techniques from network sciences. This allows us to answer a broad variety of questions on collaboration patterns. Our findings are in line with (statistical) properties of other co-authorship networks from biology, physics and mathematics as conducted earlier by pioneers of network sciences.

1 Introduction

Shortly after the invitation of the second author to give an invited talk at the 26th Conference on Implementation and Application of Automata (CIAA), the idea grew to study collaboration patterns of the co-authorship network of this conference. As said in [15] "the structure of such networks turns out to reveal many interesting features of academic communities." Co-authorship networks and collaboration patterns thereof had been subject to scientific studies long before data science became a prominent subfield of artificial intelligence research, see, e.g., [4,16]. Thus, besides the above mentioned interesting features of academic communities with such a study we familiarize ourselves with the techniques in data science and in particular in network sciences. Moreover, since the 25th jubilee of the CIAA conference passed due to the COVID-19 pandemic restrictions without further celebration, this paper may serve as a late birthday present to the whole community that is interested in implementation and application of automata.

Our study is based on collection and analysis of data gathered from open sources. The two main open sources we rely on are DBLP[1] (database systems and logic programming), which is the on-line reference for bibliographic information on major computer science publications, LNCS[2] (Lecture Notes in Computer Science), the prestigious conference proceedings series published by Springer, and the general website https://www.informatik.uni-giessen.de/ciaa/ of the conference. The raw data from these sources were obtained during January to April

---

[1] https://dblp.org.
[2] https://www.springer.com/gp/computer-science/lncs.

© Springer Nature Switzerland AG 2022
P. Caron and L. Mignot (Eds.): CIAA 2022, LNCS 13266, pp. 3–18, 2022.
https://doi.org/10.1007/978-3-031-07469-1_1

2022 and were pre- and post-processed with the help of the widely used Python[3] distribution "Anaconda,"[4] which includes a range of useful packages for scientific coding, such as `matplotlib`, `numpy`, `pandas`, etc.

Before we turn to the analysis of the co-authorship network we briefly give some history on the conference, which will obviously lack completeness. The CIAA conference actually started in 1996 as the "*Workshop on Implementation of Automata*" (WIA) in London, Ontario, Canada. The need for such a workshop was explained in [17] as follows:

"Whence WIA? Why the need for a workshop of this type? As there are already many (perhaps too many) computer science conferences and workshops, any new meeting faces a rather stiff need to justify its existence. WIA came about primarily because there is no other good forum for systems that support symbolic computation with automata. [...] In addition [...] there is a vast amount of applied work, most of it undocumented, using automata for practic applications such as protocol analysis, IC design and testing, telephony, and other situations where automata software is useful.

This is good and interesting work, and it needs a place to be exhibited and discussed. Existing journals and conferences, however, seem to have a difficult time in finding a place for what we do. Theoretical arenas sometimes treat this work as "mere" implementation, a simple working-out of the algorithms, theorems, and proofs that are the "real" contribution to the field. Systems-oriented venues, on the other hand, sometimes find this kind of work suspect because it appears to be aimed at theoreticians. It is tricky navigating between the Scylla of the too-abstract and the Charybdis of the too-practical."

At that time the general organization and orientation of WIA was governed by a Steering Committee (SC) composed of (in alphabetical order) Stuart Margolis, Denis Maurel, Derick Wood, and Sheng Yu. Sadly, both Derick Wood and Sheng Yu, our late lamented colleagues, passed away too early on October 4, 2010 and January 23, 2012, respectively. The first four workshops were held at London, Ontario, Canada (1996 and 1997), Rouen, France (1998), and Potsdam, Germany (1999). During the general WIA meeting in 1999 it was decided to rename the meeting to "*International Conference on Implementation and Application of Automata*" (CIAA) and to hold its first CIAA in London, Ontario, Canada, in the summer of 2000. There it was part of a tri-event conference together with the workshop on "*Descriptional Complexity of Automata, Grammars and Related Structures*" (DCAGRS) and a special day devoted to the 50th anniversary of automata theory, which was called "*A Half Century of Automata Theory.*" It is worth mentioning that CIAA is rarely co-located with other conferences. An exception was the Conference on "*Finite-State Methods and Natural Language Processing*" (FSMNLP) in 2011 in Rouen, France.

---

[3] https://www.python.org.
[4] https://www.anaconda.com.

Already after around half a decade the conference became mature and started its way all around the globe: Pretoria, South Africa (2001), Tours, France (2002), Santa Barbara, California, USA (2003), Kingston, Ontario, Canada (2004), Nice, France (2005), Taipei, Taiwan (2006), Prague, Czech Republic (2007), San Francisco, California, USA (2008), Sydney, Australia (2009), Winnipeg, Manitoba, Canada (2010), Blois, France (2011), Porto, Portugal (2012), Halifax, Nova Scotia (2013), Giessen, Germany (2014), Umeå, Sweden (2015), Seoul, South Korea (2016), Marne-la-Vallée, France (2017), Charlottetown, Prince-Edward-Island (2018), Košice, Slovakia (2019), and Bremen, Germany (2021), which was held as a virtual event due to the COVID-19 pandemic. The 2020 conference, planned at Loughborough, United Kingdom, was canceled and thus was also a victim of the pandemic crisis. This year, CIAA takes place again in Rouen, France, where it was last held 22 years ago. A distribution of the locations w.r.t. the continents is depicted in Fig. 1. There is a slight overhang on the number of locations for Europe (14) followed by North America (9). Then there is a large drop for Asia (2), Africa (1), and Australia/Oceania (1). South America and Antarctica have never been visited by CIAA, and for Antarctica, we personally think that there is no chance to organize it there. The current SC is encouraged to further globalize the conference and to fill the white or say gray spots on the continents' landscape.

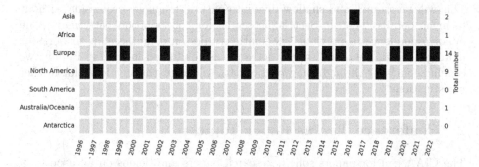

Fig. 1. CIAA destinations in relation to their continent locations.

Since the first WIA event in 1996, the proceedings appeared in the Springer LNCS series. This was not the case for the sister conferences "*Developments in Language Theory*" (DLT) and "*Descriptional Complexity of Formal Systems*" (DCFS), formerly known as "*Descriptional Complexity of Automata, Grammars and Related Structures*" (DCAGRS), that started slightly earlier than WIA. The authors of the best paper of the actual conference are awarded a monetary grant since 2004 (except for 2021). Until 2008, this was sponsored by the University of California at Santa Barbara and later by the conference itself. By acclamation the best paper award was subtitled "*Sheng Yu Award*" at the general CIAA meeting in 2012 and first awarded with this naming in 2014. So far, only five authors had the privilege of receiving the "Best Paper Award" twice. These are (in alphabetical order) Janusz Brzozowski (2017 and 2018), Markus Holzer (2009 and 2015), Lisa Kaati (2006 and 2008), Lila Kari (2004 and 2018), and Mikhail V. Volkov (2007 and 2012). Since the renaming to CIAA in 2000, extended versions of selected papers from the proceedings of the conference series are usually retained for publication in special issues of either *International Journal of Foundations of Computer Science* (IJFCS) or *Theoretical Computer Science* (TCS), alternating each year.

The legacy of CIAA continues—the event is in its 26th edition and the expectations raised in [17] have been widely fulfilled:

> "Providing a forum for this work is a useful goal, and a sufficient one for WIA [CIAA]. But I think WIA [CIAA] is part of something more fundamental, and a process I want to encourage: the re-appraisal of the value of programming in computer science."

Nowadays the general organization and orientation of CIAA is directed by the SC members (in alphabetical order) Markus Holzer, Oscar H. Ibarra, Sylvain Lombardy, Nelma Moreira, Kai Salomaa, and Hsu-Chun Yen. Enough of the historical overview. Now let us concentrate on what can be deduced from the data that we extracted from the web.

The paper is organized as follows: In Sect. 2 we first briefly take a look on the topics of CIAA as communicated by the call for papers and the published papers. This will be a quick and shallow dive into natural language processing without to much details. Then in Sect. 3 the search for collaboration patterns is done in correspondence to previous systematic studies on co-authorship networks or more general on social real-world networks as conducted in [13,14]. Finally, we conclude our tour through the world of data-science with some ideas for further investigations.

2   Conference *Versus* Paper Topics

The CIAA call for papers solicits research papers and demos on all aspects of implementation and application of automata and related structures, including theoretical aspects, as but not limited to:

- bioinformatics,
- complexity of automata operations,
- compilers,
- computer-aided verification,
- concurrency,
- data structure design for automata,
- data and image compression,
- design and architecture of automata software,
- digital libraries,
- DNA/molecular/membrane computing,
- document engineering,
- editors, environments,
- experimental studies and practical experiences,
- industrial applications,
- natural language processing,
- networking,
- new algorithms for manipulating automata,

- object-oriented modeling,
- pattern-matching,
- quantum computing,
- speech and speaker recognition,
- structured and semi-structured documents,
- symbolic manipulation environments for automata,

- teaching,
- text processing,
- techniques for graphical display of automata,
- very large-scale integration (VLSI) research,
- viruses, related phenomena, and
- world-wide web (WWW).

How do the topics in the call for papers compare to the topics of the actual papers? To answer this question, we take a look at word clouds.

Word clouds have become a staple of data-visualization for analyzing texts. Usually words (unigrams) and bigrams, and the importance of each are shown with fontsize and/or color. Since the list of CIAA topics is condensed and limited one may consider all CIAA publications as a natural resource for natural language processing techniques. The decision to use only DBLP as data source considerably limits the analysis of the CIAA texts, because DBLP does not offer all relevant features of publications. For instance, the access to abstracts is not possible *via* DBLP. For such, information the relevant Springer websites have to be contacted. The only meaningful textual data DBLP provides is the title of a publication. With these titles, one can easily prepare a word cloud with the help of Python's `wordcloud` library. To this end the frequency of uni- and bigrams are determined. For a word the frequency is defined as the quotient of how often the word appears in the text and the number of all words of the text in question. Normalization is done by dividing with the maximal frequency. Usually preprocessing of the text incorporates removing of stopwords, such as, e.g., are, is, and, or, etc., stemming and lemmatization (word normalization). The word cloud obtained from the titles of all CIAA publications is depicted on the left of Fig. 2, where only the removing of stopwords was applied. Words and bigrams related to automata and expressions attain high ranks. It is worth mentioning that the missing words "implementation" and "application" from the conference name CIAA appear on rank 12 and 22, respectively, with normalized frequencies 0.1215 and 0.0841, respectively.

3   Collaboration Patterns

In general the *co-authorship network* or *co-authorship graph*, for short, is an undirected graph built from a set of publications P restricted to a set of authors A from these publications with the following properties: (i) the set of nodes corresponds to the set of authors A and (ii) two authors are connected by an undirected edge if there is at least one publication in P jointly co-authored by them. We call such a network a P-A co-authorship network. There are several ways to generalize co-authorship graphs, for instance, to introduce edge and node weights reflecting measures for collaboration (e.g., Newman's weighting scheme) and impact/productivity (e.g., h-index/number of papers), respectively. Note

word/bigram	frequency
automata	1.0000
finite automata	0.2850
language	0.2617
finite state	0.2196
algorithm	0.1963
weighted	0.1636
regular expression	0.1636
complexity	0.1402
transducer	0.1355
tree	0.1308

Fig. 2. (Left) Word cloud generated from all titles published at CIAA with standard stopwords and (right) the words and bigrams with the highest normalized frequencies.

that co-authorship graphs are quite different from citation graphs. The latter is yet another important type of graph related to network sciences, but is not considered here.

We investigate (i) the publication venue co-authorship network of CIAA by using all publications of CIAA and hence all authors that ever published a paper at the conference (CIAA-CIAA co-authorship network) and (ii) the field co-authorship network, where all publications, not limited to the conference in question, of CIAA authors are used to construct the graph to be investigated (ALL-CIAA co-authorship network). For better comparability, we only take papers into account that appeared in 1996 or later when constructing the ALL-CIAA network. We think that the differentiation of these two graphs is important, because the conference only cannot describe the community behind CIAA completely. This may lead to different results of the analysis. As already mentioned earlier, for the analysis we decided to use only one data source, namely DBLP. This, in particular reduces the bias and simplifies identification problems such as, e.g., author identification, since we are acting within a closed world, namely DBLP. On the other hand, DBLP will not offer all relevant features of publications and authors as one would like to have. The raw data for the two networks contains lists of papers, including authors names and possibly other information such as title, pagination and so forth, but no information on abstract or affiliation of the authors, because these data are not communicated by DBLP. The construction of the co-authorship networks is straightforward by using Python's networkx[5] library and leads us to some basic results, which we report next.

The findings on the basic results for our two co-authorship networks are summarized in Table 1. Let us comment on these numbers. The total number of papers is 688 respectively 38, 250. As a curious fact, for the CIAA-CIAA data set there are exactly two papers with the same title and authors, namely "Size Reduction of Multitape Automata" by Hellis Tamm, Matti Nykänen, and Esko

---

[5] https://networkx.org.

Table 1. Summary of results of the analysis of the CIAA-CIAA and ALL-CIAA co-authorship network.

	Co-authorship network	
	CIAA-CIAA	ALL-CIAA
total papers	688	38,250
total authors	839	839
mean papers per author	1.81	59.12
mean authors per paper	2.22	3.35
mean collaborators per author	2.57	43.80
size of giant component	192	696
as a percentage	22.76%	83.4%
2nd largest component	41	8
clustering coefficient	0.55	0.49
mean distance[a]	8.36	4.71
maximum distance[a]	22	12

[a]Since the CIAA-CIAA and ALL-CIAA co-authorship networks are not connected, the values are only computed for the largest connected component.

Ukkonen that appeared in 2004 and 2005. Concerning the number of authors, as already said, the identification problem such as mentioned in [7] is not relevant to our study, thanks to the use of DBLP as the single source of truth for authors. DBLP does an excellent job in author name disambiguation, as reported in [9]. Author name disambiguation at DBLP is achieved by the combined effort of algorithms and humans, as described in [12]. For instance, the DBLP database identifies Kees Hemerik and C. Hemerik as the same person, while by relying on names only, one would rather count them as separate individuals. We are quite sure that the CIAA-CIAA data set is approximately correct w.r.t. the identification problem of authors. Hence, a bias from an incorrect identification is negligible for us. The average number of papers per author is 1.81 and the distribution of papers per author follows a power law. This was first observed by Lotka [10] and later confirmed by several studies, and is nowadays known as "Lokta's Law of Scientific Productivity"—see Fig. 3.

Simply speaking, if one plots two quantities against each other where both axes are logarithmically scaled (log-log scaled) and they show a linear relationship, this indicates that the two quantities have a power law distribution. Such a line can be described by $\ln f(x) = -\alpha \ln x + c$ and by taking exponentials we end up with

$$f(x) = C \cdot x^{-\alpha},$$

where $C = e^c$. Distributions of this form are said to follow a *power law* and α is called the *exponent* of the power law. Observe, that a positive exponent α induces a negative slope on the straight line in the log-log plot. Mostly the constant C

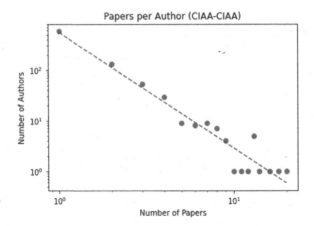

Fig. 3. Plot of the number of papers written by authors in the CIAA-CIAA co-authorship network. The plot is log-log scaled. The corresponding plot for the ALL-CIAA co-authorship network is similar but not shown due to space constraints.

is not of particular interest. Power law distributions occur in an extraordinarily wide range of phenomena, e.g., [1,3,8,10,11,18]. The distribution of papers per author follows a power law with exponent α approximately 2 in general [10] and we have $\alpha \approx 2.28$.

Now we turn to the ALL-CIAA co-authorship network. For many papers, DBLP identifies that an author name is shared by different authors, yet is not able to make an educated guess to which person the paper should be attributed. In that case, the author link in the DBLP record of the paper points to a disambiguation page, which lists the papers of all authors with that name. In our data set, we used the disambiguation page to serve as a list of papers by that author if DBLP cannot determine the author. In total, we have to deal with 11 disambiguation pages. While this number is quite modest compared to the total number of authors, these eleven pages list an amount of 2035 publications in total. So the average number of publications per disambiguation page is 185. Since those disambiguation pages list papers that are sometimes produced by many different actual persons, the disambiguation pages may introduce a sizable distortion in averages such as "papers per author" and "number of collaborators per author." For a moment, let us assume that each disambiguation page stands for an actual author who published only 1 paper overall - this will certainly underestimate the actual state of affairs. Then we have 839 authors and $(38250 - 2035 + 11)$ papers, which yields a figure of 43.12 papers per author on average, which is seizably lower but still in the same ballpark. So another explanation for the unusually high scores is in order. We will propose a hypothesis below, where we look at the top 10 in various different aspects.

In the first column of Table 2, we list the most frequent authors of both the CIAA-CIAA and ALL-CIAA co-authorship network. For the ALL-CIAA network, we observe that some CIAA authors are highly prolific writers, drawn

Table 2. The authors with the highest numbers of papers, fractional number of papers, and numbers of co-authors in the CIAA-CIAA and ALL-CIAA co-authorship network. Italicized items are disambiguation pages, i.e., possibly several actual authors.

		number of papers		fractional no. of papers		number of co-workers
CIAA-CIAA	20	Martin Kutrib	9.08	Andreas Maletti	22	Jean-Marc Champarnaud
	18	Jean-Marc Champarnaud	9.00	Bruce W. Watson	16	Nelma Moreira
	16	Markus Holzer	8.20	Martin Kutrib	14	Kai Salomaa
	14	Kai Salomaa	7.58	Oscar H. Ibarra	13	Martin Kutrib
	13	Andreas Maletti	7.00	Markus Holzer	13	Borivoj Melichar
	13	Borivoj Melichar	6.87	Mehryar Mohri	13	Sheng Yu
	13	Mehryar Mohri	6.82	Jean-Marc Champarnaud	12	Rogério Reis
	13	Bruce W. Watson	6.23	Borivoj Melichar	11	Johanna Björklund
	13	Sheng Yu	6.00	Kai Salomaa	11	Markus Holzer
	12	Oscar H. Ibarra	5.75	Sheng Yu	11	Sylvain Lombardy
ALL-CIAA	695	Alois C. Knoll	269.8	Moshe Y. Vardi	1082	*Cheng Li*
	609	Václav Snásel	229.5	Gonzalo Navarro	875	Alois C. Knoll
	577	Gonzalo Navarro	222.0	B. Sundar Rajan	532	*Fei Xie*
	569	Moshe Y. Vardi	175.1	William I. Gasarch	516	*Bin Ma*
	501	B. Sundar Rajan	175.0	Alois C. Knoll	420	Václav Snásel
	475	Thomas A. Henzinger	167.6	Václav Snásel	374	*Xiaoyu Song*
	466	*Bin Ma*	162.6	Thomas A. Henzinger	365	Axel Legay
	438	Kim G. Larsen	152.2	Henning Fernau	359	*Yong Sun*
	438	Axel Legay	140.1	Jeffrey O. Shallit	341	Madhav V. Marathe
	384	*Cheng Li*	137.2	Andrzej Pelc	323	Kim G. Larsen

from diverse fields in computer science: Robotics (Alois C. Knoll), artificial intelligence (Václav Snásel), string algorithms (Gonzalo Navarro), logic and verification (Moshe Y. Vardi), network coding (B. Sundar Rajan), to list the fields of the five most prolific authors. While only few of them regularly contribute to CIAA, this shows that the conference helps bringing the various applied fields of computer science together.

Admittedly, among the top ten CIAA authors with most collaborators, five are actually DBLP disambiguation pages: Cheng Li, Fei Xie, Bin Ma, Xiaoyu Song and Yong Sun.[6] But as explained above, the amount of distortion due to fuzziness in the data is not too high. Together with the facts explained in the

---

[6] The interested readers who is able to help with disambiguation is invited to suggest corrections to the DBLP team.

preceding paragraph, this may explain why the CIAA authors have, on average, very high scores regarding both research output and collaboration.

We thus identified two factors that may serve as a partial explanation for the very high scores in the ALL-CIAA network. Another factor is probably the way we construct the ALL-CIAA data set: we include the 839 CIAA authors and all their publications, but we exclude most of the co-authors that contributed to those publications. For comparison, the analysis carried out for computer science as a whole in [14] included all authors that were coauthors of at least one paper in the data set. For the community of the ACM SIGMOD conference, an analysis of the co-authorship graph was carried out in [13]. The network they construct is analogous to our CIAA-CIAA network, and there again, the considered set of authors is implied by the papers that were selected. In the ALL-CIAA network, we deliberately zoomed in on the set of CIAA authors, and as a consequence, the number of authors is much smaller than the number of publications we consider. Yet, as a *Gedankenexperiment*, let us extend the set of authors to all authors listed as co-author in papers of the ALL-CIAA network. Then we obtain a total of 24717 authors—and the average number of papers per author drops to 1.55. Then again, this figure appears too low—after all, we included only a fraction of the papers by those authors that collaborated with a CIAA author.

The alternative to counting the total number of papers is fractional number of papers. Each paper co-authored by a given author adds an amount of $\frac{1}{n}$ to the fractional number of papers instead of 1 as for number of papers, where n is the total number of authors on the paper. The rationale behind this choice is that in an ideal world, an authors collective equally divides the writing between all n authors who work on a paper. The fractional number of papers became famous among theoretical computer scientists by the author ranking to the "*International Colloquium on Automata, Languages, and Programming*" (ICALP) prepared by the late Manfred Kudlek and published in the EATCS Bulletin series. As expected, there is substantial overlap between the authors with a large number of papers and those with a large fractional number of papers.

By empirical results from the literature it is awaited that a power law also applies for the authors per paper and collaborators per author. Both distributions are shown in Fig. 4. The average number of authors per paper is 2.22, which is in perfect fit with the average value 2.22 for computer science as a whole [14]. The largest number of authors on a single paper is 7 ("In Vitro Implementation of Finite-State Machines" by Max H. Garzon, Y. Gao, John A. Rose, R. C. Murphy, Russell J. Deaton, Donald R. Franceschetti, and Stanley Edward Stevens Jr.). In the CIAA-CIAA network, the mean on number of collaborators is 2.55 and this somewhat less than 3.59 for computer science as report in [14]. The distributions of the number of collaborators are depicted in Fig. 4. The third column of Table 2 shows the authors of the CIAA-CIAA and ALL-CIAA co-authorship network with the largest numbers of collaborators.

In the CIAA-CIAA network, it is remarkable that although Jean-Marc Champarnaud is already retired and has published his last CIAA paper in 2012, i.e., a decade ago, he still has the highest number of 22 co-workers. His co-workers

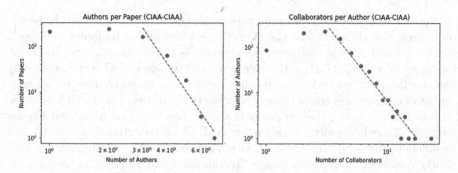

Fig. 4. Plots of the (i) number of authors per paper and (ii) number of collaborators per author in the CIAA-CIAA co-authorship network. Both plots are log-log scaled. The corresponding plots for the ALL-CIAA co-authorship network are similar.

are (in alphabetical order) Philippe Andary, Pascal Caron, Fabien Coulon, Tibor Csáki, Jean-Philippe Dubernard, Gérard Duchamp, Jason Eisner, Jacques Farré, Marianne Flouret, Tamás Gaál, Franck Guingne, Hadrien Jeanne, André Kempe, Éric Laugerotte, Jean-Francis Michon, Ludovic Mignot, Florent Nicart, Faissal Ouardi, Thomas Paranthoën, Jean-Luc Ponty, Are Uppman, and Djelloul Ziadi.

Next let us come to more graph theoretical properties and measures that are relevant in the network analysis community. The obvious measures of a graph are the number of nodes n and the number of (undirected) edges m. Both measures give rise to the density, which is defined as $d = 2m/(n(n-1))$. The CIAA-CIAA co-authorship network with $n = 839$ nodes and $m = 1077$ edges has density $d = 0.0031$. The values for the ALL-CIAA co-authorship network are $n = 839$, $m = 2150$, and thus $d = 0.0061$. Hence both networks are sparsely connected. Density is a measure in the theory of graphs with limited meaning for real-world networks. Real-world networks are unlike random graph or regular lattices, and, as empirical observation suggests, they are more like small-worlds [2]. Networks of this kind are characterized by at least two main features:

1. The diameter of the network grows logarithmically in the size of the network like in random graphs and
2. the network is highly clustered as it happens in lattices.

By the first property any two nodes can be reached from each other (if they are in the same connected component) using only a few number of steps, even if the network is large. The second trait induces that any two neighbors of a given node have a large probability of being themselves neighbors. In other words the network has the tendency to form tightly connected neighborhoods.

Both studied co-authorship networks are disconnected. The CIAA-CIAA co-authorship network contains 219 connected components, and the giant component is built by 192 nodes, which is approximately 22.76% of the whole graph. The ALL-CIAA co-authorship network contains 73 connected components, and the giant component has 696 nodes (83.35%).

Further basic concepts of graph theory are the diameter and the clustering coefficient. The diameter and the clustering coefficient can be found in Table 1 and they are defined as follows: the *diameter* is the maximum eccentricity of the nodes of a graph G. Here the *eccentricity of a node v* of G is the maximum distance from a given node v to all other nodes in the graph G. The *periphery* is the set of nodes whose eccentricity is equal to the diameter. For the CIAA-CIAA co-authorship network the periphery is the set that contains Mohamed Faouzi Atig and Antonio Restivo, while for the ALL-CIAA co-authorship network the members of the periphery are Juan Otero Pombo, Leandro Rodríguez Liñares, Gloria Andrade, Niels Bjørn Bugge Grathwohl, Ulrik Terp Rasmussen, Lasse Nielsen, and Kenny Zhuo Ming Lu. The diameter of the giant component in CIAA-CIAA network and the ALL-CIAA network is 22 and 12, respectively. The *clustering coefficient C* for a graph G with vertex set V is the average

$$C = \frac{1}{n} \sum_{v \in V} c_v,$$

where n is the number of nodes of G and c_v is defined as the fraction of possible triangles through that node that exist,

$$c_v = \frac{2\,T(v)}{deg(v)(deg(v) - 1)},$$

where $T(v)$ is the number of triangles through node v and $deg(v)$ is the degree of the node v. The clustering coefficient of the CIAA-CIAA network and the ALL-CIAA network is 0.55 and 0.49, respectively. The obtained values are in correspondence to previous empirical results for diameters and clustering coefficients obtained from real-world co-authorship networks [14].

In order to identify the most influential individuals in (small-world) networks one may take a closer look on the measure of betweenness. Loosely speaking betweenness is an indicator who bridges the flow of information between most others. In the literature one can find several competing definitions of betweenness, see, e.g., [5], which cover different aspects of being important. In our analysis we rely on the following definition: the *betweenness*, or *betweenness centrality*, of a node v in the graph G with vertex set V is the sum of the fraction of all-pairs shortest paths that pass through v, namely

$$c_B(v) = \sum_{s,t \in V} \frac{\sigma(s, t \mid v)}{\sigma(s, t)},$$

where V is the set of nodes, $\sigma(s, t)$ is the number of shortest (s, t)-paths, and the value $\sigma(s, t \mid v)$ is the number of those paths passing through some node v other than s or t. If $s = t$, then $\sigma(s, t) = 1$, and if $v \in \{s, t\}$, then $\sigma(s, t \mid v) = 0$. The first column of Table 3 summarize our findings on betweenness.

Now let us come to the strength of collaboration. Cooperation in co-authorship networks is measured in several different ways in the literature [19, Chapter 5]. We will only consider two measures that can be seen as counterparts

Table 3. The authors with the highest betweenness, the strongest straight collaboration weight, and the strongest Newman's collaboration weight in the two co-authorship networks. Non-CIAA-authors are italicized.

	betweenness ($\times 10^{-2}$)		collaboration weight (straight)		collaboration weight (Newman)	
CIAA-CIAA	2.98	Stavros Konstantinidis	9	Nelma Moreira/ Rogério Reis	6.00	Markus Holzer/ Martin Kutrib
	2.91	Lila Kari	8	Markus Holzer/ Martin Kutrib	4.25	Cyril Allauzen/ Mehryar Mohri
	2.51	Galina Jirásková	7	Martin Kutrib/ Andreas Malcher	4.25	Martin Kutrib/ Andreas Malcher
	2.48	Juraj Sebej	7	Sylvain Lombardy/ Jacques Sakarovitch	4.17	Sylvain Lombardy/ Jacques Sakarovitch
	2.45	Kai Salomaa	7	Kai Salomaa/ Sheng Yu	3.75	Martin Kutrib/ Matthias Wendlandt
	2.40	Markus Holzer	6	Cyril Allauzen/ Mehryar Mohri	3.75	Nelma Moreira/ Rogério Reis
	2.33	Yo-Sub Han	6	Martin Kutrib/ Matthias Wendlandt	3.67	Kai Salomaa/ Sheng Yu
	2.30	Michal Hospodár	5	Jean-Marc Champarnaud/ Djelloul Ziadi	3.50	Yo-Sub Han/ Sang-Ki Ko
	2.07	Derick Wood	4	Cyrill Allauzen/ Michael Riley	2.83	Jean-Marc Champarnaud/ Djelloul Ziadi
	1.81	Jean-Luc Ponty	4	Jurek Czyzowicz/ Wojciech Fraczak	2.75	Cyril Allauzen/ Michael Riley
ALL-CIAA	6.49	Bruce W. Watson	223	Luiza de Macedo Mourelle/ Nadia Nedjah	151.87	Luiza de Macedo Mourelle/ Nadia Nedjah
	5.36	Andreas Maletti	184	Shunsuke Inenaga/ Masayuki Takeda	69.33	Martin Kutrib/ Andreas Malcher
	5.14	Moshe Y. Vardi	181	Hideo Bannai/ Shunsuke Inenaga	63.12	*Sanjay Jain/ Frank Stephan*
	4.79	Axel Legay	167	Bin Ma/ *Haizhou Li*	59.90	Luca Aceto/ Anna Ingólfsdóttir
	4.61	Juhani Karhumäki	166	Hideo Bannai/ Masayuki Takeda	59.76	*Krishnendu Chatterjee/ Thomas A. Henzinger*
	4.13	Markus Holzer	149	Luca Aceto/ Anna Ingólfsdóttir	55.98	Markus Holzer/ Martin Kutrib
	4.07	Sheng Yu	141	*Ajith Abraham/ Václav Snásel*	51.50	Shmuel Tomi Klein/ Dana Shapira
	4.02	Jean-Marc Champarnaud	136	*Pavel Krömer/ Václac Snásel*	51.50	Shunsuke Inenaga/ Masayuki Takeda
	3.93	Jeffrey O. Shallit	132	*Jan Platos/ Václav Snásel*	50.43	*Pavel Krömer/ Václav Snásel*
	3.82	Sebastian Maneth	132	*Sanjay Jain/ Frank Stephan*	49.18	Bin Ma/ *Haizhou Li*

to the number of papers and the number of fractional papers that are assigned to the authors (nodes of the graph). The easiest way is to assign a weight to a pair of co-authors, which is an edge in the co-authorship graph, is to use the

Fig. 5. The giant component of the CIAA-CIAA co-authorship network, which contains 192 authors; names are not shown in order to keep the drawing readable. There are 647 more authors in smaller components. Application of the Clauset-Newman-Moore community structure algorithm produces 12 communities, where the three size-largest ones (top, middle, bottom) are shown by colors (blue, green, red). Node size corresponds to the number of papers and edge width to collaboration weight. (Color figure online)

number of commonly co-authored papers. This measure is called the *straight collaboration weight*. A more complex measure also takes other co-authors into account—we refer to this measure as *Newman's collaboration weight*. For a pair of co-authors it is defined as the sum over all co-authored papers of $1/(n-1)$, where n is the number of collaborators of the paper under consideration in the summing. The idea behind the choice of the value $1/(n-1)$ is that the researchers divide their time equally between the $n-1$ co-authors. Observe, that Newman's collaboration weight does not take into account the actual order in which the names appear in a publication. This is a reasonable assumption for computer science publications, since there are only around 130 CIAA publications that don't list the authors lexicographically. This is approximately 18.90 percent. The obtained results for both co-authorship networks are depicted in the second and third column of Table 3.

An important issue for real-world networks is the identification and extraction of meaningful communities in order to better understand complex networks. Common to all community definitions [19] is the idea that a community is a group of densely interconnected nodes that are only sparsely connected with the rest of the network. On the variety of algorithms, the community detection algorithm from [6] based on a measure called modularity performed best, in the sense that the identified communities fit very well with the given data. Figure 5 illustrates the result of this algorithm running on the giant component of the CIAA-CIAA co-authorship network. Overall 12 communities are detected, of sizes (in decreasing order) 28 (blue), 22 (green), 22 (red), 19, 19, 16, 13, 12, 12, 11, 10, and 8. There are 72 nodes contained in the three largest communities. This is 37.5%, and thus more than a third, of the giant component of the CIAA-CIAA co-authorship network. Take a closer look at the largest community. There is an eye-catching node with high degree. An educated guess is that this node stands for Jean-Marc Champarnaud. The analysis confirms this—the authors that from the largest community are Jean-Marc Champarnaud, his 22 collaborators already mentioned earlier, except Jacques Farreé, and (in alphabetical order) Houda Abbad, Samira Attou, Christof Baeijs, Dominique Geniet, Gaëlle Largeteau, and Clément Miklarz.

The presented results can be seen as a starting point for more complex analyses, including, e.g., analysis of the growth of the co-authorship network over time, analysis of the citation network, text analytics and natural language processing (NLP) to cluster research texts, etc. Let us close with congratulations to CIAA and all the best for the coming 25 years.

References

1. Adamic, L.A., Huberman, B.A.: The nature of markets in the world wide web. Q. J. Electron. Commer. **1**, 512 (2000)
2. Amaral, L.A.N., Scala, A., Barthélémy, M., Stanley, H.E.: Classes of small-world networks. Proc. Natl. Acad. Sci. **97**(21), 11149–11152 (2000)
3. Auerbach, F.: Das Gesetz der Bevölkerungskonzentration. Petermanns Geographische Mitteilungen **59**, 74–76 (1913)
4. Kao, R.R.: Networks and Models with Heterogeneous Population Structure in Epidemiology. In: Network Science, pp. 51–84. Springer, London (2010). https://doi.org/10.1007/978-1-84996-396-1_4
5. Brandes, U.: On variants of shortest-path betweenness centrality and their generic computation. Soc. Netw. **30**(2), 136–145 (2008)
6. Clauset, A., Newman, M.E., Moore, C.: Finding community structure in very large networks. Phys. Rev. E **70**(6), 066111 (2004)
7. Grossman, J.W., Ion, P.D.F.: On a portion of the well-known collaboration graph. Congr. Numer. **108**, 129–132 (1995)

8. Gutenberg, B., Richter, R.F.: Frequency of earth-quakes in California. Bull. Seismol. Soc. Am. **34**, 185–188 (1944)

9. Kim, J.: Evaluating author name disambiguation for digital libraries: a case of DBLP. Scientometrics **116**(3), 1867–1886 (2018). https://doi.org/10.1007/s11192-018-2824-5

10. Lotka, A.J.: The frequency distribution of scientific productivity. J. Wash. Acad. Sci. **16**(12), 317–324 (1926)

11. Lu, E.T., Hamilton, R.J.: Avalanches of the distribution of solar flares. Astrophys. J. **380**, 89–92 (1991)

12. Müller, M.-C., Reitz, F., Roy, N.: Data sets for author name disambiguation: an empirical analysis and a new resource. Scientometrics **111**(3), 1467–1500 (2017). https://doi.org/10.1007/s11192-017-2363-5

13. Nascimento, M.A., Sander, J., Pound, J.: Analysis of SIGMOD's co-authorship graph. SIGMOD Rec. **32**(3), 8–10 (2003)

14. Newman, M.E.J.: The structure of scientific collaboration networks. Proc. Natl. Acad. Sci. **98**, 404–409 (2001)

15. Newman, M.E.J.: Coauthorship networks and patterns of scientific collaboration. Proc. Nat. Acad. Sci. **101**(suppl_1), 5200–5205 (2004)

16. Newman, M.E.J.: Network: An Introduction. Cambridge University Press, Cambridge (2010)

17. Raymond, D.: WIA and the practice of theory in computer science. In: Raymond, D., Wood, D., Yu, S. (eds.) WIA 1996. LNCS, vol. 1260, pp. 1–5. Springer, Heidelberg (1997). https://doi.org/10.1007/3-540-63174-7_1

18. de Solla Price, D.J.: Networks of scientific papers. Science **149**, 510–515 (1965)

19. Savić, M., Ivanović, M., Jain, L.C.: Analysis of enriched co-authorship networks: methodology and a case study. In: Complex Networks in Software, Knowledge, and Social Systems. ISRL, vol. 148, pp. 277–317. Springer, Cham (2019). https://doi.org/10.1007/978-3-319-91196-0_8

Manipulation of Regular Expressions Using Derivatives: An Overview

Nelma Moreira[✉] and Rogério Reis

CMUP & DCC, Faculdade de Ciências da Universidade do Porto,
Rua do Campo Alegre, 4169-007 Porto, Portugal
{nelma.moreira,rogerio.reis}@fc.up.pt

Abstract. The notions of derivative and partial derivative of regular expressions revealed themselves to be very powerful and have been successfully extended to many other formal language classes and algebraic structures. Although the undisputed elegance of this formalism, its efficient practical use is still a challenging research topic. Here we give a brief historical overview and summarise some of these aspects.

1 Preliminares

Regular expressions are the common choice to represent regular languages due to their succinctness and clear syntax. Deterministic finite automata are an excellent representation for testing equivalence, containment, or membership, as these problems are easily solved for this model. However, minimal deterministic finite automata (DFA) can be exponentially larger than the associated regular expression, while corresponding nondeterministic finite automata (NFA) are only linearly larger. The computational and descriptional complexity of regular expressions and of conversions to and from finite automata are well studied. Good surveys on the subject are [39,40]. In recent years, the average size of different NFA constructions from regular expressions were studied using the framework of analytic combinatorics [14,17,63]. For the average case, the uniform distribution on the set of regular expressions is considered although that does not imply a uniform representation of regular languages. In this survey, we focus on the derivative and partial derivative based constructions. First, we recall some basic notions and fix notation.

Given an alphabet $\Sigma = \{\sigma_1, \ldots, \sigma_k\}$ of size $k \geq 1$, a *language* L is a subset of the free monoid $\Sigma^\star$. The *left-quotient* of a language L by a word $w \in \Sigma^\star$, is the language $w^{-1}L = \{x \mid wx \in L\}$.

The set $\mathcal{R}_k$ of (standard) *regular expressions* r over Σ is composed by $\emptyset$ plus the expressions defined by the following context-free grammar:

$$r := \varepsilon \mid \sigma_1 \mid \cdots \mid \sigma_k \mid (r + r) \mid (r \odot r) \mid (r^\star), \tag{1}$$

Research supported by CMUP through FCT project UIDB/00144/2021.

P. Caron and L. Mignot (Eds.): CIAA 2022, LNCS 13266, pp. 19–33, 2022.
https://doi.org/10.1007/978-3-031-07469-1_2

where the symbol $\odot$ is normally omitted and represents concatenation. The (regular) *language* represented by an expression $r \in \mathcal{R}_k$ is denoted by $\mathcal{L}(r)$ and is inductively defined as follows for $r, r' \in \mathcal{R}_k$: $\mathcal{L}(\emptyset) = \emptyset$, $\mathcal{L}(\varepsilon) = \{\varepsilon\}$, $\mathcal{L}(\sigma) = \{\sigma\}$, $\mathcal{L}(r + r') = \mathcal{L}(r) \cup \mathcal{L}(r')$, $\mathcal{L}(r \odot r') = \mathcal{L}(r)\mathcal{L}(r') = \{wv \mid w \in \mathcal{L}(r) \wedge v \in \mathcal{L}(r')\}$, and $\mathcal{L}(r^\star) = \mathcal{L}(r)^\star = \bigcup_{n \in \mathbb{N}}(\mathcal{L}(r)^n)$. For the *size* of a regular expression r, denoted by $\|r\|$, we consider the size of its syntactic tree, i.e., the number of symbols in r, not counting parentheses but including $\odot$. The *alphabetic size* of r, denoted by $|r|_\Sigma$, is just the number of alphabetic symbols in r. We define $\varepsilon(r) = \varepsilon$ if $\varepsilon \in \mathcal{L}(r)$, and $\varepsilon(r) = \emptyset$, otherwise. The function $\varepsilon()$ is easily defined inductively in the structure of r. Two expressions r and s are *equivalent* if their languages are the same, and we write $r = s$. With this interpretation, the algebraic structure $(\mathcal{R}_k, +, \cdot, \emptyset, \varepsilon)$ is a idempotent semiring that with $\star$ forms a Kleene algebra.

A *nondeterministic finite automaton* (NFA) is a quintuple $\mathcal{A} = \langle Q, \Sigma, \delta, I, F \rangle$ where Q is a finite set of states, Σ is a finite alphabet, $I \subseteq Q$ is the set of initial states, $F \subseteq Q$ is the set of final states, and $\delta : Q \times \Sigma \to 2^Q$ is the transition function. The *language accepted* by $\mathcal{A}$ is $\mathcal{L}(\mathcal{A}) = \{w \in \Sigma^\star \mid \delta(I, w) \cap F \neq \emptyset\}$. When $I = \{q_0\}$, we use $I = q_0$. If $|I| = 1$ and $|\delta(q, \sigma)| \leq 1$, for all $q \in Q, \sigma \in \Sigma$, $\mathcal{A}$ is *deterministic* (DFA). For a DFA $\mathcal{A}$, $w \in \mathcal{L}(\mathcal{A})$ if $\delta(q_0, w) \in F$. Two NFAs $\mathcal{A}$ and $\mathcal{A}'$ are *equivalent* if their languages are the same. An automaton $\mathcal{A}$ is equivalent to a regular expression r if $\mathcal{L}(\mathcal{A}) = \mathcal{L}(r)$. We can convert an NFA $\mathcal{A}$ into an equivalent DFA $D(\mathcal{A})$ by the *determinisation* operation D, using the well-known subset construction. An equivalence relation $\equiv$ on Q is *right invariant* w.r.t. an NFA $\mathcal{A}$ if and only if $\equiv \subseteq (Q - F)^2 \cup F^2$ and $\forall p, q \in Q, \sigma \in \Sigma$, if $p \equiv q$ then $\forall p' \in \delta(p, \sigma) \; \exists q' \in \delta(q, \sigma)$ such that $p' \equiv q'$. The *quotient automaton* $\mathcal{A}/\equiv$ is given by $A/\equiv = \langle Q/\equiv, \Sigma, \delta/\equiv, I/\equiv, F/\equiv \rangle$, where $\delta/\equiv([p], \sigma) = \{[q] \mid q \in \delta(p, \sigma)\} = \delta(p, \sigma)/\equiv$. It is easy to see that $\mathcal{L}(\mathcal{A}/\equiv) = \mathcal{L}(\mathcal{A})$.

2   Derivatives

In 1962, Janusz Brzozowski introduced the notion of derivative of a regular expression in his Ph.D. thesis *Regular Expression Techniques for Sequential Circuits* [22]. Based on nerve nets of McCulloch and Pitts [52], in 1956 Kleene [44] showed the equivalence of finite automata and regular expressions. Brzozowski proposed regular expressions as a simple formalism for describing the behaviour of sequential circuits as opposed to use directly finite automata (state graphs), as regular expressions are in general more readable. A theory of regular expressions was developed for the conversion of expressions to finite automata and vice-versa. Methods for converting finite automata into regular expression were already known [53, 61] but a simple method was presented, nowadays known as the *state elimination method* [21]. For the conversion from regular expressions into finite automata, there existed already methods such as the McNaughton-Yamada automaton ($\mathcal{A}_{MY}$) [53]. Brzozowski defined a deterministic finite automaton equivalent to a regular expression using the notion of derivative [22, 25]. The *derivative* by $\sigma \in \Sigma$ of a regular expression r is a regular expression $d_\sigma(r)$, inductively defined by:

$$d_\sigma(\emptyset) = d_\sigma(\varepsilon) = \emptyset, \qquad d_\sigma(r + r') = d_\sigma(r) + d_\sigma(r'),$$

$$d_\sigma(\sigma') = \begin{cases} \{\varepsilon\} & \text{if } \sigma' = \sigma, \\ \emptyset & \text{otherwise}, \end{cases} \qquad d_\sigma(rr') = \begin{cases} d_\sigma(r)r' & \text{if } \varepsilon(r) = \emptyset, \\ d_\sigma(r)r' + d_\sigma(r') & \text{otherwise}, \end{cases}$$

$$d_\sigma(r^*) = d_\sigma(r)r^*.$$

$$(2)$$

This notion can be extended to words: $d_\varepsilon(r) = r$ and $d_{\sigma w}(r) = d_w(d_\sigma(r))$. The language of $d_w(r)$ is $\mathcal{L}(d_w(r)) = \{x \mid wx \in \mathcal{L}(r)\} = w^{-1}\mathcal{L}(r)$. The set of all derivatives of r, $\{d_w(r) \mid w \in \Sigma^*\}$, may not be finite. For finiteness, Brzozowski considered the quotient of that set modulo some regular expression equivalences, namely the associativity, commutativity, and idempotence of $+$ (ACI) and the following rules: $r\varepsilon = \varepsilon r = r$, $\emptyset r = r\emptyset = \emptyset$, and $\emptyset + r = r + \emptyset = r$.[1] Let $\mathcal{D}(r)$ be the resulting set. The *Brzozowski's automaton* for r is the DFA defined as follows

$$\mathcal{A}_B(r) = \langle \mathcal{D}(r), \Sigma, \delta_B, [r], F_B \rangle, \qquad (3)$$

where $F_B = \{[r'] \in \mathcal{D}(r) \mid \varepsilon(r') = \varepsilon\}$, and $\delta_B([r'], \sigma) = [d_\sigma(r')]$, for all $[r] \in \mathcal{D}(r)$ and $\sigma \in \Sigma$. The proof that $\mathcal{D}(r)$ is finite constitute one of the first results on state complexity bounds. A language L is recognised by a finite automaton if and only if it has a finite number of left-quotients [62], and that number is the state complexity of L. The language of a derivative is a left-quotient, but two derivatives may represent the same language. Known upper bounds for the state complexity of several operations can be obtained using derivatives by tightening the bounds of $|\mathcal{D}(r)|$ [23]. Both the size $|\mathcal{D}(r)|$ and the size of the elements of $\mathcal{D}(r)$ can grow exponentially with $\|r\|$.

Derivatives can be used to decide problems such as the word membership, universality, or equivalence of regular expressions, avoiding the automaton construction.

Membership. A word $w \in \mathcal{L}(r)$ if and only in $\varepsilon(d_w(r)) = \varepsilon$. This method can be extended to nonregular languages.

Universality. A regular expression r represents Σ^* if and only if for all $[r'] \in \mathcal{D}(r)$, $\varepsilon([r']) = \varepsilon$.

Equivalence. The correctness of the Brzozowski's automaton relies in the following equivalence

$$r = \varepsilon(r) + \sum_{\sigma \in \Sigma} \sigma d_\sigma(r), \qquad (4)$$

If $\mathcal{D}(r) = \{r = r_1, \ldots, r_n\}$, then the following system of equations is satisfied

$$r_i = \varepsilon(r_i) + \sum_{j=1}^{k} \sigma_j r_{i,j}, \qquad (5)$$

---

[1] The necessity of these equalities was pointed out by Salomaa [72].

where $r_{i,j}$ is $[d_{\sigma_j}(r_i)]$. One has that $r = s$ if and only if $\varepsilon(r) = \varepsilon(s)$ and $[d_{\sigma_j}(r)] = [d_{\sigma_j}(s)]$ for all $\sigma_j \in \Sigma$. Below we present a refutation method such that testing the equivalence of the two expressions corresponds to an iterated process of testing the equivalence of their derivatives [2,5].

```
equivP (r,s):
    S = {(r,s)}
    H = ∅
    while (r,s) = POP(S):
        if ε(r) ≠ ε(s): return False
        ` PUSH(H, (r,s))
        for σ ∈ Σ:
            (r',s') = ([dσ(r)],[dσ(s)])
            if (r',s') ∉ H: PUSH(S,(r',s'))
    return True
```

This method is related to the Hopcroft and Karp's algorithm for testing the equivalence of two deterministic finite automata that avoids their minimisation [3,41]. Ginzburg [36] argues that the above method is *cumbersome* due to the computation of derivatives and equivalence classes, and presents a similar method but using NFAs.

Regular expressions can be extended to include any Boolean operation $\oplus$ on regular languages. Brzozowski defined $d_\sigma(\oplus(r_1, \ldots, r_n)) = \oplus(d_\sigma(r_1), \ldots, d_\sigma(r_n))$, for $\sigma \in \Sigma$. In particular, $d_\sigma(r \cap r') = d_\sigma(r) \cap d_\sigma(r')$ and $d_\sigma(\neg r) = \neg d_\sigma(r)$. Again, he proved that an extended regular expression has a finite number of derivatives modulo some equivalences and thus a DFA could be constructed, solving a problem stated in [53].

In the next decades, derivatives were useful in several algebraic characterizations, for instance [24,33,48,72]; inspired conversions from expressions to automata, such as the Thompson automaton ($\mathcal{A}_{\varepsilon-T}$) [77]; or were the based of regular expression equivalence tests [36,58]. However, for practical applications, manipulation methods based directly on regular expressions were thought much more inefficients than the ones based on the conversion of regular expressions to finite automata. Also the fact that regular expressions needed to be considered modulo ACI was a disadvantage. One exception is Berry and Sethi's method of constructing the McNaughton-Yamada DFA ($\mathcal{A}_{MY}$) using derivatives [9].

3 Partial Derivatives

In 1966, Boris G. Mirkin [57] presented an algorithm for constructing an NFA that is a nondeterministic counterpart of Brzozowski's automaton. Mirkin considered a system of equations as (5) but where the $r_{i,j}$ can be sums of expressions. The solution of the system leads to a nondeterminitic automaton construction. Given a regular expression r_0, a set of expressions $\pi(r_0) = \{r_1, \ldots, r_n\}$ is a *support* of r_0 if for each $r_i \in \{r_0\} \cup \pi(r_0)$ the Eq. (5) holds where each $r_{i,j}$ is a (possibly empty) sum of elements in $\pi(r_0)$. The set $\{r_0\} \cup \pi(r_0)$ is a *pre-base* of r_0. Mirkin proved that a support of $r \in \mathcal{R}_k$ can be inductively defined as follows

$$\begin{aligned}
\pi(\emptyset) &= \emptyset, & \pi(r+s) &= \pi(r) \cup \pi(s), \\
\pi(\varepsilon) &= \emptyset, & \pi(rs) &= \pi(r)s \cup \pi(s), \\
\pi(\sigma) &= \{\varepsilon\}, & \pi(r^\star) &= \pi(r)r^\star,
\end{aligned} \tag{6}$$

where, for any $S \subseteq \mathcal{R}_k$, we define $S\emptyset = \emptyset S = \emptyset$, $S\varepsilon = \varepsilon S = S$, and $Sr' = \{rr' \mid r \in S \wedge r \neq \varepsilon\} \cup \{r' \mid \varepsilon \in S\}$ if $r' \neq \emptyset, \varepsilon$ (and analogously for $r'S$). It is easy to see that $|\pi(r)| \leq |r|_\Sigma$ and thus a relatively small NFA can be constructed. Moreover, it follows also from Mirkin's proof that set of transitions of this automaton can be inductively defined [13, 19].

Almost thirty years later, and independently, Valentin Antimirov [4] introduced partial derivatives as a (non-deterministic) generalisation of derivatives and obtained an NFA construction, called the partial derivative automaton, $\mathcal{A}_{\text{PD}}$ Champarnaud and Ziadi [27] proved that the Mirkin and Antimirov automaton constructions are equivalent. Essentially, Antimirov associates to a left-quotient of $\mathcal{L}(r)$ a set of regular expressions instead of a unique expression. For a regular expression $r \in \mathcal{R}_k$ and a symbol $\sigma \in \Sigma$, the *set of partial derivatives by σ of* r is defined inductively as follows:

$$\begin{aligned}
\partial_\sigma(\emptyset) &= \partial_\sigma(\varepsilon) = \emptyset, & \partial_\sigma(r+r') &= \partial_\sigma(r) \cup \partial_\sigma(r'), \\
\partial_\sigma(\sigma') &= \begin{cases} \{\varepsilon\} & \text{if } \sigma' = \sigma, \\ \emptyset & \text{otherwise,} \end{cases} & \partial_\sigma(rr') &= \partial_\sigma(r)r' \cup \varepsilon(r)\partial_\sigma(r'), \\
& & \partial_\sigma(r^\star) &= \partial_\sigma(r)r^\star,
\end{aligned} \tag{7}$$

where for $S \subseteq \mathcal{R}_k$ and $r \in \mathcal{R}_k$, we consider Sr or rS as above. The set of partial derivatives by a word $w \in \Sigma^\star$ of $r \in \mathcal{R}_k$ is inductively defined by $\partial_\varepsilon(r) = \{r\}$ and $\partial_{w\sigma}(r) = \partial_\sigma(\partial_w(r))$. We have that $\mathcal{L}(d_w(r)) = \mathcal{L}(\partial_w(r)) = \bigcup_{r' \in \partial_w(r)} \mathcal{L}(r')$, for $w \in \Sigma^\star$. The set of all partial derivatives of r by nonempty words is $\partial^+(r) = \bigcup_{w \in \Sigma^\star \setminus \{\varepsilon\}} \partial_w(r)$ and coincides with $\pi(r)$, i.e., $\partial^+(r) = \pi(r)$ [27]. Equation (2) can be redefined as follows

$$r = \varepsilon(r) \cup \bigcup_{\sigma \in \Sigma} \sigma\partial_\sigma(r), \tag{8}$$

where we denote the right-hand side by $\mathsf{L}_\varepsilon(r)$. This means that membership, universality, equivalence, and related decision problems can be solved, adapting the procedures given above, to sets of partial derivatives.

The *partial derivative automaton* of $r \in \mathcal{R}_k$ is defined as

$$\mathcal{A}_{\text{PD}}(r) = \langle \text{PD}(r), \Sigma, \delta_{\text{PD}}, r, F_{\text{PD}} \rangle,$$

where $\text{PD}(r) = \partial^+(r) \cup \{r\}$, $F_{\text{PD}} = \{r' \in \text{PD}(r) \mid \varepsilon(r') = \varepsilon\}$, and $\delta_{\text{PD}}(r', \sigma) = \partial_\sigma(r')$, for all $r' \in \text{PD}(r)$ and $\sigma \in \Sigma$. We have, $|\text{PD}(r)| \leq |r|_\Sigma + 1$.

Both Mirkin and Antimirov argued that the DFA obtained from $\mathcal{A}_{\text{PD}}(r)$ by determinisation, $\text{D}(\mathcal{A}_{\text{PD}}(r))$, has several advantages over $\mathcal{A}_{\text{B}}(r)$: avoids the computation of a equivalence relation; has at most $2^{|r|_\Sigma}$ states; each state of

$D(\mathcal{A}_{PD}(r))$ is a set of partial derivatives $\partial_w(r) \subseteq PD(r)$ and thus each of these sets could be defined using references to some elements of $PD(r)$.

We note that $D(\mathcal{A}_{PD}(r))$ is not isomorphic to $\mathcal{A}_B$, i.e., $D(\mathcal{A}_{PD}(r)) \not\simeq \mathcal{A}_B$. This is mainly due to the distributivity of the concatenation over a set of expressions in Eq. (7) (see [64]). In [6,11] it was shown that $D(\mathcal{A}_{PD}(r))/{\equiv_{L_\varepsilon}} \simeq \mathcal{A}_B(r)/{\equiv_{L_\varepsilon}}$ where $\equiv_{L_\varepsilon}$ is a right-invariant equivalence relation w.r.t. these automata such that $S \equiv_{L_\varepsilon} S'$ if and only if $L_\varepsilon(S) = L_\varepsilon(S')$, for $S, S' \subseteq \mathcal{R}_k$. The resulting quotient automaton can be directly obtained by the determinisation of yet another automaton construction based on partial derivatives, that we denote by $\mathcal{A}_{\overleftarrow{Pre}}$. From Eq. (8), the elements of $L_\varepsilon(r)$ are either ε or expressions of the form $\sigma r'$. Consider the function $\overleftarrow{p}_w(r)$ on words $w \in \Sigma^\star$ defined inductively by $\overleftarrow{p}_\varepsilon(r) = L_\varepsilon(r)$ and $\overleftarrow{p}_{w\sigma}(r) = \bigcup_{\sigma r' \in \overleftarrow{p}_w(r)} L_\varepsilon(r')$. It is immediate that $\mathcal{L}(\overleftarrow{p}_w(r)) = w^{-1}\mathcal{L}(r)$. The automaton $\mathcal{A}_{\overleftarrow{Pre}}(r)$ is a NFA equivalent to r defined by

$$\mathcal{A}_{\overleftarrow{Pre}}(r) = \langle \overleftarrow{Pre}(r), \Sigma, \delta_{\overleftarrow{Pre}}, L_\varepsilon(r), \varepsilon \rangle,$$

where $\overleftarrow{Pre}(r) = \bigcup_{w \in \Sigma^\star} \overleftarrow{p}_w(r)$ and $\delta_{\overleftarrow{Pre}}(r', \sigma) = L_\varepsilon(r'')$ if $r' = \sigma r''$, and $\delta_{\overleftarrow{Pre}}(r', \sigma) = \emptyset$, otherwise. Then, we have [11]

$$D(\mathcal{A}_{PD}(r))/{\equiv_{L_\varepsilon}} \simeq \mathcal{A}_B(r)/{\equiv_{L_\varepsilon}} \simeq D(\mathcal{A}_{\overleftarrow{Pre}}(r)).$$

This DFA is interesting because it is the smallest among several deterministic automata constructions obtained from regular expressions, although not always the minimal [11].

For a language $L \subseteq \Sigma^\star$ and a word $w \in \Sigma^\star$ one can also define the *right-quotient* of L by w, as $Lw^{-1} = \{ x \mid xw \in L \}$. The notions of derivative and partial-derivative can also be defined in this case, as well as the correspondent automata. However, that is tantamount to consider the left constructions in the double reverse, i.e., $\mathcal{A}(r^R)^R$ where R is the reversal operation. Of course, one has $\mathcal{L}(\mathcal{A}(r)) = \mathcal{L}(\mathcal{A}(r^R)^R) = \mathcal{L}(r)$. In particular, $\mathcal{A}_{\overleftarrow{Pre}}(r) \simeq \mathcal{A}_{Pre}(r^R)^R$ where $\mathcal{A}_{Pre}$ is the *prefix automaton* introduced by Yamamoto [78] and studied in [11,19]. Broda et al. [11] presented a taxonomy of conversions from regular expressions to finite automaton that includes the above ones and that are related with the position automaton, which we consider in the next section.

3.1   Position Automaton

The position automaton $\mathcal{A}_{POS}$, introduced by Victor Glushkov [37] in 1961, permits us to convert a regular expression r into an equivalent NFA without ε-transitions. McNaughton-Yamada 1960's automaton [53], $\mathcal{A}_{MY}$, corresponds to the determinisation of $\mathcal{A}_{POS}$ and the construction is similar. Leiss inductive automaton construction [49] leads to the same automaton [30]. This automaton is also called *standard* as it has a unique initial state which is *non-returning* [70,71]. Below we will see its connection with the partial derivative automaton, $\mathcal{A}_{PD}$.

The states in the position automaton correspond to the positions of alphabetic symbols in r plus an additional initial state. Formally, given $r \in \mathcal{R}_k$, one can mark each occurrence of a symbol $\sigma \in \Sigma$ with its position in r, considering reading it from left to right. The resulting regular expression is a *marked* regular expression $\bar{r}$ with all alphabetic symbols distinct. Then, a position $i \in [1, |r|_\Sigma]$ corresponds to the symbol σ_i in $\bar{r}$, and consequently to exactly one occurrence of σ in r. The same notation is used to remove the markings, i.e., $\bar{\bar{r}} = r$. Let $\mathsf{Pos}(r) = \{1, 2, \ldots, |r|_\Sigma\}$, and let $\mathsf{Pos}_0(r) = \mathsf{Pos}(r) \cup \{0\}$. To define the $\mathcal{A}_{\mathsf{POS}}(r)$ we consider the following sets: $\mathsf{First}(r) = \{\, i \mid \sigma_i w \in \mathcal{L}(\bar{r}) \,\}$, $\mathsf{Last}(r) = \{\, i \mid w\sigma_i \in \mathcal{L}(\bar{r}) \,\}$, and $\mathsf{Follow}(r, i) = \{\, j \mid u\sigma_i\sigma_j v \in \mathcal{L}(\bar{r}) \,\}$. Given a set $S \subseteq \mathsf{Pos}(r)$ and $\sigma \in \Sigma$, let $\mathsf{Select}(S, \sigma) = \{\, i \mid i \in S \wedge \overline{\sigma_i} = \sigma \,\}$. Then, the *position automaton* for r is

$$\mathcal{A}_{\mathsf{POS}}(r) = \langle \mathsf{Pos}_0(r), \Sigma, \delta_{\mathsf{POS}}, 0, \mathsf{Last}(r) \cup \varepsilon(r)\{0\}\rangle,$$

where $\delta_{\mathsf{POS}}(i, \sigma) = \mathsf{Select}(\mathsf{Follow}(r, i), \sigma)$.

Champarnaud and Ziadi [28] proved that $\mathcal{A}_{\mathsf{PD}}$ is a quotient of the position automaton $\mathcal{A}_{\mathsf{POS}}$ by the right-invariant equivalence relation $\equiv_c$, that we define in the following. Given a position i, for all $w \in \Sigma_{\bar{r}}^\star$, $\partial_{w\sigma_i}(\bar{r})$ is either empty or equal to the singleton $\{c(r, i)\}$, which element is called the i's c-continuation of $\bar{r}$. For $i \in \mathsf{Pos}(r)$, c-continuations are inductively defined by: $c(\emptyset, i) = c(\varepsilon, i) = \emptyset$, and $c(\sigma_i, i) = \varepsilon$. Now consider $\bar{r}$ of the form $r_1 + r_2$, $r_1 r_2$, or $r_1^\star$. If i occurs in r_1, then $c(r_1 + r_2, i) = c(r_1, i)$, $c(r_1 r_2, i) = c(r_1, i)r_2$, and $c(r_1^\star, i) = c(r_1, i)r_1^\star$. If i occurs in r_2, then $c(r_1 + r_2, i) = c(r_1 r_2, i) = c(r_2, i)$. Considering $c(r, 0) = \bar{r}$, for $i, j \in \mathsf{Pos}_0(r)$ we define $i \equiv_c j \Leftrightarrow c(r, i) = c(r, j)$.

Proposition 1 ([28]). $\mathcal{A}_{PD}(r) \simeq \mathcal{A}_{POS}(r)/{\equiv_c}$.

The proof of this proposition relies in the following relations

- $\partial^+(\bar{r}) = \{\, c(r, i) \mid i \in \mathsf{Pos}(r) \,\}$;
- $\partial_{\sigma_i}(\bar{r}) = \{c(r, i)\} \iff i \in \mathsf{First}(r)$;
- $\varepsilon(c(r, i)) = \varepsilon \iff i \in \mathsf{Last}(r)$;
- $c(r, i) \in \partial_{\sigma_i}(c(r, j)) \iff i \in \mathsf{Follow}(r, j)$.

From that, one has that $\mathcal{A}_{\mathsf{PD}}(\bar{r}) \simeq \mathcal{A}_{\mathsf{POS}}(\bar{r})/{\equiv_c'}$, where $i \equiv_c' j \Leftrightarrow c(r, i) = c(r, j)$. And, thus $\overline{\mathcal{A}_{\mathsf{PD}}(\bar{r})} \simeq \overline{\mathcal{A}_{\mathsf{POS}}(\bar{r})}/{\equiv_c'}$, where $\overline{\mathcal{A}}$ means an automaton equal to $\mathcal{A}$ but with the transition labels unmarked. Now, noting that for $\sigma \in \Sigma$, $\partial_\sigma(r) = \bigcup_{i \in \mathsf{Select}(\mathsf{Pos}(r), \sigma)} \partial_{\sigma_i}(\bar{r})$, the result follows.

4   Complexity of Partial Derivatives

Here we will focus on the partial derivative based automata constructions and, due to Proposition 1, on the position automaton. We will consider both the size of the automata, as well as, the complexity of the associated constructions. Moreover we restrict to standard regular expressions with union, concatenation, and Kleene star. First, we consider the $\mathcal{A}_{\mathsf{POS}}$.

Proposition 2 ([20,32,67]). *The position automaton $\mathcal{A}_{POS}(r)$ has $|r|_\Sigma + 1$ states and the number of transitions is $\Theta(\|r\|^2)$. It can be constructed in $O(\|r\|^2)$ time and use just $O(\|r\|)$ space.*

The *star normal form* of a regular expression r, introduced by Bruggemann-Klein [20], corresponds to ensure that in any subexpression $s^\star$ one has that $\varepsilon(s) = \emptyset$. The conversion of an expression to star normal form can be done in linear time; the $\mathcal{A}_{POS}$ of both expressions coincide; and for star normal forms its construction runs in quadratic time. Gruber and Gulan [38] extended this form to *strong star normal form* (ssnf) that is the one we will consider here.

Nicaud [63] studied the average size of $\mathcal{A}_{POS}$ for the uniform distribution. Broda et al. [13], using a variant of the computation of the ssnf(r), improved the result for the number of transitions.

Proposition 3 ([63]). *Asymptotically, and as the alphabet size grows, the average number of states in $\mathcal{A}_{POS}$ is $\frac{\|r\|}{2}$.*

Proposition 4 ([13,63]). *Asymptotically, and as the alphabet size grows, the average number of transitions in $\mathcal{A}_{POS}$ is $\|r\|$.*

Now, we turn to the complexity of partial derivatives and $\mathcal{A}_{PD}$. The next two propositions follow directly from Eq. (6).

Proposition 5 ([4,57] Th. 3.4). *For any regular expression $r \in \mathcal{R}_k$, the following inequality holds $|\partial^+(r)| \leq |r|_\Sigma$.*

Proposition 6 ([4], **Th. 3.8**). *Given $r \in \mathcal{R}_k$, a partial derivative of r is either ε or a concatenation $r_1 r_2 \cdots r_n$ such that each r_i is a subexpression of r and $n-1$ is no greater than the number of occurrences of concatenations and stars in r.*

Corollary 1. *For $r_1 \in \partial^+(r)$, the size $\|r_1\|$ is $O(\|r\|^2)$.*

In general, the same bounds apply for partial derivatives by an alphabetic symbol. To improve the computation of $\partial_\sigma(r)$, Antimirov defined the *linear form* φ of a regular expression r that allows the computation of the partial derivatives by all alphabetic symbols in a unique transversal of the expression:

$$\varphi(r) = \{ (\sigma, r') \mid r' \in \partial_\sigma(r) \}. \tag{9}$$

Proposition 7 ([4,57]). *For $r \in \mathcal{R}_k$, we have $|\varphi(r)| \leq |r|_\Sigma$ and for $(\sigma, r') \in \varphi(r)$, the size $\|r'\|$ is $O(\|r\|^2)$. If r contains no subexpression of the form $r_1^\star$, then the size $\|r'\|$ is $O(\|r\|)$.*

From the above we have

Corollary 2. *For $r \in \mathcal{R}_k$, $|\delta_{PD}(r)|$ is $O(|r|_\Sigma^2)$.*

The following examples show that the above upper bounds are attained.

Example 1. Let $r_n = a_1^\star a_2^\star \cdots a_n^\star$, with $|r|_\Sigma = n$, $n \geq 1$. Then $\partial^+(r_n) = \{ a_i^\star \cdots a_n^\star \mid 2 \leq i \leq n \}$, and $|\varphi(r_n)| = |r_n|_\Sigma = n$. The largest partial derivative has size $3n - 1$, and $|\delta_{PD}(r_n)| = \sum_{i=1}^{n-1} i = \frac{n(n+1)}{2}$.

Example 2. Consider $r_0 = a$ and $r_n = (r_{n-1}^\star a)$, for $n \geq 1$ over the unary alphabet $\{a\}$. The size of r_n is $3n + 1$, for $n \geq 0$. For $n \geq 1$, the largest partial derivative of $\partial_a(r_n) = \{\, r_i \cdots r_n \mid 1 \leq i \leq n \,\} \cup \{\varepsilon\}$ is $r_1 r_2 \cdots r_n$ whose size is

$$n - 1 + \sum_{i=1}^{n}(3i + 1) = \frac{3n^2 + 7n - 2}{2} = \Theta(n^2).$$

Although $\mathcal{A}_{\mathrm{PD}}$ is no larger than $\mathcal{A}_{\mathrm{POS}}$, the quadratic size of the partial derivatives can burden the computation of $\mathcal{A}_{\mathrm{PD}}$. Before considering the complexity of the construction algorithms, we recall some average-case estimates.

Proposition 8 ([12,13]). *Asymptotically in the size of the expression $r \in \mathcal{R}_k$, and as the alphabet size grows, the average of upper bounds of: the size of $\varphi(r)$ is the constant 6; the size of $\partial^+(r)$ is $\frac{\|r\|}{4}$; the size of $\delta_{PD}(r)$ is $\frac{\|r\|}{2}$.*

In particular, we can conclude that, asymptotically, on average the size of $\mathcal{A}_{\mathrm{PD}}$ is half the size of $\mathcal{A}_{\mathrm{POS}}$. The estimation of the average size of partial derivatives is also important and was studied by Konstantinidis et al. [46]. Moreover, if the regular expression is in ssnf, the size of partial derivatives are on average linear in the size of the expression. Let $\mathcal{S}_k$ be the set of regular expressions in ssnf, then, we have the following.

Proposition 9 ([46] **Th.3 and Th.4**). *Asymptotically and as the alphabet size grows, the average of an upper bound of the maximum size of partial derivatives of $r \in \mathcal{R}_k$ is $\frac{\sqrt{\pi}}{4}(\|r\|)^{\frac{3}{2}}$. For $s \in \mathcal{S}_k$, that value is $\frac{\|s\|}{2}$.*

Proposition 6 shows that a partial derivative is a concatenation of subexpressions of the original expression. Thus, one can estimate the average number of new concatenations when computing $\partial_\sigma(r)$ and $\partial^+(r)$.

Proposition 10 ([45,46]). *Asymptotically and as the alphabet size grows: the average of an upper bound of the number of new concatenations in a partial derivative by an alphabetic symbol of a regular expression $s \in \mathcal{S}_k$ is 14; the average of an upper bound of the number new concatenations in all partial derivatives of a regular expression $s \in \mathcal{S}_k$ is $\frac{1}{8}\sqrt{\frac{\pi}{2}}\|s\|^{\frac{3}{2}}$.*

4.1 Complexity of Building $\mathcal{A}_{\mathrm{PD}}$

Antimirov [4] presented a construction of the $\mathcal{A}_{\mathrm{PD}}$ with worst-case time complexity $O(|r|_\Sigma^3 \|r\|^2)$ and worst-case space complexity $O(|r|_\Sigma \|r\|^2)$. Mirkin's construction of $\mathcal{A}_{\mathrm{PD}}$ has a worst-case time complexity $O(\|r\|^3)$. Champarnaud and Ziadi [31] presented a quadratic algorithm to construct $\mathcal{A}_{\mathrm{PD}}$ that first builds $\mathcal{A}_{\mathrm{POS}}$ and then, using Proposition 1, computes the equivalence relation $\equiv_c$ on the set of states of $\mathcal{A}_{\mathrm{POS}}$. The set of c-continuations can be computed in $O(\|r\|^2 |r|_\Sigma)$. To compute the relation $\equiv_c$ one can lexicographically sort the set of c-continuations using Paige and Tarjan linear algorithm [66] and then compare consecutive identical expressions. Thus, the set $\partial^+(r)$ can be computed in

$O(\|r\|^2 |r|_{\Sigma})$ time and space. But several improvements can be done and Champarnaud and Ziadi showed that $\mathcal{A}_{PD}(r)$ can be computed in time and space $O(\|r\|^2)$.

An improved method was proposed by Khorsi and Ziadi [43], which has worst-case time and space complexity $O(\|r\| |r|_{\Sigma})$. The main difference is the substitution of the lexicographic sorting of the c-continuations by the minimisation of an acyclic DFA and which can be performed in time $O(\|r\|)$ [68]. More recently Ouardi et al. [65] presented a similar algorithm using the Thompson automaton, $\mathcal{A}_{\varepsilon-T}$, instead of $\mathcal{A}_{POS}$.

For practical applications, the drawbacks of these methods rely on the need to build a larger automaton and the computation of equivalence relations. Thus, it is interesting to construct the $\mathcal{A}_{PD}$ in quadratic time and linear space avoiding the computation of larger automata. Using the average estimates given above, Konstantinis et al. [45] presented an algorithm for computing $\mathcal{A}_{PD}$ which for ssnf expressions of size n uses, on average, time $O\left(n^{3/2} \sqrt[4]{\log(n)}\right)$ and space $O\left(n^{3/2}/(\log n)^{3/4}\right)$. The regular expression and the set of its partial derivatives are represented by a directed acyclic graph (DAG) with shared common subexpressions. Flajolet et al. [35] showed that a tree of size n has, in this compact form, an expected size of $O\left(n/\sqrt{\log n}\right)$. The algorithm computes $\mathcal{A}_{PD}(r)$ by constructing a DAG for r, and simultaneously builds the set of all partial derivatives by adding new concatenation nodes to the DAG. Empirical tests suggest that this algorithm can outperform Khorsi and Ziadi's algorithm.

A possible advantage of a direct method is its easy adaptation to other regular operations, such as intersection and shuffle [7,16,75], and its efficient extension to decision problems such as membership and equivalence. Partial derivatives have already been considered for solving these problems, but a fine-grain complexity analysis is needed [3,26,59,64,74].

5   Beyond Regular Languages

The notions of derivative and partial derivative are easily extended to other regularity preserving operations. We note that even for intersection and shuffle extending the position automaton is more challenging [15,18]. However, in some cases, e.g. intersection, the Mirkin's construction may lead to automata that are not initially connected [8].

As left-quotients are defined for any formal language, derivatives have been defined for context-free languages both considering grammars and μ-expressions [1,76]. Interestingly, parsing context-free grammars with derivatives can be achieved in cubic time. Parsing expression grammars (PEG) are a recognition-based formalism for which parsing can be achieved in linear time. Deterministic context-free languages are recognisable by PEGs but it is not known if all context-free grammars are recognisable, although some non-context-free languages are. Derivatives for PEGs were proposed in [60].

Derivatives of weighted rational expressions, that represent formal power series with coefficients in a semiring, have also been extensively studied

[29,50,70,71]. In this case, derivatives are also connected with the notion of quotient of a series. In the same manner, if one consider trees instead of words the above methods can be extended to tree regular expressions and tree automata [54–56].

More recently, partial derivatives for regular expressions with labels over finitely generated monoids (possible non-free) were studied by Konstantinidis et al. [47] and also by Demaille [34]. In particular, those expressions allow to represent (weighted) rational relations. In this case, using an appropriate version of the linear form of an expression, the Eqs. (8) and (6) hold and a partial derivative automaton can be defined. Lombardy and Sakarovitch [51] expanded and generalised this approach, showing that the partial derivative automaton is a quotient of position automaton, even considering weighted regular expressions over non free monoids.

Finally we briefly point to the fast literature on category theory of automata and algebraic and coalgeraic approaches to characterise general state-based systems where the notion of derivative plays also an important role [10,42,69,73].

References

1. Adams, M.D., Hollenbeck, C., Might, M.: On the complexity and performance of parsing with derivatives. In: Krintz, C., Berger, E. (eds.) Proceedings 37th ACM SIGPLAN PLDI, pp. 224–236. ACM (2016). https://doi.org/10.1145/2908080. 2908128

2. Almeida, M., Moreira, N., Reis, R.: Antimirov and Mosses' rewrite system revisited. Int. J. Found. Comput. Sci. **20**(4), 669–684 (2009). https://doi.org/10.1142/ S0129054109006802

3. Almeida, M., Moreira, N., Reis, R.: Testing equivalence of regular languages. J. Autom. Lang. Comb. **15**(1/2), 7–25 (2010). https://doi.org/10.25596/jalc-2010-007

4. Antimirov, V.M.: Partial derivatives of regular expressions and finite automaton constructions. Theoret. Comput. Sci. **155**(2), 291–319 (1996). https://doi.org/10. 1016/0304-3975(95)00182-4

5. Antimirov, V.M., Mosses, P.: Rewriting extended regular expressions. In: Rozenberg, G., Salomaa, A. (eds.) Developments in Language Theory, pp. 195–209. World Scientific (1994)

6. Asperti, A., Coen, C.S., Tassi, E.: Regular expressions, au point. CoRR abs/1010.2604 (2010). http://arxiv.org/abs/1010.2604

7. Câmpeanu, C., Manea, F., Shallit, J. (eds.): DCFS 2016. LNCS, vol. 9777. Springer, Cham (2016). https://doi.org/10.1007/978-3-319-41114-9

8. Bastos, R., Broda, S., Machiavelo, A., Moreira, N., Reis, R.: On the average complexity of partial derivative automata for semi-extended expressions. J. Autom. Lang. Comb. **22**(1–3), 5–28 (2017). https://doi.org/10.25596/jalc-2017-005

9. Berry, G., Sethi, R.: From regular expressions to deterministic automata. Theoret. Comput. Sci. **48**, 117–126 (1986)

10. Bonchi, F., Pous, D.: Checking NFA equivalence with bisimulations up to congruence. In: Giacobazzi, R., Cousot, R. (eds.) Proceedings 40th POPL 2013, pp. 457–468. ACM (2013). https://doi.org/10.1145/2429069.2429124

11. Broda, S., Holzer, M., Maia, E., Moreira, N., Reis, R.: A mesh of automata. Inf. Comput. **265**, 94–111 (2019). https://doi.org/10.1016/j.ic.2019.01.003
12. Broda, S., Machiavelo, A., Moreira, N., Reis, R.: On the average state complexity of partial derivative automata: an analytic combinatorics approach. Int. J. Found. Comput. Sci. **22**(7), 1593–1606 (2011). https://doi.org/10.1142/S012905
13. Broda, S., Machiavelo, A., Moreira, N., Reis, R.: On the average size of Glushkov and partial derivative automata. Int. J. Found. Comput. Sci. **23**(5), 969–984 (2012). https://doi.org/10.1142/S0129054112400400
14. Broda, S., Machiavelo, A., Moreira, N., Reis, R.: Average size of automata constructions from regular expressions. Bull. Eur. Assoc. Theor. Comput. Sci. **116**, 167–192 (2015). http://bulletin.eatcs.org/index.php/beatcs/article/view/352/334
15. Broda, S., Machiavelo, A., Moreira, N., Reis, R.: Position automaton construction for regular expressions with intersection. In: Brlek, S., Reutenauer, C. (eds.) DLT 2016. LNCS, vol. 9840, pp. 51–63. Springer, Heidelberg (2016). https://doi.org/10.1007/978-3-662-53132-7_5
16. Broda, S., Machiavelo, A., Moreira, N., Reis, R.: Automata for regular expressions with shuffle. Inf. Comput. **259**(2), 162–173 (2018). https://doi.org/10.1016/j.ic.2017.08.013
17. Broda, S., Machiavelo, A., Moreira, N., Reis, R.: Analytic combinatorics and descriptional complexity of regular languages on average. ACM SIGACT News **51**(1), 38–56 (2020)
18. Broda, S., Machiavelo, A., Moreira, N., Reis, R.: Location based automata for expressions with shuffle. In: Leporati, A., Martín-Vide, C., Shapira, D., Zandron, C. (eds.) LATA 2021. LNCS, vol. 12638, pp. 43–54. Springer, Cham (2021). https://doi.org/10.1007/978-3-030-68195-1_4
19. Broda, S., Maia, E., Moreira, N., Reis, R.: The prefix automaton. J. Autom. Lang. Comb. **26**(1–2), 17–53 (2021). https://doi.org/10.25596/jalc-2021-017
20. Brüggemann-Klein, A.: Regular expressions into finite automata. Theoret. Comput. Sci. **48**, 197–213 (1993)
21. Brzozowski, Jr. J.A., McCluskey, E.J.: Signal flow graph techniques for sequential circuit state diagrams. IEEE Trans. Electron. Comput. **EC-12**(2), 67–76 (1963)
22. Brzozowski, J.: Regular expression techniques for sequential circuits. Ph.D. thesis, Department of Electrical Engineering, Princeton University (1962)
23. Brzozowski, J.A.: Quotient complexity of regular languages **15**(1/2), 71–89 (2010). https://doi.org/10.25596/jalc-2010-071
24. Brzozowski, J.A., Leiss, E.L.: On equations for regular languages, finite automata, and sequential networks. Theor. Comput. Sci. **10**, 19–35 (1980). https://doi.org/10.1016/0304-3975(80)90069-9
25. Brzozowski, J.: Derivatives of regular expressions. J. ACM **11**(4), 481–494 (1964). https://doi.org/10.1145/321239.321249
26. Cardoso, E.M., Amaro, M., da Silva Feitosa, S., dos Santos Reis, L.V., Bois, A.R.D., Ribeiro, R.G.: The design of a verified derivative-based parsing tool for regular expressions. CLEI Electron. J. **24**(3) (2021). https://doi.org/10.19153/cleiej.24.3.2
27. Champarnaud, J.M., Ziadi, D.: From Mirkin's prebases to Antimirov's word partial derivatives. Fundam. Inform. **45**(3), 195–205 (2001)
28. Champarnaud, J.M., Ziadi, D.: Canonical derivatives, partial derivatives and finite automaton constructions. Theoret. Comput. Sci. **289**, 137–163 (2002). https://doi.org/10.1016/S0304-3975(01)00267-5

29. Champarnaud, J.-M., Ouardi, F., Ziadi, D.: An efficient computation of the equation $\mathbb{K}$-automaton of a regular $\mathbb{K}$-expression. In: Harju, T., Karhumäki, J., Lepistö, A. (eds.) DLT 2007. LNCS, vol. 4588, pp. 145–156. Springer, Heidelberg (2007). https://doi.org/10.1007/978-3-540-73208-2_16

30. Champarnaud, J., Ponty, J., Ziadi, D.: From regular expressions to finite automata. Int. J. Comput. Math. **72**(4), 415–431 (1999). https://doi.org/10.1080/00207169908804865

31. Champarnaud, J., Ziadi, D.: From C-continuations to new quadratic algorithms for automaton synthesis. Int. J. Alg. Comput. **11**(6), 707–736 (2001)

32. Chang, C., Paige, R.: From regular expressions to DFA's using compressed NFA's. Theor. Comput. Sci. **178**(1–2), 1–36 (1997). https://doi.org/10.1016/S0304-3975(96)00140-5

33. Conway, J.H.: Regular Algebra and Finite Machines. Chapman and Hall, London (1971)

34. Demaille, A.: Derived-term automata of multitape rational expressions. In: Han, Y.-S., Salomaa, K. (eds.) CIAA 2016. LNCS, vol. 9705, pp. 51–63. Springer, Cham (2016). https://doi.org/10.1007/978-3-319-40946-7_5

35. Flajolet, P., Sipala, P., Steyaert, J.-M.: Analytic variations on the common subexpression problem. In: Paterson, M.S. (ed.) ICALP 1990. LNCS, vol. 443, pp. 220–234. Springer, Heidelberg (1990). https://doi.org/10.1007/BFb0032034

36. Ginzburg, A.: A procedure for checking equality of regular expressions. J. ACM **14**(2), 355–362 (1967). https://doi.org/10.1145/321386.321399

37. Glushkov, V.M.: The abstract theory of automata. Russ. Math. Surv. **16**, 1–53 (1961)

38. Gruber, H., Gulan, S.: Simplifying regular expressions. In: Dediu, A.-H., Fernau, H., Martín-Vide, C. (eds.) LATA 2010. LNCS, vol. 6031, pp. 285–296. Springer, Heidelberg (2010). https://doi.org/10.1007/978-3-642-13089-2_24

39. Gruber, H., Holzer, M.: From finite automata to regular expressions and back–a summary on descriptional complexity. Int. J. Found. Comput. Sci. **26**(8), 1009–1040 (2015). https://doi.org/10.1142/S0129054115400110

40. Holzer, M., Kutrib, M.: The complexity of regular(-like) expressions. Int. J. Found. Comput. Sci. **22**(7), 1533–1548 (2011)

41. Hopcroft, J., Karp, R.M.: A linear algorithm for testing equivalence of finite automata. Technical report, TR 71–114, University of California, Berkeley, California (1971)

42. Kappé, T., Brunet, P., Luttik, B., Silva, A., Zanasi, F.: Brzozowski goes concurrent - a Kleene theorem for pomset languages. In: Meyer, R., Nestmann, U. (eds.) Proceedings 28th CONCUR 2017. LIPIcs, vol. 85, pp. 25:1–25:16. Schloss Dagstuhl - Leibniz-Zentrum für Informatik (2017). https://doi.org/10.4230/LIPIcs.CONCUR.2017.25

43. Khorsi, A., Ouardi, F., Ziadi, D.: Fast equation automaton computation. J. Discrete Algorithms **6**(3), 433–448 (2008). https://doi.org/10.1016/j.jda.2007.10.003

44. Kleene, S.C.: Representation of events in nerve nets and finite automata. In: Shannon, C.E., McCarthy, J. (eds.) Automata Studies, pp. 3–41. Princeton University Press, Princeton (1956)

45. Konstantinidis, S., Machiavelo, A., Moreira, N., Reis, R.: Partial derivative automaton by compressing regular expressions. In: Yan, Y., Ko, S. (eds.) Proceedings 23rd DCFS 2021. LNCS, vol. 13037, pp. 100–112. Springer, Cham (2021). https://doi.org/10.1007/978-3-030-93489-7_9

46. Konstantinidis, S., Machiavelo, A., Moreira, N., Reis, R.: On the size of partial derivatives and the word membership problem. Acta Informatica **58**(4), 357–375 (2021). https://doi.org/10.1007/s00236-021-00399-6

47. Konstantinidis, S., Moreira, N., Reis, R.: Partial derivatives of regular expressions over alphabet-invariant and user-defined labels. Theor. Comput. Sci. **870**, 103–120 (2021). https://doi.org/10.1016/j.tcs.2020.12.029

48. Krob, D.: Differentiation of K-rational expressions. Int. J. Algebra Comput. **2**(1), 57–88 (1992). https://doi.org/10.1142/S0218196792000062

49. Leiss, E.L.: The complexity of restricted regular expressions and the synthesis problem for finite automata. J. Comput. Syst. Sci. **23**(3), 348–354 (1981). https://doi.org/10.1016/0022-0000(81)90070-2

50. Lombardy, S., Sakarovitch, J.: Derivatives of rational expressions with multiplicity. Theor. Comput. Sci. **332**(1–3), 141–177 (2005). https://doi.org/10.1016/j.tcs.2004.10.016

51. Lombardy, S., Sakarovitch, J.: Derived terms without derivation a shifted perspective on the derived-term automaton. J. Comput. Sci. Cybern. **37**(3), 201–221 (2021). https://doi.org/10.15625/1813-9663/37/3/16263

52. McCulloch, W., Pitts, W.: A logical calculus of the ideas immanent in nervous activity. Bull. Math. Biophisics **5**, 115–133 (1943)

53. McNaughton, R., Yamada, H.: Regular expressions and state graphs for automata. IEEE Trans. Electron. Comput. **9**, 39–47 (1960)

54. Mignot, L.: A unified implementation of automata and expression structures, and of the associated algorithms using enriched categories. CoRR abs/2012.10641 (2020). https://arxiv.org/abs/2012.10641

55. Mignot, L., Sebti, N.O., Ziadi, D.: Tree automata constructions from regular expressions: a comparative study. Fundam. Informaticae **156**(1), 69–94 (2017). https://doi.org/10.3233/FI-2017-1598

56. Mignot, L., Sebti, N.O., Ziadi, D.: An efficient algorithm for the construction of the equation tree automaton. Int. J. Found. Comput. Sci. **29**(6), 951–978 (2018). https://doi.org/10.1142/S0129054118500156

57. Mirkin, B.G.: An algorithm for constructing a base in a language of regular expressions. Eng. Cybern. **5**, 51–57 (1966)

58. Mizoguchi, Y., Ohtsuka, H., Kawahara, Y.: Symbolic calculus of regular expressions. Bull. Inf. Cybern. **22**(3–4), 165–170 (1987)

59. Moreira, N., Pereira, D., de Sousa, S.M.: Deciding Kleene algebra terms (in)equivalence in Coq. J. Logical Algebraic Methods Program. **84**(3), 377–401 (2015). https://doi.org/10.1016/j.jlamp.2014.12.004

60. Moss, A.: Simplified parsing expression derivatives. In: Leporati, A., Martín-Vide, C., Shapira, D., Zandron, C. (eds.) LATA 2020. LNCS, vol. 12038, pp. 425–436. Springer, Cham (2020). https://doi.org/10.1007/978-3-030-40608-0_30

61. Myhill, J.: Finite automata and representation of events. In: Fundamental Concepts in the Theory of Systems, vol. 57. Wright Air Development Center (1957)

62. Nerode, A.: Linear automaton transformations. Proc. Am. Math. Soc. **9**, 541–544 (1958)

63. Nicaud, C.: On the average size of Glushkov's automata. In: Dediu, A.H., Ionescu, A.M., Martín-Vide, C. (eds.) LATA 2009. LNCS, vol. 5457, pp. 626–637. Springer, Heidelberg (2009). https://doi.org/10.1007/978-3-642-00982-2_53

64. Nipkow, T., Traytel, D.: Unified decision procedures for regular expression equivalence. In: Klein, G., Gamboa, R. (eds.) ITP 2014. LNCS, vol. 8558, pp. 450–466. Springer, Cham (2014). https://doi.org/10.1007/978-3-319-08970-6_29

65. Ouardi, F., Lotfi, Z., Elghadyry, B.: Efficient construction of the equation automaton. Algorithms **14**(8), 238 (2021). https://doi.org/10.3390/a14080238
66. Paige, R., Tarjan, R.E.: Three partition refinement algorithms. SIAM J. Comput. **16**(6), 973–989 (1987). https://doi.org/10.1137/0216062
67. Ponty, J.-L., Ziadi, D., Champarnaud, J.-M.: A new quadratic algorithm to convert a regular expression into an automaton. In: Raymond, D., Wood, D., Yu, S. (eds.) WIA 1996. LNCS, vol. 1260, pp. 109–119. Springer, Heidelberg (1997). https://doi.org/10.1007/3-540-63174-7_9
68. Revuz, D.: Minimisation of acyclic deterministic automata in linear time. Theoret. Comput. Sci. **92**(1), 181–189 (1992)
69. Rutten, J.: Behavioural differential equations: a coinductive calculus of streams, automata, and power series. Theoret. Comput. Sci. **208**(1–3), 1–53 (2003). https://doi.org/10.1016/S0304-3975(02)00895-2
70. Sakarovitch, J.: Elements of Automata Theory. Cambridge University Press (2009). https://doi.org/10.1017/CBO9781139195218
71. Sakarovitch, J.: Automata and rational expressions. In: Pin, J. (ed.) Handbook of Automata Theory, pp. 39–78. European Mathematical Society Publishing House, Zürich (2021). https://doi.org/10.4171/Automata-1/2
72. Salomaa, A.: Two complete axiom systems for the algebra of regular events. J. Assoc. Comput. Mach. **13**(1), 158–169 (1966)
73. Silva, A., Bonchi, F., Bonsangue, M.M., Rutten, J.J.M.M.: Quantitative Kleene coalgebras. Inf. Comput. **209**(5), 822–849 (2011). https://doi.org/10.1016/j.ic.2010.09.007
74. Sulzmann, M., Lu, K.Z.M.: Regular expression sub-matching using partial derivatives. In: Schreye, D.D., Janssens, G., King, A. (eds.) Proceedings PPDP 2012, pp. 79–90. ACM (2012). https://doi.org/10.1145/2370776.2370788
75. Sulzmann, M., Thiemann, P.: Derivatives and partial derivatives for regular shuffle expressions. J. Comput. Syst. Sci. **104**, 323–341 (2019). https://doi.org/10.1016/j.jcss.2016.11.010
76. Thiemann, P.: Partial derivatives for context-free languages. In: Esparza, J., Murawski, A.S. (eds.) FoSSaCS 2017. LNCS, vol. 10203, pp. 248–264. Springer, Heidelberg (2017). https://doi.org/10.1007/978-3-662-54458-7_15
77. Thompson, K.: Regular expression search algorithm. Commun. ACM **11**(6), 410–422 (1968)
78. Yamamoto, H.: A new finite automaton construction for regular expressions. In: Bensch, S., Freund, R., Otto, F. (eds.) 6th NCMA. books@ocg.at, vol. 304, pp. 249–264. Österreichische Computer Gesellschaft (2014)

How to Settle the ReDoS Problem: Back to the Classical Automata Theory

Sicheol Sung, Hyunjoon Cheon, and Yo-Sub Han[(✉)]

Yonsei University, Seoul, Republic of Korea
{sicheol.sung,hyunjooncheon,emmous}@yonsei.ac.kr

Abstract. Most regular-expression matching engines in practice are based on the Thompson construction and the Spencer matching algorithm. While these engines work fast and efficiently, a serious problem, the regular expression denial-of-service (ReDoS), has been reported recently. ReDoS is an algorithm complexity attack, which exploits the backtracking feature of the engine, and makes the service unresponsive indefinitely. Researchers suggested a few remedies to cope with the ReDoS problem, yet they are often ad-hoc or undesirable in practice. We instead propose a hybrid matching scheme that selects between the Thompson and the Spencer matching algorithms depending on the needed features. We also suggest to use the position construction for its intrinsic characteristics for fast matching. We evaluate the proposed approach using a benchmark dataset collected from various open-source projects, and compare the performance with the current approach. The experimental results show that a hybrid matcher reduces the ReDoS-vulnerability by 96% and 99.98% in full and partial matching, respectively. Moreover, 55% of the most problematic regular expressions become invulnerable to ReDoS by the position construction.

Keywords: Regular expressions · Denial of service · ReDoS · Position automata

1 Introduction

Regular expressions (regexes in short) are widely used in many applications such as software engineering, bioinformatics and natural language processing to describe string patterns [7,9,20]. A regex matching engine takes two inputs—a regex E and an input text T—and checks if the whole (= full matching) T or a substring (= partial matching) of T is matched by E. A typical regex engine in practice has two components: a compiler and a matcher. The compiler translates E into an internal representation of the engine. Then the matcher simulates the compiled E against T. Most regex engines rely on the Thompson construction for compilers and the Spencer algorithm for matchers [10,14].

Regexes were developed as a theoretical model for simple computations [19], and later became a popular tool for efficient pattern matching [28,29]. Then, people started to introduce additional features to serve different domain needs such

© Springer Nature Switzerland AG 2022
P. Caron and L. Mignot (Eds.): CIAA 2022, LNCS 13266, pp. 34–49, 2022.
https://doi.org/10.1007/978-3-031-07469-1_3

as backreferences or lookarounds. Thus, the gap between the original regexes and the new regexes is very large; regexes with the extended features are not regular anymore [4,5]. All regex engines with these extended features worked well until a serious problem—regular-expression denial-of-service (ReDoS) attacks—happened [31]. The ReDoS attack is an algorithmic complexity attack that produces denial-of-service by providing an input in which a regex engine takes a very long time to evaluate and becomes unresponsive.

One simple solution is to verify whether a regex is vulnerable to ReDoS prior to matching, and ask users to revise the regex if it is vulnerable. Another resolution is to design a ReDoS-resistant regex engine. Cox [10] proposed RE2 that employs a Thompson matcher and eliminates ReDoS. Since the extended features in practical regexes make matching NP-hard [2], Cox suggested removing the extended features and preserving regularity. Another line of research is to mitigate the ReDoS problem without giving up extended features. For example, Davis et al. [13] proposed to memoize the matching attempts of the Spencer matcher and reduce the computation steps, and Schmid [26] suggested several properties of regexes that guarantee poly-time matching.

We propose a hybrid matching scheme that suits both the efficient matching time and the desired features in practical regexes. For fast matching, we suggest using the position construction that has several intrinsic properties [6]. We demonstrate that these properties indeed lead to better performance and mitigate the ReDoS problem well. Our research questions are summarized as follows:

RQ1 How much do the position construction and the hybrid matching scheme improve the performance for ReDoS-vulnerable regexes?
RQ2 How much does the position construction improve the performance for ReDoS-invulnerable (= linear-matching-time) regexes?
RQ3 How often are regexes deterministic and how much is the performance improved by the position construction?
RQ4 How does the position construction affect memory usage during matching?

In Sect. 2, we give a brief background for practical regex engines and the ReDoS problem. Then, in Sect. 3, we present a hybrid matching scheme of the Thompson matcher and the Spencer matcher based on the position construction. We evaluate the proposed engine using a benchmark dataset and show the performance improvement in Sect. 4. We conclude the paper with possible future work in Sect. 5.

2   Background

2.1   Theoretical Foundations

An alphabet Σ is a set of symbols. A string w over Σ is a sequence of symbols in Σ. The length $|w|$ of w is the number of symbols of w. An empty string is denoted by λ such that $|\lambda| = 0$. We say that E is a regular expression (regex) over Σ if E is the empty set symbol $\emptyset$, an empty string λ, a single symbol $\sigma \in \Sigma$, the catenation $(E_1 E_2)$, the union $(E_1 | E_2)$ of two regular expressions E_1 and E_2, Kleene star (E_1^*) or Kleene plus (E_1^+) of a regular expression E_1.

Given a regex E, we obtain a marked regex $\overline{E}$ over an marked alphabet $\overline{\Sigma} = \{\sigma_i \mid \sigma \in \Sigma, i \in \mathbb{N}\}$, which distinguishes the occurrences of the same symbol in different positions. Then, $\mathsf{sym}(\overline{E}) \subseteq \overline{\Sigma}$ denotes the finite set of marked symbols that occur in $\overline{E}$. Let $\mathsf{first}(\overline{E})$ and $\mathsf{last}(\overline{E})$ be the sets of marked symbols that appear as the first and the last symbols of strings in $L(\overline{E})$, respectively. Similarly, let $\mathsf{follow}(\overline{E}, \sigma_i)$ be the set of marked symbols following σ_i in $L(\overline{E})$. A regex E is deterministic (one-unambiguous in Brüggemann-Klein and Wood [3]) if, for all marked symbols σ_i, τ_j and strings u, v, w over $\overline{\Sigma}$, $u\sigma_i v, u\tau_j w \in L(\overline{E})$ and $\sigma_i \neq \tau_j$ imply that the unmarked symbols σ and τ are different.

Automata Constructions: One of the most famous finite automaton (FA) constructions is the Thompson construction [29]. The construction guarantees an FA of linear size with respect to the regex size since it has one start state and one accepting state, and each state has at most two out-transitions [15]. Most regex compilers use the Thompson construction due to its easy and intuitive implementation.

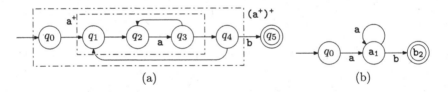

Fig. 1. (a) A Thompson FA and (b) a position FA of a regex $E = (\mathsf{a}^+)^*\mathsf{b}$. Some λ-transitions are omitted for simplicity.

The position construction [16,22] is another FA construction based on the symbol positions of a regex. Given a regex E over Σ, the position FA of E is an FA $A = (\mathsf{sym}(\overline{E}) \cup \{q_0\}, \Sigma, \delta, q_0, F)$, where $\delta(q, \sigma) = \{\tau_i \in \mathsf{first}(\overline{E}) \mid \tau = \sigma\}$ if $q = q_0$ and $\{\tau_i \in \mathsf{follow}(\overline{E}, q) \mid \tau = \sigma\}$ otherwise, and F is $\mathsf{last}(E) \cup \{q_0\}$ if $\lambda \in L(E)$ and $\mathsf{last}(E)$ otherwise. Position FAs have a few interesting properties [6]: (1) FA has no λ-transitions, (2) all incoming transitions of a state have the same symbol label and (3) the number of states is exactly $|E| + 1$. Another important property is that, if a regex is deterministic, then its position FA is always deterministic [3].

Matching Algorithms: Once we compile an FA M from a regex E, a matcher then starts to process an input string T. It checks if M has a path from the start state to an accepting state that spells out T. Thus, the matching process is closely related to how the engine processes M. The Thompson matching algorithm explores M in a breadth-first manner and determines if there is an accepting path for T [29]. The algorithm reads each symbol in T from left to right, 1) stores every next state when it reads a symbol, and 2) never reads that symbol again. Spencer [28] proposes a depth-first matching algorithm, now called the Spencer matching algorithm. This algorithm 1') chooses one next state at a time among multiple target states. If there is no path to explore further, then the algorithm 2') comes back and chooses another state in a DFS manner. This is called backtracking.

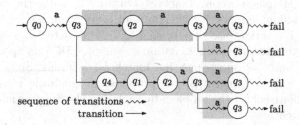

Fig. 2. An example of the Spencer matcher; the algorithm matches a regex $E = (\mathsf{a}^+)^+\mathsf{b}$ with an input string aaa using its Thompson FA in Fig. 1(a). Arrows in a blue box and a red box denote cycles $\pi_1 = q_3q_2q_3$ and $\pi_2 = q_3q_4q_1q_2q_3$, respectively.

Figure 2 shows an exponential runtime growth when matching a regex $(\mathsf{a}^+)^+\mathsf{b}$ with a string aa^k by using the Thompson FA in Fig. 1(a). Note that there are two cycles around q_3 that read a's. The exponential runtime occurs by backtracking all possible paths for reading successive a's since the number of such paths is the number of permutations with k repetitions of those cycles involving q_3.

2.2 ReDoS Problem: Regular Expression Denial-of-Service

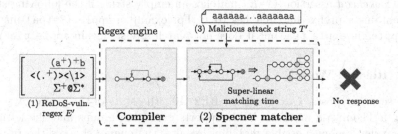

Fig. 3. Figure describing ReDoS behavior. A service is vulnerable when it uses (1) a ReDoS-vulnerable regex E', (2) a regex engine with a Spencer matcher and (3) the engine is exposed to a malicious input string T'. In practice, E' is from service developers and T' is from users.

A ReDoS attack is an algorithmic complexity attack that causes denial-of-service from a service provider by using a malicious input string that requires a super-linear time to evaluate [31]. The attack exploits the fact that most regex engines use the Spencer algorithm [28]. Figure 3 illustrates a ReDoS attack.

On July 20, 2016, an unintentional ReDoS attack caused by a post stopped Stack Overflow for 34 min.[1] The service used a pattern $\verb|^\s+|\s+$|$[2] to delete heading and trailing whitespaces on the problematic post containing 20,000 successive whitespaces. After the outage, Stack Overflow replaced the regex procedure with a simple substring function. On July 2, 2019, the domain name service of Cloudflare stopped for 27 min, and users could not visit any Cloudflare domain.[3] The service used a pattern $\Sigma^*\Sigma^*{=}\Sigma^*$ to detect cross-site scripting attacks. If a given text T does not contain a symbol =, then its Spencer matcher tries to split T into two substrings that match Σ^* as prefix. Since the matcher does not read = from T, eventually it processes in quadratic runtime without success. Cloudflare solved the problem by replacing the Spencer matcher with a Thompson matcher.

We say that a regex E has a *degree of vulnerability* $f(n)$ in a regex engine, if the regex engine takes asymptotically $O(f(n))$ time to match a string of length n with E [11]. The degree of vulnerability of E is closely related to the implementation of a regex engine and the most super-linear vulnerabilities happen due to the Spencer algorithm. Despite of the ReDoS-vulnerability, the Spencer algorithm is widely used because it supports handy features such as capturing groups, backreferences or lookaheads.

1. An engine not only finds the substring $w \in L(E)$ occurrence in T but also identifies which part of w matches which piece of E surrounded by parentheses. We call such regex pieces *capturing groups* and the matched substrings of w *captured groups*.
2. A *backreference* \n matches the nth captured group. For example, a regex E = <(head|body)></\1> matches <head></head> but does not match <head></body>.
3. A *lookahead* assertion (?=E) matches an empty string if the following string contains a prefix that matches to E. For example, apple␣(?=tea) matches apple␣ in apple␣tea, but it does not match any strings in apple␣pie.

2.3   Related Work

In a series of posts, Cox proposed RE2 [10], the state-of-the-art regex engine using a Thompson matcher. RE2 supports capturing groups and the leftmost-eager rule—among possible matching results, the engine chooses the result of highest precedence. RE2 does not support backreference and lookahead to avoid ReDoS.

---

[1] https://stackstatus.net/post/147710624694/outage-postmortem-july-20-2016.
[2] Simplified. ^ and $ match the start and the end of lines, respectively. \s matches the whitespace characters such as a space or a tab.
[3] https://blog.cloudflare.com/details-of-the-cloudflare-outage-on-july-2-2019/.

Davis et al. [11,12] collected real-world regexes from code repositories, and warned that the threat of ReDoS is widespread. They proposed using a selective memoization technique to remove redundant backtrackings of the Spencer matcher [13]. Van der Merwe et al. [23] showed that it is NP-hard to compute the smallest set of states that guarantees a linear-time matching using memoization.

Kirrage et al. [18] studied the abstract syntax tree of regexes, and proposed heuristics that identify regexes with an exponential degree of vulnerability. Their heuristics find strings (prefix, pump, suffix) such that the attack string prefix · pump^k · suffix invokes an exponential matching time. Rathnayake and Thielecke [25] later improved the heuristics that always find true positive attack strings by considering an implicit priority of matching results.

Berglund et al. [1] also investigated the priority of matching results. They proposed prioritized-NFAs (pNFAs) that annotate priorities on FA transitions, which explain Spencer matchers' behaviors. They revealed a relation between a regex's degree of vulnerability and the corresponding pNFA's ambiguity. In following study, Weideman et al. [30] developed an analyzer that identifies ReDoS-vulnerable regexes and their degree of vulnerability. Since static analysis identifies ReDoS-vulnerability without running regex engines, it might miss details and extended features that are dependent on executing the engines.

Dynamic analysis methods complement such limitations by finding reliable attack strings with engine-dependent features. Shen et al. [27] used a genetic algorithm that finds attack strings for vulnerable regexes. Their dynamic analyzer ReScue starts with strings occurring in the regex pattern, and gradually modifies the strings to maximize running time in the Java regex engine. Wüstholz et al.'s Rexploiter [32] and Lin et al.'s Revealer [21] use a combined approach. The former uses dynamic analysis for verification of attack strings that are statically generated, and the latter generates attack strings both statically and dynamically.

3   Proposed Approach

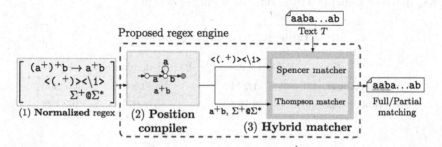

Fig. 4. An overview of our approach. We (1) normalize a regex E by reducing the number of capturing groups, (2) compile using the position construction (3) use a Spencer matcher only if it is essential.

Our first approach to mitigate ReDoS is choosing a matcher dynamically according to the regex features. Our hybrid matching scheme checks if E contains extended features and requires a Spencer matcher. If not, we use a Thompson matcher. For instance, if E contains a backreference, our only choice is to use a Spencer matcher. This selection comes with a simple normalization for groups; a pair of parentheses in E indicates a precedence and a capturing group. Thus, we support the capturing group feature if a matcher needs to handle partial matching or backreference. Otherwise, we ignore the feature and use it for representing precedence only.

Our second approach is to implement a compiler by the position construction. Because the position construction has no λ-transitions, the resulting FA might mitigate ReDoS-vulnerabilities. For example, the regex in Fig. 1 becomes invulnerable in the position construction; the states q_1, q_2, q_3 and q_4 in Fig. 1(a) merge into a_1 in Fig. 1(b), which has only one available path no matter how many consecutive a's that the input contains. This reduces the number of choices compared to the matching with the Thompson FA. Moreover, if E is deterministic, then the resulting position FA is always deterministic [3]. Being deterministic has an advantage in the Spencer matcher since we can quickly determine a matching failure without backtracking. Figure 4 depicts the overview of our approach.

4   Experimental Results and Analysis

We use the Thompson compiler and the Spencer matcher implemented by Davis et al. [13] as a baseline engine. We turn off their memoization feature in the Spencer matcher to compare the matcher performance without any optimizations.

4.1   Dataset

We use the benchmark dataset by Davis et al. [12] that consists of 537,806 regexes from 193,524 projects in 8 different programming languages [13]. From the dataset, we remove 175,078 regexes that cannot be processed by our engine, because either it takes more than one second to generate an accepting string, or it has different semantics from our regex engine design.

Table 1. The dataset summary

	ReDoS-vulnerable	ReDoS-invulnerable	Total
Original dataset [12]	51,244	486,562	537,806
Experiment dataset	48,757	313,971	362,728

Each vulnerable regex E in the dataset has prefix, pump and suffix strings that are used to produce a malicious string causing ReDoS. Thus, by fixing the number k of pumps, we produce a sufficiently long string $T = \text{prefix} \cdot \text{pump}^k \cdot \text{suffix}$ for a ReDoS attack for E.

4.2   Experiment Settings

For **RQ1**, we measure the performance of a regex on an input by both checking the matching time and counting the number of matching steps. Since experiments for **RQ2** and **RQ3** have relatively short matching time and the result largely fluctuates depending on the environment such as OS scheduling, we instead use the number of matching steps only.

For ReDoS-vulnerable regexes $E_{\text{vuln.}}$, we first match $T_k = \text{prefix} \cdot \text{pump}^k \cdot \text{suffix}$ for $1 < k \leq 11$ with $E_{\text{vuln.}}$, and approximate the matching steps in the baseline engine as a function f of the pumping number k. For each ReDoS-invulnerable regex $E_{\text{invuln.}}$, we generate at most 10 accepting strings using Xeger[4] with a 1-second time limit. We vary the number of repetitions in $E_{\text{invuln.}}$ to generate strings with variable lengths. We then randomly generate another set of rejecting strings that have the same lengths as the accepting strings.

In addition, we calculate the memory usage for answering **RQ4**. To explore both general and extreme situations, we select regexes with the following 5 criteria (given a regex E, let $|E_T|$ and $|E_P|$ be the memory size of its Thompson and position FA representations).

1. 100 regexes E with the largest $|E_T|$
2. 100 regexes E with the largest $|E_P|$
3. 100 regexes E with the largest difference of $|E_T| - |E_P|$
4. 100 regexes E with the largest difference of $|E_P| - |E_T|$
5. 100 randomly selected regexes

We measure the memory usage of these 500 regexes by calculating the maximum amount of memory allocated for the matcher via Valgrind[5].

4.3   Results and Analysis

RQ1. Vulnerable Regexes: We first study the performance improvement of substituting compilers in practical ReDoS settings. We generate input strings that are long enough to invoke 10^6 and 10^7 matching steps in the baseline engine, and measure the matching time using these strings. Note that Liu et al. [21] and Shen et al. [27] choose 10^5 and 10^8 (with fixed input length) as the threshold steps for the occurrence of ReDoS, respectively. However, we exclude experiments for 10^8 steps since matching for these inputs often exceed our 5-second time limit.

Figure 5 shows the differences of matching time in the Thompson FA and the position FA in ReDoS-attack scenarios. We observe that, with the same sets of inputs, the FAs of the position compiler show faster matching than those of the Thompson compiler on average. This result confirms that the position construction generates better FAs than the Thompson construction in terms of matching time.

---

[4] https://pypi.org/project/xeger/.
[5] https://valgrind.org/.

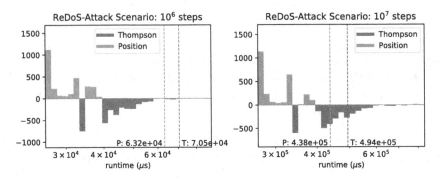

Fig. 5. Difference in matching time distribution for ReDoS attack scenarios in full matching by the Spencer matcher. Orange bars indicate that position FAs require more matching time, and the blue bars are for Thompson FAs. The blue and orange dashed lines show the average matching time in μsec.

Table 2. The number of regexes by the degree of vulnerability in full matching.

Matching	Matcher	Compiler	Degree of vulnerability				
			$\Omega(2^n)$	$\Theta(n^{\geq 4})$	$\Theta(n^3)$	$\Theta(n^2)$	$O(n)$
Full	Spencer	Thompson	139	2	119	7,935	40,562
		Position	63	2	113	7,934	40,645
	Hybrid	Thompson	2	0	0	8	48,747
		Position	2	0	0	8	48,747
Partial	Spencer	Thompson	122	18	801	43,243	4,573
		Position	97	16	778	43,263	4,603
	Hybrid	Thompson	2	0	0	9	48,746
		Position	2	0	0	9	48,746

Table 2 gives the number of regexes by the degree of vulnerability in terms of matching steps. Compared to the baseline engine using the Thompson compiler and the Spencer matcher, the hybrid matcher removes almost every vulnerability. This agrees with Cox's discovery—the Thompson matching algorithm is indeed effective for eliminating ReDoS-vulnerability. Another interesting result is that the position compiler effectively resolves vulnerability of exponential degrees. We observe that 73 regexes (out of 139 exponential-degree regexes) become to run in linear time in the position FA case. This supports our claim that the position construction is an effective ReDoS solution when the Spencer matching is inevitable.

Interestingly, few cases show increased vulnerability when using the position compiler. There are seven such cases in which the position compiler shows quadratic degree whereas the Thompson shows linear. This is due to an internal priority of the matcher for processing FAs. The following example illustrates FA matching steps for each compiler for an example regex $a^+b^*\Sigma^*b^*$. For an input string $T = \mathsf{ab}^k\mathsf{a}$, the Spencer matcher matches T with the Thompson FA in the following order:

(1) matches the first a with a^+ of the pattern,
(2) matches successive b's with the first b^*,
(3) matches the last a with Σ^* and
(4) matches an empty string with the second b^*.

On the other hand, in the case of the position FA, the Spencer matcher

(1) matches the first a with a^+ of the pattern,
(2′) matches b^k with the Σ^* (Note that the matcher skips b^* because of a predefined priority of the matcher),
(3′) fails to match the last a in T to the second b^* of the pattern and
(4′) cancels the last matching of b and Σ^*, and instead matches the b to the second b^*.

The Spencer matcher repeats step (4′) while reducing the length of string matched to Σ^*, until it matches the empty string and b^k to Σ^* and the second b^*, respectively, and fails to match the last symbol a. Then, the matching succeeds when the last a and Σ^* match. This process requires quadratic matching steps in the size of T, and the regex's degree of vulnerability becomes $\Theta(n^2)$ by the position compiler. This example shows that the precedence of matching is an important factor that causes ReDoS.

RQ2. Invulnerable Regexes: While the position construction and the hybrid matching scheme may mitigate the ReDoS vulnerability, Table 3 shows that the Spencer matcher runs faster than the Thompson matcher when a string is accepted. This is because the number of states to explore is smaller when an input is accepted, since the Spencer matcher stops matching right after finding one accepting path. However, if an input is rejected (failure matching), then the Spencer matcher becomes much slower because it often needs to repeat the same computation due to backtracking until no more states are left to explore. These differences are more notable in partial matching.

Given a regex E and a string T for partial matching, a matcher internally checks whether $T \in L(\Sigma^*(E)\Sigma^*)$. Let us assume that an accepting string T in partial matching consists of three strings x, y and z such that $T = xyz$ and $y \in L(E)$. Since the Spencer matching algorithm chooses only one state at a time, the Spencer matcher completes the processing of the first Σ^* when it starts to read y. On the other hand, when the hybrid matcher processes y with E, the hybrid matcher—especially, the embedded Thompson matcher—also keeps matching y with Σ^* at the same time. In this process, the hybrid matcher visits the states for Σ^* at least $|y|$ more times than the Spencer matcher, which results in unnecessary trial and error, until the matcher finds a matching in E.

If T is rejected, then the Spencer matcher probes every possible path until it finally tries to match T in the first Σ^* and fails. Since the Spencer matcher has no memoization mechanisms, it should compute the visited states after backtracking. The Thompson matcher, on the other hand, records its previous state

Table 3. The average number of steps for ReDoS-invulnerable regexes.

Matching	Matcher	Compiler	Matching steps	
			Accepting case	Rejecting case
Full	Spencer	Thompson	27.97	10.27
		Position	26.27	8.18
	Hybrid	Thompson	59.65	6.69
		Position	57.25	6.44
Partial	Spencer	Thompson	45.34	100.24
		Position	39.71	82.85
	Hybrid	Thompson	159.81	89.73
		Position	146.14	79.00

and never has to check the consumed input repeatedly. Thus, while the two matchers probe the same number of states, the Spencer matcher requires more computation steps.

Note that the replacement of the Thompson compiler with the position compiler always decreases the average matching step. We think this is because of the λ-transitions in a Thompson FA.

RQ3. Deterministic Regexes: We examine the practicality of deterministic regexes whose position FAs are deterministic [3,6]. There are 11,311 ReDoS-vulnerable and 256,213 ReDoS-invulnerable regexes that are deterministic in the dataset.[6] Table 4 is a comparison for different implementations when a regex is deterministic.

Table 4. The average number of steps for deterministic regexes.

Matching	Matcher	Compiler	Matching steps		
			ReDoS-vulnerable	Accepting case	Rejecting case
Full	Spencer	Thompson	3.42×10^5	22.24	2.97
		Position	76.77	21.54	2.94
	Hybrid	Thompson	166.7	42.85	4.30
		Position	127.4	40.96	4.26
Partial	Spencer	Thompson	1.13×10^7	35.23	61.98
		Position	1.04×10^7	32.49	51.01
	Hybrid	Thompson	4.00×10^4	145.80	86.09
		Position	3.64×10^4	132.65	75.17

---

[6] We have removed 359 ReDoS-vulnerable regexes in Table 1 that do not cause ReDoS behavior in both full and partial matching.

When using the Spencer matcher for ReDoS-vulnerable regexes in full matching, the position compiler reduces a large number of matching steps compared
to the Thompson compiler since the main cause of the vulnerability is capturing groups that merely record a matched text. In partial matching, however,
there is little improvement since we cannot replace capturing groups with non-
capturing ones to preserve the regex semantics and the Spencer matcher implements capturing groups by tagged λ-transitions. This forces the compiler to add
λ-transitions to the corresponding FA and removes the advantage of the position
construction for deterministic regexes.

Table 5. The reduced amount of matching steps by the position compiler when an
input is accepted. Each cell shows $1 - \mathbb{P}/\mathbb{T}$, where $\mathbb{T}$ and $\mathbb{P}$ denote the number of
matching steps in the Thompson and the position compilers, respectively.

Matching	Matcher	Reduced amount of steps (%)	
		ReDoS-invuln.	Invuln. and det.
Full	Spencer	6.1	3.1
	Hybrid	4.0	4.4
Partial	Spencer	12.4	7.8
	Hybrid	8.6	9.0

Table 5 shows the performance improvement by replacing an FA compiler
from the Thompson compiler to the position compiler when an input is accepted.
(When an input is rejected, the performance improvement is negligible, and we
omit the results.) For the hybrid matcher, we observe a performance improvement when the regex is deterministic. However, for the Spencer matcher, we
notice that the improvement is smaller for deterministic regexes. This is because
the Spencer matcher runs in a DFS manner and tends to visit a smaller number of states when an input is accepted. In other words, it stops as soon as the
Spencer matcher finds an accepting path. Thus, if no backtracking occurs, then
this makes the Spencer matcher run deterministically even for nondeterministic FAs. We also note that the Thompson compiler in the baseline engine by
Davis et al. [13] uses a variant of the Thompson construction that produces less
λ-transitions than the original Thompson construction. This implies that the
resulting FA is more succinct and reduces matching steps.

Table 6 shows the distribution of the number of operations in our benchmark
regexes. Note that deterministic regexes have the smallest number of expected
λ-transitions per operation in the corresponding Thompson FAs followed by
invulnerable and vulnerable regexes. The smaller number of λ-transitions speeds
up the matching time and, thus, reduces the advantage of the position compiler
in the deterministic case.

RQ4. Memory Usage: In low-resource systems such as IoT devices, memory
usage is an important factor. Since the matcher runs on a given input text

Table 6. No. of operation distribution in regexes. The numbers in parentheses indicate the number of λ-transitions produced by the baseline Thompson compiler [13] for each operation. #(λ) denotes the expected number of λ-transitions per operation.

	Catenation (0)	Union (2)†	Star (3)	Plus (2)	#(λ)
ReDoS-vulnerable	80.1	0.9	9.7	9.2	0.49
ReDoS-invulnerable	89.5	2.9	3.0	4.6	0.24
Deterministic	90.8	1.8	2.5	4.9	0.21

† n successive unions $(R_0|R_1|\cdots|R_n)$ produce $2n+1$ λ-transitions.

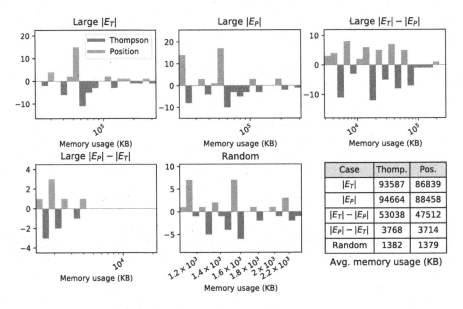

Fig. 6. Difference of memory usage distribution of the two compilers in partial matching with the Spencer matcher. Orange bars indicate that position FAs require more memory, and the blue bars are for Thompson FAs.

while the compiler does not need to run every time, we measure the maximum amount of memory during the matching procedure. Figure 6 shows the maximum memory usage of the Spencer matcher on Thompson FAs and position FAs. The position compiler shows less memory usage than the Thompson compiler on average and only marginally better when the Thompson FAs are much smaller than the position FAs.

Note that the position FA for a regex E has a quadratic size in the worst-case [3] and a linear size in the average case [24]. In our experiments, most position FAs have a linear size as well. This supports our claim that using the position construction indeed saves memory in matching as well as in representing FAs.

5   Conclusions

Recently, ReDoS has been a serious problem in various applications. The ReDoS problem exploits the fact that most regex engines are implemented based on the Spencer algorithm [28], which allows backtrackings. While the backtracking feature is handy for practical regexes, which are not regular anymore [4], sometimes the matching takes super-linear time with respect to the input size. A possible solution would be not to use the Spencer algorithm; for example, Go drops the Spencer algorithm and uses the classical Thompson algorithm [17]. However, due to its functionality, many people still want to use the current features of regexes, which require the Spencer algorithm. Therefore, the ReDoS problem can happen anytime when there are no proper precautions. We have studied the ReDoS vulnerable regexes and suggested a possible remedy founded from the classical automata theory. We have proposed using the position construction instead of the Thompson construction, and a hybrid matcher to mitigate ReDoS-vulnerable regexes.

Our experiments have showed that the proposed approach reduces about 99.88% (8,185/8,195) and 99.98% (44,173/44,184) ReDoS-vulnerabilities in full matching and partial matching, respectively. Moreover, for the baseline engine, we have demonstrated that substituting the Thompson compiler with the position compiler resolves 55% (76/139) of ReDoS-vulnerable regexes with an exponential degree without undermining the power of the Spencer matcher. Moreover, we have observed that, for ReDoS-vulnerable regexes, the position compiler always reduces the number of matching steps. It is worth noting that 74% of practical regexes are deterministic. Our position compiler removes the ReDoS-vulnerability in full matching for the deterministic case. This implies that using a position compiler and a hybrid matcher may reduce the matching time for most practical regexes since the FA representation is often deterministic.

Nevertheless, it still remains open to develop an efficient algorithm that predicts a potential ReDoS behavior or optimizes a regex. Cheon et al. [8] examined the case when a ReDoS-vulnerable regex is disguised as an infix of an ordinary regex and studied the decision problem for such cases. For the regex engines, Davis et al. [13] showed that caching the intermediate results in a selected set of states can boost the matching time. However, the hardness of determining the smallest set of states that guarantees ReDoS-invulnerability of the Spencer matcher in Thompson FAs is not known yet; only the problem on general NFAs is only known as NP-hard [23]. There are a few known heuristics for detecting ReDoS-vulnerabilities based on the syntactic properties called anti-patterns [11]. It would be an interesting problem to design efficient algorithms that detect such regexes based on anti-patterns.

Acknowledgment. This research was supported by the NRF grant (NRF-2020R1A4A3079947) funded by MIST.

References

1. Berglund, M., Drewes, F., van der Merwe, B.: Analyzing catastrophic backtracking behavior in practical regular expression matching. In: Proceedings of the 14th International Conference on Automata and Formal Languages, pp. 109–123 (2014)
2. Berglund, M., van der Merwe, B.: Regular expressions with backreferences re-examined. In: Proceedings of the Prague Stringology Conference 2017, pp. 30–41 (2017)
3. Brüggemann-Klein, A., Wood, D.: One-unambiguous regular languages. Inf. Comput. **140**(2), 229–253 (1998)
4. Câmpeanu, C., Salomaa, K., Yu, S.: A formal study of practical regular expressions. Int. J. Found. Comput. Sci. **14**(6), 1007–1018 (2003)
5. Câmpeanu, C., Salomaa, K., Yu, S.: Regex and extended regex. In: Proceedings of the 7th International Conference on Implementation and Application of Automata, pp. 77–84 (2003)
6. Caron, P., Ziadi, D.: Characterization of Glushkov automata. Theoret. Comput. Sci. **233**(1–2), 75–90 (2000)
7. Chapman, C., Stolee, K.T.: Exploring regular expression usage and context in Python. In: Proceedings of the 25th International Symposium on Software Testing and Analysis, pp. 282–293 (2016)
8. Cheon, H., Hahn, J., Han, Y.S.: On the decidability of infix inclusion problem. In: Proceedings of the 26th International Conference on Developments in Language Theory (2022, in publishing)
9. Cortes, C., Mohri, M.: Learning with weighted transducers. In: Proceedings of the 7th International Workshop on Finite State Methods and Natural Language Processing, pp. 14–22 (2008)
10. Cox, R.: Regular expression matching in the wild (2010). http://swtch.com/~rsc/regexp/regexp3.html. Accessed 7 Apr 2022
11. Davis, J.C., Coghlan, C.A., Servant, F., Lee, D.: The impact of regular expression denial of service (ReDoS) in practice: an empirical study at the ecosystem scale. In: Proceedings of the 26th ACM Joint Meeting on European Software Engineering Conference and Symposium on the Foundations of Software Engineering, pp. 246–256 (2018)
12. Davis, J.C., Michael IV, L.G., Coghlan, C.A., Servant, F., Lee, D.: Why aren't regular expressions a lingua franca? An empirical study on the re-use and portability of regular expressions. In: Proceedings of the 27th ACM Joint Meeting on European Software Engineering Conference and Symposium on the Foundations of Software Engineering, pp. 443–454 (2019)
13. Davis, J.C., Servant, F., Lee, D.: Using selective memoization to defeat regular expression denial of service (ReDoS). In: Proceedings of the 2021 IEEE Symposium on Security and Privacy, pp. 1–17 (2021)
14. Friedl, J.E.F.: Mastering Regular Expressions, 3rd edn. O'Reilly Media Inc. (2006)
15. Giammarresi, D., Ponty, J., Wood, D., Ziadi, D.: A characterization of Thompson digraphs. Discret. Appl. Math. **134**(1–3), 317–337 (2004)
16. Glushkov, V.M.: The abstract theory of automata. Russ. Math. Surv. **16**(5), 1–53 (1961)
17. Google: regexp (Go documentation). https://pkg.go.dev/regexp@go1.18. Accessed 7 Apr 2022
18. Kirrage, J., Rathnayake, A., Thielecke, H.: Static analysis for regular expression denial-of-service attacks. In: Proceedings of the 7th International Conference on Network and System Security, pp. 135–148 (2013)

19. Kleene, S.C.: Representation of events in nerve nets and finite automata. Automata Stud. **34**, 3–41 (1956)
20. Liu, T., Sun, Y., Liu, A.X., Guo, L., Fang, B.: A prefiltering approach to regular expression matching for network security systems. In: Bao, F., Samarati, P., Zhou, J. (eds.) ACNS 2012. LNCS, vol. 7341, pp. 363–380. Springer, Heidelberg (2012). https://doi.org/10.1007/978-3-642-31284-7_22
21. Liu, Y., Zhang, M., Meng, W.: Revealer: detecting and exploiting regular expression denial-of-service vulnerabilities. In: Proceedings of the 2021 IEEE Symposium on Security and Privacy, pp. 1468–1484 (2021)
22. McNaughton, R., Yamada, H.: Regular expressions and state graphs for automata. IRE Trans. Electron. Comput. **EC-9**(1), 39–47 (1960)
23. van der Merwe, B., Mouton, J., van Litsenborgh, S., Berglund, M.: Memoized regular expressions. In: Maneth, S. (ed.) CIAA 2021. LNCS, vol. 12803, pp. 39–52. Springer, Cham (2021). https://doi.org/10.1007/978-3-030-79121-6_4
24. Nicaud, C.: On the average size of Glushkov's automata. In: Dediu, A.H., Ionescu, A.M., Martín-Vide, C. (eds.) LATA 2009. LNCS, vol. 5457, pp. 626–637. Springer, Heidelberg (2009). https://doi.org/10.1007/978-3-642-00982-2_53
25. Rathnayake, A., Thielecke, H.: Static analysis for regular expression exponential runtime via substructural logics. arXiv preprint CoRR 1405.7058 (2014)
26. Schmid, M.L.: Regular expressions with backreferences: polynomial-time matching techniques. arXiv preprint CoRR 1903.05896 (2019)
27. Shen, Y., Jiang, Y., Xu, C., Yu, P., Ma, X., Lu, J.: ReScue: crafting regular expression DoS attacks. In: Proceedings of the 33rd IEEE/ACM International Conference on Automated Software Engineering, pp. 225–235 (2018)
28. Spencer, H.: A regular-expression matcher. In: Software Solutions in C, pp. 35–71. AP Professional (1994)
29. Thompson, K.: Programming techniques: regular expression search algorithm. Commun. ACM **11**(6), 419–422 (1968)
30. Weideman, N., van der Merwe, B., Berglund, M., Watson, B.: Analyzing matching time behavior of backtracking regular expression matchers by using ambiguity of NFA. In: Proceedings of the 21st International Conference on Implementation and Application of Automata, pp. 322–334 (2016)
31. Weidman, A., other contributers: Regular expression denial of service - ReDoS. https://owasp.org/www-community/attacks/Regular_expression_Denial_of_Service_-_ReDoS. Accessed 7 Apr 2022
32. Wüstholz, V., Olivo, O., Heule, M.J.H., Dillig, I.: Static detection of DoS vulnerabilities in programs that use regular expressions. In: Legay, A., Margaria, T. (eds.) TACAS 2017. LNCS, vol. 10206, pp. 3–20. Springer, Heidelberg (2017). https://doi.org/10.1007/978-3-662-54580-5_1

Conference Papers

Ordered Context-Free Grammars

Brink van der Merwe[1,2] and Martin Berglund[3,4(✉)]

[1] Department of Computer Science, Stellenbosch University,
Stellenbosch, South Africa
[2] National Institute for Theoretical and Computational Sciences,
Stellenbosch, South Africa
[3] Department of Information Science, Stellenbosch University,
Stellenbosch, South Africa
[4] Department of Computing Science, Umeå University, Umeå, Sweden
mbe@cs.umu.se

Abstract. We propose a new unambiguous grammar formalism, referred to as ordered context-free grammars, which is identical to context-free grammars, apart from the property that it also places an order on parse trees. Since only a minor modification to ordered context-free grammars is required to obtain parsing expression grammars, the relationship between context-free grammars and parsing expression grammars becomes more evident. By preserving how ordered context-free grammars support left-recursion, parsing expression grammars is modified to support left recursion in ways much more natural than current approaches.

Keywords: Ordered context-free grammars · Parsing expression grammars · unambiguous grammar formalisms

1 Introduction

Ordered context-free grammars (oCFGs), a novel grammar formalism proposed in this paper, is not only a vehicle towards understanding parsing expression grammars (PEGs) better and to propose alternative semantics for PEGs with left recursion, but also have various other useful properties. The oCFG formalism is a natural way to generalize Perl-compatible regular expression (PCRE) matching (Perl semantics is common in practice, see [1] for illustration how real-world regex matching semantics are deeply intertwined with a depth-first backtracking parsing technique), to context-free parsing. It also provides a good alternative to PEGs when an unambiguous (i.e. at most one parse tree for a given input string) grammar formalism is required. Ordered context-free grammars become unambiguous if we always select the least parse tree for a given input string (if possible) based on the order induced on parse trees by the oCFG formalism. Also, depending on the properties of the switching function of the oCFG, which provides an additional switching criterion for switching from forward search to backtracking during derivations, derivations will also produce the least parse tree as first parse tree in a derivation of the string under consideration.

© Springer Nature Switzerland AG 2022
P. Caron and L. Mignot (Eds.): CIAA 2022, LNCS 13266, pp. 53–66, 2022.
https://doi.org/10.1007/978-3-031-07469-1_4

The oCFG formalism provides an unambiguous grammar formalism with more intuitive semantics than PEGs, given that an oCFG matches exactly the same string language as the corresponding context-free grammar (CFG), again if the switching function satisfies appropriate criteria. The intuition behind PEGs is that they are obtained from context-free grammars by dictating a depth-first backtracking parsing approach, made efficient by a combination of memoization and ignoring some backtracking options. Specifically, each time a nonterminal succeeds in matching a substring it never attempts matching this substring with a different rule choice when using the given nonterminal. For example, if the first attempt to match a nonterminal A to $abab$ has it match aba, no attempt will be made to proceed by having A match ab or $abab$, even if such an attempt would lead to overall matching/parsing success. This results in somewhat unintuitive matching semantics, which is evident when considering the PEG $S \leftarrow aSa \,/\, a$, and verifying that is does not match a^5 (while matching both a^3 and a^7). A PEG parser will regard $S \leftarrow aSa$ as the locally correct rule choice for matching the third a if the first two as are consumed by applying $S \leftarrow aSa$ twice, since by doing this, the third to the fifth a will be consumed without failure, and then the PEG parser will regard $S \leftarrow aSa$ as the incorrect choice for consuming the second a, and thus switch to using $S \leftarrow a$ for matching the second a. This can be verified using either PEG matching semantics as given in [2], or interpreting the grammar as the specification of a recursive descent parser. For the latter, the nonterminal S is regarded as a function with two blocks of statements, with the first block matching a (in the input), then calling S recursively, and finally, matching a again, and the second block only matching a. The second block is called once it is determined that the first block fails, where failure is defined to be the inability to match a when required. The accepted strings and corresponding parse trees are not changed (compared to when using the CFG grammar interpretation) when considering the corresponding (unambiguous) CFG for this grammar, i.e. the CFG with productions $S \rightarrow aSa \mid a$, and rather interpreting it as an oCFG (with an appropriately defined switching function) instead of a PEG.

Although we provide our own more general definition of PEGs in Definition 9 (by making backtracking in oCFG parsing non-exhaustive), PEGs will be mentioned frequently before then. For space considerations, we can unfortunately not reproduce the definition from [2] in the next section, and thus the reader who did not find our informal introduction to PEGs sufficient should consult [2].

As pointed out in [3], the influence of PEGs can be illustrated by the fact that despite having been introduced only fifteen years ago, the number of PEG-based parser generators exceeds the number of parser generators based on any other parsing method. Despite the enthusiasm for PEGs, there are some objections, for example, proving that a given PEG matches an intended language is often more difficult than one would like. These observations provide ample motivation for proposing and studying oCFGs.

In [4] it is noted that the parser generator ANTLR uses the order of the productions in the grammar to resolve ambiguities, with conflicts resolved in favor of the rule with the lowest production number. This statement provides

additional motivation for our work, and we thus consider how this way of disambiguation can be added to CFGs in order to turn CFGs into an unambiguous
grammar formalism.

The outline of this paper is as follows. The next section provides definitions
and elementary results. Then oCFG derivations are considered, after which we
touch briefly upon various oCFG extensions. Finally, we provide our conclusions
and future work.

2   Definitions and Elementary Properties of oCFG

In this section we define oCFGs and other related required basic concepts. We
then consider a subclass of oCFGs which always have least parse trees for any
string of the language defined by the oCFG. For oCFGs we end up with a modification to CFG parsing semantics where the strings accepted and corresponding
parse trees are identical, but we obtain an order on the parse trees. From this,
the choice of name for our grammar formalism becomes evident.

In order to discuss parsing, we first define trees in a way suitable for our
purposes.

Definition 1. *The set of* ordered, rooted and ranked trees, *over a finite ranked
alphabet* $\Gamma = \cup_{i=0}^{\infty} \Gamma_i$, *denoted by* $\mathcal{T}_\Gamma$, *where* Γ_i *is the alphabet symbols of rank i,
is defined inductively as follows: (i) if $a \in \Gamma_0$, then $a \in \mathcal{T}_\Gamma$; (ii) if $a \in \Gamma_k$ and $t_i \in \mathcal{T}_\Gamma$
for $1 \le i \le k$, then $a[t_1, \ldots, t_k] \in \mathcal{T}_\Gamma$.*

Next, we define special kinds of trees, referred to as contexts. In a context we
replace a leaf node in a tree, by another tree, when this leaf node is the left-most
leaf node labelled by the special symbol □.

Definition 2. *Assume* □ *is a symbol not in the ranked alphabet* Γ, *and denote
by* $\mathcal{C}_\Gamma$ *the set of trees over the ranked alphabet* $\Gamma \cup \{\square\}$, *where* □ *is a symbol of
rank 0. The following restrictions are placed on the trees $t \in \mathcal{C}_\Gamma$: (i) t contains at
least one instance of* □; *(ii) no symbols from* Γ_0 *in t appears to the right of any
instance of* □ *(i.e. all □-labeled nodes appear as a suffix when listing the node
labels in depth-first preorder). A tree in* $\mathcal{C}_\Gamma$ *is referred to as a* context.

For $t \in \mathcal{C}_\Gamma$ and $t' \in \mathcal{T}_\Gamma \cup \mathcal{C}_\Gamma$, we denote by $t[\![t']\!]$ the tree obtained by replacing
the left-most instance of □ in t, by t'.

Next we define ordered context-free grammars. The distinction between
CFGs and oCFGs will become clear once we start discussing parse trees and
how to order these.

Definition 3. *An* ordered context-free grammar G *is a tuple* (N, Σ, P, S),
*where: (i) N is a finite set of nonterminals; (ii) Σ the input alphabet; (iii) P
is the production function and for $A \in N$, we have $P(A) = (r_1^A, \ldots, r_{n_A}^A)$, with
$r_i^A \in (N \cup \Sigma)^*$; and (iv) $S \in N$ is the start nonterminal.*

In the definition above when $P(A) = (r_1^A, \ldots, r_{n_A}^A)$, we also write $A \to r_1^A \mid \cdots \mid r_{n_A}^A$. We associate a ranked alphabet Γ_G with an ordered context-free grammar G (which we will use in parse trees) as follows. Denote by $|v|$ the length of a string v, with the length of the empty string ε taken to be 0. We let $\Sigma \cup \{\varepsilon\}$ be the elements of rank 0 in Γ_G, and if $P(A) = (r_1^A, \ldots, r_{n_A}^A)$, then A_i, for $1 \leq i \leq n_A$, is a symbol of rank $\max\{1, |r_i^A|\}$ in Γ_G. We use A_i in parse trees to encode the production choice $A \to r_i^A$.

For a tree t, denote by $y(t)$ the yield of t, i.e. the string obtained by reading the non-ε leaf symbols in t left to right. Thus, $y(t)$ is obtained by deleting ε and all symbols of rank greater than zero in the string representation of t. If all leaf symbols are equal to ε, then $y(t)$ is defined to be equal to ε as well.

Definition 4. *For an oCFG G and string $w \in \Sigma^*$, we define the set of* parse trees *of w, denoted by $\mathcal{P}_G(w)$, as all trees over the ranked alphabet Γ_G, satisfying the following criteria: (i) The root is labelled by some S_i, $1 \leq i \leq n_S$, where S is the start nonterminal of G; (ii) $y(t) = w$; (iii) the children of a node labelled by A_i, ignoring subscripts of non-terminals, are labelled, in order, by the symbols in r_i^A. As a special case, when $|r_i^A| = 0$ a node labelled by A_i will have a single child leaf labeled by ε. The* string language *defined by G, denoted by $\mathcal{L}(G)$, is the set of strings w for which $\mathcal{P}_G(w) \neq \varnothing$.*

Note that we modified the usual definition of parse trees to make it possible to directly read off the productions used to obtain a tree, from the nonterminal labels used in the tree. More precisely, when doing a preorder traversal of the non-leaf nodes of a parse tree, the nonterminals in combination with their integer subscripts, describe uniquely (with the subscript of a nonterminal indicating which production choice was made for a given nonterminal) the productions used in a left-most derivation to produce the respective parse tree. In particular, all leaf labels are uniquely determined by the label of their parent.

Remark 1. From an oCFG G we construct a context-free grammar G', with parse trees (as a CFG) almost identical to those of G. The grammar G' has nonterminals S', and A_i, with $1 \leq i \leq n_A$, for each nonterminal A in G. In G', we have the productions $S' \to S_1 \mid \ldots \mid S_{n_S}$, and $A_i \to r_{i,1}^A \mid \ldots \mid r_{i,j}^A \mid \ldots$ (with finitely many $r_{i,j}^A$), where the $r_{i,j}^A$ is obtained by replacing in r_i^A, each nonterminal B by B_l, with $1 \leq l \leq n_B$. The parse trees for G are obtained from those for G' by leaving out the root node labelled by S'.

We denote the set of parse trees of G by $\mathcal{L}_T(G)$ and refer to this set of trees as the *tree language* of G. Formally, $\mathcal{L}_T(G) = \cup_{w \in \Sigma^*} \mathcal{P}_G(w)$.

For $t \in \mathcal{L}_T(G)$, let $n(t)$ denote the sequence of integers obtained by replacing all symbols A_i in the string representation of t (as used in Definition 1 to represent trees), by i, and deleting all other symbols (i.e. '[', ']', ',' and terminal leafs) in the string representation of t.

Definition 5. *A total order $<_G$ is defined on $\mathcal{L}_T(G)$ as follows. We let $t_1 <_G t_2$ when $n(t_1)$ is smaller than $n(t_2)$ lexicographically.*

The definitions so far do not guarantee that an oCFG has a well-ordered set of parse trees for each given string, and as this is often important, we consider the following restricted cases:

Definition 6. *Let G be any oCFG. Then if for all strings w we have: (i) $\mathcal{P}_G(w)$ is either empty or has a least parse tree, we refer to G as having* least parse trees, *or simply* least trees, *whereas (ii) if $\mathcal{P}_G(w)$ is well-ordered (i.e. every subset of $\mathcal{P}_G(w)$ has a least parse tree) we say that G is* well-ordered.

Note that G being well-ordered does not mean that all of $\mathcal{L}_T(G)$ is well-ordered. An oCFG having least trees is however sufficient to turn oCFGs into an unambiguous grammar formalism by for each w selecting the least tree in $\mathcal{P}_G(w)$ as *the* canonical parse tree. The well-ordered property is strictly stronger, but turns out to be important as it is sufficient to guarantee least trees and is decidable.

Example 1. Next we provide an example of a grammar G not having least parse trees. Consider the grammar G with production $S \to S \mid a$. Then $\mathcal{L}(G) = \{a\}$. We show that for any $t \in \mathcal{P}_G(a)$, we can construct a tree $t' \in \mathcal{P}_G(w)$ with $t' <_G t$. We obtain t' from t by replacing the subtree $S_2[a]$ in t, by the subtree $S_1[S_2[a]]$. In G, the parse trees for the string a form an infinite sequence of decreasing parse trees, namely:
$S_2[a] >_G S_1[S_2[a]] >_G S_1[S_1[S_2[a]]] >_G \cdots$. Note that if we change the production to $S \to a \mid S$, we obtain the infinitely increasing sequence of parse trees:
$S_1[a] <_G S_2[S_1[a]] <_G S_2[S_2[S_1[a]]] <_G \cdots$.

Example 2. Consider G with production $S \to SS \mid \varepsilon \mid a$, for which $\mathcal{L}(G) = \{a^n \mid n \geq 0\}$. This grammar does *not* have least parse trees, since any $t \in \mathcal{P}_G(a)$ (and similarly for $t \in \mathcal{P}_G(a^n)$ in general) will have $S_1[S_1[\cdots S_1[S_1[S_2[\varepsilon], S_2[\varepsilon]], S_2[\varepsilon]], \cdots], S_3[a]] <_G t$ for *sufficiently* many nested instances of S_1.

Example 3. A grammar G' with least trees which is nonetheless not well-ordered can be obtained from either of the grammars from Example 1 or 2 by adding a new start nonterminal S' with the production $S' \to a \mid S' \mid S$ for Example 1 and $S' \to a \mid \varepsilon \mid S'S' \mid S$ for Example 2. Then $\mathcal{P}_G(w)$ has a least tree for $w = a$ or in general, $w \in \mathcal{L}(G)$, never using the nonterminal S, but the subset of $\mathcal{P}_G(w)$ where the root is labeled S'_3 in Example 1 and S'_4 in Example 2 (i.e. the parse trees that is obtained from the derivation step $S' \to S$) has no least tree, and G' is therefore not well-ordered.

It turns out that Examples 1 and 2 exhibit the only ways a grammar might not be well-ordered, that is, by ε-productions (where parse trees contain an unbounded number of leaf nodes labelled by ε), or by cycles of unit productions (where parse trees may contain monadic branches repeating nonterminals, e.g. $A[B[C[A[\cdots]]]]$). This is easy to demonstrate, since if we can bound the size of parse trees (i.e. the number of nodes) for a string w in the length of w, the string w can have only finitely many parse trees, and G must then be well-ordered.

Lemma 1. *If a grammar G does not have any ε-productions or cycles of unit productions, then G is well-ordered.*

Proof. Observe that the only way a string of length $|w|$ can have a parse tree of unbounded size (and thus infinitely many parse trees for a given input string) is if it either has parse trees with a number of leaves not bounded in $|w|$ (some of which must then be ε), or it is of height not bounded in $|w|$ (thus it must contain a monadic subtree with a repeating nonterminal). ∎

The condition in the previous lemma is however not *necessary*, for example $S \to \varepsilon \mid a \mid S$ is well-ordered (and thus also has least trees). Note that the previous lemma also implies that an oCFG in Chomsky normal form is well-ordered. Thus, we conclude that the class of string languages recognized by well-ordered oCFGs, or oCFGs with least parse trees, is precisely the context-free languages.

Example 4. In this example we give a well-ordered oCFG for arithmetic expressions (without parenthesis) over subtraction $(-)$, multiplication $(*)$ and exponentiation $(\char`\^)$, taking precedence and associativity of these three operators in the parse trees into account. Left associativity (for $-$ and $*$) is encoded as $S \to S{-}S \mid x$ and $S \to S * S \mid x$, and right associativity (for $\char`\^$) as $S \to x \mid S\char`\^S$. To take precedence into account, operators with lower precedence are specified first. Putting these observations together, we obtain $S \to S - S \mid S * S \mid x \mid S\char`\^S$ as oCFG.

Next we show the undecidability of determining whether a grammar has least parse trees.

Theorem 1. *It is undecidable whether an oCFG G has least parse trees.*

Proof. As is well-known, it is undecidable whether a CFG $G = (N, \{a, b\}, P, S_G)$ is *universal*, i.e. whether $\mathcal{L}(G) = \{a, b\}^*$ (where $\{a, b\}^*$ denotes all strings over $\{a, b\}$). Without loss of generality assume that G is in Chomsky normal form, ensuring G itself has least parse trees. We construct G' from G by adding a new start nonterminal S and a new production $S \to S_G \mid SS \mid \varepsilon \mid a \mid b$. Then G is universal if and only if G' has least parse trees. To see this, first assume G is universal. This implies that for all strings w, a parse tree can be derived using $S \to S_G$ and avoiding $S \to SS$, $S \to \varepsilon$, $S \to a$ or $S \to b$. These parse trees, making use of $S \to S_G$, are smaller that any parse tree making use of $S \to SS$, $S \to \varepsilon$, $S \to a$ or $S \to b$. Thus, G having least parse trees also implies G' has least parse trees. Conversely, assume G is not universal and let $w \notin \mathcal{L}(G)$. Then any parse tree t for w, will use $S \to SS \mid \varepsilon \mid a \mid b$ and not $S \to S_G$, and as shown in Example 2, a smaller parse tree (than t) can be derived making use of $S \to SS \mid \varepsilon \mid a \mid b$ (and not $S \to S_G$), but with the same yield as t. Thus, $\mathcal{P}_{G'}(w)$ will not contain a least parse tree. ∎

It is however decidable whether a oCFG is well-ordered, which implies that it has least parse trees, but is again not necessary.

Theorem 2. *It is decidable whether an oCFG $G = (N, \Sigma, P, S)$ is well-ordered.*

Proof (sketch). In this proof let a *free context* be a context, as in Definition 2, except we permit symbols from Γ_0 to occur to the right of any $\square$, and with a free context containing precisely one leaf node labelled by $\square$ (e.g. $(a[\square, b])[\![c[d]]\!] = a[c[d], b]$).

By definition, G is *not* well-ordered if and only if there exists some string w where $\mathcal{P}_G(w)$ has an infinite subset $\{t_1, t_2, t_3, \ldots\} \subseteq \mathcal{P}_G(w)$ having $\cdots <_G t_3 <_G t_2 <_G t_1$. We next argue that such a subset exists if and only if there exist two trees $u_1, u_2 \in \mathcal{P}_G(w)$ having $u_2 <_G u_1$, where $u_1 = c[\![t]\!]$ and $u_2 = c[\![c'[\![t]\!]]\!]$ for some tree t, a free context c, and a non-empty (i.e. containing at least one non-$\square$ node) free context c' with $y(c') = \square$.

The if direction is trivial: if $c[\![c'[\![t]\!]]\!] <_G c[\![t]\!]$ then we can choose $u_3 = c[\![c'[\![c'[\![t]\!]]\!]]\!]$, $u_4 = c[\![c'[\![c'[\![c'[\![t]\!]]\!]]\!]]\!]$ etc., these trees all have the yield w and have $\cdots <_G u_3 <_G u_2 <_G u_1$ by construction.

The only if direction can be established by a pumping argument: the set of all parse trees is described by a regular tree automaton (see [5] for the basics on tree languages) with $\mathcal{O}(|N|)$ states, and the infinite set $\{t_1, t_2, \ldots\}$ all having the same yield means that infinitely many of the trees will contain subpaths which repeat a state/nonterminal but contribute no symbols to the yield. Pick such a tree u_2 and construct $u_2 = c[\![c'[\![t]\!]]\!]$ by letting c' be (one of) the non-empty contexts resulting by extracting the shortest subpath repeating a state/nonterminal (i.e. the $\square$ must be replaced with a rule for the same nonterminal as the root of c' to be a valid parse tree). Then $u_1 = c[\![t]\!]$ is also a parse tree. We are not guaranteed that every such u_1 and u_2 has $u_2 <_G u_1$, but we are guaranteed that some pair with this property exists, or the set $\{t_1, t_2, \ldots\}$ would be finite, causing a contradiction.

Finally, if such a pair u_1 and u_2 exist then there will (for some possibly different string) exist such a pair with height bounded by $\mathcal{O}(|N|)$. Simply pick any candidate $u_2 = c[\![c'[\![t]\!]]\!]$ and observe that we can always "unpump" c and t (i.e. remove any subpaths repeating nonterminals) resulting in heights bounded by $\mathcal{O}(|N|)$. This may change the yielded string (shortening it), but as the same change happens in both the resulting trees u_1 and u_2 we retain their relationship. We can similarly unpump c' to a height bounded by $\mathcal{O}(|N|)$, noting that at most one nonterminal repetition may be needed to retain the first rule application which causes the ordering $u_2 <_G u_1$ to hold.

Putting these pieces together the resulting trees $u_2 = c[\![c'[\![t]\!]]\!]$ and $u_1 = c[\![t]\!]$ to have a height bounded by $\mathcal{O}(|N|)$. The property is then decidable by simply enumerating all possible pairs of parse trees (for any string) of height below this bound, checking if any pair disproves well-orderedness. ∎

Corollary 1. *If an oCFG $G = (N, \Sigma, P, S)$ is well-ordered then for every string w the kth smallest $t \in \mathcal{P}_G(w)$ has a height bounded by $\mathcal{O}(k|N||w|)$.*

Proof. This follows from the proof of Theorem 2. When G is well-ordered the *least* tree for any string will contain no subpath which repeats a nonterminal without deriving any terminal (otherwise that subpath would, in the terms of the proof of Theorem 2, form a free context c' which demonstrates G not well-ordered). The *second least* will, worst case, add $\mathcal{O}(|N|)$ to the height (repeating

c' once). The third least adds at most another $\mathcal{O}(|N|)$, and so on. Iterating this demonstrates this bound. ∎

It is quite natural to consider grammars which do not have least trees (or even those that are not well-ordered) to be malformed. However, since we consider the structure of parse trees important there is no generally applicable way of stating a procedure for eliminating ε- or unit productions, as this changes the parse trees produced. The fairly efficient decidability of well-orderedness does in practice mean that it is not very difficult to set out to design a well-ordered grammar, and in a suitably guided way remove any undesirable behaviors.

3   oCFG Derivations

We define in this section oCFG derivations and also show the close relationship between PEG and oCFG derivations. They are related as follows: when searching for oCFG (or equivalently, CFG) parse trees in a depth-first search (DFS) way, we obtain PEG parse trees by switching less often between backtracking and the forward search, compared to when searching for oCFG parse trees. As a result the PEG DFS is not exhaustive, not visiting all trees, where the oCFG search is exhaustive if allowed by the switching function. We obtain oCFG derivations by reformulating left-most CFG derivations to be deterministic by trying out production choices, for a given nonterminal, in the order they are specified in the oCFG. To use the next production choice, all previous production choices must first be attempted (a property shared by oCFG and PEG derivations). In our setting, derivations will be left-most, but more importantly also deterministic, in contrast to how CFG derivations are typically defined. Our derivations will also keep track of the status of the partially constructed parse tree as the derivation proceeds.

Before defining oCFG derivations for strings w over an oCFG G, we first introduce some required notation.

We let ε' be a symbol that will be associated with ε, but which is not given the empty string interpretation. Also, for $A \to r_1^A \mid \cdots \mid r_{n_A}^A$, denote by $\bar{r}_i^A$ the string that is equal to r_i^A if $r_i^A \neq \varepsilon$, and equal to ε' otherwise. Note that the rank of A^i is equal to $|\bar{r}_i^A|$.

We denote by Γ_G' the set of symbols $\Gamma_G \cup N \cup \{\varepsilon'\}$, and by $\mathcal{C}_{\Gamma_G}'$ the set of trees $\mathcal{C}_{\Gamma_G} \cup \mathcal{T}_{\Gamma_G}$. Instead of having derivation steps between strings in $(N \cup \Sigma)^*$ derivable from S, i.e. between sentential forms, we have derivation steps between elements in $\mathcal{C}_{\Gamma_G}' \times (\Gamma_G')^* \times \Sigma^*$. Derivations will be done in one of two modes: prefix mode, where parsing a prefix of the input string successfully is regarded as a success, and full mode, where the complete input string must be parsed (successfully) for the parse to be regarded as successful. The situation is similar to typical PCRE-style regular expression matchers, where the matcher can either be forced to determine if a full match is possible, or be asked to return the first prefix match possible, or all prefix matches in order.

A derivation starts with $(\square, S, w)$, and produces along the way the parse trees of prefixes v of w, as the first component $t \in \mathcal{T}_{\Gamma_G}$ of triples (t, ε, v'), where $w = vv'$

and $y(t) = v$. In full mode, we only consider trees t with $y(t) = w$ as parse trees, and essentially simply ignore all parse trees t produced along the way having $y(t)$ as a proper prefix of w. If only the first (full) parse tree is of interest, the derivation is terminated after producing the first (full) parse tree, or after failing by producing $(\square, S_{n_S}, w)$ before any parse trees. If we are interested in all parse trees, the derivation is only terminated after producing $(\square, S_{n_S}, w)$, at which stage all parse trees t would have been produced as the first component of triples of the form (t, ε, v') (if the switching function allows it). It is important to note that the number of parse trees and/or the derivation might not be finite.

There are three types of derivation steps, namely terminal or ε-shifting, rule application, and backtracking, defined next.

Definition 7. *Let* $t \in \mathcal{C}'_{\Gamma_G}$, $a \in \Sigma$, $\alpha \in (\Gamma'_G)^*$, $v \in \Sigma^*$, *and* $P(A) = (r_1^A, \ldots, r_{n_A}^A)$.

1. *A terminal shifting step has the form* $(t, a\alpha, av) \Rightarrow_t (t[\![a]\!], \alpha, v)$ *and* ε-*shifting the form* $(t, \varepsilon'\alpha, v) \Rightarrow_t (t[\![\varepsilon]\!], \alpha, v)$;
2. *A rule application step has one of the following forms:*
   (a) $(t, A\alpha, v) \Rightarrow_r (t[\![A_1[\square, \ldots, \square]]\!], \bar{r}_1^A \alpha, v)$; *or*
   (b) $(t, A_i\alpha, v) \Rightarrow_r (t[\![A_{i+1}[\square, \ldots, \square]]\!], \bar{r}_{i+1}^A \alpha, v)$ *if* $i < n_A$, *where in* $A_1[\square, \ldots, \square]$ *and* $A_{i+1}[\square, \ldots, \square]$, *the number of leaf nodes labelled by the symbol* $\square$ *is equal to the rank of* A_1 *and* A_{i+1}, *respectively.*
3. *A backtracking step has one of the following forms:*
   (a) $(t[\![a]\!], \alpha, v) \Rightarrow_b (t, a\alpha, av)$, *i.e. terminal backtracking; or*
   (b) $(t[\![\varepsilon]\!], \alpha, v) \Rightarrow_b (t, \varepsilon'\alpha, v)$, *i.e. ε-backtracking; or*
   (c) $(t[\![A_i[\square, \ldots, \square]]\!], \bar{r}_i\alpha, v) \Rightarrow_b (t, A_i\alpha, v)$, *i.e. rule backtracking.*

A derivation starts with $(\square, S, w)$ and alternates between a forward and backtracking phase, defined next, until a triple of the form $(\square, S_{n_S}, w)$ is obtained.

We generalize oCFGs to include an additional computable function $\mathcal{S}$, referred to as the *switching function*, mapping triples from $\mathcal{C}'_{\Gamma_G} \times (\Gamma'_G)^* \times \Sigma^*$ and the grammar G, to the boolean values $\{True, False\}$. The function $\mathcal{S}$ is used, in combination with other criteria (given in the next definition), in determining when to switch from the forward to the backtracking phase. We regard the switching function $\mathcal{S}$ with constant value *False* as the *default switching function*. We only consider the default switching function, and switching functions comparing $|y(t)|$ to $|w|$, for triples (t, α, v) (note that $|w|$ can be computed from (t, α, v)), but we still define $\mathcal{S}$ in this more general way for future exploration, and also state our results and definitions using this more general set-up. In fact, when not using the default switching function, we use the switching function $\mathcal{S}$ that returns *True* on (t, α, v) when $|y(t)| > |w|$ and *False* otherwise.

Definition 8.

- In the forward phase, we apply terminal or ε-shifting, or rule application steps until a triple of one of the forms (1)–(3) are obtained, or until $\mathcal{S}((t, \alpha, v), G) =$ *True* (where (t, α, v) is the current triple).
  1. $(t, a\alpha, bv)$, *with* $a, b \in \Sigma$ *and* $a \neq b$;

2. $(t, a\alpha, \varepsilon)$;

3. (t, ε, v) which implies $y(t) \in \Sigma^*$, i.e. t is a parse tree of a prefix of w.

After the forward phase, we proceed to backtracking.

- In the backtracking phase, we apply terminal and rule backtracking, but switch back to the forward phase in the following cases.

  1. Rule backtracking produced $(t, A_i\alpha, v)$ with $i < n_A$.

  2. A triple $(\square, S_i\alpha, v)$, with $i < n_S$, was produced.

  If $i = n_A$, replace A_{n_A} by A and proceed with backtracking. If $(\square, S_{n_S}, w)$ is produced, the derivation terminates.

In a derivation, if rule backtracking produced $(t, A_1\alpha, v)$, the triple $(t, A\alpha, v)$ should have appeared earlier in the derivation, and similarly, if rule backtracking produced $(t, A_{i+1}\alpha, v)$, then $(t, A_i\alpha, v)$ should have appeared earlier. The backtracking phase undoes the steps from the most recent forward phase, up to the point where an alternative production choice can be made in the forward phase. In the case where during backtracking A_{n_A} is replaced by A, backtracking will undo steps from an earlier forward phase until an earlier alternative choice. Also note that for (t, α, v) we have $|\alpha|$ equal to the number of instances of $\square$ in t.

Grammars with left recursion might lead to infinite derivations, even without producing a single parse tree. Consider for example the grammar with the following left recursive production $S \rightarrow Sa \mid a$. With the default switching function, an infinite derivation will be obtained, similar to PEGs not supporting left recursion, as defined in [2]. Various ways of extending parsing expression grammars (PEGs) to support left-recursion has been proposed, for example in [6], which is used in the Pegen implementation [7], but these approaches often leads to unexpected parsing results in corner cases, as is pointed out in the section on related work in [8]. When defining the switching function S to return True on (t, α, v), when $|y(t)| > |w|$ (and False otherwise), we avoid infinite derivations and still obtain the unique parse tree of each input string of the form a^n in the given example.

Theorem 3. *Derivations produce parse trees (not necessarily all of them) in the order determined by $<_G$. If derivations are finite and the switching function S only returns True in cases where no parse tree can be derived by continuing the current forward phase, then all parse trees are produced for the given input string.*

Proof (sketch). Induction over the height of parse trees can be used to show that all parse trees are produced for finite derivations when S has the stated property. The definition of derivations can be used to show that if (t', α', v') is produced after (t, α, v) in a forward phase of a derivation, then $t <_G t'$. ∎

Remark 2. When an oCFG G contains no ε-productions and has no cyclic (nonterminal) unit productions, and the switching function S returns True on (t, α, v) when $|y(t)| > |w|$ (and False otherwise), derivations are finite and produce all parse trees. It is left as future work to determine if it is possible to produce least parse trees (first) in derivations, by appropriately defined switching functions, when G is well-ordered.

PEGs are defined exactly as oCFGs, but production choices for a given nonterminal are given different semantics. Thus, where in oCFGs we write $A \to r_1^A \mid \cdots \mid r_{n_A}^A$, for PEGs we write $A \to r_1^A / \cdots / r_{n_A}^A$. Note that we do not follow the convention of writing PEG productions as $A \leftarrow r_1^A / \cdots / r_{n_A}^A$, i.e. we use the right arrow, instead of the left arrow.

In PEG derivations, the switching between backtracking and the forward phase happens less often than in corresponding oCFG derivations. PEGs often recognize a proper subset of the strings recognized by corresponding oCFGs, since the depth-first search performed by PEGs is not exhaustive, as it is in the case of oCFGs (if allowed by the switching function). For PEGs, the derivation is terminated after obtaining the first parse tree, since if we do not, backtracking (in a single phase), as defined for PEGs, will produce $(\Box, S, w)$ (again).

Definition 9. *Backtracking for PEGs are obtained by modifying oCFG backtracking as follows. During each backtracking phase, when encountering rule backtracking on A_i, we consider the tree rooted at this instance of A_i when we started the current backtracking phase. If the subtree rooted at A_i was not a context, i.e. it was in $\mathcal{T}_{\Gamma_G}$, we replace A_i by A, just as we would do for A_{n_A}, and then continue with the backtracking phase.*

Remark 3. Assume we use the default switching function $\mathcal{S}$, then our PEG semantics is identical to that defined by Ford in [2], at least in terms of strings being accepted. This excludes various extensions to PEGs as defined by Ford and considered in the next section. We will not prove this due to space considerations, especially since it is tedious but straightforward. On a high level, it follows from the observation that both our PEG semantics and the semantics defined by Ford, is such that a production choice is made for a given nonterminal completely based on if the choice is locally successful, but earlier production choices for the given nonterminal is not. Also, a local production choice is not changed in order to guarantee overall matching/parsing success.

Example 5. In this example we use the switching function $\mathcal{S}$ that returns *True* on (t, α, v) when $|y(t)| > |w|$, where w is the string being parsed, and *False* otherwise. Recall from Remark 2 that this switching function ensures that oCFG and PEG derivations always terminate, in contrast to PEGs as defined in [2], which beyond accepting or rejecting input strings, may also loop.

Consider the PEG with production $S \to aSa/a$, and thus no left recursion. Then a^5 is accepted, where it is not in Ford's semantics. This is due to the fact that the complete sentential form is used to determine if the current partial parse tree could still lead to a parse tree for a prefix of the input string, whereas Ford (and thus the default switching function) only makes use of terminals preceding the first nonterminal in the sentential form to determine if it is still possible to derive a parse tree.

Example 6. In this example we show the consequence of having a more eager switching (from backtracking to the forward phase) for oCFG derivations compared to PEG derivations. Let $S \to A \mid aa$; $A \to Ba$; $B \to aa \mid a$ and $w = aa$

(and '|' replaced by '/' in the corresponding PEG grammar). Assume we use the default switching function. We only consider derivations until they produce the first parse tree. The oCFG derivation produces the parse tree $S_1[A_1[B_2[a],a]]$, whereas the PEG parse tree is $S_2[a,a]$. Recall that we encode production choices as integer indices in nonterminal labels of parse trees.

Next, we show the oCFG derivation, terminated after obtaining the first parse tree. We use $\Rightarrow_r$, $\Rightarrow_s$, $\Rightarrow_b$ to indicate a rule application, terminal shifting, and backtracking steps respectively.

$$(\Box, S, aa) \Rightarrow_r (S_1[\Box], A, aa) \Rightarrow_r (S_1[A_1[\Box,\Box]], Ba, aa)$$
$$\Rightarrow_r (S_1[A_1[B_1[\Box,\Box],\Box]], aaa, aa) \Rightarrow_s \cdots \Rightarrow_s (S_1[A_1[B_1[a,a],\Box]], a, \varepsilon) \Rightarrow_b \cdots$$
$$\Rightarrow_b (S_1[A_1[\Box,\Box]], B_1 a, aa) \Rightarrow_r (S_1[A_1[B_2[\Box],\Box]], aa, aa) \Rightarrow_s \cdots$$
$$\Rightarrow_s (S_1[A_1[B_2[a],a]], \varepsilon, \varepsilon)$$

If we compare the oCFG derivation with the PEG derivation (i.e. we now change instances of '|' to '/' in the grammar), we have the following difference. The PEG derivation is identical up to the point where the oCFG derivation applies the step $(S_1[A_1[\Box,\Box]], B_1 a, aa) \Rightarrow_r (S_1[A_1[B_2[\Box],\Box]], aa, aa)$, but when we started the backtracking phase proceeding this derivation step in the oCFG derivation, the subtree $B_1[a,a]$ in $(S_1[A_1[B_1[a,a],\Box]], a, \varepsilon)$ was in $\mathcal{T}_{\Gamma_G}$, i.e. not a context. Thus, the backtracking phase in the PEG derivation is continued up to $(\Box, S_1, aa)$. From here on, the PEG derivation proceeds as follows: $(\Box, S_1, aa) \Rightarrow_r (S_2[\Box,\Box], aa, aa) \Rightarrow_s \cdots \Rightarrow_s (S_2[a,a], \varepsilon, \varepsilon)$.

4   oCFG Extensions

We sketch in this short section the relative ease with which various useful extensions can be added to oCFGs, similar to the lookahead predicates in PEGs [2]. We leave a precise description and a formal study of the properties of these extensions as future work.

First we add *positive* and *negative lookahead predicates* to oCFGs/PEGs. To accommodate lookahead predicates, our grammar productions $A \rightarrow r_1^A \mid \ldots \mid r_{n_A}^A$ or $A \rightarrow r_1^A / \ldots / r_{n_A}^A$ are extended by allowing the r_i^A to not only be a concatenation of terminal or nonterminals, but also to have subexpressions of the form $\&B$ (a positive lookahead on the nonterminal B) and $!B$ (a negative lookahead) in the concatenation, for any nonterminal B. We let lookaheads modify derivations in the case of predicates being encountered, as follows. When encountering $(t, \& A\alpha, v)$, it is determined if it is possible to parse a prefix of v with starting nonterminal A and the same productions as the original oCFG, but interpreting this grammar with starting nonterminal A as a CFG, and not a oCFG. If it is possible, we continue the original derivation with (t, α, v), otherwise we terminate the derivation. When nested lookaheads are allowed, i.e. while determining if a lookahead match, another lookahead is encountered, or when considering PEGs, lookaheads should be considered as spawning a new oCFG derivation starting with $(\Box, A, v)$, and once this newly spawned derivation succeeds at parsing a prefix of v, we continue the original derivation with (t, α, v). For negative looka-heads, when $(t, !A\alpha, v)$ is encountered, we require that it is not possible to parse a prefix of w, before continuing with (t, α, v). Note that oCFGs with lookaheads are closely related to Boolean grammars [9].

Once we have negative lookaheads, it is no longer necessary to make the distinction between prefix and full parsing, i.e. prefix parsing combined with a negative lookahead is enough to force full parsing.

Next we generalize the right-hand sides of grammar productions to be oCFG/PEG *expressions*. The expressions are one of two types. Type 1, is the concatenation of expressions of type 2, and type 2 expressions is either expres-sions of type 1 combined with the operator '|' for oCFG expressions, or combined with the operator '/' for PEG expressions. We start the inductive definition by regarding terminals, nonterminal, positive lookahead nonterminals (i.e. $\&A$ for example), and negative lookahead nonterminals (i.e. $!A$ for example) as type 2 expressions, and then alternate between constructing type 1 and type 2 expres-sions.

We provide semantics to oCFGs/PEGs with these more general type of gram-mar productions (i.e. expressions are allowed in the right-hand sides of produc-tions), by giving a nonterminal name to each type 2 expression e, say A, adding a rule $A \to e$, and then using A when building up type 1 expressions instead of e. We then continue this process, by giving a name to each type 1 expression when using these to build up type 2 expressions. Consider the grammar with the production $S \to (A \mid B)(CD \mid EF)$. Then we replace this production with the productions $S \to XY$, $X \to (A \mid B)$ and $Y \to (CD \mid EF)$. The parse trees will contain labels indicating production choices in terms of these new non-terminals, and they indicate the subexpressions used of the original oCFG in parse trees.

For oCFG expressions, one can show that concatenation is left and right dis-tributive over the operator '|', but for PEG expressions, concatenation is only left distributive over the operator '/', in terms of strings being accepted. Compar-ing the PEG G_1 with production $S \to (a/aa)b$, with G_2, having the production $S' \to ab/aab$, shows that we do not have the right distributive law for PEGs, since $aab \notin \mathcal{L}(G_1)$ but $aab \in \mathcal{L}(G_2)$

5   Conclusions and Future Work

We have shown that oCFGs, a novel unambiguous grammar formalism, provides a good way to understand the relationship between PEGs and CFGs. Ordered context-free grammars is a natural way in which to extend PCRE regex matching to an ordered context-free grammar formalism, in which it is possible to talk about the first match or least parse tree, just as in the case of PCRE regex matching. We also provided what is, in our opinion, a more natural and generic way in which to support left recursion in PEGs, by making use of switching functions to avoid infinite derivations.

Future work includes a thorough investigation into parsing complexity, and a better understanding of interesting classes of switching functions and their influence on the underlying oCFGs. Moreover, the decision algorithm provided in Theorem 2 is most likely suboptimal, and it should be possible to provide a better algorithm than simply enumerating all pairs of trees below a certain height.

References

1. Berglund, M., van der Merwe, B.: On the semantics of regular expression parsing in the wild. Theor. Comput. Sci. **679**, 69–82 (2017)
2. Ford, B.: Parsing expression grammars: a recognition-based syntactic foundation. In: Proceedings of the 31st ACM SIGPLAN-SIGACT Symposium on Principles of Programming Languages, pp. 111–122 (2004)
3. Loff, B., Moreira, N., Reis, R.: The computational power of parsing expression grammars. J. Comput. Syst. Sci. **111**, 1–21 (2020)
4. Parr, T., Fisher, K.: LL(*): the foundation of the ANTLR parser generator. In: Hall, M.W., Padua, D.A. (eds.) Proceedings of the 32nd ACM SIGPLAN Conference on Programming Language Design and Implementation, pp. 425–436 (2011)
5. Nivat, M., Podelski, A. (eds.): Tree Automata and Languages. North-Holland, Amsterdam (1992)
6. Warth, A., Douglass, J.R., Millstein, T.D.: Packrat parsers can support left recursion. In: Glück, R., de Moor, O. (eds.) Proceedings of the 2008 ACM SIGPLAN Symposium on Partial Evaluation and Semantics-based Program Manipulation, pp. 103–110 (2008)
7. Pegen. https://github.com/we-like-parsers/pegen. Accessed 28 Feb 2022
8. Medeiros, S., Mascarenhas, F., Ierusalimschy, R.: Left recursion in parsing expression grammars. Sci. Comput. Program. **96**, 177–190 (2014)
9. Okhotin, A.: Boolean grammars. Inf. Comput. **194**(1), 19–48 (2004)

Symbolic Weighted Language Models, Quantitative Parsing and Automated Music Transcription

Florent Jacquemard[(✉)] and Lydia Rodriguez de la Nava

INRIA and CNAM/Cedric Lab, Paris, France
`florent.jacquemard@inria.fr`, `lydia.rodriguez-de-la-nava@inria.fr`

Abstract. We study several classes of symbolic weighted formalisms: automata (swA), transducers (swT) and visibly pushdown extensions (swVPA, swVPT). They combine the respective extensions of their symbolic and weighted counterparts, allowing a quantitative evaluation of words over a large or infinite input alphabet.

We present properties of closure by composition, the computation of transducer-defined distances between nested words and languages, as well as a PTIME 1-best search algorithm for swVPA. These results are applied to solve in PTIME a variant of parsing over infinite alphabets. We illustrate this approach with a motivating use case in automated music transcription.

1 Introduction

Symbolic Weighted (sw) language models [13] (automata and transducers) combine two important extensions of standard models. On the one hand, symbolic extensions, like in *Symbolic Automata* (sA [9]), can handle an infinite input alphabet Σ, by guarding every transition with a predicate $\phi : \Sigma \to \mathbb{B}$. The ability of sA to compare input symbols is quite restricted, compared to other models of automata extended e.g. with registers (see [21] for a survey), however, under appropriate closure conditions on the set of predicates, all the good properties enjoyed by automata over finite alphabets are still valid for sA.

On the other hand, *Weighted Automata* (wA [10]) extend qualitative evaluation of input words to *quantitative* evaluation, by assigning to every transition a weight value in a semiring $\mathbb{S}$. The weights of the rules involved in a computation are combined using the product operator $\otimes$ of $\mathbb{S}$, whereas the sum operator $\oplus$ of $\mathbb{S}$ is used to resolve ambiguity (typically, $\oplus$ selects, amongst two computations, the best weighted one). These extensions have also been applied to evaluate hierarchical structures, like trees [10, ch. 9], or nested words, with symbolic [8], or weighted [7] extensions of Visibly Pushdown Automata (VPA [3]). With their ability to evaluate data sequences quantitatively, sw models have found various applications such as data stream processing [4], runtime verification of timed systems [24] or robustness optimization for machine learning models [16].

P. Caron and L. Mignot (Eds.): CIAA 2022, LNCS 13266, pp. 67–79, 2022.
https://doi.org/10.1007/978-3-031-07469-1_5

The sw models with data storage defined in [13], where their expressiveness is extensively studied, are very general, and cover all the models cited above, as well as those considered in this paper. Here, we consider simple models of sw-automata and transducers whose transitions are assigned *functions* $\phi : \Sigma \to \mathbb{S}$ from input symbols in an infinite alphabet Σ into a semiring $\mathbb{S}$ (Sect. 3). Such functions generalize the boolean guards of symbolic models from the Boolean codomain $\mathbb{B}$ to an arbitrary semiring $\mathbb{S}$, and the constant values of weighted models. We prove some properties of closure under composition for those sw models, generalizing classical constructions for the composition of transducers [20], and propose a polynomial time algorithm of search for a word of minimal weight for swVPA (somehow a variant of accessibility problems in pushdown automata [6]). We apply these results to the problem of parsing words over infinite alphabet (sw-*parsing*), whose goal is: given an (unstructured) input word s, to find a (structured) nested word t at a minimal distance from s, where the distance, following [18], is defined by $T(s,t) \otimes A(t)$, T being a sw-transducer (swT) and A a swVPA (Sect. 4). The notion of transducer-based distances allows to consider different infinite alphabets for the input s and output t. Moreover, the use of swVPA allows to search for an output t in the form of a nested word, as a linear representation of a parse tree; sw-*parsing* is solved with a Bar-Hillel, Perles and Shamir construction [12, ch. 13], and the best-search algorithm for swVPA. We illustrate our approach with an application that motivated this work: *automated music transcription*, i.e. the problem of converting a linear music recording given in input into a score in *Common Western Music Notation*, a representation structured hierarchically [25].

Example 1. Let us consider a short input sequence I of musical events represented by symbols of the form $e : \tau$ in an infinite alphabet Σ, where e is a MIDI key number in 21..108 [22], or the mark 'start' or 'end', and $\tau \in \mathbb{Q}$ is a duration in seconds. Such inputs typically correspond to the recording of a live performance: $I =$ start: $0.07, 69 : 0.65, 71 : 0.19, 73 : 0.14, 74 : 0.31, 76 : 0.35, 77 : 0.29,$ end: 0.

The output of parsing I is a nested word O, where separated notes are grouped into hierarchical patterns. It is made of symbols $a : \tau'$ in an alphabet Δ, where a is either a *note name*, (e.g., A_4, G_5, etc.), a *continuation* symbol '$-$', or a *markup* symbol (opening or closing parenthesis). The time value τ' is a musical duration. For instance, the music score ♯ is represented by the nested word: $O = \lceil_m : 2, \lceil_2 : 1, A_4 : \frac{1}{2}, \lceil_2 : \frac{1}{2}, - : \frac{1}{4}, \lceil_2 : \frac{1}{4}, B_4 : \frac{1}{8}, C\sharp_5 : \frac{1}{8}, \rceil_2 : \frac{1}{4}, \rceil_2 : \frac{1}{2}, \rceil_2 : 1,$ $\lceil_m : 1, \lceil_3 : 1, D_5 : \frac{1}{3}, E_5 : \frac{1}{3}, F_5 : \frac{1}{3}, \rceil_3 : 1, \rceil_m : 1, \rceil_m : 2$ (see Fig. 1). The symbol $\lceil_m$ marks the opening of a *measure* (a time interval of duration 1), while the subsequences of O between markups $\lceil_d : \ell$ and $\rceil_d : \ell$, for some natural number d, represent the division of a duration ℓ by d. The sequence $O \in \Delta^*$ is a candidate solution for the transcription of $I \in \Sigma^*$. Let us consider another candidate ♯, represented by $O' = \lceil_m : 2, \lceil_2 : 1, A_4 : \frac{1}{2}, \lceil_2 : \frac{1}{2}, - : \frac{1}{4}, B_4 : \frac{1}{4}, \rceil_2 : \frac{1}{2}, \rceil_2 : 1, \lceil_m : 1, \lceil_3 : 1, 'C\sharp'_5 : 0, D_5 : \frac{1}{3},$ $E_5 : \frac{1}{3}, F_5 : \frac{1}{3}, \rceil_3 : 1, \rceil_m : 1, \rceil_m : 2$. The quoted symbol '$C\sharp_5$' represents an *appogiatura*, i.e. an ornamental note of theoretical duration 0. Roughly, sw-parsing associates a weight value to each candidate, depending of its temporal distance to I and notational complexity. Our goal is to find a best candidate.   ◇

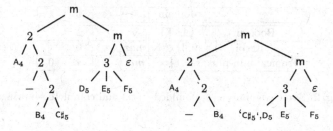

Fig. 1. Tree representation of the scores of Example 1, linearized respectively into O and O'.

2   Preliminary Notions

Semirings. We shall consider weight values in a *semiring* $\langle S, \oplus, 0, \otimes, 1 \rangle$: a structure of domain S, equipped with two associative binary operators $\oplus$ and $\otimes$, with respective neutral elements 0 and 1, such that $\oplus$ is commutative, $\otimes$ distributes over $\oplus$: $\forall x, y, z \in S, x \otimes (y \oplus z) = (x \otimes y) \oplus (x \otimes z)$, and $(x \oplus y) \otimes z = (x \otimes z) \oplus (y \otimes z)$, 0 is absorbing for $\otimes$: $\forall x \in S, 0 \otimes x = x \otimes 0 = 0$.

A semiring S is *commutative* if $\otimes$ is commutative. It is *idempotent* if for every $x \in S$, $x \oplus x = x$. Every idempotent semiring S induces a partial ordering $\leq_\oplus$ called the *natural ordering* of S [17], defined by: for every $x, y \in S, x \leq_\oplus y$ iff $x \oplus y = x$. It is sometimes defined in the opposite direction [10, ch. 1]; we follow here the direction that coincides with the usual ordering on the Tropical semiring *min-plus* (Fig. 2). An idempotent semiring S is called *total* if $\leq_\oplus$ is total, i.e. when for every $x, y \in S$, either $x \oplus y = x$ or $x \oplus y = y$.

Lemma 1 (Monotony, [17]). *If* $\langle S, \oplus, 0, \otimes, 1 \rangle$ *is idempotent, for every* $x, y, z \in S, x \leq_\oplus y$ *implies* $x \oplus z \leq_\oplus y \oplus z, x \otimes z \leq_\oplus y \otimes z$ *and* $z \otimes x \leq_\oplus z \otimes y$.

We say that S is *monotonic* wrt $\leq_\oplus$. Another important semiring property in the context of optimization is *superiority* ((i) of Lemma 2), which generalizes the *non-negative weights* condition in Dijkstra's shortest-path algorithm. Intuitively, it means that combining elements with $\otimes$ always increases their weight.

Lemma 2 (Superiority, Boundedness). *Let* $\langle S, \oplus, 0, \otimes, 1 \rangle$ *be an idempotent semiring. The two following statements are equivalent: (i) for all* $x, y \in S, x \leq_\oplus x \otimes y$ *and* $y \leq_\oplus x \otimes y$ *(ii) for all* $x \in S, 1 \oplus x = 1$.

The property (i) of superiority implies that $1 \leq_\oplus z \leq_\oplus 0$ for all $z \in S$ (by setting $x = 1$ and $y = 0$ in Lemma 2). From an optimization point of view, it means that 1 is the best value, and 0 the worst. A semiring S with property (ii) of Lemma 2 is called *bounded* in [17] and in the rest of the paper.

Lemma 3 ([17], Lemma 3). *Every bounded semiring is idempotent.*

	domain	$\oplus$	$\otimes$	0	1
Boolean	$\{\bot, \top\}$	$\vee$	$\wedge$	$\bot$	$\top$
Viterbi	$[0,1] \subset \mathbb{R}$	max	$\times$	0	1
Tropical min-plus	$\mathbb{R}_+ \cup \{\infty\}$	min	$+$	∞	0

Fig. 2. Some commutative, bounded, total and complete semirings.

We need to extend $\oplus$ to infinitely many operands. A semiring $\mathbb{S}$ is called *complete* [10, ch. 1] if it has an operation $\bigoplus_{i \in I} x_i$ for every family $(x_i)_{i \in I}$ of elements in the domain of $\mathbb{S}$, over an index set $I \subseteq \mathbb{N}$, such that:

i. *infinite sums extend finite sums:* $\forall j, k \in \mathbb{N}, j \neq k$,
$$\bigoplus_{i \in \emptyset} x_i = 0, \quad \bigoplus_{i \in \{j\}} x_i = x_j, \quad \bigoplus_{i \in \{j,k\}} x_i = x_j \oplus x_k,$$

ii. *associativity and commutativity:* for all partition $(I_j)_{j \in J}$ of I,
$$\bigoplus_{j \in J} \bigoplus_{i \in I_j} x_i = \bigoplus_{i \in I} x_i,$$

iii. *distributivity of products over infinite sums:* for all $I \subseteq \mathbb{N}$, $\forall x, y \in \mathbb{S}$,
$$\bigoplus_{i \in I} (x \otimes y_i) = x \otimes \bigoplus_{i \in I} y_i, \text{ and } \bigoplus_{i \in I} (x_i \otimes y) = \left(\bigoplus_{i \in I} x_i \right) \otimes y.$$

Label Theories. The functions labelling the transitions of sw-automata and transducers generalize the Boolean algebras of [9]. We consider *alphabets*, which are non-empty countable sets of symbols denoted by Σ, Δ... and write Σ^* for the set of finite sequences (*words*) over Σ, ε for the empty word, $\Sigma^+ = \Sigma^* \setminus \{\varepsilon\}$, and uv for the concatenation of $u, v \in \Sigma^*$.

Given a semiring $\langle \mathbb{S}, \oplus, 0, \otimes, 1 \rangle$, a *label theory* $\bar{\Phi}$ over $\mathbb{S}$ is an indexed family of sets Φ_Σ, resp. $\Phi_{\Sigma,\Delta}$, containing recursively enumerable functions of type $\Sigma \to \mathbb{S}$, resp. $\Sigma \times \Delta \to \mathbb{S}$, and such that if $\Phi_{\Sigma,\Delta} \in \bar{\Phi}$, then $\Phi_\Sigma \in \bar{\Phi}$ and $\Phi_\Delta \in \bar{\Phi}$, every $\Phi_\Sigma, \Phi_{\Sigma,\Delta} \in \bar{\Phi}$ contains all the constant functions of $\Sigma \to \mathbb{S}$, resp. $\Sigma \times \Delta \to \mathbb{S}$, for all $\Phi_{\Sigma,\Delta} \in \bar{\Phi}$, $\eta \in \Phi_{\Sigma,\Delta}$, $a \in \Sigma$, $b \in \Delta$, the partial application $x \mapsto \eta(x,b)$ is in Φ_Σ and the partial application $y \mapsto \eta(a,y)$ is in Φ_Δ, and $\bar{\Phi}$ is closed under the following operators, derived from the operations of $\mathbb{S}$:

- For all $\Phi_\Sigma \in \bar{\Phi}$, all $\phi \in \Phi_\Sigma$, and $\alpha \in \mathbb{S}$, $\alpha \otimes \phi : x \mapsto \alpha \otimes \phi(x)$, and $\phi \otimes \alpha : x \mapsto \phi(x) \otimes \alpha$ are in Φ_Σ, and similarly for $\oplus$ and for $\Phi_{\Sigma,\Delta}$.
- For all $\Phi_\Sigma \in \bar{\Phi}$, all $\phi, \phi' \in \Phi_\Sigma$, $\phi \otimes \phi' : x \mapsto \phi(x) \otimes \phi'(x)$ is in Φ_Σ.
- For all $\Phi_{\Sigma,\Delta} \in \bar{\Phi}$, all $\eta, \eta' \in \Phi_{\Sigma,\Delta}$, $\eta \otimes \eta' : x, y \mapsto \eta(x,y) \otimes \eta'(x,y)$ is in $\Phi_{\Sigma,\Delta}$.
- For all $\Phi_\Sigma, \Phi_{\Sigma,\Delta} \in \bar{\Phi}$, all $\phi \in \Phi_\Sigma$ and $\eta \in \Phi_{\Sigma,\Delta}$, $\phi \otimes_1 \eta : x, y \mapsto \phi(x) \otimes \eta(x,y)$ and $\eta \otimes_1 \phi : x, y \mapsto \eta(x,y) \otimes \phi(x)$ are in $\Phi_{\Sigma,\Delta}$.
- For all $\Phi_\Delta, \Phi_{\Sigma,\Delta} \in \bar{\Phi}$, all $\psi \in \Phi_\Delta$ and $\eta \in \Phi_{\Sigma,\Delta}$, $\psi \otimes_2 \eta : x, y \mapsto \psi(y) \otimes \eta(x,y)$ and $\eta \otimes_2 \psi : x, y \mapsto \eta(x,y) \otimes \psi(y)$ are in $\Phi_{\Sigma,\Delta}$.
- Analogous closures hold for $\oplus$.

Example 2. We go back to Example 1. In order to align an input in Σ^* with a music score in Δ^*, we must account for the expressive timing of human performance that results in small time shifts between an input event of Σ and a notational event in Δ. These shifts can be weighted as a distance in $\Phi_{\Sigma,\Delta}$, defined in the tropical min-plus semiring by $\delta(e: \tau, a: \tau') = |\tau' - \tau|$ if a corresponds to e (e.g. e is the MIDI key 69 and a is the note A_4), or 0 otherwise. $\diamond$

3 SW Visibly Pushdown Automata and Transducers

Let $\langle S, \oplus, 0, \otimes, 1 \rangle$ be a commutative and complete semiring and let Σ and Δ be countable alphabets called *input* and *output* respectively, such that Δ is partitioned into three disjoint subsets of symbols Δ_i, Δ_c and Δ_r, called respectively *internal*, *call* and *return* [3]. Let $\bar{\Phi}$ be a label theory over S, consisting of $\Phi_e = \Phi_\Sigma$, $\Phi_i = \Phi_{\Delta_i}$, $\Phi_c = \Phi_{\Delta_c}$, $\Phi_r = \Phi_{\Delta_r}$, $\Phi_{ei} = \Phi_{\Sigma,\Delta_i}$ and $\Phi_{cr} = \Phi_{\Delta_c,\Delta_r}$.

Definition 1 (swVPT). *A Symbolic Weighted Visibly Pushdown Transducer over Σ, Δ, S, and $\bar{\Phi}$ is a tuple $T = \langle Q, P, \text{in}, \bar{w}, \text{out} \rangle$, where Q is a finite set of states, P is a finite set of stack symbols, $\text{in}: Q \to S$ (respectively $\text{out}: Q \to S$) are functions defining the weight for entering (respectively leaving) a state, and $\bar{w}$ is a tuplet composed of the transition functions : $w_{10}: Q \times Q \to \Phi_e$, $w_{01}: Q \times Q \to \Phi_i$, $w_{11}: Q \times Q \to \Phi_{ei}$, $w_c: Q \times Q \times P \to \Phi_c$, $w_r: Q \times P \times Q \to \Phi_{cr}$, $w_r^e: Q \times Q \to \Phi_r$.*

For convenience, we extend the above transition functions as follows, for every $q, q' \in Q$, $p \in P$, $e \in \Sigma$, $a \in \Delta_i$, $c \in \Delta_c$, $r \in \Delta_r$, overloading their names:

$$\begin{aligned}
w_{10}(q, e, \varepsilon, q') &= \phi(e) & \text{where } \phi &= w_{10}(q, q'), \\
w_{01}(q, \varepsilon, a, q') &= \phi(a) & \text{where } \phi &= w_{01}(q, q'), \\
w_{11}(q, e, a, q') &= \eta(e, a) & \text{where } \eta &= w_{11}(q, q'), \\
w_c(q, \varepsilon, c, q', p) &= \phi(c) & \text{where } \phi &= w_c(q, q', p), \\
w_r(q, c, p, \varepsilon, r, q') &= \eta(c, r) & \text{where } \eta &= w_r(q, p, q'), \\
w_r^e(q, \varepsilon, r, q') &= \phi(r) & \text{where } \phi &= w_r^e(q, q').
\end{aligned}$$

The swVPT T computes asynchronously on pairs $\langle s, t \rangle \in \Sigma^* \times \Delta^*$. Intuitively, a transition $w_{ij}(q, e, a, q')$, with $i, j \in \{0, 1\}$ and $e \in \Sigma \cup \{\varepsilon\}$, $a \in \Delta_i \cup \{\varepsilon\}$, is interpreted as follows: when reading e and a in the input and output words, it increments the current position in the input word if and only if $i = 1$, and in the output word iff $j = 1$, and changes state from q to q'. When $e = \varepsilon$ (resp. $a = \varepsilon$), the current symbol in the input (resp. output) is not read. These transitions ignore the stack.

A transition of $w_c(q, \varepsilon, c, q', p)$ reads the call symbol $c \in \Delta_c$ in the output word, pushes it to the stack along with $p \in P$, and changes state from q to q'. As for $w_r(q, c, p, \varepsilon, r, q')$ and $w_r^e(q, \varepsilon, r, q')$ (used when the stack is empty), they read the return symbol r in the output word and change state from q to q'. Additionally, w_r reads and pops from the stack a pair $\langle c, p \rangle$ and the symbol c is compared to r by the function $\eta = w_r(q, p, q') \in \Phi_{cr}$.

Formally, the computations of the transducer T are defined with an intermediate function weight_T. A configuration $q[\gamma]$ is composed of a state $q \in Q$ and a stack content $\gamma \in \Gamma^*$, where $\Gamma = \Delta_c \times P$, and weight_T is a function from $[Q \times \Gamma^*] \times \Sigma^* \times \Delta^* \times [Q \times \Gamma^*]$ into $\mathbb{S}$, whose recursive definition enumerates each of the possible cases for reading $e \in \Sigma$, $a \in \Delta_i$, $c \in \Delta_c$, or $r \in \Delta_r$ (the empty stack is denoted by $\perp$, and the topmost symbol is the last pushed pair):

$$\text{weight}_T\left(q[\gamma], \varepsilon, \varepsilon, q'[\gamma']\right) = \mathbb{1} \text{ if } q = q', \gamma = \gamma' \text{ and } \mathbb{0} \text{ otherwise} \tag{1}$$

$$\text{weight}_T\left(q[\gamma], e\,u, \varepsilon, q'[\gamma']\right) = \bigoplus_{q'' \in Q} w_{10}(q, e, \varepsilon, q'') \otimes \text{weight}_T\left(q''[\gamma], u, \varepsilon, q'[\gamma']\right)$$

$$\text{weight}_T\left(q[\gamma], \varepsilon, a\,v, q'[\gamma']\right) = \bigoplus_{q'' \in Q} w_{01}(q, \varepsilon, a, q'') \otimes \text{weight}_T\left(q''[\gamma], \varepsilon, v, q'[\gamma']\right)$$

$$\text{weight}_T\left(q[\gamma], e\,u, a\,v, q'[\gamma']\right) = \bigoplus_{q'' \in Q} w_{10}(q, e, \varepsilon, q'') \otimes \text{weight}_T\left(q''[\gamma], u, a\,v, q'[\gamma']\right)$$

$$\oplus \bigoplus_{q'' \in Q} w_{01}(q, \varepsilon, a, q'') \otimes \text{weight}_T\left(q''[\gamma], e\,u, v, q'[\gamma']\right)$$

$$\oplus \bigoplus_{q'' \in Q} w_{11}(q, e, a, q'') \otimes \text{weight}_T\left(q''[\gamma], u, v, q'[\gamma']\right)$$

$$\text{weight}_T\left(q[\gamma], u, c\,v, q'[\gamma']\right) = \bigoplus_{\substack{q'' \in Q \\ p \in P}} w_c(q, \varepsilon, c, q'', p) \otimes \text{weight}_T\left(q'' \begin{bmatrix} \langle c, p \rangle \\ \gamma \end{bmatrix}, u, v, q'[\gamma']\right)$$

$$\text{weight}_T\left(q \begin{bmatrix} \langle c, p \rangle \\ \gamma \end{bmatrix}, u, r\,v, q'[\gamma']\right) = \bigoplus_{q'' \in Q} w_r(q, c, p, \varepsilon, r, q'') \otimes \text{weight}_T\left(q''[\gamma], u, v, q'[\gamma']\right)$$

$$\text{weight}_T\left(q[\perp], u, r\,v, q'[\gamma']\right) = \bigoplus_{q'' \in Q} w_r^e(q, \varepsilon, r, q'') \otimes \text{weight}_T\left(q''[\perp], u, v, q'[\gamma']\right)$$

The weight associated by T to an input/output pair $\langle s, t \rangle \in \Sigma^* \times \Delta^*$ is defined according to empty stack semantics:

$$T(s, t) = \bigoplus_{q, q' \in Q} \text{in}(q) \otimes \text{weight}_T\left(q[\perp], s, t, q'[\perp]\right) \otimes \text{out}(q') \tag{2}$$

Since $\mathbb{0}$ is absorbing for $\otimes$, and neutral for $\oplus$ in $\mathbb{S}$, if a transition's weight is equal to $\mathbb{0}$, then the entire term is $\mathbb{0}$, meaning the transition is impossible. This is analogous to the case of a transition's guard not satisfied in symbolic models [9].

Symbolic Weighted Visibly Pushdown Automata. swVPA are the particular case of swVPT that do not read in the input word, i.e. where all w_{10} and w_{11} are constant functions equal to $\mathbb{0}$, or $\Sigma = \emptyset$ (see [1, §C]). They are a weighted extension of sVPA [8], from Boolean semirings to arbitrary semiring domains. A relationship between swVPA and sw-Tree Automata is presented in [1, §F].

Example 3. We consider a swVPA A over Δ^*, with $P = Q$, computing a value of *notational complexity* for a given score. In a sequence $O \in \Delta^*$ like in Example 1, Δ_i contains timed notes and continuations, and Δ_c and Δ_r contain respectively opening and closing parentheses. To a call symbol $\lceil_n : \ell$, for some duration value ℓ, let us associate a transition for the division of ℓ by n: $w_c(q_\ell, \varepsilon, \lceil n : \ell, q_{\frac{\ell}{n}}, q') = \alpha_n \in S$. And to the matching return symbol $\rceil_n : \ell$, we associate a transition of weight $\mathbb{1}$: $w_r(q_{\frac{\ell}{n}}, \lceil n : \ell, q', \varepsilon, \rceil_n : \ell, q') = \mathbb{1}$, which jumps to the state q' stored in the stack. The choice of weight values for the call transitions can express some preferences in term of the expected output notation: if we want to prioritize pairs over triplets, in the Tropical min-plus semiring, then we would let $\alpha_2 < \alpha_3$. It is able to compute on several representations of a piece of music, estimating for each one a weight value depending on the preferences that we set. The algorithm of Theorem 4 then allows to select the best weighted representation.   ◇

Symbolic Weighted Transducers. swT are the particular case of swVPT that do not use the stack during their computations, because all w_c, w_r and w_r^e are constant functions equal to $\mathbb{0}$, or because $\Delta_c = \Delta_r = \emptyset$ (see [1, § C]).

The four first lines in expression (1) can be seen as a stateful definition of an edit-distance between a word $s \in \Sigma^*$ and a word $t \in \Delta_i^*$, see also [18]. Intuitively, in this vision, $w_{10}(q, e, \varepsilon, q')$ is the cost of the deletion of the symbol $e \in \Sigma$ in s, $w_{01}(q, \varepsilon, a, q')$ is the cost of the insertion of $a \in \Delta_i$ in t, and $w_{11}(q, e, a, q')$ is the cost of the substitution of $e \in \Sigma$ by $a \in \Delta_i$. Following (2), the cost of a sequence of such operations transforming s into t is the product in terms of $\otimes$ of the individual costs of the operations involved, and the distance between s and t is the sum in terms of $\oplus$ of all possible products.

Example 4. We propose a swT over Σ and Δ_i that computes the distance between an input $I \in \Sigma^*$ and an output $O \in \Delta_i^*$ like in Example 1 (for δ, see Example 2):

$$w_{11}(q_0, e : \tau, a : \tau', q_0) \text{ and } w_{11}(q_1, e : \tau, a : \tau', q_0) = \delta(e : \tau, a : \tau') \quad \text{if } a \neq -$$
$$w_{01}(q_0, \varepsilon, - : \tau', q_0) = \mathbb{1} \quad w_{01}(q_1, \varepsilon, - : \tau', q_0) = \mathbb{1} \quad w_{10}(q_0, e : \tau, \varepsilon, q_1) = \alpha$$

The continuation symbol '$-$' (e.g. in *ties* ♩♪, or *dots* ♩) is skipped with no cost (w_{01}). We also want to consider performing errors, by switching to an error state q_1. Reading an extra event e is handled by w_{10} that switches to q_1, with a fixed $\alpha \in S$, then w_{11} and w_{01} can switch back to q_0. Finally, we let q_0 be the initial and final state, with $\text{in}(q_0) = \text{out}(q_0) = \mathbb{1}$, and $\text{in}(q_1) = \text{out}(q_1) = \mathbb{0}$.   ◇

Symbolic Weighted Automata. swA are particular cases of swT omitting the output symbols, or equivalently, swVPA without markups ($\Delta_c = \Delta_r = \emptyset$).

4   Symbolic Weighted Parsing

Parsing is the problem of structuring a linear representation (a finite word) according to a language model [12]. We shall consider in this section the problem of parsing over an infinite alphabet. Let S Σ, Δ, and $\bar{\Phi}$ be like in Sect. 3. We assume to be given the following input:

– a swT T over Σ, Δ_i, S, and $\bar{\Phi}$, defining a measure $T : \Sigma^* \times \Delta_i^* \to S$,

– a swVPA A over Δ, $\mathbb{S}$, and $\bar{\Phi}$, defining a measure $A : \Delta^* \to \mathbb{S}$,
– an (unstructured) input word $s \in \Sigma^*$.

For every $u \in \Sigma^*$ and $t \in \Delta^*$, let $d_T(u,t) = T\big(u, t|_{\Delta_i}\big)$, where $t|_{\Delta_i} \in \Delta_i^*$ is the projection of t onto Δ_i, obtained from t by removing all symbols in $\Delta \setminus \Delta_i$. Given the above input, *symbolic weighted parsing* aims at of finding a (structured) nested word $t \in \Delta^*$ that minimizes $d(s,t) \otimes A(t)$ wrt $\leq_\oplus$, i.e. such that:

$$d_T(s,t) \otimes A(t) = \bigoplus_{v \in \Delta^*} d_T(s,v) \otimes A(u) \tag{3}$$

In the terminology of [18], sw-parsing is the problem of computing the distance (3) between the input word s and the weighted language over the output alphabet defined by A, and returning a witness t.

Example 5. In the running example, the input is as follows: the swT T evaluates a "fitness measure", i.e. a temporal distance between a performance and a nested-word representation of a music score (Example 4). The swVPA A expresses a weight related to the complexity of music notation (Example 3). The input word is I of Example 1. The notation ♯ , will be favored over ♯ when the weight assigned to the call $\lceil_2$ is less than the difference of weight between the appogiatura 'c♯$_5$' and the standard note c♯$_5$. The sw-parsing framework, applied to music transcription, finds an optimal solution considering both the fitness of the output to the input, and its notational complexity.   ◇

Nested words in Δ^* can represent linearizations of labeled trees, and to any Weighted Regular Tree Grammar (wRTG), we can associate in polynomial time a swVPA computing the same weight (see [1, § F]). Therefore, instead of a swVPA in input, we may be given a wRTG, or a weighted CFG (wCFG), for a definition closer to conventional parsing. The sw-parsing problem hence generalizes the problem of searching for the best derivation tree of a wCFG G that yields a given input word w, with an infinite input alphabet instead of a finite one and transducer-defined distances instead of equality. It is however uncomparable to the related problems of *semiring parsing* [11], and *weighted parsing* [19].

   In Sect. 5, we present results on swVPT and subclasses (automata construction and best-search algorithm) that can be applied for solving sw-parsing.

Theorem 1. *The problem of Symbolic Weighted Parsing can be solved in PTIME in the size of the input swT T, swVPA A and input word s, and the computation time of the functions and operators of the label theory.*

Proof. We follow an approach of *parsing as intersection* [12, ch. 13]. First, we associate to T and A a swVPT called $(T \otimes A)$, computing the product of the respective weights for the two models (Theorem 2): i.e. $(T \otimes A)(u,t) = d_T(u,t) \otimes A(t)$. Then, we construct a swVPA computing, for $t \in \Delta^*$, $(T \otimes A)(s,t) = d_T(s,t) \otimes A(t)$ (Theorem 3). Finally, with the algorithm of Theorem 4, we find a *best* $t \in \Delta^*$ minimizing the latter value wrt $\leq_\oplus$, i.e. a solution of sw-parsing. □

5 Properties and Best-Search Algorithm

In the following results, we assume that the functions of a label theory $\bar{\bar{\Phi}}$ are given in a finite representation (e.g. Turing machine) in the definitions of swVPT, and provide complexity bounds parameterized by the semiring operators and the operators of Sect. 2 over the functions of $\bar{\bar{\Phi}}$ (the latter might be represented symbolically by structures like Algebraic Decision Diagrams [5]).

Similarly to VPA [3] and sVPA [8], the class of swVPT is closed under the binary operators of the underlying semiring.

Proposition 1. *Let T_1, T_2 be two swVPT over the same Σ, Δ, commutative $\mathbb{S}$ and $\bar{\bar{\Phi}}$. There exist two effectively constructible swVPT $T_1 \oplus T_2$ and $T_1 \otimes T_2$, such that for every $s \in \Sigma^*$ and $t \in \Delta^*$, $(T_1 \oplus T_2)(s,t) = T_1(s,t) \oplus T_2(s,t)$ and $(T_1 \otimes T_2)(s,t) \doteq T_1(s,t) \otimes T_2(s,t)$.*

Proof. Classical Cartesian product construction, similar to the case of the Boolean semiring [8], see [1, §B] for details. □

The following result shows how to compose, in a single swVPT, the two measures as input of sw-parsing: the swT computing input-output distance and the swVPA expressing the weight of parse trees' linearization.

Theorem 2. *Given a swT T over Σ, Δ_i, commutative $\mathbb{S}$, and $\bar{\bar{\Phi}}$, and a swVPA A over Δ, $\mathbb{S}$, $\bar{\bar{\Phi}}$, one can construct in PTIME a swVPT $T \otimes A$, over Σ, Δ, $\mathbb{S}$, $\bar{\bar{\Phi}}$, such that $\forall s \in \Sigma^*$, $t \in \Delta^*$, $(T \otimes A)(s,t) = T(s,t|_{\Delta_i}) \otimes A(t)$.*

Proof. (sketch, see [1, §C]). The state set of $T \otimes A$ is the Cartesian product of the state sets of T and A, and every transition of $T \otimes A$ is either a transition of T or a transition of A of the same kind (in these cases the state of the other machine remains the same), or a product of two transitions w_{11} of T and A. □

The next result is the construction, as a swVPA, for the partial application of a swVPT, setting an input word s as its first argument.

Theorem 3. *Given a swVPT T over Σ, Δ, commutative, complete and idempotent $\mathbb{S}$, and $\bar{\bar{\Phi}}$, and given $s \in \Sigma^*$, there exists an effectively constructible swVPA $T(s)$ over Δ, $\mathbb{S}$, and $\bar{\bar{\Phi}}$, such that for every $t \in \Delta^*$, $T(s)(t) = T(s,t)$.*

Proof. (sketch, see [1, §D]). We construct an automaton that simulates, while reading an output word $t \in \Delta^*$, the synchronized computation of T on s and t. The main difficulty comes from the transitions of T of the form w_{10}, which read in input s and ignore the output t. Since the automaton $A(T)$ only reads the output word t, we add to $A(T)$ a corresponding ε-transition, and show how to remove the ε-transitions from a swVPA while preserving its language. □

We present now a procedure for searching a word of minimal weight for a swVPA A, a variant of reachability problems in pushdown automata [6].

First of all, for a complete semiring S, we consider the following operators on the functions of a label theory $\bar{\Phi}$:

$$\oplus_\Sigma : \Phi_\Sigma \to S, \ \phi \mapsto \bigoplus_{a \in \Sigma} \phi(a), \quad \oplus^1_\Sigma : \Phi_{\Sigma,\Delta} \to \Phi_\Delta, \ \eta \mapsto \left(y \mapsto \bigoplus_{a \in \Sigma} \eta(a,y)\right),$$

$$\oplus^2_\Delta : \Phi_{\Sigma,\Delta} \to \Phi_\Sigma, \ \eta \mapsto \left(x \mapsto \bigoplus_{b \in \Delta} \eta(x,b)\right).$$

Intuitively, $\oplus_\Sigma$ returns the global minimum, wrt $\leq_\oplus$, of a function ϕ of Φ_Σ, and $\oplus^1_\Sigma$, $\oplus^2_\Delta$ return partial minimums of a function η of $\Phi_{\Sigma,\Delta}$. A label theory is called *effective* when the three above operators applied on its functions are recursively enumerable, and there exists a function returning a witness symbol that reaches the minimum. In the complexity bounds, we assume a constant time evaluation for these operators. Effectiveness of label theories is a strong restriction, although realistic for the case study presented in this paper. It is satisfied e.g. by functions with a codomain $\{0, \alpha\}$, with $\alpha <_\oplus 0$, generalizing the boolean guards of [8,9] to *filters* returning null or constant weight values.

Theorem 4. *For a swVPA A over Δ, S commutative, complete, bounded and total, and $\bar{\Phi}$ effective, one can construct in PTIME a word $t \in \Delta^*$ such that $A(t)$ is minimal wrt the natural ordering $\leq_\oplus$ for S.*

Proof. Let $A = \langle Q, P, \mathsf{in}, \bar{\mathsf{w}}, \mathsf{out} \rangle$. For every $q, q' \in Q$, let $b_\perp(q, q')$ be the minimum, wrt $\leq_\oplus$, of the function $\beta_{q,q'} : t \mapsto \mathsf{weight}_A(q[\perp], \varepsilon, t, q'[\perp])$. By definition of $\leq_\oplus$, and since S is complete and total, it holds that: $b_\perp(q, q') = \bigoplus_{t \in \Delta^*} \mathsf{weight}_A(q[\perp], \varepsilon, t, q'[\perp])$ (see (1) for the definition of weight_A). Following (2), and the algebraic properties of $\otimes$ and $\oplus$, the minimum of $A(t)$ wrt $\leq_\oplus$ is:

$$\bigoplus_{t \in \Delta^*} A(t) = \bigoplus_{t \in \Delta^*, q,q' \in Q} \mathsf{in}(q) \otimes \beta_{q,q'}(t) \otimes \mathsf{out}(q') = \bigoplus_{q,q' \in Q} \mathsf{in}(q) \otimes b_\perp(q, q') \otimes \mathsf{out}(q')$$
$$(4)$$

Hence, in order to prove Theorem 4, it is sufficient to show that for all $q, q' \in Q$, we can compute $b_\perp(q, q')$ in PTIME. We proceed by searching for a best weighted derivation in a S-labeled hypergraph $\mathcal{G}_A$ associated to the swVPA A. It has a set of vertices $V_A = (Q \times \{\perp, \top\} \times Q)$, where $\top$ is a new symbol representing a non-empty stack, a set of hyperedges $E_A = (V_A \times V_A) \cup (V_A \times V_A \times V_A)$, and an hyperedge labelling function $\eta_A : E_A \to S$ defined as follows, for $q_0, q'_0, q_1, q_2, q_3 \in Q$, ($\mathsf{w}_\mathsf{i}$ is another name for w_{01}, like in [1, §C]):

$$\langle q_0, \perp, q_1 \rangle, \langle q'_0, \gamma, q_2 \rangle \mapsto 0 \quad \text{if } \gamma = \top \text{ or } (\gamma = \perp \text{ and } q'_0 \neq q_0)$$

$$\langle q_0, \perp, q_1 \rangle, \langle q_0, \perp, q_2 \rangle \mapsto \bigoplus_{\Delta_\mathsf{i}} \mathsf{w}_\mathsf{i}(q_1, q_2) \oplus \bigoplus_{\Delta_\mathsf{r}} \mathsf{w}^\mathsf{e}_\mathsf{r}(q_1, q_2)$$

$$\langle q_1, \top, q_2 \rangle, \langle q_0, \perp, q_3 \rangle \mapsto \bigoplus_{p \in P} \bigoplus_{\Delta_\mathsf{c}} \left[\mathsf{w}_\mathsf{c}(q_0, q_1, p) \otimes \bigoplus^2_{\Delta_\mathsf{r}} \mathsf{w}_\mathsf{r}(q_2, p, q_3) \right]$$

$$\langle q_1, \top, q_2 \rangle, \langle q_0, \top, q_3 \rangle \mapsto \left[\bigoplus_{q_1 = q_0} \bigoplus_{\Delta_\mathsf{i}} \mathsf{w}_\mathsf{i}(q_2, q_3) \right] \oplus$$
$$\left[\bigoplus_{p \in P} \bigoplus_{\Delta_\mathsf{c}} \left[\mathsf{w}_\mathsf{c}(q_0, q_1, p) \otimes_2 \bigoplus^2_{\Delta_\mathsf{r}} \mathsf{w}_\mathsf{r}(q_2, p, q_3) \right] \right]$$

$$\langle q_0, \gamma_1, q_1 \rangle, \langle q_1, \gamma_2, q_2 \rangle, \langle q_0, \gamma, q_2 \rangle \mapsto \mathbb{1} \quad \text{if } \gamma_1 = \gamma_2 = \gamma \text{ or } 0 \text{ otherwise.}$$

Intuitively, a vertex $v = \langle q, \bot, q' \rangle$ (resp. $v = \langle q, \top, q' \rangle$) of $\mathcal{G}_A$ represents computations of $\mathcal{A}$ starting in state q with an empty stack (resp. non-empty stack γ), and ending in state q' with an empty stack (resp. the same non-empty stack γ). The best weight of such computations is the best cumulated weight of hyperedges along a derivation to v. More precisely, a *derivation* of $\mathcal{G}_A$ is a V_A-labeled binary tree of the form, v, $v(\theta_1)$ or $v(\theta_1, \theta_2)$, where θ_1 and θ_2 are sub-derivations, and its weight is defined by (for $i = 1, 2$, the root of θ_i, is labeled with $v_i \in V_A$):

- $\mathsf{weight}(\langle q, \bot, q \rangle) = \mathsf{weight}(\langle q, \top, q \rangle) = \mathbb{1}$,
- $\mathsf{weight}(\langle q, \bot, q' \rangle) = \mathsf{weight}(\langle q, \top, q' \rangle) = \mathbb{0}$ if $q \neq q'$,
- $\mathsf{weight}(v(\theta_1)) = \mathsf{weight}(\theta_1) \otimes \eta_A(v_1, v)$,
- $\mathsf{weight}(v(\theta_1, \theta_2)) = \mathsf{weight}(\theta_1) \otimes \mathsf{weight}(\theta_2) \otimes \eta_A(v_1, v_2, v)$.

With $\mathcal{D}(\mathcal{G}_A, v)$ denoting the set of derivations of $\mathcal{G}_A$ with root labeled with $v \in V_A$, it holds that ([1, § E]): for all $q, q' \in Q$, $b_\bot(q, q') = \bigoplus\limits_{\theta \in \mathcal{D}(\mathcal{G}_A, \langle q, \bot, q' \rangle)} \mathsf{weight}(\theta)$.

Therefore, computing $b_\bot(q, q')$ reduces to the search for a smallest weighted derivation of $\mathcal{G}_A$ (wrt $\leq_\oplus$) rooted with $\langle q, \bot, q' \rangle$, a problem solvable in PTIME [14], because S is monotonic wrt $\leq_\oplus$ and superior (Lemma 2). Therefore, by (4), the minimum of $t \mapsto A(t)$, wrt $\leq_\oplus$, can be computed in PTIME.

Moreover, a witness $t \in \Delta^*$ for this minimum can be associated to the appropriate best derivation, with no additional cost, see [1, § E] for details.   □

Conclusion

We presented closure properties and one decision algorithm for three classes of Symbolic Weighted language models: swVPT, swT and swVPA, and applied these results to the problem of parsing with infinitely many input symbols (typically timed events). In our approach to parsing, words are compared by computing a distance between them, defined by a given sw-transducer, which allows to consider finer word relationships than strict equality.

The application to automated music transcription suggested in a toy example has been implemented in a C++ library [2], following the principles of the present sw-parsing framework, although with some differences; e.g. the automata constructions are performed on-the-fly during best-search for efficiency reasons. One advantage of this swVPA approach is the *global view* provided by the stack during transcription, as opposed to other HMM-based approaches [23].

This work can be extended in several directions. The best-search algorithm for swVPA could be generalized from 1-best to n-best [15], and to k-*closed* semirings [17] (instead of *bounded*, which corresponds to 0-*closed*). One could also study the generalization of the best-search algorithm of Theorem 4 to the computation of the best possible output of a swVPT for a given input, or even to the more general models of [13].

Finally, the best-search algorithm presented here works offline, whereas an on-the-fly approach coupling automata construction and best-search would be interesting e.g. for online XML validation or filtering, or program monitoring [8].

Acknowledgments. The authors would like to thank the reviewers at CIAA for their useful remarks.

References

1. Extended version of this article. https://hal.archives-ouvertes.fr/hal-03647675
2. Library qparse for music transcription. https://qparse.gitlabpages.inria.fr
3. Alur, R., Madhusudan, P.: Adding nesting structure to words. J. ACM **56**(3), 1–43 (2009)
4. Alur, R., Mamouras, K., Stanford, C.: Automata-based stream processing. In: 44th ICALP. Schloss Dagstuhl-Leibniz-Zentrum für Informatik (2017)
5. Bahar, R.I., et al.: Algebraic decision diagrams and their applications. Formal Methods Syst. Des. **10**(2–3), 171–206 (1997)
6. Bouajjani, A., Esparza, J., Maler, O.: Reachability analysis of pushdown automata: application to model-checking. In: Mazurkiewicz, A., Winkowski, J. (eds.) CONCUR 1997. LNCS, vol. 1243, pp. 135–150. Springer, Heidelberg (1997). https://doi.org/10.1007/3-540-63141-0_10
7. Caralp, M., Reynier, P.-A., Talbot, J.-M.: Visibly pushdown automata with multiplicities: finiteness and K-boundedness. In: Yen, H.-C., Ibarra, O.H. (eds.) DLT 2012. LNCS, vol. 7410, pp. 226–238. Springer, Heidelberg (2012). https://doi.org/10.1007/978-3-642-31653-1_21
8. D'Antoni, L., Alur, R.: Symbolic visibly pushdown automata. In: Biere, A., Bloem, R. (eds.) CAV 2014. LNCS, vol. 8559, pp. 209–225. Springer, Cham (2014). https://doi.org/10.1007/978-3-319-08867-9_14
9. D'Antoni, L., Veanes, M.: The power of symbolic automata and transducers. In: Majumdar, R., Kunčak, V. (eds.) CAV 2017. LNCS, vol. 10426, pp. 47–67. Springer, Cham (2017). https://doi.org/10.1007/978-3-319-63387-9_3
10. Droste, M., Kuich, W., Vogler, H.: Handbook of Weighted Automata. Springer, Heidelberg (2009). https://doi.org/10.1007/978-3-642-01492-5
11. Goodman, J.: Semiring parsing. Comput. Linguist. **25**(4), 573–606 (1999)
12. Grune, D., Jacobs, C.J.H.: Parsing Techniques. MCS, Springer, New York (2008). https://doi.org/10.1007/978-0-387-68954-8
13. Herrmann, L., Vogler, H.: Weighted symbolic automata with data storage. In: Brlek, S., Reutenauer, C. (eds.) DLT 2016. LNCS, vol. 9840, pp. 203–215. Springer, Heidelberg (2016). https://doi.org/10.1007/978-3-662-53132-7_17
14. Huang, L.: Advanced dynamic programming in semiring and hypergraph frameworks. In: COLING (2008)
15. Huang, L., Chiang, D.: Better k-best parsing. In: Proceedings of the 9th International Workshop on Parsing Technology. ACL (2005)
16. Ma, M., Du, D., Liu, Y., Wang, Y., Li, Y.: Efficient adversarial sequence generation for RNN with symbolic weighted finite automata. In: Proceedings of the Workshop on Artificial Intelligence Safety (SafeAI), vol. 3087 (2022)
17. Mohri, M.: Semiring frameworks and algorithms for shortest-distance problems. J. Autom. Lang. Comb. **7**(3), 321–350 (2002)
18. Mohri, M.: Edit-distance of weighted automata: general definitions and algorithms. Int. J. Found. Comput. Sci. **14**(06), 957–982 (2003)
19. Mörbitz, R., Vogler, H.: Weighted parsing for grammar-based language models. In: 14th International Conference on Finite-State Methods and Natural Language Processing. ACL (2019)

20. Rozenberg, G., Salomaa, A. (eds.): Handbook of Formal Languages. Springer, Heidelberg (1997). https://doi.org/10.1007/978-3-642-59136-5
21. Segoufin, L.: Automata and logics for words and trees over an infinite alphabet. In: Ésik, Z. (ed.) CSL 2006. LNCS, vol. 4207, pp. 41–57. Springer, Heidelberg (2006). https://doi.org/10.1007/11874683_3
22. Selfridge-Field, E. (ed.): Beyond MIDI: The Handbook of Musical Codes. MIT Press (1997). http://beyondmidi.ccarh.org/beyondmidi-600dpi.pdf
23. Shibata, K., Nakamura, E., Yoshii, K.: Non-local musical statistics as guides for audio-to-score piano transcription. Inf. Sci. **566**, 262–280 (2021)
24. Waga, M.: Online quantitative timed pattern matching with semiring-valued weighted automata. In: André, É., Stoelinga, M. (eds.) FORMATS 2019. LNCS, vol. 11750, pp. 3–22. Springer, Cham (2019). https://doi.org/10.1007/978-3-030-29662-9_1
25. Yust, J.: Organized Time. Oxford University Press, Oxford (2018)

A Similarity Measure for Formal Languages Based on Convergent Geometric Series

Florian Bruse[(✉)], Maurice Herwig, and Martin Lange

University of Kassel, Kassel, Germany
`florian.bruse@uni-kassel.de`

Abstract. We present a distance metric on formal languages based on the accumulated weight of words in their symmetric difference. The contribution of an individual word to this weight decreases exponentially in its length, guaranteeing the distance between languages to be a real value between 0 and 1. We show that this distance is computable for regular languages. As an application, we show how the similarity measure derived from a modification of this metric can be used in automatic grading of particular standard exercises in formal language theory classes.

1 Introduction

A similarity measure is a function that associates a numerical value to two objects of some class in order to quantify how similar they are. Such a measure typically satisfies certain properties, for instance symmetry, since A should be as similar to B as B is to A. It should be monotonic in the sense that the numerical similarity of A and B should be higher than that of A and C, when C appears to be more different to A than B does. The triangular inequality ensures that the numerical values measure similarity evenly throughout the entire class: C cannot be appear to be less similar to A than the sum of the values indicating the similarity of C to B and that of B to A. Finally, it should satisfy a maximality condition ensuring that no B can be more similar to A than A itself.

There is not an established theory of similarity measures, probably because of its close connection to the established theory of *distance* in metric spaces. In fact, similarity can be seen as the absence of distance in such a space. In other words, one can typically obtain a similarity measure satisfying the properties above by inverting a distance metric on such objects.

Similarity measures are heavily used in many applications, not at all restricted to formal language theory or even computer science. They play vital roles in psychology [3] and educational sciences [11] but also in other fields within computer science, for example image processing [9], bioinformatics [13] and data science [5]. In fact, it is the recent resurgence of machine learning and the progress it has brought to many applications areas which has created new

© Springer Nature Switzerland AG 2022
P. Caron and L. Mignot (Eds.): CIAA 2022, LNCS 13266, pp. 80–92, 2022.
https://doi.org/10.1007/978-3-031-07469-1_6

interest in the study of similarity measures. Supervised learning relies on a thorough understanding of similarity between objects, for example images, in order to guarantee reliable classification results by trained neural networks.

Fundamental formal language theory provides results and concepts which may apply to other areas through the encoding of their primary objects of study by words and languages, cf. modelling of DNA sequences or program runs as words over a finite alphabet. Similarity measures and, more specifically, distance metrics have therefore been studied in the context of formal language theory, mainly on words. Essentially all known types of distance/similarity like Euclidian, Manhattan, Cosine, Hamming, Levenshtein, Jaccard, etc. can be used to turn the set of words over some alphabet into a metric space.

A distance measure d on words naturally induces a distance $\hat{d}$ on languages via $\hat{d}(L_1, L_2) := \min\{d(w_1, w_2) \mid w_i \in L_i\}$. This is unsuitable as a basis for a similarity measure on languages for many applications, though, as it ignores the inner structure of these languages. Worst of all, it considers two languages to be closest, and therefore most similar, already when their intersection is nonempty. For example, $\{a^n b^n \mid n \geq 1\}$ and $a^* b^*$ would be as similar as $a^* b^*$ is to itself. A more involved definition lifts these distance notions from words to languages using the Hausdorff distance, i.e. $\hat{d}(L_1, L_2) = \max\left(\{\tilde{d}(L_1, w) \mid w \in L_2\} \cup \{\tilde{d}(L_2, w') \mid w' \in L_1\}\right)$ where $\tilde{d}(L, w) = \min\{d(w', w) \mid w' \in L\}$. This notion assigns distance 0 only to equal sets, yet one quickly runs into undecidability problems using this definition [4].

In this paper we propose a new distance metric for formal languages, based on the sparsity of the symmetric difference between two languages. This is standard; however, given that the symmetric difference can be of infinite size, there is no standard way to obtain a finite numerical distance value from this. We define the distance as the accumulated weight of all words in the symmetric difference, where the weight of a word is exponential in the inverse of its length. This guarantees well-definedness of the distance metric, as it is bounded from above by a convergent geometric series.

In Sect. 2 we recall necessary preliminaries, present the formal definition of this distance metric, discuss its most important algebraic and computational properties, and compare it to other proposals from the literature. In Sect. 3 we show its usefulness in a particular application scenario: the similarity measure derived from this distance metric can be used to automatically assess and grade students' solutions to exercises of the form "construct an NFA/DFA/regular expression for the language $L = \ldots$" We show how this measure can be modified to better suit the needs of this application scenario, describe its implementation and how an empirical evaluation can be used to tweak the measure's parameters. Section 4 concludes with remarks on further work.

2 Distance Based on a Convergent Geometric Series

2.1 Formal Languages and Metrics

We briefly recall a few preliminaries about formal languages, finite automata and metric spaces.

An *alphabet* is a finite nonempty set $\Sigma = \{a, b, \dots\}$ of *letters*. A (finite) Σ-*word* is a sequence $w = a_1 \cdots a_n$ of letters. Its length $|w|$ is n. The empty word is denoted by ε and has length 0. Σ^* is the set of all Σ-words; Σ^n denotes the set of Σ-words of length n. A Σ-*language* is an $L \subseteq \Sigma^*$. We write $L^{(n)}$ for $L \cap \Sigma^n$, $L^{(\leq n)}$ for $\bigcup_{i \leq n} L^{(i)}$ and $L^{(>n)}$ for $\bigcup_{i > n} L^{(i)}$. As usual, for $a \in \Sigma$ and $L \subseteq \Sigma^*$ we write aL for the language $\{aw \mid w \in L\}$.

A *nondeterministic finite automaton* (NFA) is an $\mathcal{A} = (Q, \Sigma, \delta, Q_I, Q_F)$ where Q is a finite non-empty set of *states*, Σ is an alphabet, $\delta \colon Q \times \Sigma \to 2^Q$ is the *transition relation* and $Q_I, Q_F \subseteq Q$ are the sets of *initial*, resp. *final* states.

The extended transition relation $\hat{\delta} \colon Q \times \Sigma^* \to 2^Q$ can be obtained via $\hat{\delta}(q, \varepsilon) = \{q\}$ and $\hat{\delta}(q, wa) = \bigcup_{q' \in \hat{\delta}(q,w)} \delta(q', a)$. As usual $L(\mathcal{A}) := \{w \mid \text{ex. } q \in Q_I \text{ s.t. } \hat{\delta}(q, w) \cap Q_F \neq \emptyset\}$ is the language of words accepted by $\mathcal{A}$. An $L \subseteq \Sigma^*$ is *regular* if it is accepted by some NFA.

An NFA is called *deterministic*, or a DFA, if $|\delta(q, a)| = 1$ for all $q \in Q, a \in \Sigma$ and $|Q_I| = 1$. It follows by induction that $|\hat{\delta}(q, w)| = 1$ for all $q \in Q, w \in \Sigma$ and that the automaton accepts iff $\hat{\delta}(q, w) \in Q_F$ for the unique $q \in Q_I$. For an underlying DFA we simply write $\hat{\delta}(q, w) = q'$ instead of $\hat{\delta}(q, w) = \{q'\}$, etc.

It is folklore that for every NFA there is a DFA that accepts the same language, and that the regular languages are closed under the usual operations, in particular union, intersection, complementation, Kleene star, etc. [10].

Finally, we recall the definition of a *metric space*, i.e. a pair (M, d) of a set M and a function $d \colon M^2 \to \mathbb{R}^{\geq 0}$ satisfying the following properties for all $x, y, z \in M$:

- $d(x, y) = 0$ iff $x = y$ (identity of indiscernibles),
- $d(x, y) = d(y, x)$ (symmetry),
- $d(x, z) \leq d(x, y) + d(y, z)$ (the triangular inequality).

2.2 Formal Definition of the Distance Metric

Let Σ be an alphabet. The distance metric presented in the following is defined as $d(L_1, L_2) = \omega_\lambda(L_1 \vartriangle L_2)$ where $L_1 \vartriangle L_2$ is the symmetric difference of L_1 and L_2 and $\omega_\lambda \colon 2^{\Sigma^*} \to [0, 1]$ is a sum-based weight function that assigns a real number to each language, depending on a parameter $\lambda \in \mathbb{Q}$ with $0 < \lambda < 1$.

Let $L \subseteq \Sigma^*$ be a language. Let $f_L \colon \mathbb{N} \to \mathbb{Q} \cap [0, 1]$ be defined as

$$f_L(n) = \frac{|L^{(n)}|}{|\Sigma^n|}$$

i.e. f_L assigns to each number the fraction of all words in Σ^n that are in L. The value of $\omega_\lambda(L)$ depends on the values of $f_L(n)$ for all $n \in \mathbb{N}$ and, hence, all of L. In order to derive a finite value from the generally infinite sequence $(f_L(n))_{n \in \mathbb{N}}$, we use the fact that the geometric series $\sum_{i=0}^{\infty} \lambda^i$ converges to $\frac{1}{1-\lambda}$ for all $\lambda \in [0, 1)$. Hence, if we discount the elements of the sequence $(f_L(n))_{n \in \mathbb{N}}$ by the corresponding terms of the geometric series, we obtain a finite value, i.e. for all $\lambda \in [0, 1)$, the infinite sum $\sum_{i=0}^{\infty} \lambda^i \cdot f_L(i)$ is well-defined and yields a value between 0 and $\frac{1}{1-\lambda}$. Clearly, this value is only interesting when $\lambda > 0$. Boundedness of the infinite sum follows from the fact that $\sum_{i=0}^{\infty} \lambda^i$ converges for $\lambda \in [0, 1)$ and $0 \leq f_L(i) \leq 1$ for all i.

In order to use the above for a similarity measure on languages that has a fixed range, we normalise the value obtained in the infinite sum to $[0, 1]$. This yields, for each $\lambda \in (0, 1)$, the following definition for a function $\omega_\lambda \colon 2^{\Sigma^*} \to [0, 1]$.

Definition 1. *Let $\lambda \in (0, 1)$ and let Σ be an alphabet. Then the sum-based measure ω_λ is defined via*

$$\omega_\lambda(L) = (1 - \lambda) \cdot \sum_{i=0}^{\infty} \lambda^i \cdot f_L(i) = (1 - \lambda) \cdot \sum_{i=0}^{\infty} \lambda^i \cdot \frac{|L^{(i)}|}{|\Sigma^i|}.$$

We drop the parameter λ if it is clear from context or not important, and simply write $\omega(L)$. We will use both the characterisation using $f_L(i)$ and that using the fraction, depending on which presentation is more useful in the situation.

Observation 1. *For all $\lambda \in (0, 1)$, we have that $\omega_\lambda(L) = 0$ iff $L = \emptyset$ and $\omega_\lambda(L) = 1$ iff $L = \Sigma^*$. Moreover, ω_λ is strictly monotone, i.e. if $L \subsetneq L'$ then $\omega_\lambda(L) < \omega_\lambda(L')$. The converse, is not true: $\omega_\lambda(L) < \omega_\lambda(L')$ does not imply $L \subsetneq L'$ as can easily be seen from the example where $L = \{\varepsilon, a\}$ and $L' = \{a, aa\}$ over the alphabet $\{a\}$. We have $\omega_{0.5}(L) = \frac{3}{4} > \frac{3}{8} = \omega_{0.5}(L')$.*
   Finally, if $L = L_1 \dot\cup L_2$, then $\omega_\lambda(L) = \omega_\lambda(L_1) + \omega_\lambda(L_2)$.

From this observation, we conclude that ω_λ is well-defined:

Lemma 1. *Let Σ be an alphabet and let $\lambda \in (0, 1)$ and let the sum-based function $d_\lambda \colon 2^{\Sigma^*} \times 2^{\Sigma^*} \to [0, 1]$ be defined via $d_\lambda(L_1, L_2) = \omega_\lambda(L_1 \triangle L_2)$. Then d_λ is a metric on the space of all Σ-languages.*

Proof. By Observation 1, $d_\lambda(L_1, L_2) = 0$ iff $L_1 = L_2$. Next, the definition of d_λ is clearly inherently symmetric since $L_1 \triangle L_2 = L_2 \triangle L_1$. Hence, it only remains to show that d_λ satisfies the triangular inequality.

Let $L_1, L_2, L_3 \subseteq \Sigma^*$. We have to show that $d_\lambda(L_1, L_2) + d_\lambda(L_2, L_3) \geq d_\lambda(L_1, L_3)$. Since $d_\lambda(L_1, L_3)$ is defined as $\omega_\lambda(L_1 \triangle L_3)$ and since ω_λ is monotone by Observation 1, it is sufficient to observe that if $w \in L_1 \triangle L_3$ then $w \in L_1 \triangle L_2$ or $w \in L_2 \triangle L_3$ whence $L_1 \triangle L_3$ can be divided into $L_1 \triangle L_3 = D_1 \dot\cup D_2$ such that $D_1 \subseteq L_1 \triangle L_2$ and $D_2 \subseteq L_2 \triangle L_3$. $\qquad\square$

We now show that $\omega_\lambda(L)$ is computable if L is regular and, hence, d_λ constitutes a computable distance metric on the regular languages. Since the class of regular languages is closed under all Boolean operations – in particular symmetric differences – and distances are invariant under the formalism used to represent a language, it suffices to show that, for a DFA $\mathcal{A} = (Q, \Sigma, \delta, q_i, Q_F)$, the value $\omega_\lambda(L(\mathcal{A}))$ is computable.

For $q \in Q$, let L_q be the language defined by the automaton $\mathcal{A}_q = (Q, \Sigma, \delta, q, Q_F)$, i.e. the DFA that results from $\mathcal{A}$ by making q the unique starting state. It is well-known that the languages L_q can be characterised recursively via $L_q = \chi_q \cup \bigcup_{a \in \Sigma} a L_{\delta(q,a)}$ with $\chi_q = \{\varepsilon\}$ if $q \in Q_F$ and $\chi_q = \emptyset$ otherwise. We can use a similar characterisation for the computation of the values of $\omega_\lambda(L_q)$ for all q. First, by definition we have

$$\omega_\lambda(L_q) = (1 - \lambda) \cdot \sum_{i=0}^{\infty} \lambda^i \cdot \frac{|L_q^{(i)}|}{|\Sigma^i|} \ .$$

The individual terms of this infinite sum are all computable, for example $\frac{|L_q^{(0)}|}{|\Sigma^0|}$ is 1 if L_q contains the empty word, and 0 otherwise. For $i \geq 1$, a word in $L_q^{(i)}$ is of the form aw where $w \in L_{\delta(q,a)}^{(i-1)}$. Hence, the fraction $\frac{|L_q^{(i)}|}{|\Sigma^i|}$ can be rewritten as

$$\frac{|L_q^{(i)}|}{|\Sigma^i|} = \frac{|\bigcup_{a \in \Sigma} a L_{\delta(q,a)}^{(i-1)}|}{|\Sigma^i|} = \frac{\sum_{a \in \Sigma} |L_{\delta(q,a)}^{(i-1)}|}{|\Sigma^i|} . \tag{1}$$

It follows that the infinite sum for $\omega_\lambda(L_q)$ can also be rewritten as

$$\omega_\lambda(L_q) = (1 - \lambda)\left(|L_q^{(0)}| + \sum_{i=1}^{\infty} \lambda^i \cdot \frac{|L_q^{(i)}|}{|\Sigma^i|}\right)$$

$$= (1 - \lambda) \cdot |L_q^{(0)}| + (1 - \lambda) \cdot \sum_{i=1}^{\infty} \lambda^i \cdot \frac{\sum_{a \in \Sigma} |L_{\delta(q,a)}^{(i-1)}|}{|\Sigma^i|}$$

$$= (1 - \lambda) \cdot |L_q^{(0)}| + \lambda \cdot (1 - \lambda) \cdot \sum_{i=1}^{\infty} \lambda^{i-1} \cdot \frac{\sum_{a \in \Sigma} |L_{\delta(q,a)}^{(i-1)}|}{|\Sigma| \cdot |\Sigma^{i-1}|}$$

$$= (1 - \lambda) \cdot |L_q^{(0)}| + \frac{\lambda}{|\Sigma|} \cdot \sum_{a \in \Sigma} (1 - \lambda) \cdot \sum_{i=0}^{\infty} \lambda^i \cdot \frac{|L_{\delta(q,a)}^{(i)}|}{|\Sigma^i|}$$

$$= (1 - \lambda) \cdot |L_q^{(0)}| + \frac{\lambda}{|\Sigma|} \cdot \sum_{a \in \Sigma} \omega_\lambda(L_{\delta(q,a)})$$

We write $t_{q,q'}$ for $\frac{|\{a \in \Sigma | \delta(q,a) = q'\}|}{|\Sigma|}$ and e_q for $|L_q^{(0)}|$, i.e. $e_q = 1$ if $q \in Q_F$ and $e_q = 0$ otherwise. Assume that $Q = \{q_1, \ldots, q_n\}$ for some n. Then the above equation can be rewritten as

$$\omega_\lambda(L_q) = (1 - \lambda) \cdot e_q + \lambda \cdot t_{q,q_1} \omega_\lambda(L_{q_1}) + \cdots + \lambda \cdot t_{q,q_n} \omega_\lambda(L_{q_n}). \tag{2}$$

From this we derive the following equation system relating the values of $\omega_\lambda(L_q)$:

$$-(1-\lambda) \cdot e_{q_1} = (\lambda \cdot t_{q_1,q_1} - 1) \cdot \omega_\lambda(L_{q_1}) \quad + \cdots + \lambda \cdot t_{q_1,q_n} \cdot \omega_\lambda(L_{q_n})$$

$$\vdots \quad \vdots \qquad\qquad\qquad \ddots \qquad \vdots \tag{3}$$

$$-(1-\lambda) \cdot e_{q_n} = \lambda \cdot t_{q_n,q_1} \cdot \omega_\lambda(L_{q_1}) \qquad + \cdots + (\lambda \cdot t_{q_n,q_n} - 1) \cdot \omega_\lambda(L_{q_n})$$

By the above, this system is satisfied by the individual L_q and their weights. Uniqueness of a solution can be shown in a standard way.

Lemma 2. *Let $\mathcal{A}$ be a DFA and let $\mathcal{E}$ be the set of equations associated to it as in Eq. 3. Then $\mathcal{E}$ possesses a unique solution.*

It follows that $\omega_\lambda(L)$ is computable if L is regular.

Theorem 2. *Let $\mathcal{A}$ be a DFA with n states. Then $\omega_\lambda(L(\mathcal{A}))$ can be computed in time $\mathcal{O}(n^3)$.*

The given runtime follows from the well-known complexity of e.g. Gaussian elimination. This does of course not preclude asymptotically better procedures based on other equation solvers.

It is a standard exercise to construct a DFA for the symmetric difference from two given DFA via the product construction. This then yields computability of both the weight function ω_λ and the distance metric d_λ on regular languages.

Corollary 1. *Let L_1, L_2 be regular and given as a DFAs with n, resp. m states. Then $d_\lambda(L_1, L_2)$ can be computed in time $\mathcal{O}((n \cdot m)^3)$.*

Clearly, computability holds also for any other representation that can be translated into DFA like NFA, (extended) regular expressions, formulas of Monadic Second-Order Logic, etc. with corresponding effect on the overall runtime. A fair question here concerns the feasibility of this approach for NFA directly without prior determinisation. The problem is that in an NFA a word aw accepted from some state q may have more than one accepting run. In particular, there may be different successors q', q'' s.t. $w \in L_{q'} \cap L_{q''}$. Since the weight of a language accumulates weights of all words in it, the approach sketched above would either count w several times and thus include aw into L_q with a wrong weight; or there would have to be some mechanism that intuitively subtracts $|L_{q'} \cap L_{q''}|$ from the nominators occurring in the corresponding terms in the equations above which, as such, is not well-defined as this set may be infinite.

It is possible to pinpoint exactly where this approach fails for NFA: the second equality in Eq. 1 simply does not hold for genuinely nondeterministic automata.

2.3 A Comparison with Other Metrics

The sum-based distance metric defined in Lemma 1 is based on the sum-based weight function $\omega(L)$ which accumulates the fractions $f_L(n)$ of how many words of length n are included in L. These infinitely many fractions are then condensed into a single value by giving non-zero, but exponentially less weight to fractions associated to longer words. This places a lot of emphasis on whether short words are in L or not. Thus, finite languages that contain only short words might end up with a higher weight than infinite languages that contain all but a few short words, depending on the value of λ.

A different approach to derive one finite value from the infinite sequence $(f_L(n))_{n \in \mathbb{N}}$ is to look at possible limits of this sequence, or of similar sequences. Clearly, already for regular languages the limit $\lim_{n \to \infty} f_L(n)$ need not exist at all (e.g. for the language containing only words of even length). However, this limit, resp. an asymmetric approximation to it has seen some use in automatic grading of homework assignments [2]. A related version of this approach relates not the number of words in $L^{(n)}$ to Σ^n, but $\log |L^{(n)}|$ to n, where convergence still is not guaranteed. However, in certain settings convergence exists; this goes back to Shannon [14] under the name *channel capacity*, see also [6] for an investigation w.r.t. regular languages. In [8], the upper limit $\limsup_{n \to \infty} \frac{|L^{(n)}|}{n}$ is taken to obtain a size measure for languages, and this is computable for regular languages. Another related notion is that of (conditional) *language density* [12] where the denominator langauge in the fraction $f_L(n)$ can be any regular language.

As mentioned in the introduction, one can derive distance measures on languages from distances on words for instance via $d(L_1, L_2) := \min\{d(w_1, w_2) \mid w_i \in L_i\}$. This results in a distance measure with very different properties compared to the one defined in the previous section. Since such measures are quite useless for the application presented in the next section, we do not elaborate any further on them. Another possible way is to construct a distance measure on languages based on properties of the shortest word in their symmetric difference. Again, this completely ignores the structure of the difference except for a finite part which we discard here for the same reason. Using the Hausdorff distance yields better properties but the resulting metric is often undecidable [4].

Finally, one can construct distance measures on languages based on syntactic criteria of their *representations*. Such measures also have their place in e.g. automated grading of homework (cf. [2]) but suffer from their inherent flaw that two representations of the same language may and often will have positive distance. Moreover, they can often be cheated by taking two objects clearly representing different languages, but drowning the difference in useless padding, e.g. by adding similar but unreachable components to two NFAs accepting different languages.

3   Similarity in Formal Language Exercises

3.1   Automatic Assessment and Grading

Formal language theory is a standard part of the syllabi of computer science programs at universities worldwide. One of the basic competencies taught in corresponding courses is to understand the representation of a possibly infinite language by finite means like automata. A standard exercise on the way to achieving such competencies gives a description of a formal language and asks students to construct an automaton recognising exactly this language. Constructivistic learning theories require the students to be given adequate feedback on their solution attempts in order to initiate error-driven learning cycles that will eventually result in the acquisition of said competencies.

Feedback can be a counterexample to a wrong solution, a hint on where to look for errors, or – in the simplest form – a grade that puts a numerical value onto the assessment of how well the task was solved. Exmploying automatic grading yields several advantages: scalability makes it possible to keep up with growing student numbers and increased demand for exercises, while digitisation yields its typical benefits like increased fairness, faster response times and more focused learning efforts in the absence of human correctors.

Automatic assessment of exercises is an important application for similarity measures on formal languages. As mentioned in the introduction, any distance measure can be turned into a similarity measure by inverting (and possibly scaling) it. In the following, we use sim for the similarity measure on languages obtained as $sim(L_1, L_2) = s(1 - d_\lambda(L_1, L_2))$ for the distance measure d_λ defined in the previous section and some monotonic function s that maps the interval $[0, 1]$ to a (typically discrete) range of grades or points. We will not discuss the choice of the scaling function s, as this is highly dependent on the context dictated by the point scale in use and what teachers may consider to be a "good enough" solution etc. We discuss the choice of a good discounting factor λ below.

In comparison to other similarity measures found in the literature and mentioned in the previous section, sim features some good properties for the grading task, like well-definedness, effective computability, and – most of all – the fact that it considers two languages to be very similar when they deviate on few words only. However, the exponential decline in the weight function w.r.t. word length puts disproportionately high weights onto short words. Hence, students could achieve high marks already by covering the shortest words inside and outside of that language. Worst of all, this would give false learning incentives comparable to what can occur in test-based automatic grading, often to be observed for instance in the context of programming exercises [7].

There are two ways to remedy this: one can employ a non-linear scaling function s. This can have undesired effects, as it does not distinguish between the two situations in which low grades are achieved either by getting many long words or only some shorts words wrong. We therefore amend sim by redistributing weights of short words. This requires students' solutions to capture much larger parts of the target language in order to achieve high numerical similarity values.

3.2   Redistribution of Weights on Short Words

While some rebalancing of the individual weights associated to words can be obtained by adjusting the value λ that controls how much weight is given to each Σ^n, this still will assign an exponentially smaller weight to words of length $n + 1$ compared to those of length n, since all words of length $n + 1$ together share λ times the weight as those of length n, but there are $|\Sigma|$ times more of them. Hence, we aim to equalise the weight of all words up to a certain length η, yielding a weighting scheme defined via

$$w_\lambda^\eta(L) = w_\lambda'(L^{(\leq \eta)}) + w_\lambda(L^{(> \eta)})$$

where w_λ' satisfies the following.

- $w_\lambda'(\{w\}) = w_\lambda'(\{v\})$ for all $w, v \in L^{(\leq \eta)}$, i.e. all words of length up to η contribute equally to the weight of a language;
- $w_\lambda'(\Sigma^*) = w_\lambda(\Sigma^*)$, i.e. on the set of all words this really is a redistribution.

For any $L \subsetneq \Sigma^*$, though, we generally have $w_\lambda^\eta(L) \neq w_\lambda(L)$, and depending on the distribution of words in $L^{(\leq \eta)}$, this rearrangement of weights of words can result in a higher or lower weight of the overall language. We discuss suitable choices for η in Sect. 3.4.

In order to compute the rebalancing, we only need the overall weight of all words of length up to η, and the values of the respective $f_L(n)$ for $0 \leq n \leq \eta$. The first value can be computed straightforwardly as $(1-\lambda) \cdot \sum_{i=0}^{\eta} \lambda^i = 1 - \lambda^{\eta+1}$. Since there are $\sum_{i=0}^{\eta} |\Sigma|^i$ many words of length between 0 and η, the weight of an individual word of such length is $\frac{1-\lambda^{\eta+1}}{\sum_{i=0}^{\eta} |\Sigma|^i}$ under the new weighting scheme. The values of the individual $f_L(n)$ are known to be computable [6,14]; we give a short proof tailored to our notions.

Lemma 3. *Let $\mathcal{A} = (Q, \Sigma, \delta, q_i, Q_F)$ be a DFA such that $L = L(\mathcal{A})$ and let $n \in \mathbb{N}$. Then the values of $f_L(0), \ldots, f_L(n)$ are computable in combined time $\mathcal{O}(n \cdot |Q|^3 + |Q|^2 \cdot |\Sigma|)$.*

Proof. Recall the values $t_{q,q'}$ and e_q used in Eq. 3. Note that the $t_{q,q'}$ define a $|Q| \times |Q|$ matrix M. Let $t_{q,q'}^k$ denote the entry in M^k in the row for q and the column for q'. Then $t_{q,q'}^1 = t_{q,q'}$. We claim that

$$t_{q,q'}^k = \frac{|\{w \in \Sigma^k \mid \hat\delta(q, w) = q'\}|}{|\Sigma|^k} \tag{$\dagger$}$$

holds for all $k \in \mathbb{N}$. For $k \leq 1$ this is straightforward. Assume that $\dagger$ holds for $k \geq 1$, we show that it holds for $k+1$. By the definition of matrix multiplication,

$$t_{q,q'}^{k+1} = \sum_{q'' \in Q} t_{q,q''}^k t_{q'',q'} = \frac{|\{w \in \Sigma^k \mid \hat\delta(q, w) = q''\}|}{|\Sigma|^k} \cdot \frac{|\{a \in \Sigma \mid \delta(q'', a) = q'\}|}{|\Sigma|}$$

$$= \frac{|\{wa \in \Sigma^{k+1} \mid \hat\delta(q, wa) = q'\}|}{|\Sigma|^{k+1}}$$

which proves $\dagger$ for $k+1$. But then $f_L(k)$ is easily computed as $\sum_{q \in Q_F} t_{q_0,q}^k$.

Creating the matrix M^1 is done via computing all the $t_{q,q'}$ which takes time in $\mathcal{O}(|Q|^2 \cdot |\Sigma|)$. Computing $f_L(k)$ from M^k takes time in $\mathcal{O}(|Q|)$. The main cost is generated when computing $M^2, \ldots, M^n$. Individual matrix multiplication can be done in time $\mathcal{O}(|Q|^3)$ which yields a time of $\mathcal{O}(n \cdot |Q|^3)$ for all matrices.[1] $\square$

---

[1] Actual matrix multiplication can be done in time $\mathcal{O}(|Q|^{2.37286})$, cf. e.g. [1]. We state the cubic runtime here for the sake of readability.

If all the $f_L(k)$ are known for $k \leq \eta$, the rebalanced weight of L is obtained via subtracting the sum of the weights of words under the old weight and re-adding them with their new weight, which yields

$$\omega_\lambda^\eta(L) = \omega_\lambda(L) - \sum_{i=0}^\eta f_L(i) \cdot \lambda^i + \sum_{i=0}^\eta f_L(i) \cdot c_\lambda^\eta \cdot |\Sigma|^i,$$

where $c_\lambda^\eta = \frac{1-\lambda^{\eta+1}}{\sum_{j=0}^\eta |\Sigma|^j}$ is the weight of an individual word of length η or less under the new weighting scheme.

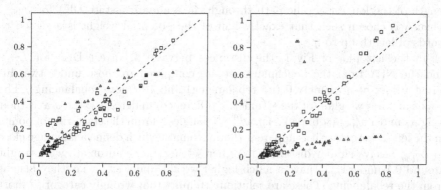

Fig. 1. Comparison of the weights of symmetric difference of the submitted automata and $L_{\overline{abba}}$ using $\omega_{0.87}^5$ on the x-axis. Left plot: weight using $\omega_{0.87}^0$ (blue), resp. $\omega_{0.87}^{10}$ (red) on the y-axis. Right plot: weight using $\omega_{0.5}^5$ (blue), resp. $\omega_{0.99}^5$ (red) on the y-axis. (Color figure online)

3.3   An Implementation and Test Cases

There is an implementation of a procedure that computes similarity values between regular languages based on the weight functions ω_λ^η, or just the weights of such languages. Inputs are accepted as NFA in a straight-forward format; these are turned into DFA using the standard powerset construction. The implementation is written in Python3 and is publicly available.[2]

Also included are various methods for visualising the effect that different choices of η and λ have on weight distributions. These can help to determine optimal parameter values in a concrete use case. Finally, we also provide, in this repository, a data set of 754 NFA taken from students' homework exercises asking for the construction of an NFA for some particular language.

On average, similarity of one of these submissions to a model solution was computed in 0.089 s for a total of 754 submissions on a desktop PC with four 2.40 GHz Cores and 8 GB RAM. The tests are run on a single core under Windows 10. Calculations for most automata were made significantly faster than 0.089 s with only a few showing runtimes in the range of seconds.

---

[2] https://github.com/maurice-herwig/wofa.git.

3.4   Empirical Determination of Good Parameter Values

We close this section with a brief discussion on what are good values for the parameters η and λ in the context of automated grading of homework assignments, using the collected data for the target language $L_{\overline{abba}} := \Sigma^* \setminus \Sigma^* abba\Sigma^*$, where $\Sigma = \{a, b\}$, as a benchmark. Out of the 174 submissions for this exercise, 75 correctly capture $L_{\overline{abba}}$ and are omitted from this discussion, as their distance is 0 under any parameter configuration.

In Fig. 1, we plot the weights of all these automata under different settings for η and λ. The default values are $\lambda = 0.87$ and $\eta = 5$, the latter chosen as the length of the longest acyclic path through the standard 5-state DFA for $L_{\overline{abba}}$. Then λ is chosen such that exactly half of the potential weight is assigned to words of length up to η.

In the left plot of Fig. 1, the distances between a correct DFA for $L_{\overline{abba}}$ and the NFA from the benchmark set are compared to those under two different values of η, namely 0 (no rebalancing) and 10 (more rebalancing). The x-axis denotes weights (of the symmetric difference) under $\omega_{0.87}^5$; the y-axis their weights under $\omega_{0.87}^0$ (squares) resp. $\omega_{0.87}^{10}$ (triangles). From the clustering of points in the left lower corner it is apparent that automata which define a language close to $L_{\overline{abba}}$ receive similar distances in either setting. Some automata with weight around 0.1 under $\omega_{0.87}^5$ have a much higher weight under $\omega_{0.87}^0$, i.e. they benefit from the rebalancing. These are solution attempts that wrongly categorise short words such as ε, which the rebalancing penalises less strongly. For most other automata, rebalancing increases the weight. This is due to mistakes which only manifest themselves on longer words, in particular those that induce cycles in the automata. We conclude from this data set that rebalancing all words up to at least the length of the longest cycle-free path in the automaton is a viable way to make the distance metric put weight onto words more evenly.

For variations of the parameter λ (right plot in Fig. 1), we obtain a different picture. Here, the x-axis represents automata weights under $\omega_{0.87}^5$, and the y-axis shows their weights under $\omega_{0.5}^5$ (squares) resp. $\omega_{0.99}^5$ (triangles). There is little difference between $\lambda = 0.5$ and $\lambda = 0.87$ in the presence of moderate rebalancing. However, the extreme choice of $\lambda = 0.99$ pushes most of the potential weigh out of the rebalancing zone and heavily de-emphasises short words. However, almost all long words do not belong to $L_{\overline{abba}}$ (cf. the limit based distance metrics discussed in Sect. 2.3), whence any automaton that rejects many words due to any reason will receive a low weight under this scheme. The few automata with high weight under this scheme all reject almost no words. Hence, extremely high values of λ may not make for a good and levelled similarity measure, especially when many deviations from the target language manifest themselves already on short words, i.e. those that use only one or two cycles in the automaton. All in all, the exact choice of λ appears to be less important in the presence of rebalancing.

4 Conclusion

We have introduced a new distance metric for formal languages based on convergent geometric series. This guarantees some nice properties, in particular well-definedness and effective computability for regular languages. The techniques employed here are not new; the use of discounting of values of words that decrease exponentially in their lengths can be seen in various concepts found in formal language theory. Yet, the distance metric introduced here, resp. the similarity measures drawn from it, especially after rebalancing the weights of short words, seem to be the first to be used in the application domain of automatic grading, and which provide properties like well-definedness etc.

Work in this area can be continued in several ways. An obvious question that arises asks for an effective way to compute distances between languages represented by nondeterministic models, without explicitly determinising them first. As argued at the end of Sect. 2.2, the method presented here cannot be applied to NFA directly. However, the argument leaves open the possibility that it may work for unambiguous NFA. Besides that, it of course remains to be seen whether the weight of a language of a truly nondeterministic finite automaton can be calculated directly, as this may be useful for efficiency purposes in other application areas. Another question to investigate concerns the nature of the equation systems representing the weights of languages per DFA state. It remains to be seen if these fall into some class for which better solving methods are known, like sparse matrices for instance.

References

1. Alman, J., Williams, V.V.: A refined laser method and faster matrix multiplication. In: Proceedings ACM-SIAM Symposium on Discrete Algorithms, SODA 2021, pp. 522–539. SIAM (2021). https://doi.org/10.1137/1.9781611976465.32
2. Alur, R., D'Antoni, L., Gulwani, S., Kini, D., Viswanathan, M.: Automated grading of DFA constructions. In: Proceedings 23rd International Joint Conference on Artificial Intelligence, IJCAI 2013, pp. 1976–1982. IJCAI/AAAI (2013)
3. Ashby, F.G., Ennis, D.M.: Similarity measures. Scholarpedia 2(12), 4116 (2007)
4. Choffrut, C., Pighizzini, G.: Distances between languages and reflexivity of relations. Theor. Comput. Sci. 286(1), 117–138 (2002). https://doi.org/10.1016/S0304-3975(01)00238-9. Mathematical Foundations of Computer Science
5. Choi, S., Cha, S.H., Tappert, C.: A survey of binary similarity and distance measures. J. Syst. Cybern. Inf. 8 (2009)
6. Chomsky, N., Miller, G.A.: Finite state languages. Inf. Control. 1(2), 91–112 (1958). https://doi.org/10.1016/S0019-9958(58)90082-2
7. Combéfis, S.: Automated code assessment for education: review, classification and perspectives on techniques and tools. Software 1(1), 3–30 (2022). https://doi.org/10.3390/software1010002
8. Cui, C., Dang, Z., Fischer, T.R., Ibarra, O.H.: Similarity in languages and programs. Theor. Comput. Sci. 498, 58–75 (2013). https://doi.org/10.1016/j.tcs.2013.05.040

9. Furht, B. (ed.): Distance and Similarity Measures, pp. 207–208. Springer, Boston (2006). https://doi.org/10.1007/0-387-30038-4_63
10. Hopcroft, J.E., Ullman, J.D.: Introduction to Automata Theory, Languages, and Computation. Addison-Wesley, N. Reading (1979)
11. Ifenthaler, D.: Measures of similarity. In: Seel, N.M. (Ed.) Encyclopedia of the Sciences of Learning, pp. 2147–2150. Springer, New York (2012). https://doi.org/10.1007/978-1-4419-1428-6_503
12. Kozik, J.: Conditional densities of regular languages. Electr. Notes Theor. Comput. Sci. **140**, 67–79 (2005). https://doi.org/10.1016/j.entcs.2005.06.023
13. Pearson, W.R.: An introduction to sequence similarity ("homology") searching. Current Protoc. Bioinf. **42**(1), 3.1.1–3.1.8 (2013). https://doi.org/10.1002/0471250953.bi0301s42
14. Shannon, C.E.: A mathematical theory of communication. Bell Syst. Tech. J. **27**(3), 379–423 (1948). https://doi.org/10.1002/j.1538-7305.1948.tb01338.x

Hybrid Tree Automata and the Yield Theorem for Constituent Tree Automata

Frank Drewes[1], Richard Mörbitz[2](✉), and Heiko Vogler[2]

[1] Umeå University, Umeå, Sweden
[2] Technische Universität Dresden, Dresden, Germany
richard.moerbitz@tu-dresden.de

Abstract. We introduce an automaton model for recognizing sets of hybrid trees, the hybrid tree automaton (HTA). Special cases of hybrid trees are constituent trees and dependency trees, as they occur in natural language processing. This includes the cases of discontinuous constituent trees and non-projective dependency trees. In general, a hybrid tree is a tree over a ranked alphabet in which symbols can additionally be equipped with an index, i.e., a natural number which indicates the position of that symbol in the yield of the hybrid tree. As a special case of HTA, we define constituent tree automata (CTA) which recognize sets of constituent trees. We show that the set of yields of a CTA-recognizable set of constituent trees is an LCFRS language, and vice versa.

1 Introduction

In order to specify the syntax of natural languages in a finite manner, two very prominent types of formal grammars have been considered: context-free grammars (CFG) [2] and linear context-free rewriting systems (LCFRS) [7,13,14].

Although being string grammars, each parse of a natural language sentence by such a grammar results in a tree-like analysis of the sentence, which can be viewed as the description of its syntactic structure. Due to the ambiguity of natural language, parsing a sentence can lead to a whole set of such analyses. The forms of analyses in which we are interested in this paper are constituent trees [11] and dependency trees [9,10]. They can be discontinuous or non-projective, respectively, as shown in Fig. 1. There, the order in which the words occur in a natural language phrase or sentence is indicated by indices next to the symbols, e.g., helpen$\langle 5 \rangle$ means that the word "helpen" occupies position 5 of the phrase. Constituent trees and dependency trees are special cases of hybrid trees [5]. In general, a hybrid tree ξ is a tree over some ranked alphabet of symbols and of indexed symbols such that no two positions of ξ carry the same index.

The question arises, for which classes of hybrid tree languages there exist automaton models which directly recognize these classes. For the class generated by CFG (i.e., continuous constituent trees), finite-state tree automata (FTA) [4,6] serve this purpose. The following might be called the yield theorem for FTA [1,3]: a string language L is context-free if and only if there exists an FTA

© Springer Nature Switzerland AG 2022
P. Caron and L. Mignot (Eds.): CIAA 2022, LNCS 13266, pp. 93–105, 2022.
https://doi.org/10.1007/978-3-031-07469-1_7

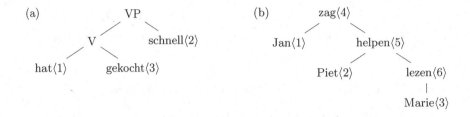

Fig. 1. (a) Discontinuous constituent tree for the German phrase "hat schnell gekocht", (b) non-projective dependency tree for the Dutch phrase "Jan Piet Marie zag helpen lezen" where we have ignored dependency labels at the edges.

$\mathcal{A}$ such that L is equal to the set of yields of trees recognized by $\mathcal{A}$ (where the yield of a tree is obtained by concatenating its leaf labels from left to right).

We introduce hybrid tree automata (HTA) as a generalization of FTA. Each HTA recognizes a set of hybrid trees. In each transition, the HTA can constrain the indices occurring in subtrees below the current tree position and at this position. The yield of a tree is generalized to hybrid trees by arranging the indexed symbols in the order of their indices and ignoring symbols which do not carry an index. By means of examples, we demonstrate that HTA can be used to specify and recognize sets of constituent trees and dependency trees. Since index constraints are unrestricted, HTA are computationally very powerful.

As a restriction of HTA, we define constituent tree automata (CTA) which are mild extensions of FTA. A CTA recognizes a set of constituent trees. We introduce an inductively defined semantics of CTA for which we establish a yield theorem: the set of yields of a CTA-recognizable hybrid tree language is an LCFRS language, and vice versa. Moreover, we consider the projection of hybrid trees to ordinary trees (by removing the indices). We show that the class of such projections of CTA-recognizable hybrid tree languages is the class of FTA-recognizable tree languages.

As another restriction of HTA, we can define dependency tree automata (DTA). Interesting questions for further research are the existence of a yield theorem for DTA and their relationship to FTA. Here we do not deal with DTA.

2   Preliminaries

The Set $\mathbb{N}$ and Intervals. The set $\{0, 1, \ldots\}$ of all natural numbers is denoted by $\mathbb{N}$; and $\mathbb{N}_+ = \mathbb{N} \setminus \{0\}$. For every $k, \ell \in \mathbb{N}$, we let $[k, \ell] = \{i \in \mathbb{N} \mid k \leq i \leq \ell\}$. Thus $[k, \ell] = \emptyset$ for $k > \ell$. We abbreviate $[1, \ell]$ by $[\ell]$.

The set $\mathbb{I}$ of all *intervals (of $\mathbb{N}_+$)* is given by $\mathbb{I} = \{[k, \ell] \mid k, \ell \in \mathbb{N}_+ \text{ and } k \leq \ell\}$. For all $I, I' \in \mathbb{I}$, the expression $I < I'$ holds if $\max I < \min I'$, and the expression $I \frown I'$ holds if $\max I + 1 = \min I'$. Thus $I \frown J$ implies $I < J$.

Strings. The set of all strings over some set A is denoted by A^*; ε is the empty string. For $w = a_1 \cdots a_k$ in A^* with $k \in \mathbb{N}$ and $a_1, \ldots, a_k \in A$, the *length of w*, denoted by $|w|$, is k. For each $k \in \mathbb{N}$, the set of strings of length k over A is denoted by A^k. We identify strings of length k and k-tuples, e.g., we identify the string $abbc$ and the tuple (a, b, b, c). Then, also, we have $(abb, cb, aa) \in (A^*)^*$.

Trees. A *ranked set* is a non-empty set Σ together with a mapping $\text{rk}: \Sigma \to \mathbb{N}$ (rank mapping). A ranked set is a *ranked alphabet* if its set is finite. For each $k \in \mathbb{N}$, we let $\Sigma^{(k)} = \text{rk}^{-1}(k)$. In examples we will show the rank of a symbol as a superscript in parentheses, e.g., $a^{(k)}$ if $\text{rk}(a) = k$.

The set T_Σ of *trees over Σ* is defined in the usual way, i.e., a tree has the form $a(\xi_1, \ldots, \xi_k)$ where $k \in \mathbb{N}$, $a \in \Sigma^{(k)}$, and $\xi_1, \ldots, \xi_k$ are trees. The *set of positions* of trees is defined by the function $\text{pos}: \text{T}_\Sigma \to \mathcal{P}((\mathbb{N}_+)^*)$ in the usual way. For the tree ξ' in Fig. 2 (right), we have $\text{pos}(\xi') = \{\varepsilon, 1, 11, 111, 112, 2, 21, 22\}$. Let $\xi \in \text{T}_\Sigma$ and $w \in \text{pos}(\xi)$. Also the *label of ξ at w*, denoted by $\xi(w)$, and the *subtree of ξ at w*, denoted by $\xi|_w$, are defined as usual.

Indexed Symbols and Hybrid Trees. The *ranked set of indexed Σ-symbols*, denoted by $\Sigma\langle\mathbb{N}_+\rangle$, is the ranked set such that $\Sigma\langle\mathbb{N}_+\rangle^{(k)} = \{a\langle n\rangle \mid a \in \Sigma^{(k)}, n \in \mathbb{N}_+\}$. An element $a\langle n\rangle$ is an *indexed symbol* and n is the *index of $a\langle n\rangle$*. The ranked set $(\Sigma, \mathbb{N}_+)$ is defined by $(\Sigma, \mathbb{N}_+)^{(k)} = \Sigma^{(k)} \cup \Sigma\langle\mathbb{N}_+\rangle^{(k)}$ for each $k \in \mathbb{N}$. (We assume that Σ and $\Sigma\langle\mathbb{N}_+\rangle$ are disjoint.) The mapping $(.)_\Sigma: (\Sigma, \mathbb{N}_+) \to \Sigma$ maps each $\alpha \in (\Sigma, \mathbb{N}_+)$ to its Σ-component; the mapping $(.)_\mathbb{N}: (\Sigma, \mathbb{N}_+) \to \mathcal{P}(\mathbb{N}_+)$ maps each $a\langle n\rangle$ to $\{n\}$ and each a to $\emptyset$. These mappings are generalized in a canonical way to mappings $(.)_\Sigma: \text{T}_{(\Sigma, \mathbb{N}_+)} \to \text{T}_\Sigma$ and $(.)_\mathbb{N}: \text{T}_{(\Sigma, \mathbb{N}_+)} \to \mathcal{P}(\mathbb{N}_+)$ (cf. Fig. 2).

A tree $\xi \in \text{T}_{(\Sigma, \mathbb{N}_+)}$ is a *hybrid tree* if, for all distinct positions $w, w' \in \text{pos}(\xi)$, it holds that $(\xi(w))_\mathbb{N} \cap (\xi(w'))_\mathbb{N} = \emptyset$ (e.g., ξ in Fig. 2 is a hybrid tree). Thus, in a hybrid tree each index occurs at most once. The set of all hybrid trees over Σ is denoted by H_Σ. Any set of hybrid trees is called a *hybrid tree language*.

The mapping $\text{yield}: \text{H}_\Sigma \to (\Sigma^*)^*$ is defined such that $\text{yield}(\xi)$ is the tuple of strings obtained from the set of all indexed symbols occurring in ξ as follows. We sequentialize this set according to its indices (turning each gap into a comma), and then we drop the indices. For the hybrid tree ξ in Fig. 2, the set of indexed symbols is $\{b\langle 2\rangle, a\langle 3\rangle, a\langle 4\rangle, d\langle 7\rangle, c\langle 9\rangle\}$, its sequentialization is $(b\langle 2\rangle a\langle 3\rangle a\langle 4\rangle, d\langle 7\rangle, c\langle 9\rangle)$, and thus $\text{yield}(\xi) = (baa, d, c)$.

Intuitively, a hybrid tree $\xi \in \text{H}_\Sigma$ is continuous if it has no subtree ξ' such that an index outside of ξ' is interleaved into the set of indices of ξ'. Moreover, at each node the indices of the ith subtree are smaller than those in the $(i+1)$st subtree. Formally, we say that ξ is *continuous* if for each $w \in \text{pos}(\xi)$:

(i) there do not exist $m \in (\xi)_\mathbb{N} \setminus (\xi|_w)_\mathbb{N}$ and $n, n' \in (\xi|_w)_\mathbb{N}$ with $n < m < n'$ and
(ii) if $\xi|_w = \alpha(\xi_1, \ldots, \xi_k)$, then $(\xi_i)_\mathbb{N} < (\xi_j)_\mathbb{N}$ for all $i, j \in [k]$ with $i < j$.

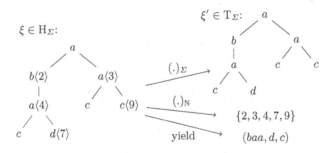

Fig. 2. Illustration of several mappings defined on $T_{(\Sigma, \mathbb{N}_+)}$.

Thus, the hybrid trees in Fig. 1 and Fig. 2 are not continuous.

Constituent Trees and Dependency Trees. A hybrid tree $\xi \in H_\Sigma$ is a *constituent tree* if each leaf is labeled by an element of $\Sigma\langle\mathbb{N}_+\rangle$ and each non-leaf is labeled by a symbol of Σ (i.e., $\xi \in H_\Sigma \cap T_\Delta$ where $\Delta = \Sigma^{(0)}\langle\mathbb{N}_+\rangle \cup \Sigma \setminus \Sigma^{(0)}$, Fig. 1(a)). We note that, for each continuous constituent tree ξ for which $(\xi)_\mathbb{N}$ is an interval, yield(ξ) is the usual concatenation of leaf labels from left to right. A hybrid tree $\xi \in H_\Sigma$ is a *dependency tree* if each position of ξ is labeled by an element of $\Sigma\langle\mathbb{N}_+\rangle$ (i.e., $\xi \in H_\Sigma \cap T_{\Sigma\langle\mathbb{N}_+\rangle}$, Fig. 1(b)).

FTA. A *finite-state tree automaton* (for short: FTA) is defined in the usual way as a tuple $\mathcal{A} = (Q, \Sigma, \delta, F)$ where Q is a finite set of *states*, Σ is a ranked alphabet of *input symbols*, $\delta \subseteq \bigcup_{k \in \mathbb{N}} Q^k \times \Sigma \times Q$ is a set of *transitions*, and $F \subseteq Q$ is a set of *final states*.

Let $\xi \in T_\Sigma$. A *run* of $\mathcal{A}$ on ξ is a mapping $\rho: \mathrm{pos}(\xi) \to Q$. It is *valid* if for all $w \in \mathrm{pos}(\xi)$ with $\xi(w) \in \Sigma^{(k)}$ it holds that $(\rho(w{\cdot}1) \cdots \rho(w{\cdot}k), \xi(w), \rho(w)) \in \delta$, and it is *accepting* if it is valid and $\rho(\varepsilon) \in F$. The *tree language recognized by* $\mathcal{A}$, denoted by $L(\mathcal{A})$, is the set of all trees over Σ for which there is an accepting run.

LCFRS. We recall the concept of linear context-free rewriting systems (LCFRS). For instance, we consider the LCFRS $\mathcal{G}$ which has the rules as shown in Fig. 3. The symbols S, D, A, B are the nonterminals and a, b are the terminals of $\mathcal{G}$. Each nonterminal X has a fanout fo(X) and it generates a tuple of fo(X) terminal strings. The variable x_i^j represents the jth component of the tuple of strings which is generated by the ith nonterminal of the right-hand side of the rule.

We allow an LCFRS to have a set of initial nonterminals, each of fanout 1. The finite set of terminal symbols is Δ. Each rule has the form $A \to e(A_1, \dots, A_k)$ where e is a tuple of fo(A) words over Δ and the set $\mathbb{X}_{(\mathrm{fo}(A_1),\dots,\mathrm{fo}(A_k))} = \{x_i^j \mid i \in [k], j \in [\mathrm{fo}(A_i)]\}$ of variables; each variable in that set occurs exactly once in e. For each $\kappa \in (\mathbb{N}_+)^k$ with $k \in \mathbb{N}$, we denote by $\mathbb{W}_\kappa^n(\Delta)$ the set of all such word tuples of length n with variables from $\mathbb{X}_\kappa$, for short: (n, κ)-word tuples. For instance, $(x_1^1 x_2^1, x_1^2 x_2^2) \in \mathbb{W}_{(2,2)}^2(\emptyset)$ and $(a) \in \mathbb{W}_{()}^1(\{a\})$. An (n, κ)-word tuple e is *monotone* if for every $x_i^{j_1}, x_i^{j_2} \in \mathbb{X}_\kappa$, if $j_1 < j_2$, then $x_i^{j_1}$ occurs left of $x_i^{j_2}$ in e.

$$S \rightarrow (x_1^1 x_2^1 x_1^2 x_2^2)(D, D)$$
$$D \rightarrow (x_1^1 x_2^1, x_1^2 x_2^2)(D, D)$$
$$D \rightarrow (x_1^1, x_2^1)(A, A)$$
$$D \rightarrow (x_1^1, x_2^1)(B, B)$$
$$A \rightarrow (a)$$
$$B \rightarrow (b)$$

$$S \rightarrow (x_1^1 x_2^1 x_1^2 x_2^2)(D, D)$$

$$D \rightarrow (x_1^1, x_2^1)(A, A) \qquad D \rightarrow (x_1^1, x_2^1)(B, B)$$

$$A \rightarrow a \qquad A \rightarrow a \qquad B \rightarrow b \qquad B \rightarrow b$$

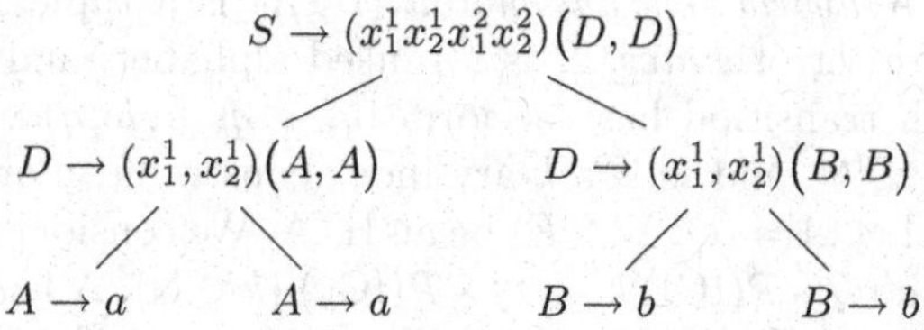

Fig. 3. The rules of the example LCFRS $\mathcal{G}$ where S is the initial nonterminal and $\mathrm{fo}(S) = \mathrm{fo}(A) = \mathrm{fo}(B) = 1$ and $\mathrm{fo}(D) = 2$, and a rule tree $d \in \mathrm{RT}_{\mathcal{G}}$ with $\pi(d) = abab$.

Each word tuple determines how the strings contained in the tuples generated by the nonterminals on the right-hand side are combined into a tuple of strings for the left-hand side nonterminal. For instance, the word tuple $e = (bx_2^1 ax_1^1 x_2^3, acx_2^2 x_1^2 a)$ in $\mathbb{W}_{(2,3)}^2(\{a, b, c, d\})$ induces the word function $[\![e]\!]: (\Delta^*)^2 \times (\Delta^*)^3 \rightarrow (\Delta^*)^2$ with $[\![e]\!]((w_1^1, w_1^2), (w_2^1, w_2^2, w_2^3)) = (bw_2^1 aw_1^1 w_2^3, acw_2^2 w_1^2 a)$.

We consider each rule $A \rightarrow e(A_1, \ldots, A_k)$ as a k-ary symbol. The set $\mathrm{RT}_{\mathcal{G}}$ of *rule trees of* $\mathcal{G}$ is the set of all trees over R such that, if a node has the label $A \rightarrow e(A_1, \ldots, A_k)$, then the rules labeling its k children have left-hand sides $A_1, \ldots, A_k$ (Fig. 3). The mapping $\pi \colon \mathrm{RT}_{\mathcal{G}} \rightarrow (\Delta^*)^*$ applies in a bottom-up manner, at each position w of the rule tree d, the word function $[\![e]\!]$ where e is the word tuple in the rule $d(w)$. The *language* $\mathrm{L}(\mathcal{G})$ *generated by* $\mathcal{G}$ is the set of all strings $w \in \Delta^*$ such that there exists a rule tree $d \in \mathrm{RT}_{\mathcal{G}}$ with an initial rule (i.e., a rule whose left-hand side is an initial nonterminal) at its root and $\pi(d) = w$. The language generated by our example LCFRS $\mathcal{G}$ is $\{ww \mid w \in \{a, b\}^+, |w| \geq 2\}$.

Let $\mathcal{G}$ be an LCFRS. We call $\mathcal{G}$ an n-LCFRS if the maximum of the fanout of its nonterminals is n. We call $\mathcal{G}$ *simple* if, for each rule $A \rightarrow e(A_1, \ldots, A_k)$ with $k \geq 1$, the word tuple e does not contain terminal symbols and, for each rule $A \rightarrow e$ (i.e., $k = 0$), we have $\mathrm{fo}(A) = 1$ and $e = (a)$ for some terminal symbol a. We call $\mathcal{G}$ *monotone* if the word tuple of each rule is monotone. In particular, a context-free grammar is nothing else but a monotone 1-LCFRS.

3   The Basic Model

Intuitively, a hybrid tree automaton is an FTA in which each transition on a k-ary input symbol contains an additional k-ary index constraint. Such a constraint ic is a set of pairs $(U_1 \cdots U_k, U)$ where $U_1, \ldots, U_k, U$ are pairwise disjoint sets of indices with $|U| \in \{0, 1\}$. Now the transition is only applicable to an input tree ξ at position w if the sets of indices of the subtrees of $\xi|_w$ and the set of indices of the symbol $\xi(w)$ satisfy the constraint ic, i.e., if $((\xi|_{w \cdot 1})_{\mathbb{N}} \cdots (\xi|_{w \cdot k})_{\mathbb{N}}, \xi(w)_{\mathbb{N}}) \in ic$.

Formally, we let $\mathrm{IC} = \bigcup_{k \in \mathbb{N}} \mathrm{IC}_k$ where $\mathrm{IC}_k = \mathrm{IC}_{k,0} \cup \mathrm{IC}_{k,1}$ and $\mathrm{IC}_{k,i}$ (for $i \in \{0, 1\}$) is the set of all $(U_1 \cdots U_k, U) \in \mathcal{P}(\mathbb{N}_+)^k \times \mathcal{P}(\mathbb{N}_+)$ in which $U_1, \ldots, U_k, U$ are pairwise disjoint and $|U| = i$. Thus, e.g., $\mathrm{IC}_{0,1} = \{(\varepsilon, \{i\}) \mid i \in \mathbb{N}_+\}$. A k-*ary index constraint* is a subset of IC_k.

A *hybrid tree automaton* (HTA) is a tuple $\mathcal{A} = (Q, \Sigma, \delta, F)$ where Q is a finite set of *states*, Σ is a ranked alphabet, and δ is a finite set of *transitions*; each transition has the form $(q_1 \cdots q_k, a, ic, q)$ where $k \in \mathbb{N}$, $q_1, \ldots, q_k, q \in Q$, $a \in \Sigma^{(k)}$, and ic is a k-ary index constraint; moreover, $F \subseteq Q$ (*final states*).

Let $\mathcal{A} = (Q, \Sigma, \delta, F)$ be an HTA. We consider $Q \times \mathcal{P}(\mathrm{IC})$ as a ranked alphabet with $(Q \times \mathcal{P}(\mathrm{IC}))^{(k)} = Q \times \mathcal{P}(\mathrm{IC}_k)$ ($k \in \mathbb{N}$). A *run of* $\mathcal{A}$ is a tree over $Q \times \mathcal{P}(\mathrm{IC})$. Let $\xi \in \mathrm{T}_{(\Sigma, \mathbb{N}_+)}$. A run ρ is a *run on* ξ if $\mathrm{pos}(\rho) = \mathrm{pos}(\xi)$. For a pair $p \in Q \times \mathcal{P}(\mathrm{IC})$, let us denote the projections onto its components by p_Q and p_{IC}, respectively. A run ρ on ξ is *valid* or *consistent* if the respective property holds for each $w \in \mathrm{pos}(\xi)$:

- *valid for* ξ: $\big(\rho(w{\cdot}1)_Q \cdots \rho(w{\cdot}k)_Q, \xi(w)_\Sigma, \rho(w)_{\mathrm{IC}}, \rho(w)_Q\big) \in \delta$ and
- *consistent for* ξ: $\big((\xi|_{w{\cdot}1})_{\mathbb{N}} \cdots (\xi|_{w{\cdot}k})_{\mathbb{N}}, \xi(w)_{\mathbb{N}}\big) \in \rho(w)_{\mathrm{IC}}$.

Since $\rho(w)_{\mathrm{IC}}$ is an index constraint, the sets $(\xi|_{w{\cdot}1})_{\mathbb{N}}, \ldots, (\xi|_{w{\cdot}k})_{\mathbb{N}}, \xi(w)_{\mathbb{N}}$ are pairwise disjoint for each $w \in \mathrm{pos}(\xi)$. Hence the existence of a consistent run on $\xi \in \mathrm{T}_{(\Sigma, \mathbb{N}_+)}$ guarantees that $\xi \in \mathrm{H}_\Sigma$. A run ρ of $\mathcal{A}$ on ξ is *accepting* if ρ is valid and consistent for ξ and $\rho(\varepsilon)_Q \in F$. The sets of valid runs and accepting runs of $\mathcal{A}$ on ξ are denoted by $\mathrm{R}^{\mathrm{v}}_{\mathcal{A}}(\xi)$ and $\mathrm{R}^{\mathrm{a}}_{\mathcal{A}}(\xi)$ respectively. The hybrid tree language *recognized by* $\mathcal{A}$ is the set $\mathrm{L}(\mathcal{A}) = \{\xi \in \mathrm{H}_\Sigma \mid \mathrm{R}^{\mathrm{a}}_{\mathcal{A}}(\xi) \neq \emptyset\}$. A hybrid tree language $L \subseteq \mathrm{H}_\Sigma$ is *recognizable* if there exists an HTA $\mathcal{A}$ such that $L = \mathrm{L}(\mathcal{A})$.

Example 1. Let $\Sigma = \{c^{(2)}, a^{(0)}, b^{(0)}\}$. We define an HTA $\mathcal{A}$ such that $\mathrm{L}(\mathcal{A})$ is a set of constituent trees and $\mathrm{yield}(\mathrm{L}(\mathcal{A})) = \{uu \mid u \in \{a, b\}^+, |u| \geq 2\}$. We let $\mathcal{A} = (\{q_a, q_b, q, q_f\}, \Sigma, \delta, \{q_f\})$ where δ consists of the transitions $(\varepsilon, z, ic_1, q_z)$ and $(q_z q_z, c, ic_2, q)$ for each $z \in \{a, b\}$, and (qq, c, ic_3, q) and (qq, c, ic_4, q_f);

$$ic_1 = \mathrm{IC}_{0,1},$$
$$ic_2 = \{(\{i\}\{j\}, \emptyset) \in \mathrm{IC}_{2,0} \mid i, j \in \mathbb{N}_+, i < j\},$$
$$ic_3 = \{((I \cup J)(I' \cup J'), \emptyset) \in \mathrm{IC}_{2,0} \mid I, I', J, J' \in \mathbb{I}, I \frown I' < J \frown J'\}, \text{ and}$$
$$ic_4 = \{((I \cup J)(I' \cup J'), \emptyset) \in \mathrm{IC}_{2,0} \mid I, I', J, J' \in \mathbb{I}, I \frown I' \frown J \frown J'\}.$$

Intuitively, ic_3 expresses that the yield of the first subtree consists of two substrings u_1 and u_2 (i.e., the respective sets I and J of positions form two intervals), and the same holds for the second subtree (with u_1', u_2', I', and J'); moreover, u_1 and u_1' can be put together (due to $I \frown I'$), and the same holds for u_2 and u_2' (due to $J \frown J'$); in the complete yield, $u_1 u_1'$ occurs left of $u_2 u_2'$ (due to $I' < J$).

In Fig. 4 we illustrate a hybrid tree ξ and an accepting run ρ of $\mathcal{A}$ on ξ. For instance, at position 2 the HTA $\mathcal{A}$ can apply the transition (qq, c, ic_3, q) because $(\{2, 5\}\{3, 6\}, \emptyset) \in ic_3$ (using $I = \{2\}$, $J = \{5\}$, $I' = \{3\}$, $J' = \{6\}$). We have $\mathrm{yield}(\xi|_2) = (bb, bb)$. The final transition (qq, c, ic_4, q_f) guarantees that $(\xi)_{\mathbb{N}}$ is an interval, thus $\mathrm{yield}(\xi) = abbabb$. In general, for every $\xi \in \mathrm{L}(\mathcal{A})$ and $w \in \mathrm{pos}(\xi)$ with $\xi(w) = c$, there exists $u \in \{a, b\}^+$ with $\mathrm{yield}(\xi|_w) \in \{uu, (u, u)\}$. □

Example 2. Let $\Sigma = \{a_2^{(2)}, b_2^{(2)}, a_1^{(1)}, b_1^{(1)}, a_0^{(0)}, b_0^{(0)}\}$, where subscripts distinguish differently ranked versions of a and b. We define an HTA $\mathcal{A}$ such that $\xi \in \mathrm{L}(\mathcal{A})$

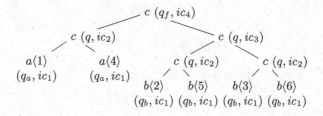

Fig. 4. A visualization of a constituent tree ξ and an accepting run $\rho \in \mathrm{R}_{\mathcal{A}}^{\mathrm{a}}(\xi)$, where the states and index constraints of ρ are written next to or below the positions of ξ.

if the following four properties hold. (1) ξ is a dependency tree. (2) ξ is a left-growing comb of which the spine finishes with a unary symbol (cf. Fig. 5). (3) Ignoring subscripts, the two strings obtained from ξ by reading from left to right (a) the leaf labels and (b) the spine labels, respectively, are the same (e.g., for ξ in Fig. 5 this string is aab). (4) yield$(\xi) = uu$ for some $u \in \{a,b\}^+$ with $|u| \geq 2$.

We let $\mathcal{A} = (\{q_a, q_b, q, q_f\}, \Sigma, \delta, \{q_f\})$ where δ consists (for each $z \in \{a,b\}$) of the transitions $(\varepsilon, z_0, ic_1, q_z)$, (q_z, z_1, ic_2, q), (qq_z, z_2, ic_3, q), and (qq_z, z_2, ic_4, q_f);

$$ic_1 = \mathrm{IC}_{0,1},$$
$$ic_2 = \{(\{i\}, \{j\}) \in \mathrm{IC}_{1,1} \mid i,j \in \mathbb{N}_+, i < j\},$$
$$ic_3 = \{((I \cup J)\{i\}, \{j\}) \in \mathrm{IC}_{2,1} \mid i,j, \in \mathbb{N}_+, I, J \in \mathbb{I}, I \curvearrowright \{i\}, J \curvearrowright \{j\}\}, \text{ and}$$
$$ic_4 = \{((I \cup J)\{i\}, \{j\}) \in \mathrm{IC}_{2,1} \mid i,j, \in \mathbb{N}_+, I, J \in \mathbb{I}, I \curvearrowright \{i\} \curvearrowright J \curvearrowright \{j\}\}.$$

Figure 5 shows a dependency tree ξ and an accepting run ρ of $\mathcal{A}$ on ξ. For instance, the automaton $\mathcal{A}$ can apply at position 1 the transition (qq_a, a_2, ic_3, q) because $(\{1,4\}\{2\}, \{5\}) \in ic_3$ with $I = \{1\}$ and $J = \{4\}$. We have yield$(\xi|_1) = (a_0a_0, a_1a_2)$ and yield$(\xi) = a_0a_0b_0a_1a_2b_2$.   □

4   Constituent Tree Automata

In index constraints, the relationship between the index sets is not per se restricted and may thus not even be computable. Thus, HTA are very powerful and must be restricted to constitute meaningful models of computation. In this section, we introduce constituent tree automata as particular HTA in which the index constraints are restricted: the index constraint of transitions on non-nullary symbols is determined by means of a word tuple e over $\emptyset$ (as for simple LCFRS) and assignments of intervals to variables in e; transitions on nullary symbols use as index constraint the full set $\mathrm{IC}_{0,1}$.

Formally, let e be in $\mathbb{W}_{\kappa}^n(\emptyset)$ with $\kappa = (\ell_1, \ldots, \ell_k)$ in $(\mathbb{N}_+)^k$ and $k \in \mathbb{N}_+$. A κ-*assignment* is a mapping $\varphi \colon \mathbb{X}_{\kappa} \to \mathbb{I}$ such that $\varphi(x) \cap \varphi(y) = \emptyset$ for every $x, y \in \mathbb{X}_{\kappa}$ with $x \neq y$. We let seq(φ) denote the string $U_1 \cdots U_k$ where $U_i = \bigcup_{j \in [\ell_i]} \varphi(x_i^j)$. We say that φ *models* e, denoted by $\varphi \models e$, if the following expression e' holds: e' is obtained from e by (a) writing $\curvearrowright$ between each two consecutive

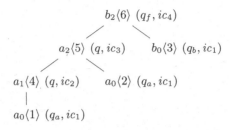

Fig. 5. A visualization of a dependency tree ξ and an accepting run $\rho \in \mathrm{R}_{\mathcal{A}}^{\mathrm{a}}(\xi)$, where the states and index constraints of ρ are written next to the positions of ξ.

variables, (b) replacing each comma by $<$, and (c) replacing each variable x_i^j by $\varphi(x_i^j)$. For instance, for $e = (x_2^1 x_1^1 x_2^3, x_2^2 x_1^2)$ in $\mathbb{W}_{(2,3)}^2(\emptyset)$ and the $(2,3)$-assignment $\varphi(x_1^1) = \{2,3\}$, $\varphi(x_1^2) = \{8,9\}$, $\varphi(x_2^1) = \{1\}$, $\varphi(x_2^2) = \{7\}$, and $\varphi(x_2^3) = \{4\}$, we have that $e' = \{1\} \frown \{2,3\} \frown \{4\} < \{7\} \frown \{8,9\}$ holds. We denote by $\mathrm{IC}(e)$ the index constraint $\{(\mathrm{seq}(\varphi), \emptyset) \mid \varphi$ a κ-assignment and $\varphi \models e\}$; note that $\mathrm{IC}(e) \subseteq \mathrm{IC}_\kappa$.

An HTA $\mathcal{A} = (Q, \Sigma, \delta, F)$ is a *constituent tree automaton* (CTA) if there exists a mapping $\mathrm{fo} \colon Q \to \mathbb{N}_+$ (*fanout-mapping*) such that, for each transition $(q_1 \cdots q_k, a, ic, q)$ in δ, the following holds:

- if $k = 0$, then $\mathrm{fo}(q) = 1$ and $ic = \mathrm{IC}_{0,1}$,
- if $k > 0$, then there is an $e \in \mathbb{W}_{(\mathrm{fo}(q_1), \ldots, \mathrm{fo}(q_k))}^{\mathrm{fo}(q)}(\emptyset)$ such that $ic = \mathrm{IC}(e)$; in this case, we specify the transition by $(q_1 \cdots q_k, a, e, q)$.

Let $\mathcal{A} = (Q, \Sigma, \delta, F)$ be a CTA. It is *final state normalized* if $\mathrm{fo}(F) = \{1\}$. It is a *n-CTA* $(n \in \mathbb{N}_+)$ if $\max \mathrm{fo}(Q) \leq n$. It is *monotone* if the word tuple in each transition is monotone.

Example 3. We consider the string language $L = \{uu \mid u \in \{a,b\}^+, |u| \geq 2\}$ from Example 1 and construct a 2-CTA $\mathcal{A}$ such that $\mathrm{yield}(\mathrm{L}(\mathcal{A})) = L$. We let $\mathcal{A} = (\{q_a, q_b, q, q_f\}, \Sigma, \delta, \{q_f\})$ where $\Sigma = \{c^{(2)}, a^{(0)}, b^{(0)}\}$, the fanout of the states q_a, q_b, and q_f is 1 and $\mathrm{fo}(q) = 2$. For each $z \in \{a,b\}$, δ contains the transitions $(\varepsilon, z, \mathrm{IC}_{0,1}, q_z)$, $(q_z q_z, c, (x_1^1, x_2^1), q)$, $(qq, c, (x_1^1 x_2^1, x_1^2 x_2^2), q)$, and $(qq, c, (x_1^1 x_2^1 x_1^2 x_2^2), q_f)$. In fact, $\mathcal{A}$ is final state normalized and monotone. $\square$

Inspired by the semantics of LCFRS, we wish to define an inductive semantics for CTA. Let us consider a CTA $\mathcal{A}$, a constituent tree ξ, and a valid run ρ of $\mathcal{A}$ on ξ. Now we wish to define inductively a family

$$\mathrm{P}(\xi, \rho) = \big((\Theta_w, \widehat{\varphi}_w) \mid w \in \mathrm{pos}(\xi) \setminus \mathrm{leaves}(\xi)\big) \cup \big(\Theta_w \mid w \in \mathrm{leaves}(\xi)\big)$$

such that the following is true at every position $w \in \mathrm{pos}(\xi)$, where n is the fanout of $\rho(w)_Q$ and $\kappa = (\mathrm{fo}(\rho(w\cdot 1)_Q) \cdots \mathrm{fo}(\rho(w\cdot \mathrm{rk}(\xi(w)))_Q)$:

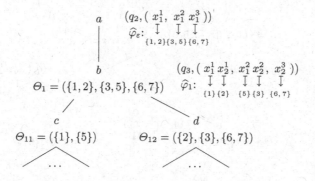

Fig. 6. Fragments of a constituent tree ξ, a run of some (unspecified) CTA $\mathcal{A}$ on ξ, and the family $\Theta = (\Theta_w \mid w \in \mathrm{pos}(\xi))$.

(i) $\Theta_w = (\Theta_w^1, \ldots, \Theta_w^n)$ is the partitioning of $(\xi|_w)_\mathbb{N}$ into n intervals such that (a) if w is a leaf, then $\Theta_w = ((\xi|_w)_\mathbb{N})$ (recall that, in this case, $n = 1$ and $(\xi|_w)_\mathbb{N}$ is a singleton) and (b) if w is not a leaf, then

$$\Theta_w^\ell = \bigcup(\Theta_{w \cdot i}^j \mid x_i^j \text{ occurs in the } \ell\text{th component of } \rho(w)_{\mathrm{IC}}).$$

(ii) if w is not a leaf, then $\widehat{\varphi}_w$ is the unique κ-assignment where $\widehat{\varphi}_w(x_i^j)$ is the jth interval in the partitioning $\Theta_{w \cdot i}$ for all $i \in [k]$ and $j \in [\mathrm{fo}(\rho(w \cdot i)_Q)]$, and

(iii) if w is not a leaf, then $\widehat{\varphi}_w \models \rho(w)_{\mathrm{IC}}$.

Items (i) and (ii) are used for the induction, which is performed by starting at the leaves (as the induction base) and proceeding to a position w once $(\Theta_{w \cdot i}, \widehat{\varphi}_{w \cdot i})$ has been defined for each child position $w \cdot i$ of w.

This construction of $\mathrm{P}(\xi, \rho)$ may face two obstacles, which then makes $\mathrm{P}(\xi, \rho)$ undefined. First, it may happen that there is a Θ_w^ℓ which is not an interval; then Θ_w^ℓ cannot appear in the image of an assignment. (E.g., in Fig. 6 at $w = 1$, the component $\Theta_1^2 = \{3, 5\}$ is not an interval. Thus, one level higher up, $\widehat{\varphi}_\varepsilon$ is not a κ-assignment as $\widehat{\varphi}_\varepsilon(x_1^2) = \{3, 5\}$.) Second, even if, for some non-leaf position w, the partitions $\Theta_{w \cdot 1}, \ldots, \Theta_{w \cdot k}$ at the children of w only have intervals in their components, the resulting $\widehat{\varphi}_w$ may not satisfy $\rho(w)_{\mathrm{IC}}$, i.e., that (iii) is violated. For instance, in Fig. 6 at $w = 1$, the assignment $\widehat{\varphi}_1$ does not model $\rho(1)_{\mathrm{IC}}$ because $\rho(1)_{\mathrm{IC}}$ contains the substring $x_1^2 x_2^2$, which translates to the requirement $\widehat{\varphi}_1(x_1^2) \frown \widehat{\varphi}_1(x_2^2)$ whereas, in fact, $\widehat{\varphi}_1(x_1^2) = \{5\} \not\frown \{3\} = \widehat{\varphi}_1(x_2^2)$. In contrast, the $(2, 3)$-assignment φ' defined by

$$x_1^1 \mapsto \{1\} \quad x_1^2 \mapsto \{5\} \quad x_2^1 \mapsto \{2, 3\} \quad x_2^2 \mapsto \{6\} \quad x_2^3 \mapsto \{7\}$$

models $\rho(1)_{\mathrm{IC}}$ and thus ρ is still a consistent run on ξ.

These considerations lead us to the following definition. Let $\xi \in H_\Sigma$ be a constituent tree and $\rho \in \mathrm{R}_{\mathcal{A}}^{\mathrm{v}}(\xi)$. We call ρ *inductively consistent* for ξ if the family $\mathrm{P}(\xi, \rho)$ is defined. Clearly, every inductively consistent run of $\mathcal{A}$ on ξ is

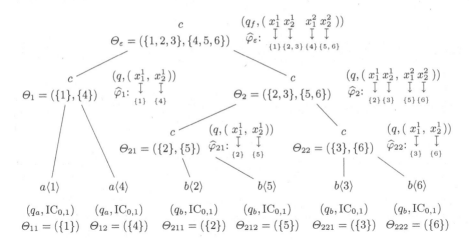

Fig. 7. Inductively consistent run of the CTA of Example 3 on the constituent tree of Fig. 4.

also consistent. The *inductive semantics* of $\mathcal{A}$, denoted by $\mathrm{L}_{\mathrm{ind}}(\mathcal{A})$, is the set of all constituent trees $\xi \in \mathrm{H}_\Sigma$ such that there exists an accepting run $\rho \in \mathrm{R}^{\mathrm{a}}_{\mathcal{A}}(\xi)$ which is inductively consistent for ξ. Thus $\mathrm{L}_{\mathrm{ind}}(\mathcal{A}) \subseteq \mathrm{L}(\mathcal{A})$. For the monotone CTA $\mathcal{A}$ in Example 3 we have $\mathrm{L}_{\mathrm{ind}}(\mathcal{A}) = \mathrm{L}(\mathcal{A})$ (Fig. 7).

Future work may investigate the questions: (a) Is it true that $\mathrm{L}_{\mathrm{ind}}(\mathcal{A}) = \mathrm{L}(\mathcal{A})$ for each monotone CTA? (b) Does there exist a CTA $\mathcal{A}$ such that $\mathrm{L}(\mathcal{A}) \setminus \mathrm{L}_{\mathrm{ind}}(\mathcal{A}) \neq \emptyset$? (c) For which CTA $\mathcal{A}$ does $\mathrm{yield}(\mathrm{L}_{\mathrm{ind}}(\mathcal{A})) = \mathrm{yield}(\mathrm{L}(\mathcal{A}))$ hold?

Now we turn to our first main result (yield theorem for CTA): the yield of the inductive semantics of CTA characterizes the class of LCFRS languages.

Theorem 1. *Let L be a string language and $n \in \mathbb{N}_+$. Then there exists a monotone and final state normalized n-CTA $\mathcal{A}$ such that $L = \mathrm{yield}(\mathrm{L}_{\mathrm{ind}}(\mathcal{A}))$ if and only if there exists an n-LCFRS $\mathcal{G}$ such that $L = \mathrm{L}(\mathcal{G})$.*

Due to space restrictions, we only present a proof sketch. Since each LCFRS can be transformed into an equivalent simple and monotone LCFRS [8,12] (disregarding ε) the central idea is as follows. We will establish a relation between:

(1) a monotone final state normalized n-CTA $\mathcal{A}$ over the ranked alphabet Σ and
(2) the so-called Σ-extension $\mathrm{ext}_\Sigma(\mathcal{G})$ of a simple monotone n-LCFRS $\mathcal{G}$ over Δ.

The Σ-extension adds information about the non-nullary symbols of Σ to the nonterminals of $\mathcal{G}$ (cf. the superscripts in Fig. 8). Of course, $\mathrm{L}(\mathcal{G}) = \mathrm{L}(\mathrm{ext}_\Sigma(\mathcal{G}))$.

We prove that, if $\mathcal{A}$ and $\mathrm{ext}_\Sigma(\mathcal{G})$ are related, then $\mathrm{yield}(\mathrm{L}_{\mathrm{ind}}(\mathcal{A})) = \mathrm{L}(\mathcal{G})$. Since for each $\mathcal{A}$ of type (1) there exists a related $\mathrm{ext}_\Sigma(\mathcal{G})$ of type (2), and vice versa, this equality implies the theorem. We say that $\mathcal{A}$ and $\mathrm{ext}_\Sigma(\mathcal{G})$ are *related* if the following holds. The nullary symbols of Σ are the elements of Δ. The states of $\mathcal{A}$ correspond to the nonterminals of $\mathcal{G}$ (preserving the fanout); thus

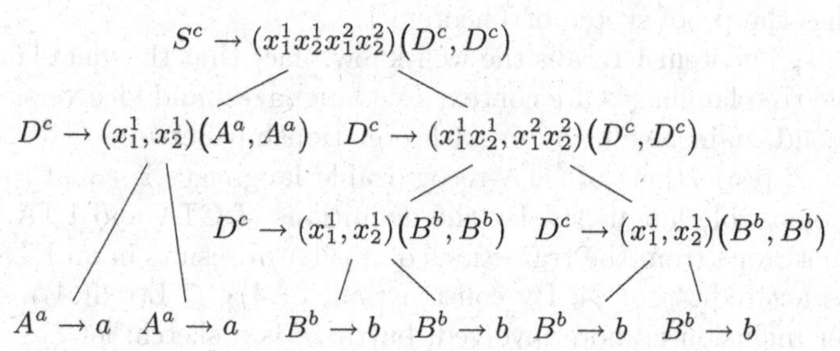

$$S^c \rightarrow (x_1^1 x_2^1 x_1^2 x_2^2)(D^c, D^c)$$

$$D^c \rightarrow (x_1^1, x_2^1)(A^a, A^a) \quad D^c \rightarrow (x_1^1 x_2^1, x_1^2 x_2^2)(D^c, D^c)$$

$$D^c \rightarrow (x_1^1, x_2^1)(B^b, B^b) \quad D^c \rightarrow (x_1^1, x_2^1)(B^b, B^b)$$

$$A^a \rightarrow a \quad A^a \rightarrow a \quad B^b \rightarrow b \quad B^b \rightarrow b \quad B^b \rightarrow b \quad B^b \rightarrow b$$

Fig. 8. A rule tree of the LCFRS $\text{ext}_\Sigma(\mathcal{G})$, where $\mathcal{G}$ is the LCFRS of Fig. 3 and Σ is the ranked alphabet of the CTA $\mathcal{A}$ of Example 3.

the final states of $\mathcal{A}$ have fanout 1, just as the initial nonterminals of $\text{ext}_\Sigma(\mathcal{G})$. The transitions of $\mathcal{A}$ correspond to the rules of $\text{ext}_\Sigma(\mathcal{G})$. The fact that the LCFRS is simple reflects the form of the index constraints in the transitions of the CTA. For instance, the CTA over Σ of Example 3 and the Σ-extension of the LCFRS $\mathcal{G}$ of Fig. 3 are related (identifying the states q_f, q, q_a, and q_b, with the nonterminals S, C, A, and B, respectively).

Let $\text{TR}_\mathcal{A}$ be the set of all pairs (ξ, ρ) consisting of a constituent tree ξ and an inductively consistent run ρ of $\mathcal{A}$ on ξ. We define a bijection $\psi \colon \text{TR}_\mathcal{A}/{\sim} \rightarrow \text{RT}_{\text{ext}(\mathcal{G})}$ where $\sim$ is the equivalence relation on $\text{TR}_\mathcal{A}$ such that $(\xi, \rho) \sim (\xi', \rho')$ if $(\xi)_\Sigma = (\xi')_\Sigma$ and $\rho = \rho'$. This factorizes out the indices from the pair (ξ, ρ), which is necessary because they are not contained in a rule tree. For instance, for the constituent tree ξ and the inductively consistent run ρ on ξ of Fig. 7, we have that $\psi([(\xi, \rho)]_\sim)$ is the rule tree of Fig. 8.

Injectivity of ψ is easy to show. The proof of surjectivity is more involved. Moreover, monotonicity of $\mathcal{A}$ and $\mathcal{G}$ is a necessary condition for surjectivity. We can show that ψ preserves yields in a certain sense. For this, we define the mapping $\text{cc} \colon (\Sigma^*)^* \rightarrow \Sigma^*$ which concatenates the components of a tuple of strings into one string (by removing the commas). Using the assumption that ρ is inductively consistent for ξ, we can show that $\text{cc}(\text{yield}(\xi)) = \text{cc}(\pi(\psi([(\xi, \rho)]_\sim)))$. Since $\mathcal{A}$ is final state normalized, this statement implies

$$\text{yield}(\xi) = \pi(\psi([(\xi, \rho)]_\sim)) \tag{1}$$

whenever $\rho(\varepsilon)_Q$ is a final state. Then, for each $w \in \Delta^*$,

$w \in \text{yield}(\text{L}_{\text{ind}}(\mathcal{A}))$

$\Leftrightarrow (\exists(\xi, \rho) \in \text{TR}_\mathcal{A}, \rho \text{ accepting}) \colon w = \text{yield}(\xi)$ \hfill (by definition)

$\Leftrightarrow (\exists(\xi, \rho) \in \text{TR}_\mathcal{A}, \rho \text{ accepting}) \colon w = \pi(\psi([(\xi, \rho)]_\sim))$ \hfill (by (1))

$\Leftrightarrow (\exists d \in \text{RT}_{\text{ext}_\Sigma(\mathcal{G})}, d(\varepsilon) \text{ initial}) \colon w = \pi(d)$ \hfill (because ψ is bijective)

$\Leftrightarrow w \in \text{L}(\text{ext}_\Sigma(\mathcal{G}))$ \hfill (by definition)

$\Leftrightarrow w \in \text{L}(\mathcal{G})$. \hfill (since $\text{L}(\mathcal{G}) = \text{L}(\text{ext}_\Sigma(\mathcal{G}))$)

This finishes the proof sketch of Theorem 1.

For $n = 1$, Theorem 1 recalls the well-known fact that the yield languages of recognizable tree languages are context-free languages, and vice versa [1,3].

Our second main result concerns the relationship between CTA and FTA: the class of Σ-projections of CTA-recognizable languages is equal to the class of FTA-recognizable languages. By the definitions of CTA and FTA, dropping all index contraints from the transitions of a CTA $\mathcal{A}$ results in an FTA. We call it the Σ-reduct red($\mathcal{A}$) of $\mathcal{A}$. By construction, $L(\mathcal{A})_\Sigma \subseteq L(\text{red}(\mathcal{A}))$. The proof of the other inclusion is more involved, but here is a sketch: let $\xi \in T_\Sigma$ and ρ be a valid and consistent run of red($\mathcal{A}$) on ξ. By the definition of red, for every $w \in \text{pos}(\xi)$ there exists an (n, κ)-word tuple which we can add to $\rho(w)$ such that we obtain a valid run ρ' of $\mathcal{A}$. Then we add indices to the leaves of ξ such that we obtain a constituent tree ξ' and ρ' is consistent for ξ'. The non-obvious part of the proof is to show that such indices always exist.

Vice versa, the *CTA-embedding of an FTA* $\mathcal{A} = (Q, \Sigma, \delta, F)$ is the monotone 1-CTA emb($\mathcal{A}$) $= (Q, \Sigma, \delta', F)$ such that, if $a \in \Sigma^{(0)}$ and $(\varepsilon, a, q) \in \delta$, then $(\varepsilon, a, IC_{0,1}, q) \in \delta'$, and if $k \in \mathbb{N}_+$, $a \in \Sigma^{(k)}$, and $(q_1 \cdots q_k, a, q) \in \delta$, then $(q_1 \cdots q_k, a, (x_1^1 \cdots x_k^1), q) \in \delta'$. Since we have $\mathcal{A} = \text{red}(\text{emb}(\mathcal{A}))$, the language $L(\mathcal{A})$ is the Σ-projection of $L(\text{emb}(\mathcal{A}))$.

Theorem 2. *1. For every CTA $\mathcal{A}$, we have $L(\mathcal{A})_\Sigma = L(\text{red}(\mathcal{A}))$.*
2. For every FTA $\mathcal{A}$, we have $L(\mathcal{A}) = L(\text{emb}(\mathcal{A}))_\Sigma$.

We note that Theorem 2 does not hold if we replace $L(\mathcal{A})$ by $L_{\text{ind}}(\mathcal{A})$.

References

1. Brainerd, W.S.: Tree generating regular systems. Inform. Control **14**, 217–231 (1969)
2. Chomsky, N.: Context-free grammars and pushdown storage. Technical report, MIT Research Lab. in Electronics, Cambridge, MA (1962)
3. Doner, J.: Tree acceptors and some of their applications. J. Comput. Syst. Sci. **4**, 406–451 (1970)
4. Engelfriet, J.: Tree automata and tree grammars. Technical report, DAIMI FN-10, Institute of Mathematics, University of Aarhus, Department of Computer Science, Denmark (1975). arXiv:1510.02036v1 [cs.FL], 7 October 2015
5. Gebhardt, K., Nederhof, M.J., Vogler, H.: Hybrid grammars for parsing of discontinuous phrase structures and non-projective dependency structures. Comput. Linguist. **43**(3), 465–520 (2017)
6. Gécseg, F., Steinby, M.: Tree Automata. Akadémiai Kiadó, Budapest (1984). arXiv:1509.06233v1 [cs.FL], 21 September 2015
7. Kallmeyer, L.: Parsing Beyond Context-Free Grammars. Springer, Heidelberg (2010). https://doi.org/10.1007/978-3-642-14846-0
8. Kracht, M.: The Mathematics of Language, vol. 63. Walter de Gruyter (2003)
9. Kübler, S., McDonald, R., Nivre, J.: Dependency Parsing, Synthesis Lectures on Human Language Technologies, vol. 2(1). Morgan & Claypool Publishers LLC (2009)

10. Kuhlmann, M.: Mildly non-projective dependency grammar. Comput. Linguist. **39**(2), 355–387 (2013)
11. McCawley, J.: Parentheticals and discontinuous constituent structure. Linguist. Inq. **13**(1), 91–106 (1982)
12. Seki, H., Matsumura, T., Fujii, M., Kasami, T.: On multiple context-free grammars. Theoret. Comput. Sci. **88**(2), 191–229 (1991)
13. Vijay-Shanker, K., Weir, D., Joshi, A.: Charaterizing structural descriptions produced by various grammatical formalisms. In: Proceedings 25th Annual Meeting of the ACL, pp. 104–111. Association for Computational Linguistics (1987)
14. Weir, D.: Characterizing mildly context-sensitive grammar formalisms. Ph.D. thesis, University of Pennsylvania (1988)

Some Results Concerning Careful Synchronization of Partial Automata and Subset Synchronization of DFA's

Jakub Ruszil[(✉)] [iD]

Jagiellonian University, Cracow, Poland
ruszil@ii.uj.edu.pl

Abstract. The goal of this paper is to present a family of partial automata that achieve length $\Theta(3^{\frac{n}{3}})$ of the shortest carefully synchronizing words, but using $\frac{2}{9}n + 2$ letters, thus substantially improving the result obtained in [19], which is $\frac{1}{3}n + 1$ letters. Additionally, modifying our idea we obtain a family of automata over a three letter alphabet and a subexponential length of the shortest carefully synchronizing words and, as a corollary of that construction, a series of binary automata with a subexponential length of word reducing set of states to a particular subset.

Keywords: Černý Conjecture · Automata synchronization

1 Introduction

The concept of synchronization of finite automata is essential in various areas of computer science. It consists in regaining control over a system by applying a specific set of input instructions. These instructions lead the system to a fixed state no matter in which state it was at the beginning. The idea of synchronization has been studied for many classes of complete deterministic finite automata (DFA) [1,2,8,12,13,22,24,26–30] and non-deterministic finite automata [10,20]. One of the most famous longstanding open problems in automata theory, known as Černý Conjecture, states that for a given synchronizing DFA with n states one can always find a synchronizing word of length at most $(n-1)^2$. This conjecture was proven for numerous classes of automata, but the problem is still not solved in general case. The concept of synchronization has been also considered in coding theory [5,11], parts orienting in manufacturing [8,21], testing of reactive systems [25] and Markov Decision Processes [14,15].

Allowing no outgoing transitions from some states for certain letters helps us to model a system for which certain actions cannot be accomplished while being in a specified state. This leads to the problem of finding a synchronizing word for a finite automaton, where transition function is not defined for all states. Notice that this is the most frequent case, if we use automata to model real-world systems. In practice, it rarely happens that a real system can be modeled

© Springer Nature Switzerland AG 2022
P. Caron and L. Mignot (Eds.): CIAA 2022, LNCS 13266, pp. 106–115, 2022.
https://doi.org/10.1007/978-3-031-07469-1_8

with a DFA where transition function is total. The transition function is usually a partial one. This fact motivated many researchers to investigate the properties of partial finite automata relevant to practical problems of synchronization.

We know that, in general case, checking if a partial automaton can be synchronized is PSPACE-complete [17] even for binary alphabet [31]. In this paper we investigate the case of deterministic finite automata such that transition from state to state is not necessary defined for all states. We refer to this model as *partial finite automaton* (PFA). We will say that a word which synchronizes a PFA is *carefully synchronizing* word. There exists also different definition of synchronization of PFA's, for example in here [3]. Our particular interest lies in the following question: what is the influence of alphabet size on the length of the carefully synchronizing word? Namely, we investigate the problem of reducing the alphabet size in carefully synchronizing automata and maximizing at the same time the length of the carefully synchronizing words. The problem of estimating the length of a shortest carefully synchronizing word for PFA was considered, among others, by Rystsov [23], Ito and Shikishima-Tsuji [20], Martyugin [18,19], Gazdag et al. [32] and de Bondt et al. [6]. Martyugin established a lower bound on the length of such words of size $\Theta(3^{n/3})$ and Rystsov [23] established an upper bound of size $O((3 + \epsilon)^{n/3})$, where n is the number of states of the automaton.

The second problem that we study in this paper is a synchronization of a DFA to a subset. Having a subset S of the set of states of a DFA, one can understand a problem synchronization to a subset as seeking for a word, such that no matter which state we apply it to, the result will be always in S. Our motivation lies in the fact, that synchronization to a subset is a generalization of synchronization of automata and is frequently used as an immediate step in algorithms that find short synchronizing words. It was proven in [4] that deciding whether the given DFA can be synchronized to a given subset of its states is PSPACE-complete even in the case of strongly connected automata. This concept has also been studied for example in [7,9].

2   Preliminaries

A *partial finite automaton* (PFA) is an ordered tuple $\mathcal{A} = (\Sigma, Q, \delta)$ where Σ is a finite set of letters, Q is a finite set of states and $\delta : Q \times \Sigma \to Q$ is a transition function, not everywhere defined. For $w \in \Sigma^*$ and $q \in Q$ we define $\delta(q, w)$ inductively: $\delta(q, \epsilon) = q$ and $\delta(q, aw) = \delta(\delta(q, a), w)$ for $a \in \Sigma$, where ϵ is the empty word and $\delta(q, a)$ is defined. A word $w \in \Sigma^*$ is called *carefully synchronizing* if there exists $\overline{q} \in Q$ such that for every $q \in Q$, $\delta(q, w) = \overline{q}$ and all transitions are defined. A PFA is called *carefully synchronizing* if it admits any carefully synchronizing word. For a given $\mathcal{A}$ we define *power-automaton* $\mathcal{P}(\mathcal{A}) = (2^Q, \Sigma, \tau)$, where 2^Q stands for the set of all subsets of Q, and alphabet Σ is defined as in $\mathcal{A}$. Transition function $\tau : 2^Q \times \Sigma \to 2^Q$ is defined as follows: let $Q' \subseteq Q$, for every $a \in \Sigma$ we define $\tau(Q', a) = \bigcup_{q \in Q'} \delta(q, a)$ if $\delta(q, a)$ is defined for all states in $q \in Q$, otherwise $\tau(Q', a)$ is not defined. We also consider a *deterministic finite automaton* DFA. The only difference to a PFA is that the transition function is total in this case. All definitions regarding PFA also apply to DFA, but we speak rather about *synchronization* than *careful synchronization* in the case of DFA. Consider DFA $\mathcal{A} = (Q, \Sigma, \delta)$ and $S \subseteq Q$. We say that $\mathcal{A}$ is *synchronizable* to S (or S in *reachable* in $\mathcal{A}$), if there exists a word $w \in \Sigma^*$, such that $\delta(Q, w) = S$. We also can say that w *synchronizes automaton* $\mathcal{A}$ to a *subset* S. We can now state obvious fact, useful to decide whether a given PFA is carefully synchronizing, whether given DFA is synchronizing or whether a given DFA is synchronizable to a given subset.

Fact 1. *Let $\mathcal{A}$ be a PFA and $\mathcal{P}(\mathcal{A})$ be its power automaton. Then $\mathcal{A}$ is synchronizing (resp. synchronizable to $S \subseteq Q$) if and only if for some state $q \in Q$ (resp. for S) there exists a labelled path in $\mathcal{P}(\mathcal{A})$ from Q to $\{q\}$ (resp. to S). The shortest synchronizing word (resp. word synchronizing Q to S) for $\mathcal{A}$ corresponds to the shortest labelled path in $\mathcal{P}(\mathcal{A})$ as above.*

An example of the carefully synchronizing automaton $\mathcal{A}_{car}$ is depicted in Fig. 1. Its shortest carefully synchronizing word w_{car} is $abc(ab)^2c^2a$, which can be easily checked via the power automaton construction.

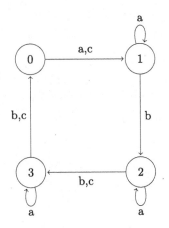

Fig. 1. A carefully synchronizing $\mathcal{A}_{car}$

Let $\mathcal{L}_n = \{\mathcal{A} = (\Sigma, Q, \delta) : \mathcal{A}$ *is carefully synchronizing and* $|Q| = n\}$. Notice that $\mathcal{L}_n$ does not depend on alphabet size. We define $d(\mathcal{A}) = \min\{|w| : w$ *is a carefully synchronizing word for* $\mathcal{A}\}$ and $d(n) = \max\{d(\mathcal{A}) : \mathcal{A} \in \mathcal{L}_n\}$. It can be easily verified from Fig 1. that the Černý Conjecture is not true for PFAs, since $|w_{car}| = 10 > (4-1)^2 = 9$.

3   Reducing the Number of Letters

In this section we provide a construction of series of automata with reduced number of letters, comparing to Martyugin construction, but with the same asymptotic length of shortest carefully synchronizing words. In particular we construct an infinite family of automata with number of states equal to n, and number of letters equal to $\frac{2}{9}n + 2$ with shortest carefully synchronizing words of length $\Theta(3^{\frac{n}{3}})$.

This is an improvement in a number of letters, since the best known construction (Martyugin) uses $\frac{1}{3}n + 1$ letters to achieve shortest words of the same length. It is worth mentioning that family of automata in [19] has shortest carefully synchronizing words of length $3^{\frac{n}{3}} - 1$ where n is a number of states, which is exactly the same result as presented in this paper. In [6] the authors obtained infinite family of PFA's over binary alphabet having the shortest carefully synchronizing words of length $\Omega(\frac{2^{n/3}}{n^{3/2}})$ and over ternary alphabet of length $\Omega(\frac{2^{2n/5}}{n})$ what is asymptotically smaller than our result.

The idea of construction is similar as in [19] but by choosing different method of "dividing" the set of states we obtain significantly (linear factor) lower alphabet size. In order to make proofs easier for a reader we assume that $n = 9k$ for $k \in \mathbb{N}$, but it is easy to modify it to work in general case. Consider the automaton $\mathcal{A}_3$ depicted in Fig. 2.

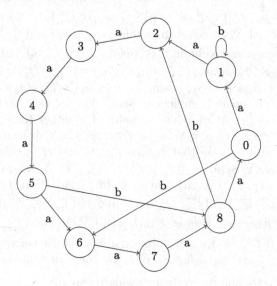

Fig. 2. Automaton $\mathcal{A}_3$

Let $\mathcal{A}_3^n = (Q, \Sigma, \delta)$ such that $Q = Q_1 \cup ... \cup Q_k$ where $Q_i = \{q_0^i, .., q_8^i\}$, We define $\Sigma = \{c, a_1, b_1, a_2, b_2, .., a_k, b_k, d\}$. The transition function is defined as follows:

1 $\delta(q_{3m+i}^j, c) = q_i^j$ for $m \in \{0, 1, 2\}$ and $i \in \{0, 1, 2\}$
2 δ on $\{a_i, b_i\}$ imitates $\mathcal{A}_3$ on subset of states Q_i
3 $\delta(q_0^i, a_j) = q_0^i$, $\delta(q_5^i, a_j) = q_1^i$, $\delta(q_7^i, a_j) = q_2^i$ for $i < j$

4 $\delta(q_0^i, b_j) = q_0^i$, $\delta(q_5^i, b_j) = q_1^i$, $\delta(q_7^i, b_j) = q_2^i$ for $i < j$

5 $\delta(q_l^i, a_j) = \delta(q_l^i, b_j) = q_l^i$, for $i > j$ and for all $l \in \{0,..,8\}$

6 $\delta(q_0^i, d) = \delta(q_5^i, d) = \delta(q_7^i, d) = q_0^1$

Denote any $\{q_f^i, q_g^i, q_h^i\} = Q_s^i$, where $\{f, g, h\}$ is a state in $\mathcal{P}(\mathcal{A}_3)$, and s is a length of a path from $\{0, 1, 2\}$ to $\{f, g, h\}$. For example $\{q_3^i, q_4^i, q_5^i\} = Q_3^i$. It can be verified with Fig. 3. Also denote $S_b = \bigcup_{i=1}^{k} Q_0^i$ and $S_f = \bigcup_{i=1}^{k} Q_{26}^j$. The intuition behind the construction is that after applying letter c to the state Q in a power automaton, we obtain state S_b. Then we treat $Q_i' \subset Q_i$ such that $|Q_i'| = 3$ and $Q_i' \subset S_b$ as i-th position of 0 in a k digit number of base 3^3. Any consecutive letter of the shortest carefully synchronizing word of that automaton acts like incrementing the former number by one. Namely we implement base 27 counter with the power automaton of $\mathcal{A}_3^n$.

Lemma 1. *The shortest $w \in \Sigma^*$ such that $\tau(S_b, w) = S_f$ has length $(3^3)^k - 1$.*

Proof. The result follows by induction on k.

Let $k = 1$. Then the result is easily verified with Fig. 3. Now assume that statement holds for $k - 1$. It means that there exists w' such that $\tau(\bigcup_{i=1}^{k-1} Q_0^i, w') = \bigcup_{i=1}^{k-1} Q_{26}^i$. We can easily verify from the definition of δ (Point 5), that also $\tau((\bigcup_{i=1}^{k-1} Q_0^i) \cup Q_i^k, w') = (\bigcup_{i=1}^{k-1} Q_{26}^i) \cup Q_i^k$ for $0 \le i < 27$. From the definition of δ (Point 3) we can deduce that $\tau(S_b, w'a_k) = (\bigcup_{i=1}^{k-1} Q_0^i) \cup Q_1^k$. We can repeat this reasoning to obtain $\tau(S_b, (w'a_k)^8) = (\bigcup_{i=1}^{k-1} Q_0^i) \cup Q_8^k$. Notice that $\tau(S_b, (w'a_k)^9) = S_b$. However $\tau(S_b, (w'a_k)^8 w'b_k) = (\bigcup_{i=1}^{k-1} Q_0^i) \cup Q_9^k$. Acting like that we obtain $\tau(S_b, w) = S_f$, where $w = (w'a_k)^8 w'b_k (w'a_k)^8 w'b_k (w'a_k)^8 w'$. To prove minimality of w it suffices to show that for each prefix v of w and for each $e \in \Sigma$ such that ve is not a prefix of w either there exists a prefix u of v such that $\tau(S_b, ve) = \tau(S_b, u)$ or $\tau(S_b, ve)$ is not defined. Straight from the definition of δ we obtain that $\tau(S_b, vc) = S_b$ and $\tau(S_b, vd)$ is not defined. Consider the state $\tau(S_b, v) = (\bigcup_{i=1}^{l-1} Q_{p_i}^i) \cup (\bigcup_{j=l}^{k} Q_{r_j}^j)$, where $l \in \{1, ..., k\}$, $p_i \in \{8, 17, 26\}$, $r_j \in \{0, ..., 26\}$ and $r_l \notin \{8, 17, 26\}$. Notice that if $m > l$, transitions $\tau((\bigcup_{i=1}^{l-1} Q_{p_i}^i) \cup (\bigcup_{j=l}^{k-1} Q_{r_j}^j), a_m)$ and $\tau((\bigcup_{i=1}^{l-1} Q_{p_i}^i) \cup (\bigcup_{j=l}^{k-1} Q_{r_j}^j), b_m)$ are undefined. Otherwise, if $m < l$ then $\tau((\bigcup_{i=1}^{l-1} Q_{26}^i) \cup (\bigcup_{j=l}^{k-1} Q_{r_j}^j), a_m)$ and $\tau((\bigcup_{i=1}^{l-1} Q_{26}^i) \cup (\bigcup_{j=l}^{k-1} Q_{r_j}^j), b_m)$ results in states visited before, which can be verified from Fig. 3 and the definition of δ. We conclude that the lemma holds.

Now we can state and prove the following theorem.

Theorem 1. *For each $n > 0$ the automaton $\mathcal{A}_3^n$ has shortest carefully synchronizing word of length $3^{\frac{n}{3}} + 1$ and uses $\lfloor \frac{2}{9}n \rfloor + 2$ letters.*

Proof. It is easy to observe from definition of δ that only letter c is defined for all states, so all synchronizing words must start with this letter. Also, we have $\tau(Q_i, c) = Q_0^i$ for all $i \in \{1, .., k\}$, so $\tau(Q, c) = S_b$. From Lemma 1 we deduce that there exists a word w with $|w| = (3^3)^k - 1$, such that $\tau(S_b, w) = S_f$ and w is shortest word with that property. Letter d is defined for S_f and also $\tau(S_f, d) = q_0^1$. Observe also, that for any proper prefix w' of w we have that $\tau(Q, cw'c) = S_b$ and $\tau(Q, cw'd)$ is not defined. From all that we claim the theorem holds.

In [6] there were presented several families of PFA's with constant alphabet size and exponentially long shortest carefully synchronizing words, but asymptotically smaller than in construction presented here. Observe also that our construction achieves asymptotically the same lower bound for the shortest carefully synchronizing word as in [18] and the same length of the shortest carefully synchronizing word as in [19] but with reduced alphabet comparing to those results.

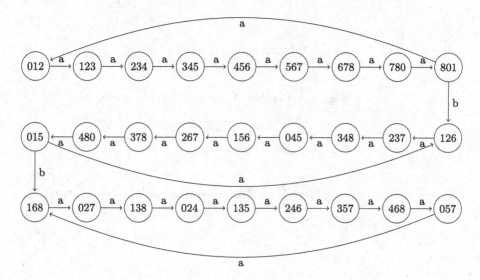

Fig. 3. Path from 012 to 057 in $\mathcal{P}(\mathcal{A}_3)$

4   Constant Number of Letters and Subset Synchronization

In this section we provide a construction of automata for a given partition of a number n. Notice that although this construction does not improve the result established in [6], where authors obtained the best known lower bounds for $d(n)$ with a restriction of constant alphabet size, it can be also used to establish a lower bound for subset synchronization in DFA.

Let $p = (k_1, .., k_s)$ be such that $\sum_{i=1}^{s} k_i = n$. Let $n > 1$, $Q^i = \{0_i, 1_i, .., (k_i - 1)_i\}$, $Q = \bigcup_{i=1}^{s} Q^i$ and $\Sigma = \{a, b, c\}$. We define a partial transition function $\delta : Q \times \Sigma \to Q$ for $\mathcal{A}_p = (\Sigma, Q, \delta)$ as follows:

1. $\delta(y_i, a) = 0_i$, $y_i \in Q^i$, $i \in \{1, .., s\}$
2. $\delta(y_i, b) = ((y + 1) \ mod \ k_i)_i$, $y_i \in Q^i$, $i \in \{1, .., s\}$
3. $\delta((k_i - 1)_i, c) = 0_1$, $j \in \{1, .., s\}$

In Fig. 4 we can see $\mathcal{A}_p$ for $p = (2, 2, 3)$ and in Fig. 5 is depicted $\mathcal{P}(\mathcal{A}_p)$.

We state and prove the following theorem.

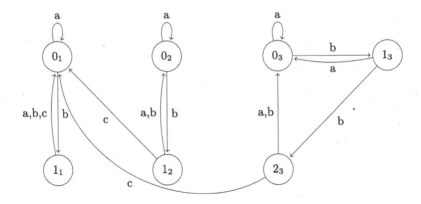

Fig. 4. Automaton $\mathcal{A}_p$ for $p = (2,2,3)$

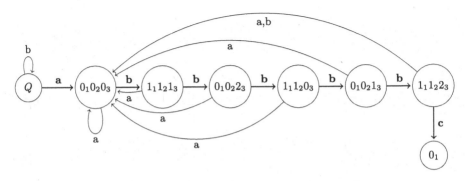

Fig. 5. Power automaton $\mathcal{P}(\mathcal{A}_p)$ with a path from Q to 0_1 (bolded arrows)

Theorem 2. $\mathcal{A}_p$ *is carefully synchronizing, and the length of its shortest carefully synchronizing word is* $lcm(k_1, .., k_s) + 1$.

Proof. First, observe that a and b are defined for all states in Q and, since b is a bijection, we have $\tau(Q, b) = Q$ and $\tau(Q, a) = \{0_1, 0_2, .., 0_s\} = Q_0$. We can also deduce that the permutation type induced by the action of b on a set of states is $[k_1^1 k_2^1 .. k_s^1] = r$, and from that we have $\tau(Q_0, b^r) = Q_0$ and for any $p < q < r$ holds $\tau(Q_0, b^p) \neq \tau(Q_0, b^q)$. Denote $\tau(Q, b^p) = Q_p$. From the definition of δ we deduce that for any p we have $\tau(Q_p, a) = Q_0$, since for any $i \in \{1, .., s\}$ we have $|Q_p \cap Q_i| = 1$. Letter c is defined only for $Q_p = Q_{r-1} = \{(k_1 - 1)_1, .., (k_s - 1)_s\}$, which can be verified by analysing the definition of δ. On the other hand, it is well-known that r is an order of permutation induced by b, and by that we have $r = lcm(k_1, .., k_s)$. So $\tau(Q, ab^{r-1}c) = 0_1$ and we claim that the theorem holds.

Corollary 1. *Let n be the number of states. There exists p_n such that* $d(\mathcal{A}_{p_n}) \propto e^{\sqrt{n \ln n}}$.

Proof. Using Theorem 2 we can construct an automaton for any given cycle decomposition of a permutation. On the other hand, we know that Landau's function [16], for a given n, is the largest order of an element of S_n. Denote it as $g(n)$. The way to obtain such a family for any n is by taking a permutation p_n with the largest order of all in S_n and constructing an automaton like in Theorem 5. It is well-known that $g(n) \propto e^{\sqrt{n \ln n}}$ and by that the corollary holds.

We can also consider above construction with removed transition labelled with letter c. Denote such automaton as $\mathcal{B}_p$ for a given partition p. Now we can formulate the following corollary.

Corollary 2. *Let $\mathcal{B}_p$ be defined as above and let $S = \{(k_1 - 1)_1, .., (k_s - 1)_s\}$. Then $\mathcal{B}_p$ is a DFA synchronizable to S, and the shortest $w \in \Sigma^*$ such that $\delta(Q, w) = S$ is of length $O(e^{\sqrt{n \ln n}})$.*

5   Conclusions and Further Work

We improved the result from [19] and gave a family of automata that has the same asymptotical length of shortest carefully synchronizing word, but we reduced significantly the number of letters. We also described how to use our method to construct the family of automata over three-letter alphabet with the shortest synchronizing word of length $O(e^{\sqrt{n \ln n}})$. As a corollary of that construction we gave an infinite series of binary DFA with a set that is reachable with a word of length $O(e^{\sqrt{n \ln n}})$ at least.

Notice that the construction from Sect. 4 gives us the DFA which are not strongly connected. We would like to investigate the case of synchronization to a subset in with strongly connected DFA's. In [9] there is a construction of automata having longer words synchronizing automaton to a subset, but the alphabet size in this construction is exponential and resulting automata are synchronizing. In the future work we are going to deal with the case of non-synchronizing automata and small number of letters.

References

1. Berlinkov, M.V.: On two algorithmic problems about synchronizing automata. In: Shur, A.M., Volkov, M.V. (eds.) DLT 2014. LNCS, vol. 8633, pp. 61–67. Springer, Cham (2014). https://doi.org/10.1007/978-3-319-09698-8_6
2. Berlinkov, M., Szykuła, M.: Algebraic synchronization criterion and computing reset words. Inf. Sci. **369**, 718–730 (2016)
3. Berlinkov, M.V., Ferens, R., Ryzhikov, A., Szykuła, M.: Synchronizing strongly connected partial DFAs. In: Bläser, M., Monmege, B. (eds.) 38th International Symposium on Theoretical Aspects of Computer Science (STACS 2021). Leibniz International Proceedings in Informatics (LIPIcs), vol. 187, pp. 12:1–12:16. Schloss Dagstuhl - Leibniz-Zentrum für Informatik, Dagstuhl, Germany (2021). https://doi.org/10.4230/LIPIcs.STACS.2021.12. https://drops.dagstuhl.de/opus/volltexte/2021/13657

4. Berlinkov, M.V., Ferens, R., Szykuła, M.: Preimage problems for deterministic finite automata. J. Comput. Syst. Sci. **115**, 214–234 (2021). https://doi.org/10.1016/j.jcss.2020.08.002. https://www.sciencedirect.com/science/article/pii/S0022000020300805

5. Biskup, M.T., Plandowski, W.: Shortest synchronizing strings for Huffman codes. Theoret. Comput. Sci. **410**, 3925–3941 (2009)

6. de Bondt, M., Don, H., Zantema, H.: Lower bounds for synchronizing word lengths in partial automata. Int. J. Found. Comput. Sci. **30**, 29–60 (2019)

7. Don, H.: The Černý conjecture and 1-contracting automata. Electron. J. Comb. **23** (2016)

8. Eppstein, D.: Reset sequences for monotonic automata. SIAM J. Comput. **19**, 500–510 (1990)

9. Gonze, F., Jungers, R.M.: Hardly reachable subsets and completely reachable automata with 1-deficient words. J. Automata Lang. Comb. **24**(2–4), 321–342 (2019). https://doi.org/10.25596/jalc-2019-321

10. Imreh, B., Steinby, M.: Directable nondeterministic automata. Acta Cybern. **14**, 105–115 (1999)

11. Jürgensen, H.: Synchronization. Inf. Comput. **206**, 1033–1044 (2008)

12. Kari, J.: A counter example to a conjecture concerning synchronizing word in finite. EATCS Bull. **73**, 146–147 (2001)

13. Kari, J.: Synchronizing finite automata on Eulerian digraphs. Theoret. Comput. Sci. **295**, 223–232 (2003)

14. Doyen, L., Massart, T., Shirmohammadi, M.: Robust synchronization in Markov decision processes. In: Baldan, P., Gorla, D. (eds.) CONCUR 2014. LNCS, vol. 8704, pp. 234–248. Springer, Heidelberg (2014). https://doi.org/10.1007/978-3-662-44584-6_17

15. Doyen, L., Massart, T., Shirmohammadi, M.: The complexity of synchronizing Markov decision processes. J. Comput. Syst. Sci. **100**, 96–129 (2019)

16. Landau, E.: Über die maximalordnung der permutationen gegebenen grades. Arch. Math. Phys. **3** (1903)

17. Martyugin, P.: Computational complexity of certain problems related to carefully synchronizing words for partial automata and directing words for nondeterministic automata. Theory Comput. Syst. **54**, 293–304 (2014). https://doi.org/10.1007/s00224-013-9516-6

18. Martyugin, P.: A lower bound for the length of the shortest carefully synchronizing words. Russ. Math. **54**, 46–54 (2010)

19. Martyugin, P.V.: Careful synchronization of partial automata with restricted alphabets. In: Bulatov, A.A., Shur, A.M. (eds.) CSR 2013. LNCS, vol. 7913, pp. 76–87. Springer, Heidelberg (2013). https://doi.org/10.1007/978-3-642-38536-0_7

20. Ito, M., Shikishima-Tsuji, K.: Some results on directable automata. In: Karhumäki, J., Maurer, H., Păun, G., Rozenberg, G. (eds.) Theory Is Forever. LNCS, vol. 3113, pp. 125–133. Springer, Heidelberg (2004). https://doi.org/10.1007/978-3-540-27812-2_12

21. Natarajan, B.K.: An algorithmic approach to the automated design of parts orienters. In: 27th Annual Symposium on Foundations of Computer Science, pp. 132–142 (1986)

22. Pin, J.E.: On two combinatorial problems arising from automata theory. In: Proceedings of the International Colloquium on Graph Theory and Combinatorics, vol. 75, pp. 535–548 (1983)

23. Rystsov, I.K.: Asymptotic estimate of the length of a diagnostic word for a finite automaton. Cybernetics **16**, 194–198 (1980)

24. Rystsov, I.K.: Reset words for commutative and solvable automata. Theoret. Comput. Sci. **172**, 273–279 (1997)
25. Sandberg, S.: 1 Homing and synchronizing sequences. In: Broy, M., Jonsson, B., Katoen, J.-P., Leucker, M., Pretschner, A. (eds.) Model-Based Testing of Reactive Systems. LNCS, vol. 3472, pp. 5–33. Springer, Heidelberg (2005). https://doi.org/10.1007/11498490_2
26. Szykuła, M.: Improving the upper bound on the length of the shortest reset word. In: STACS 2018, pp. 56:1–56:13 (2018)
27. Trahtman, A.: The Černý conjecture for aperiodic automata. Discrete Math. Theor. Comput. Sci. **9**, 3–10 (2007)
28. Černý, J.: Poznámka k homogénnym eksperimentom s konečnými automatami. Mat. Fyz. Cas. Slovens. Akad. Vied. **14**, 208–216 (1964)
29. Volkov, M.: Synchronizing automata and the Černý conjecture. Lang. Automata Theor. Appl. **5196**, 11–27 (2008)
30. Volkov, M.: Slowly synchronizing automata with idempotent letters of low rank. J. Autom. Lang. Comb. **24**, 375–386 (2019)
31. Vorel, V.: Subset synchronization and careful synchronization of binary finite automata. Jour. Found. Comput. Sci. **27**, 557–578 (2016)
32. Gazdag, Z., Ivan, I., Nagy-Gyorgy, J.: Improved upper bounds on synchronizing nondeterministic automata. Inf. Processi. Lett. **109**, 986–990 (2009)

A Toolkit for Parikh Matrices

Laura K. Hutchinson, Robert Mercaş[(✉)] [iD], and Daniel Reidenbach[iD]

Department of Computer Science,
Loughborough University, Loughborough LE11 3TU, UK
{L.Hutchinson,R.G.Mercas,D.Reidenbach}@lboro.ac.uk

Abstract. The Parikh matrix mapping is a concept that provides information on the number of occurrences of certain (scattered) subwords in a word. Although Parikh matrices have been thoroughly studied, many of their basic properties remain open. In the present paper, we describe a toolkit that has been developed to support research in this field. Its functionality includes elementary and advanced operations related to Parikh matrices and the recently introduced variants of $\mathbb{P}$-Parikh matrices and $\mathbb{L}$-Parikh matrices.

Keywords: Toolkit · Parikh matrices · $\mathbb{P}$-Parikh matrices · $\mathbb{L}$-Parikh matrices · Amiable words

1 Introduction

The Parikh vector (also referred to as *abelianization*) – i.e., a vector that, for a given word w, contains the number of occurrences of all letters in the w – is a classical concept in language and automata theory [17]. It can be easily computed and is guaranteed to be logarithmic in the size of the word it represents, but it is almost always ambiguous; that is, multiple words typically share the same Parikh vector.

Parikh matrices [15] were introduced to address this problem. They are an extension of Parikh vectors, and they do not only contain the Parikh vector of the word, but also the frequencies of some of the word's (scattered) subwords. The specific subwords that are considered are all factors of the word $a_1 a_2 a_3 \cdots a_n$, where $\{a_1, a_2, a_3, \ldots, a_n\}$ is the ordered alphabet of all distinct letters occurring in the word. For example, if $w = abcaba$ and we consider the usual lexicographical order, then its Parikh matrix contains the counts of a, b, c, ab, bc, and abc. A Parikh matrix is always an upper triangular matrix with 1 on the main diagonal; the frequencies of subwords of length 1 (corresponding to the Parikh vector) on the 1-diagonal; frequencies of subwords of length 2 on the 2-diagonal; and so on. Hence, for our above example word w, we have the following Parikh matrix:

$$\begin{pmatrix} 1 & 3 & 3 & 1 \\ 0 & 1 & 2 & 1 \\ 0 & 0 & 1 & 1 \\ 0 & 0 & 0 & 1 \end{pmatrix}$$

Parikh matrices have the same asymptotic compactness as Parikh vectors and are associated to a significantly smaller number of words. However, they do

© Springer Nature Switzerland AG 2022
P. Caron and L. Mignot (Eds.): CIAA 2022, LNCS 13266, pp. 116–127, 2022.
https://doi.org/10.1007/978-3-031-07469-1_9

not normally remove ambiguity entirely. Our above example matrix has two associated words, namely *abcaba* and *abacba*; such words, which share a Parikh matrix, are called *amiable*.

Despite intensive research (see, e. g., [1–6, 9, 10, 13, 18–21]), many fundamental problems for Parikh matrices are still open. These include the following questions:

- When is a matrix a Parikh matrix? Only some upper triangular matrices with 1 on the main diagonal and non-negative integers in the upper triangle are indeed Parikh matrices. While it is possible to decide this problem by enumerating and testing all words that have the Parikh vector that is specified by the 1-diagonal of a given "candidate" matrix, it is open if there is an effective characterisation of Parikh matrices that yields a more efficient decision procedure.
- When are two words amiable? What are the words associated to a given Parikh matrix? These problems can again be solved via brute-force algorithms, but comprehensive characterisations of amiable words have so far not been found.
- When is a word uniquely described by a Parikh matrix? What potential variations or extensions of Parikh matrices can reduce their ambiguity effectively?

Progress on these questions has been impeded by the fact that the manual construction and analysis of Parikh matrices is tedious and error-prone. We have therefore designed and implemented a toolkit that automises a range of the most important operations, so that research hypotheses can be tested more efficiently.[1] Our tool includes functionality to calculate the Parikh matrix and all amiable words for a given word, decide on whether a given matrix is a Parikh matrix, and mechanisms to investigate concepts that can reduce the ambiguity of Parikh matrices. The latter are based on the recently introduced $\mathbb{P}$-Parikh matrices and $\mathbb{L}$-Parikh matrices [7]. The main idea of these approaches is to apply a simple modification to a given word (namely a projection or the construction of the Lyndon conjugate, respectively) and to store the Parikh matrices of both the original and the modified word. The combination of these two matrices then typically has a significantly smaller number of associated words than the standard Parikh matrix alone.

A detailed description of the functionality and underlying algorithmic and design decisions of the toolkit is provided in the main Sect. 3 of this paper. Before we present these details, we describe the formal foundations of the tool in Sect. 2.

2   Preliminaries

We refer to a string of arbitrary letters as a *word* which is formed by the concatenation of letters. The set of all letters used to create our word is called an

---

[1] The software is implemented in Java, it is open-source and has been made available under the MIT License. It is available online at www.github.com/LHutch1/Parikh-Matrices-Toolkit.

alphabet. We represent an *ordered alphabet* as $\Sigma_k = \{a_1 < a_2 < \cdots < a_k\}$, where $k \in \mathbb{N}$ is the *size* of the alphabet, and by convention a_i is the ith letter in the Latin alphabet. Whenever the alphabet size is irrelevant or understood, we omit this from notation, using only Σ. All alphabets referred to in this thesis have an order imposed on them. The *Kleene star*, denoted *, is the operation that, once applied to a given alphabet, generates the set of all finite words that result from concatenating any letters from that alphabet.

We denote the concatenation of two words u and v as uv. The *length* of a word is the total number of, not necessarily distinct, letters it contains and the *empty word*, of length zero, is referred to as ε.

We say that v is a *factor* of w if and only if w can be written as $w = w_1 v w_2$ for some $w_1, w_2 \in \Sigma^*$. If $w_1 = \varepsilon$, then we also call v a *prefix* of w, and if $w_2 = \varepsilon$, then v is a *suffix* of w. A word $u = u[1]u[2]\cdots u[m]$, where $u[1], u[2], \ldots, u[m] \in \Sigma$, is a *subword* of a word v if there exists factors $v_0, v_1, \ldots, v_m \in \Sigma^*$ such that $v = v_0 u[1] v_1 u[2] \cdots v_{m-1} u[m] v_m$. We use $|v|_u$ to denote the number of distinct occurrences of u as a subword in v. We say that a word $u \in \Sigma^*$ is *lexicographically smaller* than a word $v \in \Sigma^*$, denoted $u <_{lex} v$, if $u \neq v$ and either u is a prefix of v or, for the smallest i satisfying $u[i] \neq v[i]$, the letter $u[i]$ precedes the letter $v[i]$ in the order on Σ.

We say that two words w and w' are *conjugates* if we can write $w = uv$ and $w' = vu$. For a word w, the *conjugacy class of w*, denoted $C(w)$, is the class of all of its possible conjugates.

·The *Parikh vector* [17] associated with a word $w \in \Sigma_k^*$ is obtained through a mapping $\phi : \Sigma_k^* \to (\mathbb{N} \cup \{0\})^k$, defined as $\phi(w) = [|w|_{a_1}, |w|_{a_2}, \ldots, |w|_{a_k}]$. For a matrix M of size $k \times k$, the *j-diagonal* is defined as all elements of M that are in the position $M_{i,i+j}$, for $i = 1, 2, \ldots, k - j$.

Unlike what is suggested in Sect. 1, the formal definition of a Parikh matrix is based on the multiplication of the Parikh matrices of the individual letters in the order in which they appear in the word:

Definition 1 ([15]). *Let M_{k+1} denote the set of all square matrices of size $(k+1) \times (k+1)$, where k is the size of the ordered alphabet $\Sigma = a_1 < a_2 < \cdots < a_k$. The Parikh matrix mapping is the morphism $\Psi : \Sigma^* \to M_{k+1}$, defined as follows. For $a_q \in \Sigma$ with q representing where in the ordered alphabet the letter lies, if $\Psi(a_q) = (m_{i,j})_{1 \leq i,j \leq k+1}$, then for each $1 \leq i \leq k + 1$, $m_{i,i} = 1$, $m_{q,q+1} = 1$, and all other elements of the matrix $\Psi(a_q)$ are zero.*

This elegant definition, which is also used as the basis of the related algorithm in our toolkit, then leads to the more intuitive structure of Parikh matrices as described in Sect. 1:

Theorem 1 ([16]). *Let $\Sigma = \{a_1 < a_2 < \cdots < a_k\}$ be an ordered alphabet, where $k \geq 1$, and assume that $w \in \Sigma^*$. The matrix $\Psi(w)$ has the following properties:*

1. $m_{i,j} = 0$, for all $1 \leq j < i \leq (k + 1)$;
2. $m_{i,i} = 1$, for all $1 \leq i \leq (k + 1)$;
3. $m_{i,j} = |w|_u$ where $u = a_i a_{i+1} \ldots a_{j-2} a_{j-1}$, for all $1 \leq i < j \leq (k + 1)$.

One notion we introduce in this paper relies on a change in alphabet. As such, to emphasise the alphabet Σ used for obtaining a Parikh matrix, we write $\Psi_\Sigma(w)$. If no confusion arises, we shall omit the alphabet from the notation, in favour of legibility, and write $\Psi(w)$.

An example illustrating Definition 1 is given in Sect. 3.1. For conciseness, when presenting specific examples of Parikh matrices in the remainder of this paper, we omit all entries that are immutable across all Parikh matrices, i.e., we only show the upper triangle. For example, the full Parikh matrix given in Sect. 1 is therefore displayed as follows:

$$\Psi(abcaba) = \left\langle \begin{smallmatrix} 3 & 3 & 1 \\ & 2 & 1 \\ & & 1 \end{smallmatrix} \right\rangle$$

As explained in Sect. 1, a Parikh matrix can be common to multiple words, and we call words *amiable* if they are associated to the same Parikh matrix. If two or more words are associated to a single Parikh matrix, we say that the matrix is *ambiguous*. This potential ambiguity has been a focus of research on Parikh matrices, and our toolkit implements methods related to $\mathbb{P}$-Parikh matrices and $\mathbb{L}$-Parikh matrices [7], which often allow for a reduction in ambiguity. These two approaches are based on the idea that the standard Parikh matrix of a word w is considered alongside the Parikh matrix of a simple modification of w, and that the combination of these two matrices is associated to fewer words than the standard Parikh matrix.

The $\mathbb{P}$-Parikh matrix is in essence the Parikh matrix of a projection of a word, and represents a special case of the extension of the Parikh matrix mapping presented in [21]. Formally, for $n \in \mathbb{N}$, $w \in \Sigma_n^*$ and $S \subset \Sigma_n$, the $\mathbb{P}$-Parikh matrix of w with respect to S is defined as follows.

Definition 2. *For* $m, n \in \mathbb{N}$ *with* $1 \leq m \leq n$, *let* $S \subset \Sigma_n$ *such that* $S = \{a_{k_1}, a_{k_2}, \ldots, a_{k_m}\}$, *where* $0 < k_1 < k_2 < \cdots < k_m \leq n$. *We define the* $\mathbb{P}$-*Parikh matrix of the word* w *with respect to* S *as* $\Psi_S(\pi_S(w))$, *where the morphism* $\pi : \Sigma_n^* \to \Sigma_m^*$ *is defined as*

$$\pi_S(a_i) := \begin{cases} a_i & : a_i \in S, \\ \varepsilon & : a_i \notin S. \end{cases}$$

An example of a $\mathbb{P}$-Parikh matrix can be found in Sect. 3.3.

An $\mathbb{L}$-Parikh matrix of a word w is the Parikh matrix of the *Lyndon conjugate* of w (denoted $L(w)$), i.e., it is the Parikh matrix of the conjugate of w that is lexicographically smallest based on the order on the alphabet:

Definition 3. *Given a word* w, *we define its* $\mathbb{L}$-Parikh *matrix,* $\Psi_{\ell ex}$, *as the Parikh matrix associated with its Lyndon conjugate,* $L(w)$.

An example of an $\mathbb{L}$-Parikh matrix is given in Sect. 3.2.

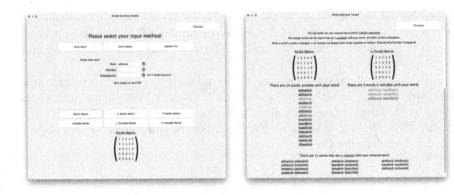

Fig. 1. Two screenshots of the user interface.

3 Toolkit

Our toolkit is accessible on GitHub[2] either as an executable .jar file, or as a collection of individual Java classes, which can be downloaded, compiled and run together to allow the user to make changes to the code to suit their individual needs. It is an open-source software, licensed with the MIT License. Two screenshots of the user interface are given in Fig. 1.

In the present section we shall explain and discuss the eight different functions that can be computed as a part of this toolkit:

1. *'Parikh Matrix'* - Calculate the Parikh matrix of a given word.
2. *'L-Parikh Matrix'* - Calculate the L-Parikh matrix of a given word.
3. *'P-Parikh Matrix'* - Calculate the P-Parikh matrix of a given word using a given set of letters.
4. *'Amiable Words'* - Find all words that are amiable with a given word.
5. *'L-Amiable Words'* - Find all words that share a Parikh matrix and an L-Parikh matrix with a given word.
6. *'P-Amiable Words'* - Find all words that share a Parikh matrix and a P-Parikh matrix with a given word using a given set of letters.
7. *'Is It Parikh?'* - Determine if a given matrix is a Parikh matrix.
8. *'Associated Words'* - Find all words associated with a given Parikh matrix.

3.1 Parikh Matrix

This function takes a word as input and outputs the Parikh matrix of that word. To calculate the Parikh matrix of a word, we first determine the Parikh matrix of each letter in the alphabet that the word uses, according to Definition 1. We then multiply the matrix of each letter in the order that they appear. The following example illustrates this method:

---
[2] www.github.com/LHutch1/Parikh-Matrices-Toolkit

Example 1. Let $w = cbbab \in \Sigma_3$. Then we have: $\Psi(a) = \left\langle \begin{smallmatrix} 1 & 0 & 0 \\ & 0 & 0 \\ & & 0 \end{smallmatrix} \right\rangle$, $\Psi(b) = \left\langle \begin{smallmatrix} 0 & 0 & 0 \\ & 1 & 0 \\ & & 0 \end{smallmatrix} \right\rangle$, $\Psi(c) = \left\langle \begin{smallmatrix} 0 & 0 & 0 \\ & 0 & 0 \\ & & 1 \end{smallmatrix} \right\rangle$. Now we calculate the Parikh matrix of w:

$$\Psi(cbbab) = \Psi(c) \times \Psi(b) \times \Psi(b) \times \Psi(a) \times \Psi(b)$$

$$= \left\langle \begin{smallmatrix} 0 & 0 & 0 \\ & 0 & 0 \\ & & 1 \end{smallmatrix} \right\rangle \times \left\langle \begin{smallmatrix} 0 & 0 & 0 \\ & 1 & 0 \\ & & 0 \end{smallmatrix} \right\rangle \times \left\langle \begin{smallmatrix} 0 & 0 & 0 \\ & 1 & 0 \\ & & 0 \end{smallmatrix} \right\rangle \times \left\langle \begin{smallmatrix} 1 & 0 & 0 \\ & 0 & 0 \\ & & 0 \end{smallmatrix} \right\rangle \times \left\langle \begin{smallmatrix} 0 & 0 & 0 \\ & 1 & 0 \\ & & 0 \end{smallmatrix} \right\rangle = \left\langle \begin{smallmatrix} 1 & 1 & 0 \\ & 3 & 0 \\ & & 1 \end{smallmatrix} \right\rangle$$

◁

While the function requires n matrix multiplications of size $(m+1) \times (m+1)$, where n is the length of the word and m is the size of the alphabet, we note that the Parikh matrices corresponding to the letters are *transvection* matrices, i.e., identity matrices with a single value replacing one of the zeroes. Thus, rather than using the naïve method or Strassen's algorithm [22] for matrix multiplication, we make use the of the shear transformations; note that the transvection matrices are generators for the special linear group $SL_k(\mathbb{Z})$ [11]. That is, the composition to the right of a matrix A with a transvection matrix that has a value c at position (i, j) implies adding to the jth column of A the cth multiple of the column i of A. This leads to a time complexity of only $O(mn)$.

3.2   L-Parikh Matrix

To calculate the L-Parikh matrix of a word, we begin by finding the Lyndon conjugate of that word. To this end, we make use of Duval's algorithm [8], which runs in linear time with respect to n. The algorithm finds the Lyndon factorisation of any given word w, that is, the factorisation $w = w_1 w_2 \cdots w_p$ where the lexicographically ordered sequence $w_1 \geq w_2 \geq \cdots \geq w_p$ consists of Lyndon words w_i, i.e., words strictly smaller than any of their conjugates. In [8], it is shown that the Lyndon conjugate of any Lyndon word u can be found by first finding the Lyndon factorisation of uu (since this concatenation must contain the Lyndon conjugate as a factor), and then choosing the first Lyndon factor of length n that we find. We can easily first find the root u of our word w, and then run the above strategy to find u's Lyndon conjugate starting position, and thus the starting position of the Lyndon conjugate of w, which we are interested in. We then calculate the Parikh matrix of the Lyndon conjugate of w in the same way as with the *Parikh Matrix* function.

Example 2. Let $w = (cbbabc)^3$ be the input word. We first find the root $u = cbbabc$ and then the Lyndon factorisation of the word $uu = cbbabccbbabc$: $u_1 = c$, $u_2 = bb$, $u_3 = abccbb$, $u_4 = abc$. The only of these words that is of equal size to u is $abccbb$, and so we now must find the Parikh matrix of the word $(abccbb)^3$, which is $\Psi((abccbb)^3) = \left\langle \begin{smallmatrix} 3 & 12 & 24 \\ & 9 & 27 \\ & & 6 \end{smallmatrix} \right\rangle$. Note that we have $\Psi(w) = \left\langle \begin{smallmatrix} 3 & 18 & 36 \\ & 9 & 24 \\ & & 6 \end{smallmatrix} \right\rangle$.   ◁

This function works in a very similar way as the *Parikh Matrix* function. We know that it takes $O(mn)$ time to calculate a Parikh matrix, which we do twice in this function. Since finding both the roots and then the Lyndon conjugates takes linear time $O(n)$, as explained above, the total time complexity of this function is $O(mn)$.

3.3 ℙ-Parikh Matrix

For the ℙ-Parikh matrix, we first calculate the word's projection using the mapping given below, taken from the definition of a ℙ-Parikh matrix, Definition 2.

Definition 4. *For* $1 \leq p \leq m \in \mathbb{N}$, *let* $S \subset \Sigma_m$ *such that* $S = \{a_{k_1}, a_{k_2}, \ldots, a_{k_p}\}$, *where* $0 < k_1 < k_2 < \cdots < k_p \leq m$. *The morphism* $\pi_S : \Sigma_m^* \to \Sigma_p^*$ *is defined as* $\pi_S(a_i) := a_i$ *if* $a_i \in S$ *and* $\pi_S(a_i) := \varepsilon$ *if* $a_i \notin S$.

We then calculate the Parikh matrix of the new word using the same method as described in Definition 1.

Example 3. Let $w = cbbabc$ and $S = \{a, c\}$. Then we first find the projection of w as $\pi_S(w) := cac$. Finally, we calculate the Parikh matrix of the projected word to obtain the ℙ-Parikh matrix of w. This yields $\Psi(\pi_S(w)) = \langle 1 \, {}^1_2 \rangle$.

The time required by this function is just as before $O(mn)$, since the time needed to obtain the projection word is linear $O(n)$.

3.4 Amiable Words

A brute force approach that finds all words that are amiable with an input word w of length n produces a list of all permutations of w and then compares the Parikh matrix of each of these $n!$ words to that of w. Since finding the Parikh matrix as discussed above can be done in $O(mn)$, while each comparison is done in at most $O(m^2)$ time, such an approach would require $O(m \times n!)$ time. Note that the size of the considered alphabet can by de facto be considered smaller than the length of the word in this case, since the extra symbols of the whole alphabet can easily be ignored, i.e., $m \leq n$.

The implementation of our toolkit is based on a more sophisticated approach, namely on an algorithm by [12] that finds the 2-binomial equivalence class of a word and reduces the number of words for which we must calculate the Parikh matrix. The algorithm finds all words that have the same number of subwords $a_i a_j$, such that $i < j$ and $a_i, a_j \in \Sigma$, as a given word. Since the Parikh matrix contains counts of a subset of these factors (namely those where $i + 1 = j$), we conclude that all words amiable with our entered word w are contained in the output of this algorithm. We can then calculate the Parikh matrices of all of these words and compare them to $\Psi(w)$ to see if they are equal.

The algorithm is based on a certain type of transformations:

Definition 5. *Let* $w_1, w_2, u, v \in \Sigma_m^*$ *where* $w_1 = ua_i a_j v$, *with* $i < j$ *and* $a_i, a_j \in \Sigma_m$. *We say that a* Switch Transformation *has been applied to* w_1 *to obtain* w_2 *if* $w_2 = ua_j a_i v$, *and denote this as* $w_1 \xrightarrow{S} w_2$.

Note that applying a Switch Transformation on the factor $a_i a_j$ reduces the number of occurrences of the subword $a_i a_j$ by 1.

We can now state the algorithm given in [12] that forms the basis of our implementation. However, the below method is a simplified version of that algorithm, as Lejeune et al. also incorporate a term to monitor the longest common

---

Algorithm 1 [12]

Input: A word $w \in \Sigma_m^*$
Output: A list α of words with equal occurrences of the subword $a_i a_{i+1}$ as w

1: Let $\chi(w) = (|w|_{a_1 a_2}, |w|_{a_2 a_3}, \cdots, |w|_{a_{m-1} a_m})$
2: Let β be the list of all words found during our search
3: Let w_1 be the lexicographically smallest word such that $\phi(w) = \phi(w_1)$.
4: Add w_1 to β
5: **while** $|\beta|$ has increased from the previous iteration **or** $|\beta| = 0$ **do**
6:    **for** each word w_k in β that was found in the previous iteration **do**
7:       **for** all factors $a_i a_j$ in w_k, where $a_i < a_j$ **do**
8:          $w_k \xrightarrow{S} u$ {using the factor $a_i a_j$ in w_k}
9:          **if** $\chi(w) == \chi(u)$ **then**
10:             Add u to α
11:          **if** $\chi(u) \geq \chi(w)$ **then**
12:             Add u to β

---

prefix of two finite words. This helps to impose an order in which the Switch Transformations should be applied, and prevents any word from appearing in their search multiple times. In our implementation, we mimic this effect by storing the words that are constructed by the algorithm in a Java object called *TreeSet*. Without removing duplicates in the process, the worst-case complexity of the algorithm would be $O(n^{n^2})$ and, hence, exceed the complexity of the brute force approach.

We now consider an example of the effect of the above algorithm on the search space of potentially amiable words.

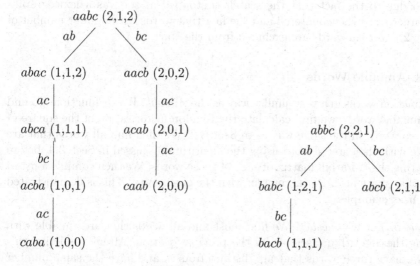

Fig. 2. Tree of single Switch Transformations for *aabc*, used in Example 4.

Fig. 3. Tree of single Switch Transformations for *abbc*, used in Example 7.

Example 4. Let $w = caba$. If we used a brute force approach to generate and test all words with the same Parikh vector as w, then we would have to compare the Parikh matrices of 11 words to that of w. We now show how the use of the above algorithm reduces the number of comparisons that need to be performed.

The lexicographically smallest word with the same Parikh vector as w is $aabc$, so this will be the starting point of our search. Since the word is ternary, $ab \rightarrow ba$, $bc \rightarrow cb$ and $ac \rightarrow ca$ are the only possible Switch Transformations.

We will represent the process in the form of a tree, where each child represents a word that can be obtained by performing a single Switch Transformation on the parent (see Fig. 2). We also record the number of subwords ab, bc and ca at each node in the form $(|w|_{ab}, |w|_{bc}, |w|_{ac})$. Note that $|w|_{ab} = 1, |w|_{bc} = 0$ and $|w|_{ac} = 0$. We can therefore stop searching once any further transformations would result in less than 1 subword ab, 0 subwords bc and 0 subwords ac, and we do not pursue any paths with duplicate words.

In this example, removing duplicate entries prevents us from switching ab in $acab$ (which would lead to $acba$, and this word is already in the tree), and from switching ab in $caab$ (since $caba$ is already in the tree).

Finally, we now collect any word in the tree that has 1 occurrence of the subword ab and 0 occurrences of the subword bc. These are $acba$ and our input word $caba$. We then calculate the Parikh matrices of the words, and since they are the same, $acba$ is the only word that is amiable with $caba$.   ◁

The worst-case complexity of the implemented algorithm is $O(n!)$ and therefore equivalent to the brute force approach described at the beginning of this sub-section. However, this worst case only occurs in the special situation when the word we consider is the lexicographically largest word with a given Parikh vector. The average case of our approach is therefore superior to the brute force method due to the fact that the search is stopped as soon as a lexicographically larger word is encountered and the fact that words with a lower number of specific 2-letter subwords are excluded from the start.

3.5   L-Amiable Words

This function works in a very similar way as the *Amiable Words* function. To find all L-amiable words, we first calculate the Lyndon factorisation of the square of our given word, in the same way as in Sect. 3.2. We then find all words that are amiable with the entered word using the algorithm discussed in Sect. 3.4, before calculating the L-Parikh matrix of each of those words. We then compile a list of words that share an L-Parikh matrix with the given word. This is demonstrated in the next example.

Example 5. Let $w = abbacc$. We first must find all words that are amiable with w using the algorithm discussed in the previous section. After completing this step, we have three words that are distinct from w and have the same number of occurrences of the subwords ab and bc as w, namely $abbcac$, $abbcca$, and *baabcc*. We now calculate the Parikh matrices of w and these words: $\Psi(abbacc) = \left\langle \begin{smallmatrix} 2 & 2 & 4 \\ & 2 & 4 \\ & & 2 \end{smallmatrix} \right\rangle$, $\Psi(baabcc) = \left\langle \begin{smallmatrix} 2 & 2 & 4 \\ & 2 & 4 \\ & & 2 \end{smallmatrix} \right\rangle$, $\Psi(abbcac) = \left\langle \begin{smallmatrix} 2 & 2 & 4 \\ & 2 & 4 \\ & & 2 \end{smallmatrix} \right\rangle$, $\Psi(abbcca) = \left\langle \begin{smallmatrix} 2 & 2 & 4 \\ & 2 & 4 \\ & & 2 \end{smallmatrix} \right\rangle$.

Since all four matrices are equal, all words output by the algorithm are amiable with w. Now we calculate the $\mathbb{L}$-Parikh matrices of these four words.

$$\Psi(L(abbacc)) = \Psi(abbacc) = \left\langle \begin{smallmatrix} 2 & 2 & 4 \\ & 2 & 4 \\ & & 2 \end{smallmatrix} \right\rangle \qquad \Psi(L(baabcc)) = \Psi(aabccb) = \left\langle \begin{smallmatrix} 2 & 4 & 4 \\ & 2 & 2 \\ & & 2 \end{smallmatrix} \right\rangle$$

$$\Psi(L(abbcac)) = \Psi(abbcac) = \left\langle \begin{smallmatrix} 2 & 2 & 4 \\ & 2 & 4 \\ & & 2 \end{smallmatrix} \right\rangle \qquad \Psi(L(abbcca)) = \Psi(aabbcc) = \left\langle \begin{smallmatrix} 2 & 4 & 8 \\ & 2 & 4 \\ & & 2 \end{smallmatrix} \right\rangle$$

There is one word that is distinct from w that shares both a Parikh and $\mathbb{L}$-Parikh matrix with it. Hence the word that is $\mathbb{L}$-amiable with *abbacc* is *abbcac*.   ◁

As this algorithm utilises the algorithm discussed in Sect. 3.4, it has asymptotically identical time complexity.

3.6 $\mathbb{P}$-Amiable Words

To find all words that are $\mathbb{P}$-amiable with a given word, we apply a similar method as described in Sect. 3.5, except instead of finding the Lyndon conjugate of the entered word, we find its projection. Let us demonstrate this using the same word explored in Example 5.

Example 6. Consider $w = abbacc$. Let us find all words that are $\mathbb{P}$-amiable with w using $S = \{a, c\}$. As shown in Example 5, there are three words amiable with w: *baabcc*, *abbcac* and *abbcca*. Now we find the Parikh matrices of the projections of w and these words.

$$\Psi(\pi_S(abbacc)) = \Psi(aacc) = \left\langle \begin{smallmatrix} 2 & 4 \\ & 2 \end{smallmatrix} \right\rangle \qquad \Psi(\pi_S(baabcc)) = \Psi(aacc) = \left\langle \begin{smallmatrix} 2 & 4 \\ & 2 \end{smallmatrix} \right\rangle$$

$$\Psi(\pi_S(abbcac)) = \Psi(acac) = \left\langle \begin{smallmatrix} 2 & 3 \\ & 2 \end{smallmatrix} \right\rangle \qquad \Psi(\pi_S(abbcca)) = \Psi(acca) = \left\langle \begin{smallmatrix} 2 & 2 \\ & 2 \end{smallmatrix} \right\rangle$$

Only one word shares a Parikh and $\mathbb{P}$-Parikh matrix with w. Therefore the word that is $\mathbb{P}$-amiable with w using the set S is *baabcc*.   ◁

As with $\mathbb{L}$-Parikh matrices, since this function uses the same algorithm as the *Amiable Words* function, the time complexity is the same as described previously.

3.7   Is It Parikh?

This function takes a matrix as input and determines if it is the Parikh matrix of a word. Before performing complex operations, we first run some initial tests on the entered matrix to check if it meets some basic necessary conditions for a matrix to be Parikh:

– The matrix is square.
– The diagonal of the matrix only contains 1's.
– There are only zeroes under the diagonal.

– Let $m_{i,j}$ represent the element on the ith row and jth column of a matrix. If $i < j$ then $m_{i+1,j} \times m_{i,j-1} \leq m_{i,j}$.

Note that it was proven in [14] that a matrix must be Parikh if it is of size 3×3 and all four of these points are true. Therefore to reduce computation time, we simply terminate the calculation immediately after these checks if the matrix is of size 3×3, and output that the matrix is Parikh if all four criteria are met, otherwise we output that the matrix is not Parikh.

To determine if a given matrix M of size $(m \times m)$, with $m > 3$, is Parikh, we find the lexicographically smallest word such that the Parikh vector of that word is equal to the 1-diagonal of M. Next, we proceed as with the strategy for *Amiable Words*, see Sect. 3.4. That is, we apply Switch Transformations as long as we can without obtaining fewer 2-letter subwords than the numbers on the 2-diagonal of M. Then we construct the Parikh matrices of all words that are enumerated in this process, and M is Parikh iff it is identical to at least one of these matrices.

Example 7. Consider the matrix $\left\langle \begin{smallmatrix} 1 & 1 & 0 \\ & 2 & 1 \\ & & 1 \end{smallmatrix} \right\rangle$. Let us determine if this matrix is Parikh. First we ensure that the standard criteria of a Parikh matrix have been met. This matrix is square, contains only ones on the diagonal and only zeroes underneath it. Furthermore, there does not exist an element in the upper triangle of the matrix that is greater than the product of the elements to its immediate left and immediately below it. Therefore this matrix could be Parikh.

Next, we consider the lexicographically smallest word with one occurrence of a, two of b and one of c, namely $abbc$. Now we apply Switch Transformations as long as we do not obtain fewer than one ab and one bc. See Fig. 3 for a visualisation. Observe that $\Psi(bcab) = \left\langle \begin{smallmatrix} 1 & 1 & 0 \\ & 2 & 1 \\ & & 1 \end{smallmatrix} \right\rangle$, which is identical to our given matrix, and this allows us to conclude that it is indeed Parikh. This example illustrates that, in the worst case, our approach merely involves constructing the Parikh matrices of the 4 words in our Switch Tree, whereas a brute force method would have had to consider the Parikh matrices of all 12 permutations of $abbc$. ◁

As this algorithm utilises the algorithm discussed in Sect. 3.4, it has asymptotically identical time complexity, namely $O(n!)$.

3.8 Associated Words

The *Associated Words* function works in a very similar way to the *Is It Parikh?* function. Namely, it takes a Parikh matrix as input and performs the same series of tests on it to determine if the matrix firstly meets the given criteria to be Parikh, and secondly if there are any words associated with it. The only difference between these two functions is the output, as it outputs any associated words it finds.

Acknowledgements. The authors wish to thank the anonymous referees for their thorough and helpful comments and suggestions.

References

1. Alazemi, H.M.K., Černý, A.: Several extensions of the Parikh matrix L-morphism. J. Comput. Syst. Sci. **79**, 658–668 (2013)
2. Atanasiu, A.: Parikh matrix mapping and amiability over a ternary alphabet. In: Discrete Mathematics and Computer Science in Memoriam Alexandru Mateescu (1952–2005), pp. 1–12 (2014)
3. Atanasiu, A., Atanasiu, R., Petre, I.: Parikh matrices and amiable words. Theoret. Comput. Sci. **390**, 102–109 (2008)
4. Atanasiu, A., Martín-Vide, C., Mateescu, A.: On the injectivity of the Parikh matrix mapping. Fund. Inform. **49**, 289–299 (2002)
5. Atanasiu, A., Teh, W.C.: A new operator over Parikh languages. Int. J. Found. Comput. Sci. **27**, 757–769 (2016)
6. Bera, S., Mahalingam, K.: Some algebraic aspects of Parikh q-matrices. Int. J. Found. Comput. Sci. **27**, 479–500 (2016)
7. Dick, J., Hutchinson, L.K., Mercaş, R., Reidenbach, D.: Reducing the ambiguity of Parikh matrices. Theoret. Comput. Sci. **860**, 23–40 (2021)
8. Duval, J.P.: Factorizing words over an ordered alphabet. J. Algorithms **4**, 363–381 (1983)
9. Egecioglu, O., Ibarra, O.H.: A matrix Q-analogue of the Parikh map. In: Levy, J.-J., Mayr, E.W., Mitchell, J.C. (eds.) TCS 2004. IIFIP, vol. 155, pp. 125–138. Springer, Boston (2004). https://doi.org/10.1007/1-4020-8141-3_12
10. Fossé, S., Richomme, G.: Some characterizations of Parikh matrix equivalent binary words. Inf. Process. Lett. **92**, 77–82 (2004)
11. Hall, B.C.: Lie Groups, Lie Algebras, and Representations. GTM, vol. 222. Springer, Cham (2015). https://doi.org/10.1007/978-3-319-13467-3
12. Lejeune, M., Rigo, M., Rosenfeld, M.: On the binomial equivalence classes of finite words. Int. J. Algebra Comput. **30**, 1375–1397 (2020)
13. Mahalingam, K., Subramanian, K.G.: Product of Parikh matrices and commutativity. Int. J. Found. Comput. Sci. **23**, 207–223 (2012)
14. Mateescu, A., Salomaa, A.: Matrix indicators for subword occurrences and ambiguity. Int. J. Found. Comput. Sci. **15**, 277–292 (2004)
15. Mateescu, A., Salomaa, A., Salomaa, K., Yu, S.: On an extension of the Parikh mapping. Turku Centre for Computer Science (2000)
16. Mateescu, A., Salomaa, A., Salomaa, K., Yu, S.: A sharpening of the Parikh mapping. RAIRO-Theor. Inf. Appl. **35**, 551–564 (2001)
17. Parikh, R.J.: On context-free languages. J. ACM **13**, 570–581 (1966)
18. Poovanandran, G., Chean Teh, W.: Strong (2·t) and strong (3·t) transformations for strong M-equivalence. Int. J. Found. Comput. Sci. **30**, 719–733 (2019)
19. Salomaa, A., Yu, S.: Subword occurrences, Parikh matrices and Lyndon images. Int. J. Found. Comput. Sci. **21**, 91–111 (2010)
20. Şerbănuţă, T.F.: Extending Parikh matrices. Theoret. Comput. Sci. **310**, 233–246 (2004)
21. Şerbănuţă, V.N.: On Parikh matrices, ambiguity, and prints. Int. J. Found. Comput. Sci. **20**, 151–165 (2009)
22. Strassen, V.: Gaussian elimination is not optimal. Numer. Math. **13**, 354–356 (1969)

Syntax Checking Either Way

Martin Kutrib[1][✉][iD] and Uwe Meyer[2][iD]

[1] Institut für Informatik, Universität Giessen, Arndtstr. 2, 35392 Giessen, Germany
kutrib@informatik.uni-giessen.de
[2] Technische Hochschule Mittelhessen, Wiesenstr. 14, 35390 Giessen, Germany
uwe.meyer@mni.thm.de

Abstract. We consider parsers of deterministic context-free languages and study the sizes of their syntax checking components. More precisely, we allow the input processing from left to right or, alternatively, from right to left, whatever is best for the given language. We establish an infinite sequence of deterministic context-free languages L_k, for $k \geq 1$, such that there is an exponential size trade-off between a deterministic pushdown automaton that reads its input from right to left and another one that reads its input from left to right. Concerning the constructibility of such a parser out of a given deterministic context-free language, it is shown that it is undecidable whether the reversal of a given deterministic context-free language is again deterministic context free. Furthermore, we study the expressive capacity of the family of languages whose reversals are deterministic context free. Finally, we turn to the family of deterministic context-free languages whose reversals are also deterministic context free and collect several of their closure properties.

1 Introduction

In the process of constructing a compiler for programming or other languages a parser has to be built. A parser takes some input text and translates it to some kind of parse tree or abstract syntax tree, while it checks for the correct syntax of the input. It is evident that the size of the parser is one of its most important properties. Since the translation process performed by the parser is often closely linked with the syntax analysis, the size of the component that checks the syntax is dominant.

A first step in this connection is the description of the syntax of the language, which is in most cases deterministic context free. Two standard methods for syntax representation are context-free grammars (the usual approach in compiler construction) and deterministic pushdown automata. But which method can represent the context-free language more succinctly? Does it depend on the language? This question is addressed in [6]. A partial answer is given as follows. For every pair of positive integers $n \geq 2$ and p, there is a language that can be accepted by a real-time deterministic pushdown automaton with n states and p pushdown symbols and size $O(np)$, for which every context-free grammar must have at least n^2p+1 nonterminals and hence must have size at least proportional

© Springer Nature Switzerland AG 2022
P. Caron and L. Mignot (Eds.): CIAA 2022, LNCS 13266, pp. 128–139, 2022.
https://doi.org/10.1007/978-3-031-07469-1_10

to n^2p. It follows that some context-free languages can be defined much more concisely by deterministic pushdown automata than by context-free grammars. These results direct our interest to the pushdown automata or parser.

Two important types of parsers check the syntax of the input in a top-down or bottom-up fashion. These deterministic pushdown automata are based on LL(k) [13] and LR(k) grammars [12]. While even LR(1) grammars characterize the family of deterministic context-free languages, their parsing strategy has an impact on their structure and, thus, on their sizes. In [2] it is shown that there can be exponential differences between the size of an arbitrary deterministic pushdown automaton for a language and the size of any deterministic pushdown automaton which behaves as an LR(1) parser for the same language.

These results raise the question of whether a parser can represent a deterministic context-free language still more succinctly than a grammar when it has to obey the LR(k) strategy. How much larger must a deterministic LL(k) or LR(k) parser be than the context-free grammar it parses? This question is addressed in [16]. Trade-off results concerning the economy of description for parsers when the ability for early error detection varies and for LR(k) grammars when the length of the lookahead k varies are established in [15].

Here we focus on another aspect that may have an impact on the size of deterministic pushdown automata which check the syntax of a deterministic context-free language. In particular, it is well known that the family of deterministic context-free languages is not closed under reversal. The LL(k) as well as the LR(k) parsers read their inputs from left to right. So, what if we allow the input processing from left to right or, alternatively, from right to left, whatever is best for the given language? If we know which direction is better, this seems to be a cheap maneuver from a practical point of view.

The paper is organized as follows. Section 3 is devoted to the question whether the idea to allow the syntax checking either way makes sense at all. In order to answer this question in the affirmative, we present an infinite sequence of deterministic context-free languages L_k, for $k \geq 1$, such that each L_k is accepted by a deterministic pushdown automaton of size $O(2^k \cdot k)$, whereas any deterministic pushdown automaton accepting L_k^R, that is by processing the input from right to left, has size $\Omega(2^{2^k})$. So, we obtain an exponential trade-off. In Sect. 4 we turn to the question for the constructibility of such a parser out of a given deterministic context-free language. Starting with a simpler question one can ask more precisely if it is decidable for a given deterministic context-free language, whether or not its reversal is again deterministic context free? This question is answered negatively. Then we turn to the expressive capacity of the family of languages whose reversals are deterministic context free. We consider the relationships with unambiguous languages, with the family of deterministic context-free languages whose reversals are also deterministic context free, and with further restrictions to languages accepted by one-turn pushdown automata. Finally, in Sect. 6 we collect several closure properties of the family of deterministic context-free languages whose reversals are also deterministic context free.

2 Definitions and Preliminaries

Let Σ^* denote the *set of all words* over the finite alphabet Σ. The *empty word* is denoted by λ, and $\Sigma^+ = \Sigma^* \setminus \{\lambda\}$. The set of words of length at most $k \geq 0$ is denoted by $\Sigma^{\leq k}$. For convenience, we use Σ_λ for $\Sigma \cup \{\lambda\}$. The reversal of a word w is denoted by w^R and for the length of w we write $|w|$. Set inclusion is denoted by $\subseteq$, and strict set inclusion by $\subset$.

A *nondeterministic pushdown automaton* (NPDA, for short) is a system $M = \langle Q, \Sigma, \Gamma, \delta, q_0, \bot, F \rangle$, where Q is a finite set of internal states, Σ is a finite input alphabet, Γ is a finite pushdown alphabet, $q_0 \in Q$ is the initial state, $\bot \in \Gamma$ is a particular pushdown symbol, called the bottom-of-pushdown symbol, $F \subseteq Q$ is the set of accepting states, and δ is a mapping from $Q \times \Sigma_\lambda \times \Gamma$ to finite subsets of $Q \times \Gamma^*$ called the transition function.

A *configuration* of a pushdown automaton is a triple (q, w, γ), where q is the current state, w the unread part of the input, and γ the current content of the pushdown store, the leftmost symbol of γ being the top symbol. If p, q are in Q, a is in Σ_λ, w is in Σ^*, γ and β are in Γ^*, and Z is in Γ, then we write $(q, aw, Z\gamma) \vdash (p, w, \beta\gamma)$, if the pair (p, β) is in $\delta(q, a, Z)$. In order to simplify matters, we require that during any computation the bottom-of-pushdown symbol appears only at the bottom of the pushdown store. Formally, we require that if (p, β) is in $\delta(q, a, Z)$, then either β does not contain $\bot$ or $\beta = \beta'\bot$, where β' does not contain $\bot$, and $Z = \bot$. As usual, the reflexive transitive closure of $\vdash$ is denoted by $\vdash^*$.

The *language accepted* by M with accepting states is

$$L(M) = \{\, w \in \Sigma^* \mid (q_0, w, \bot) \vdash^* (q, \lambda, \gamma), \text{ for some } q \in F \text{ and } \gamma \in \Gamma^* \,\}.$$

Special kinds of NPDAs are *deterministic* and *unambiguous* pushdown automata. A pushdown automaton $M = \langle Q, \Sigma, \Gamma, \delta, q_0, \bot, F \rangle$ is *deterministic* (DPDA) if (i) $\delta(q, a, Z)$ contains at most one element, for all a in Σ_λ, q in Q, and Z in Γ, and (ii) for all q in Q and Z in Γ: if $\delta(q, \lambda, Z)$ is not empty, then $\delta(q, a, Z)$ is empty for all a in Σ. In this case we simply write $\delta(q, a, Z) = (p, \beta)$ instead of $\delta(q, a, Z) = \{(p, \beta)\}$ assuming that the transition function is a mapping $Q \times \Sigma_\lambda \times \Gamma \to Q \times \Gamma^*$. Moreover, the NPDA M is *unambiguous* (UPDA) if for every word $w \in L(M)$ there is at most one accepting computation path, that is, the sequence of configurations seen during an accepting computation on the given word is unique.

NPDAs characterize the family of context-free languages (CFL) defined by context-free grammars. This characterization carries over to UPDAs in the sense that the family of unambiguous context-free languages (UCFL), generated by unambiguous context-free grammars, is equal to the family of languages accepted by UPDAs. Finally, the family of deterministic context-free languages (DCFL) is simply defined to be the family of all languages accepted by DPDAs (or equivalently generated by LR(k) context-free grammars). These three types of devices induce a strict hierarchy of language families [8].

The *size of a system* is measured as the length of its description in some fixed coding alphabet. So, there are only finitely many systems of the same size.

3   Syntax Checking Either Way – Could It Make Sense?

As said before, one of our main interests is the optimization of the resources needed to build a parser for deterministic context-free languages. Particularly, we are interested in the sizes of the parser components that check the syntax of the input. The idea is, for a given deterministic context-free language L, to consider the size of a DPDA that processes the input from left to right, and the size of a DPDA that processes the input from right to left, and to take the more efficient one of both, that is, the smaller one. So, the first DPDA accepts L, while the second DPDA has to accept L^R. Clearly, since the family DCFL is not closed under reversal, this is only possible for deterministic context-free languages whose reversal languages are deterministic context free as well. We denote the family of reversals of deterministic context-free languages by $DCFL^R = \{ L^R \mid L \in DCFL \}$. So, we are interested in the family $RDCFL = DCFL \cap DCFL^R$.

Let us first give evidence that this idea makes sense at all. The following example and proposition provide a language in RDCFL for which the processing of the input in one direction yields an exponentially more succinct DPDA than processing the input in the opposite direction.

Example 1. For any $k \geq 1$, the deterministic context-free language

$$L_k = \{ u\#a^n\#v\#a^n \mid n \geq 1, u \in \{a,b\}^k \cup \{\lambda\}, \text{ and } v \in (\{a,b\}^k)^* u(\{a,b\}^k)^* \}$$

is accepted by a DPDA M_k of size $O(2^k \cdot k)$.

For $u = \lambda$ any input accepted by M_k must have $\#$ as first symbol. For $u \neq \lambda$ each accepted input must have a letter from $\{a,b\}$ as first symbol. So, M_k can deterministically decide which case is. The simulation in the first case is independent of k and takes some fixed number of states.

Next, we construct the part $M_k' = \langle Q, \Sigma, \Gamma, \delta, q_0, \bot, F \rangle$ of M_k that accepts L_k if $u \neq \lambda$. To this end, we set $\Sigma = \{a,b,\#\}$, $\Gamma = \{A, \bot\}$, $F = \{q_{\text{acc}}\}$, and

$$\begin{aligned}
Q = {} & \{ q_w \mid w \in \{a,b\}^{\leq k} \} \cup \{ (q_w, +) \mid w \in \{a,b\}^k \} \\
& \cup \{ (q_w, i, h) \mid w \in \{a,b\}^k, 0 \leq i \leq k-1, h \in \{D, N\} \} \\
& \cup \{ i \mid 0 \leq i \leq k-1 \} \cup \{ q_-, q_{\text{acc}} \}
\end{aligned}$$

and $q_0 = q_\lambda$.

According to the structure of inputs from L_k the DPDA M_k works in four phases. For their implementations the different subsets of Q are used.

In the first phase, M_k gathers the prefix u symbol by symbol, whereby its correct length k is checked. For all $x, y, z \in \{a,b\}$ and all $w' \in \{a,b\}^{\leq k-1}$, $w \in \{a,b\}^k$, and $\hat{w} \in \{a,b\}^{k-1}$ we set:

$$\begin{aligned}
&(1) \quad \delta(q_{w'}, x, \bot) = (q_{w'x}, \bot) \\
&(2) \quad \delta(q_w, \#, \bot) = ((q_w, +), \bot)
\end{aligned}$$

If the length of u is different from k the computation gets stuck in this phase. Otherwise, the second phase starts with state $(q_u, +)$. In the second phase, M_k reads and pushes the following a-factor.

$$(3)\ \delta((q_w,+),a,\perp) = ((q_w,+),A\perp)$$
$$(4)\ \delta((q_w,+),a,A) = ((q_w,+),AA)$$
$$(5)\ \delta((q_w,+),\#,A) = ((q_w,0,D),A)$$

If there is no a after the first #, the computation gets stuck immediately. Otherwise, the third phase starts with state $(q_u,0,D)$ with pushdown content $A^n\perp$. In the third phase, M_k reads the factor v, checks that its length is a multiple of k, and checks whether it contains the factor u at a correct position. To this end, the states of the form (q_w,i,h) are used until the factor u has been detected. Afterwards, the states of the form i are used to check whether the remaining suffix of v has a length that is a multiple of k. While searching for u the states (q_w,i,h) are used as follows. In the first component of the state q_w we encode the word u. But u is rotated by one position in each step. So, the next symbol to be compared is the first symbol in the index. At the beginning and the end of processing a block of k symbols the index is u. The second component i is used to remember the current position in each block. The third component indicates that the checking of the current block has been successful so far. If yes, the component is D. Otherwise, it is set to N. The implementation of the searching for u is as follows.

$$(6)\quad \delta((q_{x\hat{w}},i,D),x,A) = ((q_{\hat{w}x},i+1,D),A) \quad \text{for } 0 \le i \le k-2$$
$$(7)\ \delta((q_{x\hat{w}},k-1,D),x,A) = (0,A)$$
$$(8)\quad \delta((q_{x\hat{w}},i,D),y,A) = ((q_{\hat{w}x},i+1,N),A) \text{ for } \ne y, 0 \le i \le k-2$$
$$(9)\quad \delta((q_{x\hat{w}},i,N),z,A) = ((q_{\hat{w}x},i+1,N),A) \quad \text{for } 0 \le i \le k-2$$
$$(10)\ \delta((q_{x\hat{w}},k-1,D),y,A) = ((q_{\hat{w}x},0,D),A) \quad \text{for } x \ne y$$
$$(11)\ \delta((q_{x\hat{w}},k-1,N),z,A) = ((q_{\hat{w}x},0,D),A)$$

So, if and only if factor u is found at a correct position, in this phase, the computation continues with states of the form i. As long as the search is unsuccessful states of the form (q_w,i,h) are used. In the first situation the length of the remaining suffix of v is checked.

$$(12)\quad \delta(i,x,A) = (i+1,A) \quad \text{for } 0 \le i \le k-2$$
$$(13)\ \delta(k-1,x,A) = (0,A)$$
$$(14)\quad \delta(0,\#,A) = (q_-,A)$$

If no factor u at a correct position is found before the third # appears in the input or if the length of the factor v is not a multiple of k, then the computation gets stuck. Otherwise, the fourth phase starts with state q_-, still with pushdown content $A^n\perp$. In the fourth phase, M_k compares the length of the remaining a-factor with the pushdown content, that is, with the length of the a-factor following the first #.

$$(15)\ \delta(q_-,a,A) = (q_-,\lambda)$$
$$(16)\ \delta(q_-,\lambda,\perp) = (q_{\text{acc}},\perp)$$

So, if there are too less a's in the suffix then the computation ends rejecting in state q_-. If there are too many a's in the suffix, it gets stuck in state q_{acc} but without processing the input entirely and, thus, rejecting. We conclude that the input is accepted if and only if it belongs to L_k.

Finally, we have to estimate the size of M_k. To this end, first we consider the number of states. By adding the sizes of the subsets of Q we obtain $2^{k+1} + 2^k + 2^k \cdot k \cdot 2 + k + 2 \in O(2^k \cdot k)$. Multiplying this number with the number of input symbols, the number of pushdown symbols, the number of final states, and the maximal number of symbols pushed in a single transition does not change the order of magnitude since all these sets are independent of k. Similarly, adding the size of the part of M_k that handles the case $u = \lambda$ does not change the order of magnitude, it is independent of k as well. We conclude that the size of M_k is $O(2^k \cdot k)$. ∎

Clearly, the language L_k^R is deterministic context free. So, the next step is to show a lower bound for the size of DPDAs accepting it.

Proposition 2. *Let $k \geq 1$. Any DPDA that accepts L_k^R is of size $\Omega(2^{2^k})$.*

Proof. Let $M = \langle Q, \Sigma, \Gamma, \delta, q_0, \bot, F \rangle$ be some DPDA accepting L_k^R. It is well known that any DPDA can be converted into an equivalent DPDA whose λ-transitions are all popping from the pushdown. Moreover, this conversion does not increase the size of the DPDA. So, we may safely assume that M has this property.

During the computation of M on input prefixes a^+ no combination of state and content of the pushdown store may appear twice. If

$$(q_0, a^n \#v\#a^n\#u, \bot) \vdash^* (q_1, a^{n-m_1}\#v\#a^n\#u, \gamma_1) \vdash^+ (q_1, a^{n-m_1-m_2}\#v\#a^n\#u, \gamma_1)$$

is the beginning of an accepting computation, then so is

$$(q_0, a^{n-m_2}\#v\#a^n\#u, \bot) \vdash^* (q_1, a^{n-m_1-m_2}\#v\#a^n\#u, \gamma_1),$$

but $a^{n-m_1-m_2}\#v\#a^n\#u$ does not belong to L_k^R. This implies that each height of the pushdown store may appear only finitely often, and thus, that the height increases arbitrarily. So, M runs into a cycle while processing input prefixes a^+, that is, the combination of a state and, for any fixed number h, some h topmost pushdown symbols α appear again and again. To render the cycle more precisely, let $(q, a^x\#v\#a^n\#u, \alpha\gamma)$ be a configuration of the cycle. Then there is a successor configuration with the same combination of state and topmost pushdown symbols $(q, a^{x-y}\#v\#a^n\#u, \alpha\beta)$. We may choose α so that during the computation starting in $(q, a^x\#v\#a^n\#u, \alpha\gamma)$ no symbol of γ is touched, that is, $\alpha\beta = \alpha\gamma'\gamma$. Therefore, the computation continues as $(q, a^{x-y}\#v\#a^n\#u, \alpha\gamma'\gamma) \vdash^+ (q, a^{x-2y}\#v\#a^n\#u, \alpha\gamma'\gamma'\gamma)$.

Now we turn to the input factors a^+ following the v. While M processes these input factors, no combination of state and content of the pushdown store may appear twice. If $(q_2, a^n\#u, \sigma) \vdash^* (q_3, a^{n-m_3}\#u, \sigma_1) \vdash^+ (q_3, a^{n-m_3-m_4}\#u, \sigma_1)$

results in an accepting computation, then so does $(q_2, a^{n-m_4}\#u, \sigma) \vdash^*$ $(q_3, a^{n-m_3-m_4}\#u, \sigma_1)$, but $a^n\#u\#a^{n-m_4}\#u$ does not belong to L_k^R. This implies that each height of the pushdown store may appear only finitely often. Moreover, in any accepting computation the pushdown store has to be decreased until some symbol of γ appears. Otherwise, we could set $u = \lambda$ and increase the number of a's in the prefix by y to drive M through an additional cycle while processing the input prefix. The resulting computation on $a^{n+y}\#v\#a^n\#$ would also be accepting but the input does not belong to L_k^R.

Now let us consider the infinite set of numbers n that drive M through complete cycles while processing the input prefix a^n. That is, there is a fixed state q' reached at the end of a cycle, and we consider the set

$$N = \{\, n \mid (q_0, a^n\#, \bot) \vdash^* (q', \#, \alpha(\gamma')^x\gamma) \text{ for some } x \geq 1 \,\}.$$

Let $N = \{n_1, n_2, n_3, \dots\}$ with $n_i < n_{i+1}$, for $i \geq 1$. Then, for all $v \in (\{a, b\}^k)^*$ and for some $x_i \geq 0$, the beginnings of accepting computations on $a^{n_i}\#v\#a^{n_i}\#u$ and $a^{n_{i+1}}\#v\#a^{n_{i+1}}\#u$ are $(q_0, a^{n_i}\#v\#a^{n_i}\#u, \bot) \vdash^* (q', \#v\#a^{n_i}\#u, \alpha(\gamma')^{x_i}\gamma)$ and $(q_0, a^{n_{i+1}}\#v\#a^{n_{i+1}}\#u, \bot) \vdash^* (q', \#v\#a^{n_{i+1}}\#u, \alpha(\gamma')^{x_i+1}\gamma)$. Next, we consider the configuration in which the first computation touches the topmost symbol of γ: $(q', \#v\#a^{n_i}\#u, \alpha(\gamma')^{x_i}\gamma) \vdash^* (q_v, w\#u, \gamma)$, where q_v may depend on v, and w is of the form a^*. Since M is deterministic, the second computation continues as $(q', \#v\#a^{n_{i+1}}\#u, \alpha(\gamma')^{x_i+1}\gamma) \vdash^* (q_v, a^{n_{i+1}-n_i}w\#u, \gamma'\gamma)$. Note that γ' and γ are fixed and, thus, are independent of v.

Next, we split each v into factors of length k and associate v with the subset $B_v \subseteq \{a, b\}^k$ of these factors. Finally, we claim that $q_v = q_{v'}$ if and only if $B_v = B_{v'}$. Assume contrarily that $q_v = q_{v'}$ and $B_v \neq B_{v'}$. Without loss of generality there is some factor $z \in B_v \setminus B_{v'}$. Since the computation $(q_0, a^{n_i}\#v\#a^{n_i}\#z, \bot) \vdash^* (q_v, w\#z, \gamma)$ continues accepting, the computation $(q_0, a^{n_i}\#v'\#a^{n_i}\#z, \bot) \vdash^* (q_v = q_{v'}, w\#z, \gamma)$ continues accepting as well. However, since $z \notin B_{v'}$ it is not a factor of v' and, thus, $a^{n_i}\#v'\#a^{n_i}\#z$ does not belong to L_k^R. The contradiction shows the claim.

Since there are 2^{2^k} subsets of $\{a, b\}^k$ we conclude that M has $\Omega(2^{2^k})$ states which implies that it is of size $\Omega(2^{2^k})$.   □

Though they provide just a lower bound, the previous example and the proposition already show, in fact, that the processing of the input from right to left makes sense. It can be done with an exponentially more succinct machinery.

4   Decidability – Why We Need Man-Made Proofs

We have already seen that syntax checking either way can help to save resources. This immediately raises the natural question for the constructibility of such a parser out of a given deterministic context-free language. Starting with a simpler question one can ask more precisely if it is decidable for a given deterministic context-free language, whether or not its reversal is again deterministic context free? The next theorem answers this question negatively.

In the following, we will use a reduction of a problem for Turing machines. To this end, histories of Turing machine computations are encoded into strings [9]. It suffices to consider deterministic Turing machines with one single tape and one single read-write head. Without loss of generality and for technical reasons, we assume that the Turing machines can halt only after an odd number of moves, accept by halting, make at least three moves, and cannot print blanks. A *valid computation* is a string built from a sequence of configurations that are passed through at the beginning of a computation.

Let Q be the state set of some Turing machine M, where q_0 is the initial state, T is the tape alphabet ($T \cap Q = \emptyset$) containing the blank symbol, and $\Sigma \subset T$ is the input alphabet. Then a configuration of M can be written as a word of the form T^*QT^* such that $t_1 t_2 \cdots t_i q t_{i+1} \cdots t_n$ is used to express that M is in state q, scanning tape symbol t_{i+1}, and t_1, t_2 to t_n is the support of the tape inscription. For the purpose of the following, valid computations VALC(M) are now defined as strings of the form $\$w_1\$w_2^R\$w_3\$w_4^R\$\cdots\$w_{2n-1}\$w_{2n}^R\$$, where $\$ \notin T \cup Q$, $w_i \in T^*QT^*$ are configurations of M, w_1 is an initial configuration of the form $q_0\Sigma^*$, and w_{i+1} is the successor configuration of w_i.

We consider the following decomposition of VALC(M): VALC$_1(M)$ is the set of strings of the form $\$w_1\$w_2^R\$\cdots\$w_{2n-1}\$w_{2n}^R\$$, where w_1 is an initial configuration and w_{2i+1} is the successor configuration of w_{2i}, for $1 \leq i \leq n-1$. VALC$_2(M)$ is the set of strings of the form $\$w_1\$w_2^R\$\cdots\$w_{2n-1}\$w_{2n}^R\$$, where w_1 is an initial configuration and w_{2i} is the successor configuration of w_{2i-1}, for $1 \leq i \leq n$.

Clearly, VALC$_1(M)$ and VALC$_2(M)$ as well as VALC$_1(M)^R$ and VALC$_2(M)^R$ are deterministic context-free languages, such that their deterministic pushdown automata can effectively be constructed from M.

Theorem 3. *It is undecidable whether or not the reversal of a given deterministic context-free language is again a deterministic context-free language.*

Proof. We will show the theorem by reduction of the halting problem for Turing machines on a given finite set of inputs to the problem in question. That is, given a Turing machine M and a finite set of inputs I, determine whether M halts on all $w \in I$. So, let M' be an arbitrary Turing machine of the type considered here. First, M' is modified to M as follows. Basically, M simulates M', but after having simulated one step, it marks the current position on the tape, moves to the first blank on the right, rewrites the blank by some fixed new tape symbol, moves back to the marked tape position, removes the mark, and simulates the next step, and so on. The new tape symbol plays the role of the blank symbol. Clearly, M halts on some input w if and only if M' halts on w. The effect of the modification is that during a non-halting computation the length of the support of the configurations increases arbitrarily. Now, let M have state set Q, tape alphabet T, input alphabet Σ, and let $I = \{v_1, v_2, \ldots, v_k\} \subset \Sigma^*$ with $k \geq 1$ be a finite set. Furthermore, let $\tilde{A}_1$ and $\tilde{A}_2$ be the two deterministic pushdown automata constructed from M that accept the languages VALC$_1(M)^R$ respectively VALC$_2(M)^R$. Since deterministic context-free languages are closed under intersection with regular languages, we can construct the two deterministic pushdown automata A_1 and A_2 that accept $L_1 = \mathrm{VALC}_1(M)^R \cap ((T \cup Q \cup \{\$\})^* \$ I q_0 \$)$ respectively $L_2 = \mathrm{VALC}_2(M)^R \cap ((T \cup Q \cup \{\$\})^* \$ I q_0 \$)$. We take two new symbols a and b and construct a deterministic pushdown automaton A that accepts the language $L = aL_1 \cup bL_2$.

We consider $L^R = L_1^R a \cup L_2^R b$ and claim that L^R is deterministic context free if and only if M accepts all inputs from I.

First, we consider the case that M accepts all inputs from I. The intersection $L_1^R \cap L_2^R$ contains exactly the words that encode the beginnings of computations of M on inputs from I. Since M halts on all inputs from I, there exists a longest word u such that there is no word of length $|u| + 1$ which is a prefix in both languages L_1^R and L_2^R. So, by inspecting the first $|u| + 1$ input symbols a deterministic pushdown automaton can decide to which language the input may still possibly belong. We conclude that there exists a deterministic pushdown automaton that accepts L^R.

Second, we consider the case that there is at least one input $v \in I$ such that M does not halt on input v. Then the computation of M on v implies that $L_1^R \cap L_2^R$ is infinite. In contrast to the assertion, we assume that L^R is accepted by some deterministic pushdown automaton B.

It is known that, by applying the technique of predicting machines [11], B can effectively be converted into a deterministic pushdown automaton that accepts immediately upon consuming the last input symbol, without subsequent λ-steps (see, for example, Exercise 10.7 in [11]). So, we safely may assume that B has this property. Since any word in L^R either ends with a or b and both symbols cannot appear anywhere else in an accepted word, we can modify B to B' as follows. Basically, B' simulates B. However, whenever B reads an a or a b and, thus, performs its final transition, the deterministic pushdown automaton B' does the following. It enters an accepting state and halts if and only if B would enter an accepting state on input symbols a *and* b. Otherwise, B' enters a rejecting state and halts. In this way, we have constructed a deterministic pushdown automaton B' that accepts $(L_1^R \cap L_2^R)\{a, b\}$.

Since deterministic context-free languages (for example represented by deterministic pushdown automata) are effectively closed under right quotient with regular languages, from B' we effectively obtain a deterministic pushdown automaton accepting $L_1^R \cap L_2^R$. However, since $L_1^R \cap L_2^R$ is infinite, a simple application of the pumping lemma for context-free languages shows that $L_1^R \cap L_2^R$ is not even context free.

From the contradiction we deduce that L^R cannot be accepted by any deterministic pushdown automaton if M does not accept all inputs from I.

Altogether we have that L is deterministic context free, while L^R is deterministic context free if and only if M halts on all inputs from I. Since the latter is undecidable for Turing machines the theorem follows.   □

Theorem 3 implies that one needs a representation for both deterministic context-free languages L and L^R in order to deal with syntax checking either way. Moreover, even if it exists the representation of L^R by a deterministic pushdown automaton cannot be obtained algorithmically out of L.

5   Expressive Capacity of DCFL^R

By the results of the previous sections there is a particular interest in the language family RDCFL = DCFL $\cap$ DCFL^R. While the family DCFL is well understood, only little is known about the family DCFL^R. So, here we will first turn to examine its expressive capacity. The relationships between several language families are depicted in Fig. 1 at the end of the section.

Lemma 4. *The family* DCFL $\cup$ DCFL^R *is properly included in* UCFL.

This gives an upper bound for the expressive capacity of DCFL^R. However, this upper bound is somehow uncomfortable since it is undecidable whether a given unambiguous context-free grammar or UPDA generates or accepts a deterministic context-free language [17]. Moreover, to our knowledge, the problem to decide regularity for UPDAs is an open problem.

We turn to a slightly generalized point of view. It is known that the family of deterministic context-free languages is characterized by the class of LR(k) grammars, for all $k \geq 1$ [12]. The languages accepted by an LR(k) parser with a finite number of runs, or equivalently by a finite cascade of possibly different LR(k) parsers, can be defined as the finite union of the languages accepted in each single run, or equivalently by the finite union of languages from DCFL. In other words, is the family DCFL^R included in the finite union closure of DCFL?

Proposition 5. *The families of languages* DCFL^R *and the finite union closure of* DCFL *are incomparable. In particular, there is a deterministic context-free language whose reversal cannot be represented as finite union of deterministic context-free languages.*

Proof. Since the family DCFL is not closed under reversal, there is a language in DCFL $\setminus$ DCFL^R. For the converse direction we consider the language

$$L = (\{ ca^n b^n \mid n \geq 0 \} \cup \{ da^n b^{2n} \mid n \geq 0 \})^*$$

as witness. Clearly, L belongs to DCFL.

In [14] the finite union closure of DCFL has been characterized by pushdown automata with limited nondeterminism. In particular, the family of languages accepted by pushdown automata that perform a constant number of guesses on each input coincides with the finite union closure of DCFL. However, in [5] it has been shown that any pushdown automaton accepting L^R requires a linear amount of nondeterminism (there unessentially only one letter is used instead of c and d). So, L^R cannot be represented as finite union of deterministic context-free languages. $\square$

Next, we consider a restricted version of pushdown automata. Though deterministic pushdown automata are already parsing rapidly in linear time, the additional property of being finite-turn can make them faster. A nondeterministic pushdown automaton is said to be finite turn if the height of the pushdown store alternatively increases and decreases at most a fixed bounded number

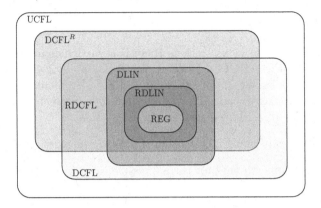

Fig. 1. Hierarchical structure of language families.

of times in any computation [4]. Such pushdown automata can reject inputs faster because the computation can be halted as soon as it exceeds the fixed bound of alternations. The families of languages accepted by finite-turn pushdown automata are also characterized, for example, by certain type of context-free grammars. Of particular interest are one-turn pushdown automata that are characterized by linear context-free grammars. The corresponding family of languages is denoted by LIN. The deterministic counterpart of one-turn pushdown automata is characterized by linear context-free grammars restricted by an LR(1) condition [10]. The corresponding family of languages is denoted by DLIN. In connection with syntax checking either way we are mainly interested in the family RDLIN = DLIN $\cap$ DLIN^R. It is well known that it is not enough to consider the intersection of LIN and DCFL to obtain DLIN [1]. We provide an example for this fact whose languages are utilized as witnesses below.

Example 6. The language $L = \{ a^k b^l a^m b^n \mid k,l,m,n \geq 1 \text{ and } k \neq l \} \cup \{ a^k b^l a^m b^n \# \mid k,l,m,n \geq 1 \text{ and } m \neq n \}$ clearly belongs to LIN $\cap$ DCFL but does not belong to DLIN. ∎

The existence of a language in DLIN whose reversal is not deterministic context free, that is, it does not belong to RDCFL is known from [3]. This shows one direction of the next proposition which justifies that we have to consider RDLIN for the purpose of syntax checking either way.

Proposition 7. *The families* DLIN *and* RDCFL *are incomparable.*

Finally, the family RDLIN can be placed into the hierarchy of languages as follows.

Proposition 8. *The family* RDLIN *is properly included in the intersection* RDCFL $\cap$ DLIN.

6   Closure Properties of RDCFL

Finally, we are going to collect several closure properties of the family RDCFL. The properties are summarized and compared with those of DCFL in Table 1.

Table 1. Closure properties of the language families DCFL and RDCFL.

Family	$-$	$\cup$	$\cap$	$\cap_{\text{REG}}$	$\cdot$	$*$	R	$h_{\text{len.pres.}}$	h^{-1}	/REG
DCFL	✓	✗	✗	✓	✗	✗	✗	✗	✓	✓
RDCFL	✓	✗	✗	✓	✗	✗	✓	✗	✓	✗

References

1. Autebert, J.-M., Berstel, J., Boasson, L.: Context-free languages and pushdown automata. In: Rozenberg, G., Salomaa, A. (eds.) Handbook of Formal Languages, pp. 111–174. Springer, Heidelberg (1997). https://doi.org/10.1007/978-3-642-59136-5_3
2. Geller, M.M., Hunt III, H.B., Szymanski, T.G., Ullman, J.D.: Economy of description by parsers, DPDA's, and PDA's. Theor. Comput. Sci. **4**, 143–153 (1977)
3. Ginsburg, S., Greibach, S.A.: Deterministic context-free languages. Inform. Control **9**, 620–648 (1966)
4. Ginsburg, S., Spanier, E.H.: Finite-turn pushdown automata. SIAM J. Contr. **4**, 429–453 (1966)
5. Goldstine, J., Leung, H., Wotschke, D.: Measuring nondeterminism in pushdown automata. J. Comput. Syst. Sci. **71**, 440–466 (2005)
6. Goldstine, J., Price, J.K., Wotschke, D.: A pushdown automaton or a context-free grammar - which is more economical? Theor. Comput. Sci. **18**, 33–40 (1982)
7. Greibach, S.A.: The unsolvability of the recognition of linear context-free languages. J. ACM **13**, 582–587 (1966)
8. Harrison, M.A.: Introduction to Formal Language Theory. Addison-Wesley, Boston (1978)
9. Hartmanis, J.: Context-free languages and Turing machine computations. In: Proceedings Symposia in Applied Mathematics, vol. 19, pp. 42–51 (1967)
10. Holzer, M., Lange, K.-J.: On the complexities of linear LL(1) and LR(1) grammars. In: Ésik, Z. (ed.) FCT 1993. LNCS, vol. 710, pp. 299–308. Springer, Heidelberg (1993). https://doi.org/10.1007/3-540-57163-9_25
11. Hopcroft, J.E., Ullman, J.D.: Introduction to Automata Theory, Languages, and Computation. Addison-Wesley (1979)
12. Knuth, D.E.: On the translation of languages from left to right. Inform. Control **8**, 607–639 (1965)
13. Knuth, D.E.: Top-down syntax analysis. Acta Inform. **1**, 79–110 (1971)
14. Kutrib, M., Malcher, A.: Context-dependent nondeterminism for pushdown automata. Theor. Comput. Sci. **376**, 101–111 (2007)
15. Leung, H., Wotschke, D.: On the size of parsers and LR(k)-grammars. Theor. Comput. Sci. **242**, 59–69 (2000)
16. Ukkonen, E.: Lower bounds on the size of deterministic parsers. J. Comput. Syst. Sci. **26**, 153–170 (1983)
17. Valiant, L.G.: A note on the succinctness of descriptions of deterministic languages. Inform. Control **32**, 139–145 (1976)

On the Power of Pushing or Stationary Moves for Input-Driven Pushdown Automata

Martin Kutrib[(✉)], Andreas Malcher, and Matthias Wendlandt

Institut für Informatik, Universität Giessen, Arndtstr. 2, 35392 Giessen, Germany
{kutrib,andreas.malcher,matthias.wendlandt}@informatik.uni-giessen.de

Abstract. Input-driven pushdown automata (IDPDAs) are pushdown automata where the next action on the pushdown store (push, pop, nothing) is solely governed by the input symbol. Nowadays such devices are usually defined such that every push operation pushes exactly one additional symbol on the pushdown store and, in addition, the devices work in real time so that stationary moves are not allowed. Here, we relax this strong definition and consider IDPDAs that may push more than one symbol in one step (push-IDPDA) or may perform stationary moves (stat-IDPDA). We study the computational power of the extended variants both in the deterministic and nondeterministic case, we investigate several decidability questions for the new automata classes, and we obtain useful interesting representations by inverse homomorphisms.

1   Introduction

Input-driven pushdown automata (IDPDAs) have been introduced in [11] and their motivation stems from the search for an upper bound for the space needed for the recognition of deterministic context-free languages. IDPDAs are a subclass of pushdown automata that work in real time and, more importantly, in an input-driven way. That is, no moves on empty input are allowed, and the actions on the pushdown store are dictated by the input symbols. The basic results in [11] and its follow-up papers [3,7] are the equivalence of nondeterministic and deterministic models and the proof that the membership problem is solvable in logarithmic space.

Input-driven pushdown automata have been revisited in [1,2], where such devices are called visibly pushdown automata or nested word automata. Some of the results comprise descriptional complexity aspects for the determinization as well as closure properties and decidability questions which turned out to be similar to those of finite automata. Further aspects such as the minimization of IDPDAs and a comparison with other subfamilies of deterministic context-free languages have been studied in [5,6]. A recent survey with many valuable references on complexity aspects of input-driven pushdown automata may be found in [12]. An extension of input-driven pushdown automata towards pushdown automata sychronized by a finite transducer has been discussed in [4].

P. Caron and L. Mignot (Eds.): CIAA 2022, LNCS 13266, pp. 140–151, 2022.
https://doi.org/10.1007/978-3-031-07469-1_11

The renewed interest in input-driven pushdown automata has also affected the definition of the devices. While in the early papers IDPDAs are defined as ordinary real-time pushdown automata whose behavior on the pushdown is solely driven by the input symbols, the definition in [1] stipulates that at most one symbol is pushed in a single push operation. Moreover, instead of getting stuck when popping from the empty pushdown it is allowed to pop from the empty pushdown by simply defining that popping from the empty pushdown results in an empty pushdown. The latter restriction has been given up in [9] where so-called *digging input-driven pushdown automata* have been introduced and studied in depth. It turned out that digging IDPDAs have similar properties as IDPDAs with regard to determinization, closure properties, and decidability questions.

In this paper, our goal is to consider variants of input-driven pushdown automata whose definition is closer to classical deterministic pushdown automata. To this end, we will further relax the restrictions of allowing only at most one symbol to be pushed in a single step and the processing of the input in real time. In detail, we consider *pushing input-driven pushdown automata* (push-IDPDAs) that are allowed to push more than one symbol in a single step. Moreover, to relax the real-time condition we consider *stationary input-driven pushdown automata* (stat-IDPDAs) where the input symbols still dictate which operation on the pushdown has to be carried out, but the transition functions determine whether the head remains on the current input symbol or moves to the right as usual. As a first result, which is in contrast to classical IDPDAs and digging IDPDAs, we obtain the nondeterministic push-IDPDAs and stat-IDPDAs are computationally stronger than their deterministic counterparts. In addition, it can be shown both in the deterministic and nondeterministic case that stat-IDPDAs are computationally stronger than push-IDPDAs which in turn are computationally stronger than classical IDPDAs. On the other hand, classical deterministic and nondeterministic pushdown automata are computationally stronger than the corresponding stat-IDPDAs. Another interesting result is that the introduced variants are well-suited for a representation by inverse homomorphism. In detail, it is shown that there is a homomorphism h_r such that every context-free language L can be represented as the inverse homomorphic image $h_r^{-1}(L') = L$ of a language L' accepted by a nondeterministic push-IDPDA. Using the same homomorphism it is also possible to obtain similar characterizations of the real-time deterministic context-free languages by deterministic push-IDPDAs and of general deterministic context-free languages by deterministic stat-IDPDAs. These characterizations can in particular be used to obtain undecidability results. It turns out that the inclusion problem for two deterministic push-IDPDAs with compatible signatures is not even semidecidable, whereas the problem is decidable for classical IDPDAs. Hence, the restriction to allow at most one symbol to be pushed is essential in order to get decidability. In the non-deterministic case, we can show that the questions of universality, equivalence, and regularity are not semidecidable for push-IDPDAs and stat-IDPDAs.

2 Definitions and Preliminaries

Let Σ^* denote the set of all words over the finite alphabet Σ. The *empty word* is denoted by λ, and $\Sigma^+ = \Sigma^* \setminus \{\lambda\}$. The set of words of length at most $n \geq 0$ is denoted by $\Sigma^{\leq n}$. The *reversal* of a word w is denoted by w^R. For the *length* of w we write $|w|$. We use $\subseteq$ for *inclusions* and $\subset$ for *strict inclusions*. We write $|S|$ for the cardinality of a set S. We say that two language families $\mathscr{L}_1$ and $\mathscr{L}_2$ are *incomparable* if $\mathscr{L}_1$ is not a subset of $\mathscr{L}_2$ and vice versa.

A classical pushdown automaton is called input-driven if the next input symbol defines the next action on the pushdown store, that is, pushing a symbol onto the pushdown store, popping a symbol from the pushdown store, or changing the state without modifying the pushdown store. To this end, the input alphabet Σ is partitioned into the sets Σ_D, Σ_R, and Σ_N, that control the actions push (D), pop (R), and state change only (N). However, if the next input symbol forces the input-driven pushdown automaton to pop a symbol from the empty pushdown then the computation does not get stuck but continues with an empty pushdown. Moreover, an input-driven pushdown automaton always works in real-time, that is, it is forced to move its input head in each step. Finally, an input-driven pushdown automaton must not push more than one symbol in a single step.

Definition 1. *A nondeterministic input-driven pushdown automaton (NIDPDA) is a system $M = \langle Q, \Sigma, \Gamma, q_0, F, \bot, \delta_D, \delta_R, \delta_N \rangle$, where Q is the finite set of internal states, Σ is the finite set of input symbols partitioned into the sets Σ_D, Σ_R, and Σ_N, Γ is the finite set of pushdown symbols, $q_0 \in Q$ is the initial state, $F \subseteq Q$ is the set of accepting states, $\bot \notin \Gamma$ is the empty-pushdown symbol, δ_D is the partial transition function mapping $Q \times \Sigma_D \times \Gamma$ to the subsets of $Q \times \{\, \text{push}(x) \mid x \in \Gamma^2 \,\}$, and $Q \times \Sigma_D \times \{\bot\}$ to the subsets of $Q \times \{\, \text{push}(x) \mid x \in \Gamma \,\}$, δ_R is the partial transition function mapping $Q \times \Sigma_R \times (\Gamma \cup \{\bot\})$ to the subsets of Q, δ_N is the partial transition function mapping $Q \times \Sigma_N \times (\Gamma \cup \{\bot\})$ to the subsets of $Q \times \{\, \text{top}(x) \mid x \in \Gamma \cup \{\bot\} \,\}$, where $(q', \text{top}(\bot)) \in \delta_N(q, a, z)$ if and only if $z = \bot$.*

A *configuration* of an NIDPDA $M = \langle Q, \Sigma, \Gamma, q_0, F, \bot, \delta_D, \delta_R, \delta_N \rangle$ is a triple (q, w, s), where $q \in Q$ is the current state, $w \in \Sigma^*$ is the unread part of the input, and $s \in \Gamma^*$ denotes the current pushdown content, where the leftmost symbol is at the top of the pushdown store. The *initial configuration* for an input string w is set to (q_0, w, λ). During the course of its computation, M runs through a sequence of configurations. One step from a configuration to its successor configuration is denoted by $\vdash$. Let $q, q' \in Q$, $a \in \Sigma$, $w \in \Sigma^*$, $z, z', z'' \in \Gamma$, and $s \in \Gamma^*$. We set

1. $(q, aw, zs) \vdash (q', w, z'z''s)$, if $a \in \Sigma_D$ and $(q', \text{push}(z'z'')) \in \delta_D(q, a, z)$,
2. $(q, aw, \lambda) \vdash (q', w, z')$, if $a \in \Sigma_D$ and $(q', \text{push}(z')) \in \delta_D(q, a, \bot)$,
3. $(q, aw, zs) \vdash (q', w, s)$, if $a \in \Sigma_R$ and $q' \in \delta_R(q, a, z)$,
4. $(q, aw, \lambda) \vdash (q', w, \lambda)$, if $a \in \Sigma_R$ and $q' \in \delta_R(q, a, \bot)$,
5. $(q, aw, zs) \vdash (q', w, z's)$, if $a \in \Sigma_N$ and $(q', \text{top}(z')) \in \delta_N(q, a, z)$,
6. $(q, aw, \lambda) \vdash (q', w, \lambda)$, if $a \in \Sigma_N$ and $(q', \text{top}(\bot)) \in \delta_N(q, a, \bot)$.

So, whenever the pushdown store is empty, the successor configuration is computed by the transition functions with the special empty-pushdown symbol $\perp$. As usual, we define the reflexive and transitive closure of $\vdash$ by $\vdash^*$.

Next, we turn to the variants of NIDPDAs that are closer to classical deterministic pushdown automata having the property that the next input symbol defines the next action on the pushdown store. First, we consider the variant that may push more than one symbol in a single step.

An input-driven pushdown automaton is a *pushing input-driven pushdown automaton* (push-NIDPDA) if its transition function δ_D maps $Q \times \Sigma_D \times \Gamma$ to the finite subsets of $Q \times \{\, \mathtt{push}(x) \mid x \in \Gamma^+\Gamma \,\}$, and $Q \times \Sigma_D \times \{\perp\}$ to the finite subsets of $Q \times \{\, \mathtt{push}(x) \mid x \in \Gamma^+ \,\}$.

Second, we consider the variant that is not forced to work in real time. To this end, it must be possible to keep the input head at its current position. Since λ-steps are somehow in conflict with the idea that the input symbol defines the action on the pushdown store, we consider stationary moves. So, an input-driven pushdown automaton is a *stationary input-driven pushdown automaton* (stat-NIDPDA) if its transition functions δ_D, δ_R, and δ_N result in additional components from $\{0, 1\}$. These components determine if the head moves to the right (1) as usual, or if it resides stationary on the current input symbol (0). In the second case the symbol is read again in the next step. This implies that the action on the pushdown store dictated by this symbol is applied again. The relation $\vdash$ is straightforwardly extended to cover these cases.

Finally, some variant of input-driven pushdown automaton is said to be deterministic (IDPDA, push-IDPDA, respectively stat-IDPDA) if $|\delta_x(q, a, z)| \leq 1$ for $x \in \{D, N, R\}$ and all $q \in Q$, $a \in \Sigma_x$, and $z \in \Gamma \cup \{\perp\}$.

The language accepted by some variant of input-driven pushdown automaton M is the set $L(M)$ of words for which there exists some computation beginning in the initial configuration and ending in a configuration in which the whole input is read and an accepting state is entered. Formally:

$$L(M) = \{\, w \in \Sigma^* \mid (q_0, w, \lambda) \vdash^* (q, \lambda, s) \text{ with } q \in F, s \in \Gamma^* \,\}.$$

In general, the family of all languages accepted by automata of some type X will be denoted by $\mathscr{L}(X)$.

Some properties of language families implied by classes of input-driven pushdown automata may depend on whether all automata involved share the same partition of the input alphabet. For easier writing, we call the partition of an input alphabet a *signature*, and say that two signatures $\Sigma = \Sigma_D \cup \Sigma_R \cup \Sigma_N$ and $\Sigma' = \Sigma'_D \cup \Sigma'_R \cup \Sigma'_N$ are *compatible* if and only if

$$\bigcup_{j \in \{D,R,N\}} (\Sigma_j \setminus \Sigma'_j) \cap \Sigma' = \emptyset \quad \text{and} \quad \bigcup_{j \in \{D,R,N\}} (\Sigma'_j \setminus \Sigma_j) \cap \Sigma = \emptyset.$$

In order to clarify these notions, we continue with an example.

Example 2. The language $L = \{\, a^n b^l c^m d^n \mid l, m, n \geq 0 \text{ and } l \geq m \,\}$ is accepted by the stat-IDPDA $M = \langle Q, \Sigma, \Gamma, q_0, F, \perp, \delta_D, \delta_R, \delta_N \rangle$ with the state set $Q' = \{q_0, q_a, q_b, r_b, q_c, r_c, q_d, q_s, q_+, q_-\}$, $\Sigma_D = \{a, b\}$, $\Sigma_R = \{c, d\}$, $\Sigma_N = \emptyset$, the set of pushdown symbols $\Gamma = \{A, A', B\}$, the set of accepting states $F = \{q_0, q_+, r_b, r_c\}$, and the transition functions specified as:

(1) $\delta_D(q_0, a, \bot) = (q_a, \text{push}(A'), 1)$

(2) $\delta_D(q_0, b, \bot) = (r_b, \text{push}(B), 1)$

(3) $\delta_R(q_0, c, \bot) = (q_-, 1)$

(4) $\delta_R(q_0, d, \bot) = (q_-, 1)$

(5) $\delta_D(q_a, a, A') = (q_a, \text{push}(AA'), 1)$

(6) $\delta_D(q_a, a, A) = (q_a, \text{push}(AA), 1)$

(7) $\delta_D(q_a, b, A') = (q_b, \text{push}(BA'), 1)$

(8) $\delta_D(q_a, b, A) = (q_b, \text{push}(BA), 1)$

(9) $\delta_R(q_a, d, A') = (q_+, 1)$

(10) $\delta_R(q_a, d, A) = (q_d, 1)$

(11) $\delta_D(q_b, b, B) = (q_b, \text{push}(BB), 1)$

(12) $\delta_R(q_b, c, B) = (q_c, 1)$

(13) $\delta_R(q_b, d, B) = (q_s, 0)$

(14) $\delta_R(q_c, c, B) = (q_c, 1)$

(15) $\delta_R(q_c, d, B) = (q_s, 0)$

(16) $\delta_R(q_c, d, A') = (q_+, 1)$

(17) $\delta_R(q_c, d, A) = (q_d, 1)$

(18) $\delta_R(q_d, d, A) = (q_d, 1)$

(19) $\delta_R(q_d, d, A') = (q_+, 1)$

(20) $\delta_R(q_s, d, B) = (q_s, 0)$

(21) $\delta_R(q_s, d, A') = (q_+, 1)$

(22) $\delta_R(q_s, d, A) = (q_d, 1)$

(23) $\delta_D(r_b, b, B) = (r_b, \text{push}(BB), 1)$

(24) $\delta_R(r_b, c, B) = (r_c, 1)$

(25) $\delta_R(r_c, c, B) = (r_c, 1)$

At the beginning of the computation three cases can be distinguished. First, if the input is empty, M accepts in state q_0. The second case is that there is some a in the input, that is, $n \geq 1$ (Transition (1)). In the third case, the first input symbol is a b, that is, $n = 0$ (Transition (2)). If the first input symbol is c, the condition $l \geq m$ is violated and the computation blocks rejecting in state q_- (Transition (3)). Similarly, if the first input symbol is d, the number of d's is not equal to the number of a's and the computation blocks rejecting in state q_- (Transition (4)).

In the third case the computation continues in states r_b and r_c by applying Transitions (23–25). Both states are accepting and the computation does not block as long as the number of c's does not exceed the number of b's. Should this happen, the computation blocks without having processed the input entirely and, thus, rejects.

The details of the second case are omitted here.   ∎

3   Homomorphic Reduction

In [10] the family of context-free languages is characterized by the closure of $\mathscr{L}(\text{IDPDA})$ under λ-free homomorphisms. Such results open the possibility to characterize certain language families by, in some sense, simpler ones and some kind of operations. Besides they shed some light on the structure of the family itself, they may be used as powerful reduction tool in order to simplify some proofs or constructions.

Here we turn to show that all context-free languages can be represented as preimages of languages from $\mathscr{L}(\text{push-NIDPDA})$ under a simple injective homomorphism. Similarly, the family of deterministic context-free languages can be represented as preimages of languages from $\mathscr{L}(\text{stat-IDPDA})$ and the family of deterministic real-time context-free languages can be represented as preimages of languages from $\mathscr{L}$(push-IDPDA). Let Σ be some alphabet and # be a fresh symbol. Then we define the homomorphism $h_r \colon \Sigma^* \to (\Sigma \cup \{\#\})^*$ as $h_r(a) = a\#^2$, for all $a \in \Sigma$. Clearly, h_r depends on Σ but it is always clear from the context which Σ is meant.

Theorem 3. *Let $L \subseteq \Sigma^*$ be accepted by some deterministic real-time pushdown automaton M. Then there exists a push-IDPDA M' such that $L = h_r^{-1}(L(M'))$.*

Let $L \subseteq \Sigma^*$ be accepted by some nondeterministic pushdown automaton M. Then there exists a push-NIDPDA M' such that $L = h_r^{-1}(L(M'))$.

Next, we turn to involve λ-transitions of the deterministic pushdown automaton. Even if we may assume that all these λ-transitions are pop moves, it may happen that the number of consecutive λ-transitions in some computation exceeds any fixed constant. So, we cannot provide enough # symbols to simulate them. Instead we are going to use stationary moves. However, the construction is more involved since a possible sequence of λ-transitions must be simulated on an input symbol # and, thus, M' has to be able to predict that M would perform λ-transitions. To this end, in certain situations the topmost pushdown symbol unequal to d has to be stored into the states.

Theorem 4. *Let $L \subseteq \Sigma^*$ be accepted by some deterministic pushdown automaton M. Then there exists a stat-IDPDA M' such that $L = h_r^{-1}(L(M'))$.*

Proof. Let language L be given by a deterministic pushdown automaton $M = \langle Q, \Sigma, \Gamma, p, F, \triangle, \delta \rangle$. As in the proof of Theorem 3 let M never remove or change the bottom-of-pushdown symbol at the bottom of the pushdown, nor push the bottom-of-pushdown symbol anywhere else in the pushdown. Moreover, we may assume that in every step M adds at most one symbol to the pushdown store. So, δ maps $Q \times (\Sigma \cup \{\lambda\}) \times (\Gamma \cup \{\triangle\})$ to $Q \times (\Gamma \cup \{\triangle\})^{\leq 2}$ obeying the restrictions concerning $\triangle$. Additionally, we may assume that all λ-transitions of M are popping (see, for example, Exercise 10.2 in [8]). We construct a stat-IDPDA $M' = \langle Q', \Sigma \cup \{\#\}, \Gamma \cup \{d, \triangle\}, p_\triangle, F', \perp, \delta_D, \delta_R, \delta_N \rangle$ that on inputs $h_r(w)$, for $w \in \Sigma^*$, simulates the computation of M on input w. Again, $d \notin \Gamma$ is a new dummy symbol and we set $\Sigma_D = \Sigma$, $\Sigma_R = \{\#\}$, and $\Sigma_N = \emptyset$. We define

$$Q' = \{\, q_z \mid q \in Q, z \in \Gamma \cup \{\triangle\}\,\} \cup \{\, q_z^{(i)} \mid q \in Q, i \in \{1,2\}, z \in \Gamma \cup \{\triangle\}\,\},$$

where the superscript expresses how many symbols d are still to be pushed and the subscript stores the topmost pushdown symbol below possible symbols d. The set of accepting states F' is then $\{\, q_z \mid q \in F, z \in \Gamma \cup \{\triangle\}\,\}$.

By the properties of M, its first move is not a λ-transition. So, the computation of M' starts in state $p_\triangle$, that is, in the initial state of M that additionally stores the topmost pushdown symbol of M's initial configuration.

Next, we define the transition function δ_D. The idea is similar to that in the proof of Theorem 3. However, here we have to handle the fact that M' must not push more than one additional symbol, and we have to implement the update of the subscript of the states.

For $p \in Q$, $a \in \Sigma$, and $z \in \Gamma$, we define δ_D for all $z' \in \Gamma \cup \{\triangle\}$ as follows. If $\delta(p, a, z) = (q, xy)$ is a push move of M, then we set

(1) $\delta_D(p_z, a, z') = (q_x^{(2)}, \text{push}(yz'), 0),$

and if $\delta(p, a, \triangle) = (q, x\triangle)$, then

(2) $\delta_D(p_\triangle, a, \perp) = (q_x^{(2)}, \text{push}(\triangle), 0).$

If $\delta(p, a, z) = (q, x)$ is a top move of M, then we set

(3) $\delta_D(p_z, a, z') = (q_x^{(1)}, \text{push}(dz'), 0),$

and if $\delta(p, a, \triangle) = (q, \triangle)$, then

(4) $\delta_D(p_\triangle, a, \perp) = (q_\triangle^{(1)}, \text{push}(d), 0).$

If $\delta(p, a, z) = (q, \lambda)$ is a pop move of M, then we set

(5) $\delta_D(p_z, a, z') = (q_{z'}, \text{push}(dd), 1).$

Furthermore, the states $q^{(1)}$ and $q^{(2)}$ are used to push one and two more dummy symbols. So, for all $q \in Q$, $a \in \Sigma$, and $z, z' \in \Gamma \cup \{\triangle\}$ we set

(6) $\delta_D(q_z^{(2)}, a, z') = (q_z^{(1)}, \text{push}(dz'), 0),$
(7) $\delta_D(q_z^{(1)}, a, d) = (q_z, \text{push}(dd), 1).$

Let us summarize what the construction yields so far. It shows that

$$(p, aw, xs) \vdash_M (q, w, ys') \text{ if and only if } (p_x, aw, s) \vdash_{M'}^+ (q_y, w, dds').$$

Now, we turn to the definition of δ_R. On the first of two adjacent symbols #, M' just pops one dummy symbol in a non-stationary move. So, for all $p \in Q$ and $z, z' \in \Gamma \cup \{\triangle\}$ we set

(8) $\delta_R(p_z, \text{\#}, d) = (p_z^{(1)}, 1).$

On the second of two adjacent symbols #, M has to pop the remaining dummy symbols (in fact, by construction, there is exactly one d left). If the next move to be simulated is a λ-transition of M, then M' performs a stationary move, otherwise not. The information about which case applies comes from the state $p_z^{(1)}$, that is, the information if $\delta(p, \lambda, z)$ is defined or not.
If $\delta(p, \lambda, z)$ is undefined, then we set

(9) $\delta_R(p_z^{(1)}, \text{\#}, d) = (p_z, 1).$

If $\delta(p, \lambda, z) = (q, \lambda)$ is defined, then we set

(10) $\delta_R(p_z^{(1)}, \text{\#}, d) = (p_z^{(1)}, 0).$

In this way, there is always one λ-transition pending, and M' can decide whether the next but one transition is again a λ-transition. So, M can perform a non-stationary move while simulating the last λ-transition in this sequence. Let $\delta(p, \lambda, z) = (q, \lambda)$. If $\delta(q, \lambda, z')$ is undefined, then we set

(11) $\delta_R(p_z^{(1)}, \#, z') = (q_{z'}, 1)$.

Let $\delta(p, \lambda, z) = (q, \lambda)$. If $\delta(q, \lambda, z') = (r, \lambda)$ is defined, then we set

(12) $\delta_R(p_z^{(1)}, \#, z') = (q_{z'}^{(1)}, 0)$.

Let us summarize what the extended construction yields. It shows that

$$(p, aw, xs) \vdash_M^+ (q, w, ys') \text{ such that } \delta(q, \lambda, y) \text{ is undefined}$$
$$\text{if and only if } (p_x, a\#\#w, s) \vdash_{M'}^+ (q_y, w, s').$$

As before, the construction of M' is finally extended such that it accepts only inputs of the form $(\Sigma\#\#)^*$. We conclude $(p, w, \triangle) \vdash_M^* (q, \lambda, zs)$ if and only if $(p_\triangle, h_r(w), \lambda) \vdash_{M'}^* (q_z, \lambda, s)$. This together with $L(M') \subseteq (\Sigma\#\#)^*$ implies $L = h_r^{-1}(L(M'))$. □

4 Computational Capacity

Here we consider the computational capacities of the different types of input-driven pushdown automata. It turns out that they form a hierarchy as shown in Fig. 1 at the end of the section. In particular, for the classes beyond classical IDPDAs nondeterminism is better than determinism. Moreover, the possibility to perform stationary moves implies stronger devices than the possibility to push more than one symbol. This is true for the deterministic as well as for the nondeterministic classes. Further relations with (non)deterministic (real-time) pushdown automata are established.

We precede the comparisons by a useful technical lemma.

Lemma 5. *Let M be any IDPDA, stat-NIDPDA, push-NIDPDA, stat-IDPDA, or push-IDPDA with input alphabet Σ that contains the symbols a and b. If $L(M) \cap a^* b^*$ is not regular then $a \in \Sigma_D$ and $b \in \Sigma_R$.*

We continue with a result that says that the restriction to push at most one symbol in each step is a serious one. As mentioned before, a DPDA can always be transformed into an equivalent one that obeys this part of a normal form, but an input-driven pushdown automaton cannot. So, this property is an essential restriction. Later it will be shown that this restriction is also unavoidable if the neat properties of IDPDAs should be obtained. A witness language for the following proper inclusion is $\{ a^n b^{2n} \mid n \geq 1 \}$.

Theorem 6. *The family of languages accepted by push-IDPDAs is a proper superset of the family of languages accepted by IDPDAs.*

By the known equality $\mathcal{L}(\text{IDPDA}) = \mathcal{L}(\text{NIDPDA})$ and Theorem 6 we immediately obtain $\mathcal{L}(\text{NIDPDA}) \subset \mathcal{L}(\text{push-IDPDA})$. Next, we climb up the next level of the automata hierarchy and compare input-driven pushdown automata that may push more than one symbol and input-driven pushdown automata that may perform stationary moves. Though the latter may push only one symbol in each move, clearly, they can simulate the former by sequences of stationary push moves.

Theorem 7. *The family of languages accepted by stat-NIDPDAs is a proper superset of the family of languages accepted by push-NIDPDAs.*

The family of languages accepted by stat-IDPDAs is a proper superset of the family of languages accepted by push-IDPDAs.

Proof. Since any push move of a push-IDPDA that pushes more than one symbol can be simulated by some stat-IDPDA that pushes the same symbols one by one in a sequence of stationary moves that is controlled by states, we have the inclusion $\mathscr{L}(\text{push-IDPDA}) \subseteq \mathscr{L}(\text{stat-IDPDA})$, and similarly the inclusion $\mathscr{L}(\text{push-NIDPDA}) \subseteq \mathscr{L}(\text{stat-NIDPDA})$.

In order to show the properness of the inclusion we use the witness language $L = \{\, a^n b^l c^m d^n \mid l, m, n \geq 0 \text{ and } l \geq m \,\}$. By Example 2, L is accepted by a stat-IDPDA.

By way of contradiction, assume now that L is accepted by a push-NIDPDA $M = \langle Q, \Sigma, \Gamma, q_0, F, \bot, \delta_D, \delta_R, \delta_N \rangle$. Applying Lemma 5 to $L \cap a^* d^*$ and to $L \cap b^* c^*$ yields that $a \in \Sigma_D$ and $b \in \Sigma_D$ must be push symbols and the symbols $c \in \Sigma_R$ and $d \in \Sigma_R$ must be pop symbols.

We consider accepting computations on words of the form $a^n b^{n+1} d^n$, for $n \geq 1$. Since there are infinitely many of those words, but $|Q| \cdot |\Gamma|$ is finite, there are two different numbers $n_1 > n_2$ such that the accepting computations on $a^{n_1} b^{n_1+1} d^{n_1}$ and $a^{n_2} b^{n_2+1} d^{n_2}$ pass through configurations in which the state and topmost pushdown symbol are identical after having processed the prefixes a^{n_1} and a^{n_2}. More precisely, we have

$$(q_0, a^{n_1} b^{n_1+1} d^{n_1}, \lambda) \vdash^+ (q_1, b^{n_1+1} d^{n_1}, z\gamma_1) \vdash^+ (q_2, d^{n_1}, \gamma_2\gamma_1) \vdash^+ (q_+, \lambda, \gamma_3\gamma_1)$$

and

$$(q_0, a^{n_2} b^{n_2+1} d^{n_2}, \lambda) \vdash^+ (q_1, b^{n_2+1} d^{n_2}, z\gamma_1') \vdash^+ (q_2', d^{n_2}, \gamma_2'\gamma_1') \vdash^+ (q_+', \lambda, \gamma_3'\gamma_1'),$$

where $q_1, q_2, q_+, q_2', q_+' \in Q$, $q_+, q_+' \in F$, $z \in \Gamma$, and $\gamma_1, \gamma_2, \gamma, \gamma_1', \gamma_2', \gamma \in \Gamma^*$. Moreover, since $b \in \Sigma_D$ we know that $|\gamma_2| \geq n_1 + 2$. So, M can perform the computation

$$(q_0, a^{n_2} b^{n_1+1} d^{n_1}, \lambda) \vdash^+ (q_1, b^{n_1+1} d^{n_1}, z\gamma_1') \vdash^+ (q_2, d^{n_1}, \gamma_2\gamma_1') \vdash^+ (q_+, \lambda, \gamma_3\gamma_1')$$

and, thus, accept $a^{n_2} b^{n_1+1} d^{n_1}$ which does not belong to L, a contradiction. $\quad\square$

The next level of the hierarchy is the top level formed by pushdown automata not obeying the input-driven property.

Theorem 8. *The family of languages accepted by NPDAs is a proper superset of the family of languages accepted by stat-NIDPDAs.*

The family of languages accepted by DPDAs is a proper superset of the family of languages accepted by stat-IDPDAs.

The family of languages accepted by real-time DPDAs is a proper superset of the family of languages accepted by push-IDPDAs.

Finally, we consider the classes depicted in Fig. 1 that are not connected by a path. Each pair of these classes describes two language families that are incomparable.

A witness language for Theorem 8 is the deterministic real-time context-free language $\{\, a^m b^m b^n a^n \mid m, n \geq 0 \,\}$. It is not accepted by any stat-NIDPDA and, thus is not accepted by any stat-IDPDA and push-IDPDA either. On the other hand, the language $\{\, a^n b^n \mid n \geq 0 \,\} \cup \{\, a^n b^{2n} \mid n \geq 0 \,\}$ is known not to be deterministic context free. But a push-NIDPDA accepting it can straightforwardly be constructed.

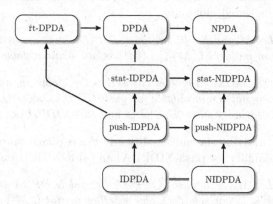

Fig. 1. Hierarchy of automata classes, where rt-DPDA denotes the class of deterministic real-time pushdown automata. An arrow indicates a proper inclusion of the induced language families. Each pair of nodes not connected by a path means that the two languages families are incomparable.

Corollary 9. *The families of languages accepted push-NIDPDA and stat-NIDPDA are both incomparable with each of the families $\mathscr{L}(rt\text{-}DPDA)$ and $\mathscr{L}(DPDA)$.*

Furthermore, from Example 2 and the proof of Theorem 7 we know that the language $\{\, a^n b^l c^m d^n \mid l, m, n \geq 0 \text{ and } l \geq m \,\}$ is accepted by a stat-IDPDA but cannot be accepted by any push-NIDPDA. Additionally, it is not accepted by any deterministic real-time pushdown automaton.

Corollary 10. *The family of languages accepted by stat-IDPDA is incomparable with the families $\mathscr{L}(push\text{-}NIDPDA)$ and $\mathscr{L}(rt\text{-}DPDA)$.*

5 Decidability Questions

In this section, we will discuss some decidability questions for push-IDPDAs, stat-IDPDAs, push-NIDPDAs, and stat-NIDPDAs. Let us recall that a decidability problem is *semidecidable* whenever the set of all instances for which the answer is "yes" is recursively enumerable. The families $\mathscr{L}$(push-IDPDA) and $\mathscr{L}$(stat-IDPDA) are effective subsets of the deterministic context-free languages. Thus, all decidability questions that are decidable for DPDAs are decidable for push-IDPDAs and stat-IDPDAs as well. Analogously, the families $\mathscr{L}$(push-NIDPDA) and $\mathscr{L}$(stat-NIDPDA) are effective subsets of the context-free languages and, hence, inherit the their positive decidability results.

Our first result is that the inclusion problem is not semidecidable for two push-IDPDAs with compatible signatures. This is in strong contrast to the result that the problem is decidable for IDPDAs and NIDPDAs. Hence, the ability of push-IDPDAs to push more than one symbol in one step turns the problem from decidability to non-semidecidability.

Theorem 11. *Let M and M' be two push-IDPDAs with compatible signatures. Then the inclusion problem $L(M) \subseteq L(M')$ is not semidecidable.*

Corollary 12. *The inclusion problem as well as the inclusion problem with compatible signatures is not semidecidable for push-IDPDAs, stat-IDPDAs and their nondeterministic variants push-NIDPDAs and stat-NIDPDAs.*

Next, we are studying the universality and the regularity problem and show its non-semidecidability for push-NIDPDAs and stat-NIDPDAs.

Theorem 13. *Let M' be a push-NIDPDA or stat-NIDPDA over some input alphabet Σ. Then it is not semidecidable whether or not $L(M') = \Sigma^*$.*

The equivalence problem with compatible signatures as well as the general equivalence problem is neither semidecidable for push-NIDPDAs nor for stat-NIDPDAs.

It is not semidecidable whether or not M' accepts a regular language.

Finally, we show that it is neither semidecidable whether a stat-NIDPDA accepts a language that is already accepted by some push-NIDPDA or IDPDA, nor whether an NPDA accepts a language that is already accepted by some stat-NIDPDA, push-NIDPDA or IDPDA, nor whether a push-NIDPDA accepts a language that is already accepted by some IDPDA. This means that it is not possible for NPDAs, stat-NIDPDAs and push-NIDPDAs to semidecide whether or not they accept languages already acceptable by weaker devices.

Theorem 14. *1. Let M' be a stat-NIDPDA. Then it is neither semidecidable whether or not $L(M')$ belongs to $\mathscr{L}$(push-NIDPDA) nor whether or not $L(M')$ belongs to $\mathscr{L}$(IDPDA).*

2. Let M' be an NPDA. Then it is neither semidecidable whether or not $L(M')$ belongs to $\mathscr{L}$(stat-NIDPDA), $\mathscr{L}$(push-NIDPDA), and $\mathscr{L}$(IDPDA).

3. Let M' be a push-NIDPDA. Then it is not semidecidable whether or not $L(M')$ belongs to $\mathscr{L}$(IDPDA).

The status of the decidability questions discussed in this section together with the results for IDPDAs, DPDAs, and NPDAs is summarized in the following Table 1.

Table 1. Decidability questions of the language families discussed. Symbols $\subseteq_c$ and $=_c$ denote inclusion and equivalence with compatible signatures. Such questions are not defined for non-input-driven devices and are marked with '—'.

	$\emptyset$	FIN	Σ^*	$\subseteq$	$\subseteq_c$	$=$	$=_c$	REG
$\mathscr{L}(\text{IDPDA})$	✓	✓	✓	✗	✓	✓	✓	✓
$\mathscr{L}(\text{push-IDPDA})$	✓	✓	✓	✗	✗	✓	✓	✓
$\mathscr{L}(\text{stat-IDPDA})$	✓	✓	✓	✗	✗	✓	✓	✓
$\mathscr{L}(\text{DPDA})$	✓	✓	✓	✗	—	✓	—	✓
$\mathscr{L}(\text{push-NIDPDA})$	✓	✓	✗	✗	✗	✗	✗	✗
$\mathscr{L}(\text{stat-NIDPDA})$	✓	✓	✗	✗	✗	✗	✗	✗
$\mathscr{L}(\text{NPDA})$	✓	✓	✗	✗	—	✗	—	✗

References

1. Alur, R., Madhusudan, P.: Visibly pushdown languages. In: Symposium on Theory of Computing (STOC 2004), pp. 202–211. ACM (2004). https://doi.org/10.1145/1007352.1007390
2. Alur, R., Madhusudan, P.: Adding nesting structure to words. J. ACM **56**(3), 1–43 (2009)
3. von Braunmühl, B., Verbeek, R.: Input-driven languages are recognized in $\log n$ space. In: Topics in the Theory of Computation, Mathematics Studies, vol. 102, pp. 1–19. North-Holland, Amsterdam (1985)
4. Caucal, D.: Synchronization of pushdown automata. In: Ibarra, O.H., Dang, Z. (eds.) DLT 2006. LNCS, vol. 4036, pp. 120–132. Springer, Heidelberg (2006). https://doi.org/10.1007/11779148_12
5. Chervet, P., Walukiewicz, I.: Minimizing variants of visibly pushdown automata. In: Kučera, L., Kučera, A. (eds.) MFCS 2007. LNCS, vol. 4708, pp. 135–146. Springer, Heidelberg (2007). https://doi.org/10.1007/978-3-540-74456-6_14
6. Crespi-Reghizzi, S., Mandrioli, D.: Operator precedence and the visibly pushdown property. J. Comput. System Sci. **78**, 1837–1867 (2012). https://doi.org/10.1016/j.jcss.2011.12.006
7. Dymond, P.W.: Input-driven languages are in $\log n$ depth. Inform. Process. Lett. **26**, 247–250 (1988)
8. Hopcroft, J.E., Ullman, J.D.: Introduction to Automata Theory, Languages, and Computation. Addison-Wesley, Reading, Massachusetts (1979)
9. Kutrib, M., Malcher, A.: Digging input-driven pushdown automata. RAIRO Theor. Informatics Appl. **55**, 6 (2021). https://doi.org/10.1051/ita/2021006
10. Kutrib, M., Malcher, A., Wendlandt, M.: Tinput-driven pushdown, counter, and stack automata. Fund. Inform. **155**, 59–88 (2017). https://doi.org/10.3233/FI-2017-1576
11. Mehlhorn, K.: Pebbling mountain ranges and its application to DCFL-recognition. In: de Bakker, J., van Leeuwen, J. (eds.) ICALP 1980. LNCS, vol. 85, pp. 422–435. Springer, Heidelberg (1980). https://doi.org/10.1007/3-540-10003-2_89
12. Okhotin, A., Salomaa, K.: Complexity of input-driven pushdown automata. SIGACT News **45**, 47–67 (2014). https://doi.org/10.1145/2636805.2636821

The Cut Operation in Subclasses
of Convex Languages
(Extended Abstract)

Michal Hospodár[1] and Viktor Olejár[1,2(✉)]

[1] Mathematical Institute, Slovak Academy of Sciences, Košice, Slovakia
olejar@saske.sk
[2] Department of Computer Science, P. J. Šafárik University, Košice, Slovakia

Abstract. The cut of two languages is a subset of their concatenation given by the leftmost maximal substring match. We study the state complexity of the cut operation assuming that both operands belong to some, possibly different, subclasses of convex languages, namely, right, left, two-sided, and all-sided ideal, prefix-, suffix-, factor-, and subword-closed, and -free languages. For all considered pairs of classes, we get the exact state complexity of cut. We show that it is m whenever the first language is a right ideal, and it is $m + n - 1$ or $m + n - 2$ if the first language is prefix-closed or prefix-free. In the other cases, the state complexity of cut is between $mn - 2n - m + 4$ and $mn - n + m$, the latter being the known state complexity of cut on regular languages. All our witnesses are described over a fixed alphabet of size at most three, except for three cases when the witness languages are described over an alphabet of size m or $m - 1$.

1 Introduction

The concept of regular expressions (regex) offers an elegant solution to a large number of string-searching problems. Specific regex matching functionality is implemented in so-called regex engines. There exist several such regex engines with different internal workings [10]. A common strategy, when it comes to implementing regex matching, is a greedy leftmost maximal substring match with the searched pattern. Such behaviour has been well defined theoretically in the context of formal languages as the cut operation [1,9]. The cut of two languages K and L is a subset of their concatenation defined as the language $K\,!\,L = \{uv \mid u \in K, v \in L,$ and $uv' \notin K$ for every non-empty prefix v' of $v\}$.

If languages K and L are accepted by the deterministic finite automata (DFAs) A and B, then $K\,!\,L$ is accepted by the cut automaton $A\,!\,B$, described by Berglund et al. [1], which has a grid-like structure similar to the product automaton. The DFA $A\,!\,B$ simulates A and starts also simulating B when a final state of A is reached, but it restarts the computation in B whenever a final state of A is reached again. If A goes to a non-final state, then $A\,!\,B$ simulates

Research supported by VEGA grant 2/0132/19 and grant APVV-15-0091.

P. Caron and L. Mignot (Eds.): CIAA 2022, LNCS 13266, pp. 152–164, 2022.
https://doi.org/10.1007/978-3-031-07469-1_12

A and B similarly as the ordinary product automaton. This construction gives the upper bound $mn - n + m$ on the state complexity of the cut operation; recall that the state complexity of a binary regular operation $\circ$ is given by the function $(m, n) \mapsto \max\{\mathrm{sc}(K \circ L) \mid \mathrm{sc}(K) \le m, \mathrm{sc}(L) \le n\}$ where $\mathrm{sc}(L)$ is the size of the minimal DFA accepting L. This upper bound is met by the binary languages $K = \{w \in \{a, b\}^* \mid |w|_a \bmod m = m - 1\}$ and $L = \{w \in \{a, b\}^* \mid |w|_b \bmod n = 0\}$ as shown by Drewes et al. [9, Theorem 3.1]. The range of attainable state complexities for this operation was investigated by Holzer and Hospodár [13] who proved that the range of possible complexities of cut of two languages with state complexities m and n is contiguous from 1 up to the upper bound in the case when an input alphabet has at least two symbols, while the values from $2\,\mathrm{m}$ to $n - 1$ are unattainable in the unary case if $2\,\mathrm{m} \le n - 1$.

Here we continue this research and study the state complexity of the cut operation assuming that its operands belong to some subclasses of convex languages, namely, right, left, two-sided and all-sided ideal, prefix-, suffix-, factor- and subword-closed, and prefix-, suffix-, factor- and subword-free languages. Our motivation for investigating this topic is two-fold.

Our first motivation is in regards to the more practical aspects of the cut operation. A number of modern regex engines heavily rely on the functionality that the cut operation models. Google's open source regex engine RE2 [8] is a prime example, which is utilized in many services and frameworks that the company provides. RE2 is a DFA-based engine with some key advantages over the backtracking-based engine counterparts, namely, reliable and fast run-time execution, bounded program stack, and avoidance of certain security vulnerabilities [2,7]. These advantages are further magnified when large amounts of data are processed, which is often the case with the company in question. Thus, even small refinements in complexity measures could present a welcome contribution.

Our second motivation comes from the fruitful research regarding operational complexity in many important subclasses of regular languages arising in theory and practice. Some suitable examples include results in the classes of prefix- and suffix-free languages by Han et al., [11,12]. Brzozowski et al. examined the classes of factor- and subword-free languages [3], ideal languages [4], and closed languages [5]. Particularly interesting are the classes of free languages since they are uniquely decodable codes arising often in practice as a result of Huffman coding [15] and other widespread coding schemes. In all these papers, the question was: What is the state complexity of an operation if the operands belong to some subclass of regular languages? It turned out that membership of languages in some classes does not decrease the state complexity of some operations. On the other hand, in some cases, the resulting complexity can be significantly smaller than in the general case of regular languages. For example, the DFAs for prefix-free languages have specific characterizations that decrease the state complexity of concatenation and star from an exponential to a linear function [12].

We can observe that if K is a right ideal, then $K\,!\,L$ is either empty or equal to K, and if K is prefix-free or L is suffix-closed, then $K\,!\,L$ is equal to KL. Hence it has little sense to consider the complexity of cut on two left ideal languages, and similar observations, which decrease the state complexity, hold for nine out of twelve considered subclasses. Therefore, unlike the above mentioned papers, in this paper we study the state complexity of the cut operation assuming that its operands belong to some, possibly different, subclasses of convex languages.

We provide the exact complexity of cut for each of 144 possible pairs of classes by grouping them in clusters that can be handled uniformly, by the same proof argument or by the same witnesses. For upper bounds, we use the properties of DFAs recognizing languages belonging to the considered classes, mainly the presence of the dead state for prefix-closed and free languages, the non-returning property for suffix-free languages, and the property of all states except dead being final for prefix-closed languages. If these properties are satisfied, some states in the resulting cut automaton are unreachable or equivalent to other states.

Having upper bounds in hand, it was not difficult to describe the corresponding witnesses over a ternary alphabet for the majority of cases. Subsequently, we were curious whether these could be further improved to binary witnesses. These improvements were then achieved with the help of some supplementary computations that we designed. As a result, all our witnesses are defined over a unary or binary alphabet, except for nine cases where we use a ternary alphabet, and three more cases where the alphabet grows linearly with m. Whenever we use a binary alphabet, it is always optimal in the sense that the corresponding upper bounds cannot be met in the unary case. In nine cases with a ternary alphabet, our computations did not result in binary witnesses attaining the state complexity upper bound for $m, n \leq 5$. The source code and supplementary computations can be accessed at https://github.com/ViktorOlejar/cut-convex-subclasses.

2 Preliminaries

We assume that the reader is familiar with the standard notation in automata theory. For details, we refer to [14,16]. We denote the set $\{0, 1, \ldots, n-1\}$ by $\mathbf{n}$.

Let Σ be a non-empty *alphabet* of symbols. Then Σ^* denotes the set of all strings over Σ, including the empty string ε. A *language* over Σ is any subset of Σ^*. The length of a string w is denoted by $|w|$, and the number of occurrences of a symbol a in w is denoted by $|w|_a$. For a regular expression r, we denote the expression $rr \cdots r$ (i-times) by r^i. Next, $r^{\leq k}$ denotes $r^0 + r^1 + \cdots + r^k$, and $r^{\geq k}$ denotes $r^k + r^{k+1} + \cdots$. The *complement* of a language L over Σ is the language $L^c = \Sigma^* \setminus L$. The *concatenation* of languages K and L is the language $KL = \{uv \mid u \in K \text{ and } v \in L\}$. The *cut* of K and L is the language

$$K \mathbin{!} L = \{uv \mid u \in K, v \in L, \text{ and } uv' \notin K \text{ for every non-empty prefix } v' \text{ of } v\}.$$

A *deterministic finite automaton* (DFA) is a quintuple $A = (Q, \Sigma, \cdot, s, F)$ where Q is a finite non-empty set of *states*, Σ is a finite non-empty *input alphabet*, $\cdot$ is the *transition function* from $Q \times \Sigma$ to Q which can be naturally extended to the domain $Q \times \Sigma^*$, $s \in Q$ is the *initial state*, and $F \subseteq Q$ is the set of *final or accepting states*. The language *accepted* by A is $L(A) = \{w \in \Sigma^* \mid s \cdot w \in F\}$.

If $p \cdot a = q$ for some states p, q and symbol a, then we speak of a *transition* (p, a, q) which is an *out-transition* of p and an *in-transition* of q. We also use $p \xrightarrow{a} q$ to denote that $p \cdot a = q$. A DFA is *non-returning* if its initial state has no in-transitions. A state q is called a *sink* state if $q \cdot a = q$ for each input symbol a. A non-final sink state is called a *dead* state. A state q is *reachable* in the DFA A if $q = s \cdot w$ for some string w. Two states p and q are *distinguishable* if there exists a string w such that $p \cdot w$ and $q \cdot w$ do not have the same finality.

If a language L is accepted by a DFA $A = (Q, \Sigma, \cdot, s, F)$, then the language L^c is accepted by the DFA $A^c = (Q, \Sigma, \cdot, s, Q \setminus F)$. For two languages accepted by DFAs A and B with m and n states, respectively, we can construct the *cut automaton* $A\,!\,B$ as described in [13, p. 193]. Let us recall this description.

Let $A = (\mathbf{m}, \Sigma, \cdot_A, 0, F_A)$ and $B = (\mathbf{n}, \Sigma, \cdot_B, 0, F_B)$ be two DFAs. Define the cut automaton $A\,!\,B = (Q, \Sigma, \cdot, s, \mathbf{m} \times F_B)$ where $Q = (\mathbf{m} \times \{\bot\}) \cup (\mathbf{m} \times \mathbf{n})$, $s = (0, \bot)$ if $\varepsilon \notin L(A)$ and $s = (0, 0)$ otherwise, and for each state (i, j) in Q and each input symbol a in Σ, we have

$$(i, \bot) \cdot a = \begin{cases} (i \cdot_A a, \bot), & \text{if } i \cdot_A a \notin F_A; \\ (i \cdot_A a, 0), & \text{otherwise;} \end{cases}$$

and

$$(i, j) \cdot a = \begin{cases} (i \cdot_A a, j \cdot_B a), & \text{if } i \cdot_A a \notin F_A; \\ (i \cdot_A a, 0), & \text{otherwise.} \end{cases}$$

By *row* i, we mean the states (i, j) with $j \in \{\bot\} \cup \mathbf{n}$, and by *column* j, we mean the states (i, j) with $i \in \mathbf{m}$. Therefore, the cut automaton has m rows and $n + 1$ columns. By the product part of $A\,!\,B$, we mean the states (i, j) with $j \neq \bot$. For each final state f of A, the states (f, j) with $j \neq 0$ are unreachable in $A\,!\,B$. This gives the upper bound $mn - n + m$ on the state complexity of the cut operation, which is known to be tight in the binary case [9, Theorem 3.1]. The following lemma presents the properties of the cut automaton under some conditions.

Lemma 1. *Let $A = (\mathbf{m}, \Sigma, \cdot_A, 0, F_A)$ and $B = (\mathbf{n}, \Sigma, \cdot_B, 0, F_B)$ be DFAs.*

(a) If $\varepsilon \in L(A)$, then the states $(i, \bot)$ are unreachable in $A\,!\,B$.

(b) If B has a dead state d, then each state (i, d) is equivalent to $(i, \bot)$.

(c) If B is non-returning, then no state $(i, 0)$ with $i \notin F_A$ is reachable, so at most m states in columns $\bot$ and 0 are reachable.

(d) If A is non-returning, then only the initial state is reachable in row 0.

Proof. (a) The initial state of $A\,!\,B$ is $(0, 0)$ and no state $(i, \bot)$ can be reached from the product part of $A\,!\,B$.

(b) Let $0 \leq i \leq m - 1$ and $j \in \{\bot, d\}$. Then for each symbol a, assuming that $i \cdot_A a = k$, each state (i, j) is sent to (k, j) on a if k is non-final in A, and it is sent to $(k, 0)$ if k is final in A. Therefore the states $(i, \bot)$ and (i, d) are equivalent.

(c) Since no transition goes to 0 in B, no transition goes to any state $(i, 0)$ in $A\,!\,B$ if i is a non-final state of A. On the other hand, if i is a final state of A, then $(i, \bot)$ is unreachable.

(d) Since no transition goes to 0 in A, no transition goes to any state $(0, j)$ in $A \, ! \, B$. Since the initial state of $A \, ! \, B$ is $(0, \bot)$ or $(0, 0)$, the claim follows.   □

A language L over Σ is a *right ideal* if $L = L\Sigma^*$, it is a *left ideal* if $L = \Sigma^* L$, it is a *two-sided ideal* if $L = \Sigma^* L \Sigma^*$, and it is an *all-sided ideal* if L is equal to the language of strings obtained from strings of L by inserting any number of alphabet symbols in any position.

For a string uxv, u is its *prefix*, x is *factor*, and v is its *suffix*. A *subword* is a possibly scattered subsequence of a string. A language L is *prefix-closed* if for every string of L, each its prefix is in L, and it is *prefix-free* if for every string of L, no its proper prefix is in L. Suffix-, factor-, and subword-closed and -free languages are defined similarly.

A language L is $\prec$-*convex* with respect to a partial order $\prec$ if for every strings u, v in L and each x with $u \prec x \prec v$, we have $x \in L$. Each prefix-free, prefix-closed, or right ideal language is prefix-convex, and similar inclusions hold also for suffix- (factor-, subword-)free, -closed, and left (two-sided, all-sided) ideal languages. The complement of a closed language is a corresponding ideal language. If a language is prefix-free, then we sometimes say that it is accepted by a prefix-free DFA; analogously for the other subclasses.

It is known that each non-empty prefix-free language is accepted by a DFA that has exactly one final state with out-transitions going to the dead state. Next, each non-empty suffix-free language is accepted by a non-returning DFA that has a dead state. The next lemma provides a sufficient condition for DFAs to be suffix-free, and the following proposition provides properties of the cut operation on some classes.

Lemma 2 (Cmorik's, *cf.* [6, Lemma 1]). *Let L be accepted by a non-returning DFA with a single final state in which no state, except for the dead state, has more than one in-transition on the same input symbol. Then L is suffix-free.*   □

Proposition 3. *Let K and L be regular languages.*
  (a) If K is a right ideal, then $K \, ! \, L = K$ if $\varepsilon \in L$, and $K \, ! \, L = \emptyset$ otherwise.
  (b) If K is prefix-free, then $K \, ! \, L = KL$.
  (c) If L is suffix-closed, then $K \, ! \, L = KL$.   □

3 Results

We start with empty or universal languages. The universal language is the only prefix-closed language whose minimal DFA has no dead state. The empty language is the only suffix-free language whose minimal DFA is not non-returning.

Proposition 4. *Let K and L be languages over Σ.*

(a) If $K = \emptyset$ or $L = \emptyset$, then $K \, ! \, L = \emptyset$ and $\mathrm{sc}(K \, ! \, L) = 1$.
(b) If $K = \Sigma^*$, then $K \, ! \, L \in \{\emptyset, \Sigma^*\}$ and $\mathrm{sc}(K \, ! \, L) = 1$.

(c) If $L = \Sigma^*$, then $K \mathop{!} L = K\Sigma^*$ and $\mathrm{sc}(K \mathop{!} L) \leq \mathrm{sc}(K)$. If moreover $\varepsilon \in K$, then $K \mathop{!} L = \Sigma^*$ and $\mathrm{sc}(K \mathop{!} L) = 1$. For $n \geq 3$ and $|\Sigma| \geq 2$, there exist all-sided ideal and subword-free languages K over Σ such that $\mathrm{sc}(K \mathop{!} \Sigma^*) = \mathrm{sc}(K) = n$.

Proof. Case (a) follows from the fact that $K \mathop{!} L \subseteq KL$ and $KL = \emptyset$ if K or L is empty. Since Σ^* is a right ideal, case (b) follows from Proposition 3(a). The upper bound in case (c) follows from Proposition 3(c) since Σ^* is suffix-closed and $\mathrm{sc}(K\Sigma^*) \leq \mathrm{sc}(K)$. For the lower bound, consider the unary all-sided ideal language $K = a^{\geq n-1}$ and the binary subword-free language $K = a^{n-2}$. In both cases we have $\mathrm{sc}(K\Sigma^*) = \mathrm{sc}(K) = n$. □

Now we assume that the first language is a right (two-sided, all-sided) ideal or prefix- (factor-, subword-) closed or -free language. The next three theorems give the exact complexity of $K \mathop{!} L$ whenever K is in these classes.

Theorem 5. *Let $K, L \subseteq \Sigma^*$ and $K, L \notin \{\emptyset, \Sigma^*\}$. Let K and L be accepted by an m-state and n-state DFA, respectively. Let K be a right ideal. Then $\mathrm{sc}(K \mathop{!} L) \leq m$, and this upper bound is met by the unary all-sided ideal $a^{\geq m-1}$ and (a) unary all-sided ideal and subword-closed language a^*, (b) unary subword-free language ε if $n \geq 2$. If $n = 1$, then $\mathrm{sc}(K \mathop{!} L) = 1$ in case (b).*

Proof. By Proposition 3(a), $K \mathop{!} L \in \{K, \emptyset\}$ and if $\varepsilon \in L$, then $K \mathop{!} L = K$. Hence $\mathrm{sc}(K \mathop{!} L) \leq m$. Next, for $K = a^{\geq m-1}$ we have $K \mathop{!} a^* = K \mathop{!} \varepsilon = K$, and $\mathrm{sc}(K) = m$, $\mathrm{sc}(a^*) = 1$, $\mathrm{sc}(\varepsilon) = 2$. If $n = 1$ and L is prefix-free or suffix-free, then $L = \emptyset$, so $K \mathop{!} L = \emptyset$ and $\mathrm{sc}(K \mathop{!} L) = 1$. □

Theorem 6. *Let $K, L \subseteq \Sigma^*$ and $K, L \notin \{\emptyset, \Sigma^*\}$. Let K and L be accepted by an m-state and n-state DFA, respectively. Let K be prefix-closed. Then we have $\mathrm{sc}(K \mathop{!} L) \leq m + n - 1$, and this bound is met by the subword-closed language $(b^*a)^{\leq m-2}b^*$ and (a) all-sided ideal $(a^*b)^{n-1}(a + b)^*$, (b) subword-closed language $(a^*b)^{\leq n-2}a^*$, and (c) prefix-free language $(a^*b)^{n-2}$. If L is suffix-free, then $\mathrm{sc}(K \mathop{!} L) \leq m + n - 2$, and this upper bound is met by the subword-closed language $a^{\leq m-2}$ and subword-free language a^{n-2}.*

Proof. Let A and B be DFAs for K and L, respectively. We may assume that all states of A are final, except for the dead state. It follows that in $A \mathop{!} B$, we have $m-1$ reset states, and at most n states in the dead state row. This gives the upper bound $m+n-1$. If, moreover, the language L is suffix-free, we may assume that B is non-returning, hence the state in the dead state row and initial state column is unreachable by Lemma 1(c). For every pair of witnesses K and L from the statement of the theorem, we use the minimal DFAs A and B for K and L, respectively, to construct the cut automaton $A \mathop{!} B$. In $A \mathop{!} B$, the corresponding number of states are reachable and pairwise distinguishable in the initial state column and in the dead state row. □

Theorem 7. *Let $K, L \subseteq \Sigma^*$ and $K, L \notin \{\emptyset, \Sigma^*\}$. Let K and L be accepted by an m-state and n-state DFA, respectively. Let K be prefix-free. Then we* have $sc(K \,!\, L) \leq m + n - 1$, and this upper bound is· met by the subword-free language a^{m-2} and (a) all-sided ideal language $(a + b)^{\geq n-1}$, (b) suffix-closed language $a^{\leq n-2} + (a + b)^* ba^{\leq n-2}$. If L is prefix-closed or prefix- or suffix-free, then $sc(K \,!\, L) \leq m + n - 2$, and this upper bound is met by the subword-free language a^{m-2} and (c) subword-closed language $a^{\leq n-2}$, (d) subword-free language a^{n-2}.

Proof. Let A and B be DFAs for K and L, respectively. We may assume that A has exactly one final state f and a dead state d such that $f \cdot a = d$ for each input symbol a. By Proposition 3(b), we have $K \,!\, L = KL$ if K is prefix-free. We can get a DFA for KL from A and B by omitting every transition (f, a, d) and merging f with the initial state of B. This gives the upper bound $m + n - 1$ in cases (a) and (b). If, moreover, the language B has a dead state, we can merge it with the dead state of A, which gives the upper bound $m + n - 2$ in cases (c) and (d). For every pair of witness languages K and L from the statement of this lemma, we construct a DFA for KL from minimal DFAs accepting K and L as described above, and we show that the resulting DFAs are minimal.   □

In the next three theorems, we assume that the first language is a left ideal, suffix-closed, or suffix-free. For lower bounds, we use languages from the list below repeatedly, so we refer to them by the lower index number. Let A_1 be the DFA from Fig. 2 (left), and A_4, A_7, and B_8 be the DFAs from Fig. 1. Next, let

$$K_i = L(A_i) \text{ for } i \in \{1, 4, 7\},$$
$$L_1 = (a^*b)^{n-1}(a + b)^*,$$
$$K_2 = (a + b + c)^*(b^*a)^{m-1}b^*,$$
$$L_2 = \{v, ucv \mid u \in \{a, b, c\}^*,$$
$$K_3 = (a + b)^*a^{\geq m-1},$$
$$v \in \{a, b\}^*, |v|_b \leq n - 2\},$$
$$K_5 = (c + (a + b)(b^*a)^{\leq m-3}b^*c)^*,$$
$$L_3 = ((a + c)^*b)^{n-2},$$
$$K_6 = a^* + (a + b)^*ba^{\geq m-1},$$
$$L_4 = b((ab^*)^{n-3}a)^*,$$
$$K_8 = a(b^*a)^{m-3}b^*(c(b^*a)^{m-3}b^*)^*,$$
$$L_5 = (b + c)(a^*b)^{n-3},$$
$$K_9 = a(bb + (ab^*)^{m-4}ab)^*,$$
$$L_6 = (ba^*)^{n-2},$$
$$K_{10} = a((ba^*)^{m-5}ba^*b)^*(ba^*)^{m-5}b,$$
$$L_7 = a^*b(a + b)^{n-3},$$
$$K_{11} = a(b^*a)^{m-3}(c(b^*a)^{m-3})^*,$$
$$L_8 = L(B_8).$$

It follows directly from the definitions of these languages that K_2 and K_3 are left ideals, L_1 is all-sided ideal, L_3 and L_7 are prefix-free, K_8, K_9, K_{10}, K_{11}, L_4, and L_6 are suffix-free, L_5 is factor-free, and K_5, K_6, and L_2 are suffix-closed. Next, K_7 and L_8 are suffix-free since DFAs A_7 and B_8 satisfy the conditions of Cmorik's Lemma. If we add a loop on b in the initial state of A_1 and mark all non-dead states of A_4 as initial, and then determinize and minimize the resulting automata, we get DFAs that are isomorphic to the original ones. It follows that K_1 is left ideal and K_4 is suffix-closed.

The next theorem gives the exact complexity of $K \,!\, L$ if K is a left ideal.

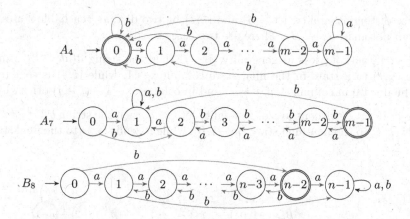

Fig. 1. The suffix-closed DFA A_4 and suffix-free DFAs A_7 and B_8.

Theorem 8. *Let $K, L \subseteq \Sigma^*$ and $K, L \notin \{\emptyset, \Sigma^*\}$. Let K and L be languages accepted by an m-state and n-state DFA, respectively. Let K be a left ideal.*

  (a) If L is an ideal or suffix-closed, then $\mathrm{sc}(K\,!\,L) \leq mn - n + m$. This bound is tight if $|\Sigma| \geq 2$ for an ideal L, and if $|\Sigma| \geq 3$ for suffix-closed L.

  (b) If L is prefix-free or prefix-closed, then $\mathrm{sc}(K\,!\,L) \leq mn - n + 1$. This bound is tight if $|\Sigma| \geq 2$ for prefix-free L, and if $|\Sigma| \geq 3$ for prefix-closed L.

  (c) If L is suffix-free, then $\mathrm{sc}(K\,!\,L) \leq mn - n - m + 2$. This bound is tight if $|\Sigma| \geq 2$ for suffix-free L, $|\Sigma| \geq 3$ for factor-free L, and $|\Sigma| \geq m$ for subword-free L.

Proof. To get upper bounds, let A and B be an m-state and n-state DFAs for K and L, respectively. The upper bound in case (a) is the same as in the case of regular languages. If L is prefix-closed or prefix-free, then we may assume that B has a dead state. Then the corresponding states in the column $\perp$ and the dead state column are equivalent by Lemma 1(b). This decreases the upper bound from case (a) by $m - 1$. If L is suffix-free, then we may assume that B is non-returning and has a dead state. Then by Lemma 1(c), there are at most m reachable states in columns $\perp$ and 0, including the states in rows corresponding to final states of A. In the other rows, there are at most $(m-1)(n-2)$ additional states, not counting the states in rows $\perp, 0$, and the dead state column. This gives at most $m + (m-1)(n-2) = mn - n - m + 2$ reachable and distinguishable states.

Now we prove lower bounds. In each of the cases (a)-(c), we consider subcases (i), (ii), and (iii) depending on L. We provide a detailed proof for case (a)(i).

(a)(i) Let us show that the languages K_1 and L_1 defined on p. 7 meet the upper bound $mn - n + m$. These languages are accepted by DFAs A_1 and B_1 from Fig. 2. The figure also shows the cut automaton $A_1\,!\,B_1$.

In the cut automaton $A_1\,!\,B_1$, each state $(i, \perp)$ with $i \neq m - 1$ and the state $(m-1, 0)$ are reached from the initial state $(0, \perp)$ by a string in b^* and each state (i, j) with $i \neq m-1$ and $j \neq \perp$ is reached from $(m-1, 0)$ by $a(ab)^j a^{m-2-i}$.

For distinguishability, let (i, j) and (k, ℓ) be two distinct reachable states of the cut automaton $A_1 \,!\, B_1$. There are two cases to consider.

Case 1: If, without loss of generality, $j < \ell$, then the string $a(ab)^{n-1-\ell}$ sends state (k, ℓ) to a state in the final state column $n - 1$, while (i, j) is sent to a non-final state in column $\perp$ if $j = \perp$, and in column $n - 1 - (\ell - j)$ otherwise.

Case 2: If $j = \ell$, without loss of generality let $i < k$, then the string $b^{m-2-i}(ab)^n$ sends (k, ℓ) to the non-final state $(m - 1, 0)$, while it sends (i, j) to the final state $(m - 2, n - 1)$.

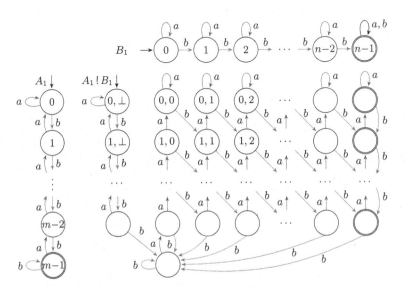

Fig. 2. The left ideal DFA A_1 and all-sided ideal DFA B_1 meeting the upper bound $mn - n + m$. In $A_1 \,!\, B_1$, the unreachable states are not shown.

The witnesses for the remaining cases are as follows: ternary left ideal K_2 and suffix-closed L_2 in case (a)(ii), binary left ideal K_1 and subword-closed L_1^c in case (b)(i), ternary left ideal K_2 and prefix-free L_3 in case (b)(ii), binary left ideal K_3 and suffix-free L_4 in case (c)(i), ternary left ideal K_2 and factor-free L_5 in case (c)(ii). In case (c)(iii) we use the alphabet $\Sigma = \{a, b_0, b_1, \ldots, b_{m-2}\}$, left ideal $K_{12} = \{a^\ell \mid \ell \geq m - 1\} \cup \bigcup_{i=0}^{m-2} \{ub_i a^\ell \mid u \in \Sigma^*, \ell \geq m - 1 - i\}$, and subword-free $L_9 = \{w \in \Sigma^* \mid |w| = n - 2\}$. $\square$

Now we examine the cases where K is suffix-closed. Notice that every closed language includes ε, and hence column $\perp$ is unreachable in the cut automaton.

Theorem 9. *Let $K, L \subseteq \Sigma^*$ and $K, L \notin \{\emptyset, \Sigma^*\}$. Let K and L be accepted by an m-state and n-state DFA, respectively. Let K be suffix-closed.*

(a) If L is ideal, closed, or prefix-free, then $\mathrm{sc}(K \,!\, L) \leq mn - n + 1$, and this bound is tight if $|\Sigma| \geq 2$ for an ideal or closed L, and if $|\Sigma| \geq 3$ for prefix-free L.

(b) If L is suffix-, factor-, or subword-free, then $\mathrm{sc}(K \,!\, L) \leq mn - n - m + 2$, and this upper bound is tight if $|\Sigma| \geq 2$ for suffix-free L, if $|\Sigma| \geq 3$ for factor-free L, and if $|\Sigma| \geq m$ for subword-free L.

Proof. To get upper bounds, let A and B be DFAs for K and L, respectively, with the initial state of B denoted by 0. Since K is suffix-closed, we have $\varepsilon \in K$. Hence the initial state of $A \,!\, B$ is in column 0 and each state in column $\perp$ is unreachable. This gives the upper bound $mn - n + 1$. Moreover, if L is suffix-free, we may assume that B is non-returning, so no state $(i, 0)$ is reachable if i is a non-final state of A. If A has $k \geq 1$ final states, this gives an upper bound $k + (m - k)(n - 1) \leq mn - m - n + 2$.

The upper bound $mn - n + 1$ in case (a) is met by the suffix-closed language K_4 and (a)(i) the all-sided ideal L_1; (a)(ii) the subword-closed language L_1^c; in sub-case (a)(iii), we use the suffix-closed language K_5 and prefix-free language L_3. The upper bound $mn - n - m + 2$ in case (b) is met by (b)(i) the binary suffix-closed language K_6 and the suffix-free language L_6; (b)(ii) the ternary suffix-closed language K_5 and the factor-free language L_5.

In case (b)(iii), we use the alphabet $\Sigma = \{a, b_0, b_1, \ldots, b_{m-2}\}$, the suffix-closed language $K_{13} = a^* \cup \bigcup_{i=0}^{m-2} \{ub_i a^\ell \mid u \in \Sigma^*, \ell \geq m - 1 - i\}$, and the subword-free language L_9. Then $\mathrm{sc}(K_{13} \,!\, L_9) = mn - n - m + 2$. □

Our last theorem examines the cases in which the first language is suffix-free, that is, it is accepted by a non-returning DFA.

Theorem 10. *Let $K, L \subseteq \Sigma^*$ and $K, L \notin \{\emptyset, \Sigma^*\}$. Let K and L be accepted by an m-state and n-state DFA, respectively. Let K be suffix-free.*

(a) If L is ideal or suffix-closed, then $\mathrm{sc}(K \,!\, L) \leq mn - 2n + m$, and this upper bound is tight if $|\Sigma| \geq 2$ for an ideal L, and if $|\Sigma| \geq 3$ for prefix-free L.

(b) If L is prefix-closed or prefix-free, then $\mathrm{sc}(K \,!\, L) \leq mn - 2n + 2$, and this upper bound is tight if $|\Sigma| \geq 2$ using a subword-closed or prefix-free language L.

(c) If L is suffix-free, then $\mathrm{sc}(K \,!\, L) \leq mn - 2n - m + 4$, and this upper bound is tight if $|\Sigma| \geq 2$ for suffix-free L, if $|\Sigma| \geq 3$ for factor-free L, and if $|\Sigma| \geq m - 1$ for subword-free L.

Proof. Let A and B be m-state and n-state DFAs for K and L, respectively. Since K is a non-empty suffix-free language, we may assume that A is non-returning. By Lemma 1(d), the only reachable state in row 0 is the initial state. This decreases the upper bound to $mn - 2n + m$ in case (a). Moreover, if L is prefix-closed or prefix-free, B has a dead state, and hence each state in the dead state column is equivalent to the corresponding state in column $\perp$ by Lemma 1(b). This decreases the upper bound from case (a) by $m - 2$ to $mn - 2n + 2$ in case (b). Finally, if L is non-empty and suffix-free, we may assume that B is non-returning and has a dead state. By Lemma 1(c), there are at most m states in columns $\perp$ and 0, and the dead state column is equivalent to column $\perp$. This results in the upper bound $m + (m - 2)(n - 2) = mn - 2n - m + 4$ in case (c).

The corresponding upper bounds are met by K_7 and L_1 in case (a)(i), by K_8 and L_2 in case (a)(ii), by K_7 and L_1^c in case (b)(i), by K_9 and L_7 in case (b)(ii), by K_{10} and L_8 in case (c)(i), and by K_{11} and L_5 in case (c)(ii). In case (c)(iii), consider the alphabet $\Sigma = \{a, b_1, b_2, \ldots, b_{m-3}, c\}$. Then the language

$$K_{14} = \{ca^\ell \mid \ell \geq m - 3\} \cup \bigcup_{i=0}^{m-2} \{cub_i a^\ell \mid u \in (\Sigma \setminus \{c\})^*, \ell \geq m - 2 - i\}$$

is suffix-free since every string in K_{14} starts with c but each proper suffix of every string in K_{14} does not start with c. Next, $L_{10} = \{w \in \Sigma^* \mid |w| = n - 2\}$ is subword-free, and $\mathrm{sc}(K_{14} \mathbin{!} L_{10}) = mn - 2n - m + 4$.   □

4   Conclusions

We investigated the state complexity of the cut operation assuming that the operands belong to some (not necessarily the same) of 12 subclasses of convex languages: right, left, two-sided, all-sided ideal, and prefix-, suffix-, factor-, subword-closed and prefix-, suffix-, factor-, and subword-free languages. In all 144 cases, we got the exact complexity of cut. Table 1 summarizes all our results, including the size of alphabet used to describe witnesses.

The complexity of cut in cases where the first operand is right ideal, prefix-closed, or prefix-free (first nine rows of the table), is m, $m + n - 1$, or $m + n - 2$ with binary or unary witnesses. The binary alphabet is optimal in the sense that the corresponding upper bounds cannot be met in the unary case since then the dead states would not be reachable.

The regular upper bound $mn - n + m$ is met only if the first language is left ideal and the second language is ideal or suffix-closed (the last row of the table). In all the remaining cases, the resulting complexity is between $mn - 2n - m + 4$ and $mn - n + m$. Except for the case when the second language is subword-free, all our witnesses are binary or ternary and result from 11 different kinds of the first language and 8 different kinds of the second language. Whenever we used the binary alphabet, it was always optimal since in the unary case the four classes of ideal, closed, and free languages coincide, so the upper bounds given in the first nine rows of the table apply.

We conjecture that the alphabet is optimal for all our ternary witnesses as well. Our computations support this hypothesis. We also think that if the second language is subword-free, the corresponding upper bounds cannot be met by any languages defined over a fixed alphabet.

Table 1. The state complexity of the cut operation on subclasses of convex languages. The dot signifies that the state complexity is the same as in the cell closest to the left. The size of alphabet used to describe witnesses is shown in brackets after the state complexity.

$K\backslash L$	Ri Li Ti Ai	Sc	Pc Fc Swc	Pf	Sf	Ff	Swf
Ri Ti Ai			m (1)				
Pc Fc Swc	$m+n-1$ (2)				$m+n-2$ (1)		
Pf Ff Swf	$m+n-1$ (2)		$m+n-2$ (1)				
Sf	$mn-2n+m$ (2)	$\cdot$(3)	$mn-2n+2$ (2)		$mn-2n-m+4$ (2)	$\cdot$(3)	$\cdot(m-1)$
Sc	$mn-n+1$ (2)	$\cdot$(2)	$mn-n+1$(2)	$\cdot$(3)	$mn-n-m+2$ (2)	$\cdot$(3)	$\cdot(m)$
Li	$mn-n+m$ (2)	$\cdot$(3)					

References

1. Berglund, M., Björklund, H., Drewes, F., van der Merwe, B., Watson, B.: Cuts in regular expressions. In: Béal, M.-P., Carton, O. (eds.) DLT 2013. LNCS, vol. 7907, pp. 70–81. Springer, Heidelberg (2013). https://doi.org/10.1007/978-3-642-38771-5_8

2. Berglund, M., Drewes, F., van der Merwe, B.: Analyzing catastrophic backtracking behavior in practical regular expression matching. Electron. Proc. Theor. Comput. Sci. **151**, 109–123 (2014). https://doi.org/10.4204/eptcs.151.7

3. Brzozowski, J., Jirásková, G., Li, B., Smith, J.: Quotient complexity of bifix-, factor-, and subword-free regular languages. Acta Cybern. **21**(4), 507–527 (2014). https://doi.org/10.14232/actacyb.21.4.2014.1

4. Brzozowski, J.A., Jirásková, G., Li, B.: Quotient complexity of ideal languages. Theor. Comput. Sci. **470**, 36–52 (2013). https://doi.org/10.1016/j.tcs.2012.10.055

5. Brzozowski, J., Jirásková, G., Zou, C.: Quotient complexity of closed languages. Theor. Comput. Syst. **54**(2), 277–292 (2013). https://doi.org/10.1007/s00224-013-9515-7

6. Cmorik, R., Jirásková, G.: Basic operations on binary suffix-free languages. In: Kotásek, Z., Bouda, J., Černá, I., Sekanina, L., Vojnar, T., Antoš, D. (eds.) MEMICS 2011. LNCS, vol. 7119, pp. 94–102. Springer, Heidelberg (2012). https://doi.org/10.1007/978-3-642-25929-6_9

7. Cox, R.: Regular expression matching in the wild, January 2007. https://swtch.com/~rsc/regexp/regexp3.html. Accessed 21 Feb 2022

8. Cox, R.: Re2: A principled approach to regular expression matching, March 2010. https://opensource.googleblog.com/2010/03/re2-principled-approach-to-regular.html. Accessed 21 Feb 2022

9. Drewes, F., Holzer, M., Jakobi, S., van der Merwe, B.: Tight bounds for cut-operations on deterministic finite automata. Fundam. Inform. **155**(1-2), 89–110 (2017). https://doi.org/10.3233/FI-2017-1577, Preliminary version in: MCU 2015.

LNCS, vol. 9288, pp. 45–60. Springer, Cham (2015). https://doi.org/10.1007/978-3-319-23111-2_4

10. Friedl, J.E.: Mastering Regular Expressions. O'Reilly Media, Inc., Newton (2006)
11. Han, Y.S., Salomaa, K.: State complexity of basic operations on suffix-free regular languages. Theor. Comput. Sci. **410**(27–29), 2537–2548 (2009). https://doi.org/10.1016/j.tcs.2008.12.054
12. Han, Y.S., Salomaa, K., Wood, D.: Operational state complexity of prefix-free regular languages. In: Ésik, Z., Fülöp, Z. (eds.) Automata, Formal Languages, and Related Topics, pp. 99–115. University of Szeged, Hungary (2009)
13. Holzer, M., Hospodár, M.: The range of state complexities of languages resulting from the cut operation. In: Martín-Vide, C., Okhotin, A., Shapira, D. (eds.) LATA 2019. LNCS, vol. 11417, pp. 190–202. Springer, Cham (2019). https://doi.org/10.1007/978-3-030-13435-8_14
14. Hopcroft, J.E., Ullman, J.D.: Introduction to Automata Theory, Languages and Computation. Addison-Wesley, Boston (1979)
15. Huffman, D.A.: A method for the construction of minimum-redundancy codes. Proc. IRE **40**(9), 1098–1101 (1952). https://doi.org/10.1109/JRPROC.1952.273898
16. Sipser, M.: Introduction to the Theory of Computation. Cengage Learning, Boston (2012)

Variations of the Separating Words Problem

Nicholas Tran[(✉)] [iD]

Department of Mathematics & Computer Science, Santa Clara University,
Santa Clara, CA 95053, USA
ntran@scu.edu

Abstract. The separating words problem seeks to determine the asymptotic growth of the minimum number of states of a deterministic finite automaton that accepts x but rejects y, where x and y are given strings. We study three natural variants of this problem which impose additional constraints on the start and/or end states: $\forall$-separation requires different end states for *every* common start state; $\forall^2$-separation requires different end states for *every pair* of start states; and $\forall^2 01$-separation requires *fixed* different end states for every pair of start states.

For distinct strings of the same length, we establish exact bounds on the number of states for $\forall^2$- and $\forall^2 01$-separation, as well as a logarithmic lower bound and a linear upper bound for $\forall$-separation.

Keywords: Separating words · DFA · Lower and upper bounds

1 Introduction

Given two strings x and y over an alphabet Σ, let $d(x, y)$ denote the minimum number of states needed for a deterministic finite automaton to accept x but reject y. For each positive integer n, define the distance functions

$$D^{\|}(n) = \max_{x \neq y \ \& \ |x|=|y|=n} d(x, y)$$

$$D^{\#}(n) = \max_{|x|<|y|=n} d(x, y)$$

to be the largest such minimum value among all pairs of distinct x and y of length n, and all pairs of x and y of different lengths whose maximum is n, respectively. The *separating words* problem is to determine the asymptotic growths of $D^{\|}(n)$ and $D^{\#}(n)$.

Goralčík and Koubek [3] were the first to study this problem. They settled the $D^{\#}(n)$ case with a tight $\Theta(\log n)$ bound for arbitrary alphabets and proved an $o(n)$ upper bound on $D^{\|}(n)$ for nonunary alphabets. Robson [4] improved their sublinear upper bound to $O(n^{2/5} \log^{3/5} n)$. Demaine et al. [2] established an $\Omega(\log n)$ lower bound on $D^{\|}(n)$ and showed that it is tight when the difference between x and y is countable with a DFA. Recently, Chase [1] improved Robson's

© Springer Nature Switzerland AG 2022
P. Caron and L. Mignot (Eds.): CIAA 2022, LNCS 13266, pp. 165–176, 2022.
https://doi.org/10.1007/978-3-031-07469-1_13

upper bound to $O(n^{1/3} \log^7 n)$. The gap between the polynomial upper bound and logarithmic lower bound on $D^{\parallel}(n)$ remains significant.

In this paper we study natural variants of the separating words problem to gain new perspectives and to obtain sharper bounds on the distance functions. First, we return to the more general definition of separation as ending in different states that was originally used in [3]; the equivalent definition involving accepting states was introduced later in [4]. Second, we impose additional conditions on the start and end states that result in a hierarchy of separation of two strings x and y by a DFA M:

- ∃-separation: for *some* common start state, M ends in different states after reading x and y (this is the problem studied in [3]);
- ∀-separation: for *every* common start state, M ends in different states after reading x and y;
- ∀²-separation: for *every pair* of start states, M ends in different states after reading x and y;
- ∀²01-separation: for *every pair* of start states, M ends in *fixed* different states after reading x and y.

For each variant $\nu \in \{\exists, \forall, \forall^2, \forall^2 01\}$, we define $d_\nu(x, y)$, $D_\nu^{\parallel}(n)$, and $D_\nu^{\sharp}(n)$ similarly to $d(x, y)$, $D^{\parallel}(n)$, and $D^{\sharp}(n)$ and seek to determine the asymptotic growths of $D_\nu^{\parallel}(n)$ and $D_\nu^{\sharp}(n)$. It is clear that $d_\exists(x, y) = d(x, y)$, $D_\exists^{\parallel}(n) = D^{\parallel}(n)$, and $D_\exists^{\sharp}(n) = D^{\sharp}(n)$.

Requiring separation for every pair of start states (∀²-separation) may seem overly restrictive or even impossible when, in addition, the end states are fixed (∀²01-separation); however, we can show that such separating automata exist iff one string is not a suffix of the other, and their maximum number of states is $1 + \min(|x|, |y|)$. In particular, we obtain exact bounds on the distance functions for ∀²- and ∀²01-separation:

$$D_{\forall^2}^{\parallel}(n) = D_{\forall^2 01}^{\parallel}(n) = n + 1$$

$$D_{\forall^2}^{\sharp}(n) = D_{\forall^2 01}^{\sharp}(n) = \infty.$$

Requiring separation for every common start state (∀-separation) is also a natural restriction of the original formulation. We show a tight $\Theta(\log n)$ bound on $D_\forall^{\sharp}(n)$ for arbitrary alphabets, as well as an $\Omega(\log n)$ lower bound and an $O(n)$ upper bound on $D_\forall^{\parallel}(n)$ for nonunary alphabets.

Requiring separation for *some* pair of start states yields an uninteresting variant. We show that a 2-state separating automaton always exists, even when $x = y$ or when they have different lengths.

The rest of this paper is organized as follows: Sect. 2 defines the various notions of separation and establishes some simple properties of the resulting separation distance functions. Section 3 proves bounds for ∀²- and ∀²01 separation, Sect. 4 proves bounds for ∀-separation, and Sect. 5 suggests some open problems for the new separation distance functions.

2   Preliminaries

$\Sigma^*/\Sigma^+/\Sigma^n$ denote the sets of strings/nonempty strings/strings of length n over alphabet Σ respectively. The ith symbol of string x is denoted by x_i. The length of a string x is denoted by $|x|$.

Define $L(n) = lcm(1, 2, \ldots, n)$ to be the least common multiple of the first positive n integers. It is known that $1.03883n > \ln(L(n))$ for $n > 0$ [5], and hence $n \in \Omega(\log(L(n)))$.

We use the following simplified definition of deterministic finite automata that does not specify an initial state or accepting states:

Definition 1. *A deterministic finite automaton (DFA) is a triple*

$$M = (Q_M, \Sigma_M, \delta_M),$$

where Q_M is a finite set of states, Σ_M is an alphabet, and $\delta_M : Q_M \times \Sigma_M \to Q_M$ is the transition function. We call the number of states of M its size and denote it with $|M|$.

The extended transition function $\delta'_M : Q_M \times \Sigma_M^* \to Q_M$ is defined recursively:

1. $\delta'_M(q, \epsilon) = q$, *where ϵ is the empty string, for $q \in Q_M$;*
2. $\delta'_M(q, xa) = \delta_M(\delta'_M(q, x), a)$ *for $a \in \Sigma_M$, $x \in \Sigma_M^*$ and $q \in Q_M$.*

The first and last state in the sequence of states of M while reading x are called the start and end state respectively.

We now introduce variants of the separating words problems which impose additional conditions on the start state(s) and/or end states.

Definition 2. *Let x and y be string over an alphabet Σ. We say a DFA M*

- $\exists$-*separates x and y if $\delta'_M(s, x) \neq \delta'_M(s, y)$ for some $s \in Q_M$;*
- $\forall$-*separates x and y if $\delta'_M(s, x) \neq \delta'_M(s, y)$ for every $s \in Q_M$;*
- $\forall^2$-*separates x and y if $\delta'_M(s_x, x) \neq \delta'_M(s_y, y)$ for every pair $s_x, s_y \in Q_M$;*
- $\forall^2 01$-*separates x and y if there exist $e_0, e_1 \in Q_M$ such that $\delta'_M(s_x, x) = e_0 \neq e_1 = \delta'_M(s_y, y)$ for every pair $s_x, s_y \in Q_M$.*

Definition 3. *Let x and y be strings over an alphabet Σ and $\nu \in \{\exists, \forall, \forall^2, \forall^2 01\}$. Define the ν-separation distance between strings x and y as follows:*

$$d_\nu(x, y) = d_\nu(y, x) = \min\{|M| : M \text{ is a DFA that } \nu\text{-separates } x \text{ and } y\}$$
$$\text{or } \infty \text{ if no such M exists.}$$

Define the ν-distance functions $D_\nu^{\|}(n)$ and $D_\nu^{\#}(n)$ as follows:

$$D_\nu^{\|}(n) = \max\{d_\nu(x, y) : x, y \in \Sigma^n, x \neq y\}$$
$$D_\nu^{\#}(n) = \max\{d_\nu(x, y) : |x| < |y| = n\}.$$

The above definitions immediately imply the following:

Proposition 1. *Let $x \neq y$, v, and w be arbitrary strings over $\Sigma \supseteq \{0, 1\}$.*

1. $d_\exists(x, y) \leq d_\forall(x, y) \leq d_{\forall^2}(x, y) \leq d_{\forall^2 01}(x, y)$;
2. $d_\nu(x, x) = \infty$, $\nu \in \{\exists, \forall, \forall^2, \forall^2 01\}$;
3. $d_\nu(x, y) \geq 2$, $\nu \in \{\exists, \forall, \forall^2, \forall^2 01\}$;
4. $d_\nu(0, 1) = 2$, $\nu \in \{\exists, \forall, \forall^2, \forall^2 01\}$;
5. *If M $\forall$-separates x and y, then M also $\forall$-separates vx and vy. Hence $d_\forall(vx, vy) \leq d_\forall(x, y)$, and this inequality is strict in some cases.*
6. *If M does not $\forall$-separate x and y, then M does not $\forall$-separate xv and yv either. Hence $d_\forall(x, y) \leq d_\forall(xv, yv)$, and this inequality is strict in some cases.*
7. *For $\nu \in \{\forall^2, \forall^2 01\}$, if M ν-separates x and y, then M also ν-separates vx and wy. Hence $d_\nu(vx, wy) \leq d_\nu(x, y)$, and this inequality is strict in some cases.*
8. *If M does not $\forall^2$-separate x and y, then M does not $\forall^2$-separate xv and yv either. Hence $d_\forall^2(x, y) \leq d_\forall^2(xv, yv)$, and this inequality is strict in some cases.*

Proof.

1. Immediate from Definition 2.
2. For every DFA M, $\delta'_M(s, x) = \delta'_M(s, x)$ for every state $s \in Q_M$, so $d_\exists(x, x) = \infty$; the rest follow from item 1.
3. Immediate from Definition 2.
4. Figure 1 shows a two-state DFA M which $\forall^2 01$-separates 0 and 1 (a stands for every symbol not 0). The rest follow from items 1 and 3.
5. Let M be a DFA with k states that $\forall$-separates x and y. For every state p,

$$\delta'_M(p, vx) = \delta'_M(\delta'_M(p, v), x) \neq \delta'_M(\delta'_M(p, v), y) = \delta'_M(p, vy),$$

   so M also $\forall$-separates vx and vy. Hence $d_\forall(vx, vy) \leq d_\forall(x, y)$, and in particular, by exhaustive search

$$d_\forall(0\ 0101, 0\ 1111) = 2 < 3 = d_\forall(0101, 1111).$$

6. Let M be a DFA with k states that does not $\forall$-separate x and y. There must be some state s such that $\delta'_M(s, x) = \delta'_M(s, y)$, so

$$\delta'_M(s, xv) = \delta'_M(\delta'_M(s, x), v) = \delta'_M(\delta'_M(s, y), v) = \delta'_M(s, yv),$$

   so M does not $\forall$-separate xv and yv either. Hence $d_\forall(x, y) \leq d_\forall(xv, yv)$, and in particular, by exhaustive search

$$d_\forall(0001, 0100) = 2 < 3 = d_\forall(0001\ 0, 0100\ 0).$$

7. Let M be a DFA with k states that $\forall^2$-separates x and y. For every pair of states p, q in Q_M,

$$\delta'_M(p, vx) = \delta'_M(\delta'_M(p, v), x) \neq \delta'_M(\delta'_M(q, w), y) = \delta'_M(q, wy),$$

so M also $\forall^2$-separates vx and wy. Hence $d_{\forall^2}(vx, wy) \leq d_{\forall^2}(x, y)$, and in particular, by exhaustive search

$$d_{\forall^2}(0\ 0101, 0\ 1111) = 2 < 3 = d_{\forall^2}(0101, 1111).$$

The same argument and example hold for $\forall^2 01$-separation.

8. Let M be DFA with k states that does not $\forall^2$-separate x and y. There exists a pair of states p, q in Q_M such that $\delta'_M(p, x) = \delta'_M(q, y)$, so

$$\delta'_M(p, xv) = \delta'_M(\delta'_M(p, x), v) = \delta'_M(\delta'_M(q, y), v) = \delta'_M(q, yv),$$

i.e., M does not $\forall^2$-separate xv and yv either. Hence $d_{\forall^2}(x, y) \leq d_{\forall^2}(xv, yv)$, and in particular, by exhaustive search

$$d_{\forall^2}(0001, 0100) = 2 < 3 = d_{\forall^2}(0001\ 0, 0100\ 0).$$

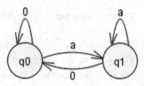

Fig. 1. A two-state DFA that $\forall^2 01$-separates 0 and 1.

$\square$

Following [2], we show that the distance functions $D_\nu^{\|}(n)$ and $D_\nu^{\#}(n)$ are independent of the alphabet size, provided it is at least 2, for $\nu \in \{\exists, \forall, \forall^2, \forall^2 01\}$.

Proposition 2. $D_\nu^{\|}(n)$ and $D_\nu^{\#}(n)$ for the binary alphabet are the same as those for larger alphabets for $\nu \in \{\exists, \forall, \forall^2, \forall^2 01\}$.

Proof. Let $D_\nu^{\|}(n, k)$ denote $D_\nu^{\|}(n)$ for alphabets of size k for $\nu \in \{\exists, \forall, \forall^2, \forall^2 01\}$. We show that $D_\nu^{\|}(n, k) = D_\nu^{\|}(n, 2)$ for $k > 2$. Since $D_\nu^{\|}(n, k)$ is the maximum ν-distance between two distinct strings of length n over an alphabet of size $k > 2$, which include the cases of distinct strings of length n over the binary alphabet, $D_\nu^{\|}(n, k) \geq D_\nu^{\|}(n, 2)$. Similarly, $D_\nu^{\#}(n, k) \geq D_\nu^{\#}(n, 2)$.

Conversely, suppose two strings x and y (not necessarily of the same length) over an alphabet Σ of size $k > 2$ differ at some position j, i.e., $x_j = 0$ and $y_j = 1$ for two different symbols 0 and 1. Replace all symbols in x and y that are not 0 with 1 to obtain strings x' and y' where $|x'| = |x|$ and $|y'| = |y|$. Let M be a DFA that ν-separates x' and y'. By adding transitions $\delta_{M'}(q, a) = \delta_M(q, 1)$ for all $q \in Q_M$ and all $a \in \Sigma - \{0\}$, we obtain a DFA M' with the same size as M that ν-separates x and y.

Now suppose x is a proper suffix of y, and let M be a DFA that ν-separates $1^{|x|}$ and $1^{|y|}$. By adding transitions $\delta_{M'}(q, a) = \delta_M(q, 1)$ for all $q \in Q_M$ and all $a \in \Sigma - \{1\}$, we obtain a DFA M' with the same size as M that ν-separates x and y.

The above two paragraphs show that $D_\nu^{\|}(n, k) \leq D_\nu^{\|}(n, 2)$ and $D_\nu^{\#}(n, k) \leq D_\nu^{\#}(n, 2)$. In combination with the inequalities shown in the first paragraph, these results show that $D_\nu^{\|}(n, k) = D_\nu^{\|}(n, 2)$ and $D_\nu^{\#}(n, k) = D_\nu^{\#}(n, 2)$ for $k > 2$ and $\nu \in \{\exists, \forall, \forall^2, \forall^2 01\}$. $\qquad\square$

The above proposition allows us to prove our subsequent results for the binary alphabet only without loss of generality.

Finally, suppose we say M $\exists^2$-separates x and y if $\delta_M'(p, x) \neq \delta_M'(q, y)$ for *some* pair of start states p and q and define $d_{\exists^2}(x, y)$ similarly to the other separation distances. The following proposition shows that a separating DFA with two states always exists, even when $x = y$ or when their lengths are different. We will not study this trivial variant further.

Proposition 3. $d_{\exists^2}(x, y) = 2$ *for every pair of strings x and y.*

Proof. Figure 2 shows a two-state DFA which $\exists^2$-separates every pair of strings x and y. Starting in the same state separates strings whose lengths have different parities; starting in different states separates strings whose lengths have the same parity.

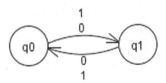

Fig. 2. A two-state DFA that $\exists^2$-separates every pair of strings.

$\qquad\square$

3 $\forall^2$-separation and $\forall^2 01$-separation

In this section, we derive exact bounds for $D_{\forall^2}^{\|}(n)$ and $D_{\forall^2 01}^{\|}(n)$ but show that $D_{\forall^2}^{\#}(n)$ and $D_{\forall^2 01}^{\#}(n)$ are unbounded. As a result, we obtain a characterization of pairs of binary strings that can be $\forall^2$- and $\forall^2 01$-separated.

To begin, we show that if x is a proper suffix of y, then no DFA can $\forall^2$- or $\forall^2 01$-separate them.

Proposition 4. $d_{\forall^2}(x, zx) = d_{\forall^2 01}(x, zx) = \infty$ *for any binary strings x and z where $|z| \geq 1$.*

Proof. For every DFA M and state $p \in Q_M$,

$$\delta'_M(p, zx) = \delta'_M(\delta_M(p, z), x),$$

so M neither $\forall^2$-separates nor $\forall^2 01$-separates zx from x. $\qquad \square$

Corollary 1. $D^{\sharp}_{\forall^2}(n) = D^{\sharp}_{\forall^2 01}(n) = \infty$ *for $n \geq 1$.*

On the other hand, the following theorem shows that $d_{\forall^2}(x, y)$ must be finite for distinct x and y of the same length, and the largest $\forall^2$-distance and $\forall^2 01$-distance between distinct strings of length n are $n + 1$.

Theorem 1. $D^{\parallel}_{\forall^2}(n) = D^{\parallel}_{\forall^2 01}(n) = n + 1$ *for $n \geq 1$.*

Proof. First we show that $D^{\parallel}_{\forall^2}(n) > n$ for $n \geq 1$. Consider an arbitrary DFA M with $k \leq n$ states on inputs 0^n and 10^{n-1}. For every $s \in Q_M$, let $t = \delta_M(s, 1)$ and $p_l = \delta'_M(t, 0^l)$ for each $l \geq 0$. There must be $0 \leq i < j \leq k$ such that $p_i = p_j$ by the pigeonhole principle.

Letting $s_y = s$ and $s_x = p_{j-i-1}$, we have

$$\begin{aligned}
\delta'_M(s_y, 10^{k-1}) &= \delta'_M(s, 10^{k-1}) \\
&= \delta'_M(\delta_M(s, 1), 0^{k-1}) \\
&= \delta'_M(t, 0^{k-1}) \\
&= p_{k-1} \\
\delta'_M(s_x, 0^k) &= \delta'_M(p_{j-i-1}, 0^k) \\
&= \delta'_M(p_j, 0^{k-i-1}) \\
&= \delta'_M(p_i, 0^{k-i-1}) \\
&= p_{k-1}.
\end{aligned}$$

Since $\delta'_M(s_y, 10^{k-1}) = \delta'_M(s_x, 0^k)$ and $k \leq n$, $\delta'_M(s_y, 10^{n-1}) = \delta'_M(s_x, 0^n)$. In other words, no DFA M with at most n states can $\forall^2$-separate 0^n and 10^{n-1}.

Next we show that $D^{\parallel}_{\forall^2 01}(n) \leq n + 1$ by induction on n.

Base case: $n = 1$. There are only two strings of length 1, and we have already seen a two-state DFA in Fig. 1 which $\forall^2 01$-separates 0 from 1.

Induction: given two different strings x and y of length n, we construct a DFA M to $\forall^2 01$-separate them with at most $n + 1$ states as follows. There are two cases:

1. The rightmost bits of x and y are different, e.g., $x = x'0$ and $y = y'1$. Then the DFA in Fig. 1 satisfies the claim.
2. The rightmost bits of x and y are the same, e.g., $x = x'b$ and $y = y'b$, where $b \in \{0, 1\}$. Since x and y are different, so are x' and y', hence, by induction hypothesis, there is a DFA M' with at most n states that $\forall^2 01$-separates x' and y', i.e., M' ends in some state e'_x after reading x' and some different state e'_y after reading y' regardless of the starting states. We construct a DFA M to $\forall^2 01$-separate x and y for three different cases based on $e_x = \delta_{M'}(e'_x, b)$ and $e_y = \delta_{M'}(e'_y, b)$:
   (a) $e_x \neq e_y$: M' always ends in e_x after reading $x = x'b$ and in e_y after reading $y = y'b$ regardless of the start states, so $M = M'$ also $\forall^2 01$-separates x and y (Fig. 3);
   (b) $e_x = e_y$ and $e_x \neq e'_x$ and $e_x \neq e'_y$: let M be obtained from M' by
      – adding a new state e, i.e., $Q_M = Q_{M'} \cup \{e\}$;
      – setting transitions from e identical to transitions from e_y, i.e., $\delta_M(e, a) = \delta_{M'}(e_y, a)$ for $a \in \{0, 1\}$;
      – changing the transition from e'_y on b to e, i.e., $\delta_M(e'_y, b) = e$.
      From any pair of start states (including the new state e), M ends in state e'_x and e'_y after reading x' and y' respectively. After reading the final bit b, M ends in state e_x and e respectively. In other words, M $\forall^2 01$-separates x and y (Fig. 4).
   (c) $e_x = e_y = e'_y$: let M be obtained from M' by
      – adding a new state e;
      – setting $\delta_M(e, b) = e$ and $\delta_M(e, 1 - b) = \delta_{M'}(e'_y, 1 - b)$;
      – changing the transition from e'_y on b (back to itself originally) to e, i.e., $\delta_M(e'_y, b) = e$.
      From any start state (including the new state e), M ends in state e'_x after reading x' and hence $e_x = e'_y$ after reading the final bit b. From any start state (including the new state e), M ends either in state e'_y or e after reading y'. In either case, M ends in state $e \neq e_x$ after reading the final bit b. In other words, M $\forall^2 01$-separates x and y (Fig. 5).

In all three cases, M has at most $n+1$ states and $\forall^2 01$-separates x and y. Since $D^{\|}_{\forall^2 01}(n) \leq n+1 \leq D^{\|}_{\forall^2}(n) \leq D^{\|}_{\forall^2 01}(n)$, we have $D^{\|}_{\forall^2}(n) = D^{\|}_{\forall^2 01}(n) = n+1$. $\square$

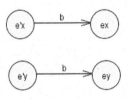

Fig. 3. If M' always ends in e'_x after reading x' and e'_y after reading y', then M' always ends in e_x after reading $x = x'b$ and e_y after reading $y = y'b$.

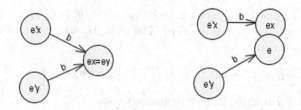

Fig. 4. If M' (left) always ends in e'_x after reading x' and e'_y after reading y', then M (right) always ends in e_x after reading $x = x'b$ and e after reading $y = y'b$. The states e and e_x have the same transitions on 0 and 1.

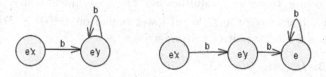

Fig. 5. If M' (left) always ends in e'_x after reading x' and e'_y after reading y', then M (right) always ends in $e_x = e'_y$ after reading $x = x'b$ and e after reading $y = y'b$. e'_y and e have the same transition on $1 - b$.

We obtain from Proposition 4 and Theorem 1 a characterization of string pairs that cannot be $\forall^2$- and $\forall^2 01$-separated:

Theorem 2. $d_{\forall^2}(x, y) = d_{\forall^2 01}(x, y) = \infty$ *iff one string is a suffix of the other for $x, y \in \{0, 1\}^*$.*
  In particular, $d_{\forall^2}(x, y) = d_{\forall^2 01}(x, y) = \infty$ for all $x, y \in \{0\}^*$.

Proof. If x is a suffix of y, i.e., $y = x$ or $y = zx$ for some $z \in \{0, 1\}^+$, then $d_{\forall^2}(x, y) = d_{\forall^2 01}(x, y) = \infty$ by Proposition 1.2 or 4.

If one string is not a suffix of the other, then we can write x and y as $x = x'0z$ and $y = y'1z$ for some string x', y' and z. There is a DFA M with at most $2 + |z|$ states to $\forall^2$- or $\forall^2 01$-separate $0z$ and $1z$ by Theorem 1. M also $\forall^2$ or $\forall^2 01$-separates x and y by Proposition 1.7. $\qquad\square$

4 ∀-separation

We establish a tight logarithmic bound on $D_{\forall}^{\#}(n)$, as well as a logarithmic lower bound and a linear upper bound on $D_{\forall}^{\|}(n)$ in this section.

A tight bound of $\Theta(\log n)$ on $d_{\exists}(x, y)$ when x and y have different lengths at most n was established in [2,3]. The same proof holds for ∀-separation.

Proposition 5. $D_{\forall}^{\#}(n) \in \Theta(\log n)$.

Proof. Let x and y be binary strings such that $|x| < |y| = n$. There is a prime $p \leq 4.4 \ln n$ such that $|y| - |x| \not\equiv 0 \pmod{p}$. The DFA M_p with p states $0, 1, \ldots, p-1$ with transition function

$$\delta_{M_p}(l, 0) = \delta_{M_p}(l, 1) = (l+1) \pmod{p}, 0 \leq l < p,$$

separates x and y starting in any (common) state.

On the other hand, for every DFA M with at most n states and for every $p \in Q_M$, $\delta'_M(p, 0^{n-1}) = \delta'_M(p, 0^{n-1+L(n)})$, so $\forall$-separating 0^{n-1} from $0^{n-1+L(n)}$ requires at least $n+1 \in \Omega(\log(n-1+L(n)))$ states. $\qquad\square$

The following theorem establishes an $\Omega(\log n)$ lower bound on $D_\forall^\|(n)$. Although it follows from the $\Omega(\log n)$ lower bound on $D^\|(n) = D_\exists^\|(n)$ in [2], our proof uses a shorter pair of witness strings.

Theorem 3. $D_\forall^\|(n) \in \Omega(\log n)$.

Proof. For $m \geq 1$, let $x = 0^{L(m)}0^{m-1}$ and $y = 1^{L(m)}0^{m-1}$, where $L(m) = lcm(1, 2, \ldots, m)$. We show that $d_\forall(x, y) = m + 1$. In comparison, it was shown in [2] that

$$d_\exists(0^{m-1}1^{m-1+L(m)}, 0^{m-1+L(m)}1^{m-1}) \geq m + 1.$$

Let M be a DFA with m states. For every start state s, define $p_l = \delta_M(s, 0^l)$ for $l \geq 0$. By the pigeonhole principle, there are $0 \leq i < j \leq m$ such that $p_i = p_j$ and $j - i \leq m$, so

$$\begin{aligned}
\delta'_M(s, 0^i) &= \delta'_M(s, 0^{i+(j-i)}) \\
&= \delta'_M(s, 0^{i+2(j-i)}) \\
&= \ldots \\
&= \delta'_M(s, 0^{i+L(m)}) \\
\delta'_M(s, 0^{i+(m-1-i)}) &= \delta'_M(s, 0^{i+L(m)+m-1-i}) \\
\delta'_M(s, 0^{m-1}) &= \delta'_M(s, 0^{L(m)+m-1}).
\end{aligned}$$

Similarly, for every start state t, define $q_l = \delta'_M(t, 1^l)$ for $l \geq 0$. There are $0 \leq i < j \leq m$ such that $q_i = q_j$ and $j - i \leq m$. But

$$\begin{aligned}
\delta'_M(q_j, 1^{L(m)}0^{m-1}) &= \delta'_M(q_j, 0^{m-1}) \\
&= \delta'_M(q_j, 0^{L(m)+m-1})
\end{aligned}$$

so M does not separate x and y when started in state q_j. This shows that $d_\forall(x, y) \geq m + 1$.

On the other hand, the following $m + 1$-state DFA S $\forall^2 01$-separates x and y:

$$\begin{aligned}
\delta_S(l, 0) &= l + 1, & 1 \leq l \leq m \\
\delta_S(m+1, 0) &= m + 1 \\
\delta_S(l, 1) &= 1, & 1 \leq l \leq m + 1
\end{aligned}$$

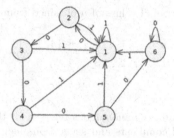

Fig. 6. A 6-state DFA S that $\forall^2 01$-separates $0^{L(5)}0^4$ and $1^{L(5)}0^4$, where $L(5) = 60$.

Figure 6 shows S for $m = 5$. It is easily seen that $\delta'_S(s, x) = m + 1$ and $\delta'_S(s, y) = 1$ for any $1 \leq s \leq m + 1$.

The asymptotic bound follows from the fact that $m \in \Omega(\ln(L(m) + m - 1))$. □

It was shown in [2] that $d_\exists(x, y) \leq p + 2$ if x and y differ at position p from the left, starting with 0. In contrast, the above proof shows that $d_\forall(x, y)$ is unbounded even when x and y differ at the leftmost position. On the other hand, the same upper bound of $p + 1$ holds for $d_\forall$ as for $d_\exists$ when x and y differ at position p from the *right*, starting with 1.

Proposition 6. *If x and y differ at position p from the right, starting with 1, then $d_\forall(x, y) \leq d_{\forall^2 01}(x, y) \leq p + 1$.*

Proof. The proof of Theorem 2 shows that there is a $p + 1$-state DFA M that $\forall^2 01$-separates two strings x and y that differ at position p from the right, starting with 1. Hence $d_\forall(x, y) \leq d_{\forall^2 01}(x, y) \leq p + 1$. □

Corollary 2. $d_{\forall^2 01}(x, y) \leq 1 + \min(|x|, |y|)$ *for all binary strings x and y such that neither is a suffix of the other.*

A linear upper bound on $D_\forall^{||}(n)$ follows from $d_\forall(x, y) \leq d_{\forall^2 01}(x, y)$:

Corollary 3. $D_\forall^{||}(n) \leq n + 1$.

5   Open Problems

We showed that $D_{\forall^2}^{||}(n) = D_{\forall^2 01}^{||}(n) = n + 1$. The remaining problem for $\forall^2$- and $\forall^2 01$-separation is to find a polynomial-time algorithm to compute $d_{\forall^2}(x, y)$ and $d_{\forall^2 01}(x, y)$ given distinct x and y of the same length.

Our lower bound and upper bound on $D_\forall^{||}(n)$ remain even farther apart than for $D_\exists^{||}(n)$, the original formulation, and need to be tightened. A feasible first step is to improve the upper bound on $D_\forall^{||}(n)$, as seemingly suggested by empirical data (Table 1):

Table 1. $D_\forall^\|(n)$ for small values of n obtained from exhaustive search.

n	1–2	3–7	8–14	15–18
$D_\forall^\|(n)$	2	3	4	5

Acknowledgments. I thank the anonymous referees for their careful reading of the manuscript. Their detailed comments and suggestions help improve the presentation of this paper.

References

1. Chase, Z.: Separating words and trace reconstruction. In: Proceedings of the 53rd Annual ACM SIGACT Symposium on Theory of Computing, pp. 21–31 (2021)
2. Demaine, E.D., Eisenstat, S., Shallit, J., Wilson, D.A.: Remarks on separating words. In: Descriptional Complexity of Formal Systems, pp. 147–157 (2011)
3. Goralčík, P., Koubek, V.: On discerning words by automata. In: International Colloquium on Automata, Languages and Programming on Automata, Languages and Programming, pp. 116–122 (1986)
4. Robson, J.: Separating strings with small automata. Inf. Process. Lett. **30**(4), 209–214 (1989)
5. Rosser, J.B., Schoenfeld, L.: Approximate formulas for some functions of prime numbers. Ill. J. Math. **6**(1), 64–94 (1962)

Homomorphisms on Graph-Walking Automata

Olga Martynova[1,2] and Alexander Okhotin[1(✉)]

[1] Department of Mathematics and Computer Science, St. Petersburg State University, 14th Line V.O., 29, Saint Petersburg 199178, Russia
{st062453,alexander.okhotin}@spbu.ru
[2] Leonhard Euler International Mathematical Institute at St. Petersburg State University, Saint Petersburg, Russia

Abstract. Graph-walking automata (GWA) analyze an input graph by moving between its nodes, following the edges. This paper investigates the effect of node-replacement graph homomorphisms on recognizability by these automata. The family of graph languages recognized by GWA is closed under inverse homomorphisms. The main result of this paper is that, for n-state automata operating on graphs with k labels of edge endpoints, the inverse homomorphic images require GWA with $kn + O(1)$ states in the worst case. The second result is that already for tree-walking automata, the family they recognize is not closed under injective homomorphisms; here the proof is based on a homomorphic characterization of regular tree languages.

1 Introduction

A graph-walking automaton moves over a labelled graph using a finite set of states and leaving no marks on the graph: this is a model of graph traversal using finite-state control. There is a classical result by Budach [3] that for every automaton there is a graph in which it cannot visit all nodes, see a modern proof by Fraigniaud et al. [6]. On the other hand, Disser et al. [5] recently proved that if such an automaton is additionally equipped with $O(\log \log n)$ memory and $O(\log \log n)$ pebbles, then it can traverse every graph with n nodes, and this amount of resources is optimal. For graph-walking automata, there are results on the construction of halting and reversible automata by Kunc and Okhotin [14], as well as recent lower bounds on the complexity of these transformations and related bounds on the state complexity of Boolean operations established by the authors [16,17].

Graph-walking automata are a generalization of two-way finite automata and tree-walking automata. Two-way finite automata are a standard model in automata theory, and the complexity of their determinization remains a major open problem, notable for its connection to the L vs. NL problem in the complexity theory [11]. Tree-walking automata (TWA) have received particular attention

This work was supported by the Ministry of Science and Higher Education of the Russian Federation, agreement 075-15-2019-1619.

P. Caron and L. Mignot (Eds.): CIAA 2022, LNCS 13266, pp. 177–188, 2022.
https://doi.org/10.1007/978-3-031-07469-1_14

in the last two decades, with important results on their expressive power established by Bojańczyk and Colcombet [1,2].

The theory of tree-walking and graph-walking automata needs further development. In particular, not much is known about their size complexity. For two-way finite automata (2DFA), only the complexity of transforming them to one-way automata has been well researched [7,8,10,12,18]. Also some bounds on the complexity of operations on 2DFA are known [9,13], which also rely on the transformation to one-way automata. This proof method has no analogue for TWA and GWA, and the complexity of operations on these models remains uninvestigated. In turn, lower bounds on the complexity of transforming GWA to halting and reversible [16] also have no analogues for TWA and 2DFA. Using these methods, state complexity of Boolean operations on graph-walking automata has recently been determined [17].

This paper continues the investigation of the state complexity of graph-walking automata, with some results extending to tree-walking automata. The goal is to study some of the few available operations on graphs: node-replacement homomorphisms, as well as inverse homomorphisms. In the case of strings, a homomorphism is defined by the identity $h(uv) = h(u)h(v)$, and the class of regular languages is closed under all homomorphisms, as well as under their inverses, defined by $h^{-1}(L) = \{\, w \mid h(w) \in L \,\}$. For the 2DFA model, the complexity of inverse homomorphisms is known: as shown by Jirásková and Okhotin [9], it is exactly $2n$ in the worst case, where n is the number of states in the original automaton. However, this proof is based on the transformations between one-way and two-way finite automata, which is a property unique for the string case. The state complexity of homomorphisms for 2DFA is known to lie between exponential and double exponential [9]. For tree-walking and graph-walking automata, no such questions were investigated before, and they are addressed in this paper.

The closure of graph-walking automata under every inverse homomorphism is easy: in Sect. 3 it is shown that, for an n-state GWA, there is a GWA with $nk + 1$ states for its inverse homomorphic image, where k is the number of labels of edge end-points. If the label of the initial node is unique, then nk states are enough. This transformation is proved to be optimal by establishing a lower bound of nk states. The proof of the lower bound makes use of a graph that is easy to pass in one direction and hard to pass in reverse, constructed in the authors' [16] recent paper.

The other result of this paper, presented in Sect. 4, is that the family of tree languages recognized by tree-walking automata is not closed under injective homomorpisms, thus settling this question for graph-walking automata as well. The result is proved by first establishing a characterization of regular tree languages by a combination of an injective homomorphism and an inverse homomorphism. This characterization generalizes a known result by Latteux and Leguy [15], see also an earlier result by Čulík et al. [4]. In light of this characterization, closure under injective homomorphisms would imply that every regular tree language is recognized by a tree-walking automaton, which would contradict the famous result by Bojańczyk and Colcombet [2].

2   Graph-walking Automata

A formal definition of graph-walking automata (GWA) requires more elaborate notation than for 2DFA and TWA. It begins with a generalization of an alphabet to the case of graphs: a *signature*.

Definition 1 (Kunc and Okhotin [14]). *A signature S is a quintuple $S = (D, -, \Sigma, \Sigma_0, (D_a)_{a \in \Sigma})$, where:*

- *D is a finite set of directions, which are labels attached to edge end-points;*
- *a bijection $-\colon D \to D$ provides an opposite direction, with $-(-d) = d$ for all $d \in D$;*
- *Σ is a finite set of node labels;*
- *$\Sigma_0 \subseteq \Sigma$ is a non-empty subset of possible labels of the initial node;*
- *$D_a \subseteq D$, for every $a \in \Sigma$, is the set of directions in nodes labelled with a.*

Like strings are defined over an alphabet, graphs are defined over a signature.

Definition 2. *A graph over a signature $S = (D, -, \Sigma, \Sigma_0, (D_a)_{a \in \Sigma})$ is a quadruple $(V, v_0, +, \lambda)$, where:*

- *V is a finite set of nodes;*
- *$v_0 \in V$ is the initial node;*
- *edges are defined by a partial function $+\colon V \times D \to V$, such that if $v + d$ is defined, then $(v + d) + (-d)$ is defined and equals v;*
- *node labels are assigned by a total mapping $\lambda\colon V \to \Sigma$, such that $v + d$ is defined if and only if $d \in D_{\lambda(v)}$, and $\lambda(v) \in \Sigma_0$ if and only if $v = v_0$.*

The set of all graphs over S is denoted by $L(S)$.

In this paper, all graphs are finite and connected.

A graph-walking automaton is defined similarly to a 2DFA, with an input graph instead of an input string.

Definition 3. *A (deterministic) graph-walking automaton (GWA) over a signature $S = (D, -, \Sigma, \Sigma_0, (D_a)_{a \in \Sigma})$ is a quadruple $A = (Q, q_0, F, \delta)$, where*

- *Q is a finite set of states;*
- *$q_0 \in Q$ is the initial state;*
- *$F \subseteq Q \times \Sigma$ is a set of acceptance conditions;*
- *$\delta\colon (Q \times \Sigma) \setminus F \to Q \times D$ is a partial transition function, with $\delta(q, a) \in Q \times D_a$ for all a and q where δ is defined.*

A computation of a GWA on a graph $(V, v_0, +, \lambda)$ is a uniquely defined sequence of configurations (q, v), with $q \in Q$ and $v \in V$. It begins with (q_0, v_0) and proceeds from (q, v) to $(q', v + d)$, where $\delta(q, \lambda(v)) = (q', d)$. The automaton accepts by reaching (q, v) with $(q, \lambda(v)) \in F$.

On each input graph, a GWA can accept, reject or loop. The set of all graphs accepted is denoted by $L(A)$.

The operation on graphs investigated in this paper is a *node-replacement homomorphism*, which replaces nodes with subgraphs.

Definition 4. *Let S and $\widehat{S}$ be two signatures, with the set of directions of S contained in the set of directions of $\widehat{S}$. A mapping $h\colon L(S) \to L(\widehat{S})$ is a homomorphism, if, for every graph G over S, the graph $h(G)$ is constructed out of G as follows. For every node label a in S, there is a connected subgraph $h(a)$ over the signature $\widehat{S}$, which has an edge leading outside for every direction in D_a; these edges are called* external. *Then, $h(G)$ is obtained out of G by replacing every node v with a subgraph $h(v) = h(a)$, where a is the label of v, so that the edges that come out of v in G become the external edges of this copy of $h(a)$.*

The subgraph $h(a)$ must contain at least one node. It contains an initial node if and only if the label a is initial.

3   Inverse Homomorphisms: Upper and Lower Bounds

Given a graph-walking automaton A and a homomorphism h, the inverse homomorphic image $h^{-1}(L(A))$ can be recognized by another automaton that, on a graph G, simulates the operation of A on the image $h(G)$. A construction of such an automaton is presented in the following theorem.

Theorem 1. *Let S be a signature with $k \geqslant 1$ directions, and let $\widehat{S}$ be a signature containing all directions from S. Let $h\colon L(S) \to L(\widehat{S})$ be a graph homomorphism between these signatures. Let A be a graph-walking automaton with n states that operates on graphs over $\widehat{S}$. Then there exists a graph-walking automaton B with $nk + 1$ states, operating on graphs over S, which accepts a graph G if and only if A accepts its image $h(G)$. If S contains a unique initial label, then it is sufficient to use nk states.*

In order to carry out the simulation of A on $h(G)$ while working on G, it is sufficient for B to remember the current state of A and the direction in which A has entered the image in $h(G)$ of the current node of B. The full construction is omitted due to space constraints.

It turns out that this expected construction is actually optimal, as long as the initial label is unique: the matching lower bound of nk states is proved below.

Theorem 2. *For every $k \geqslant 9$, there is a signature S with k directions and a homomorphism $h\colon L(S) \to L(S)$, such that for every $n \geqslant 4$, there exists an n-state automaton A over the signature S, such that every automaton B, which accepts a graph G if and only if A accepts $h(G)$, has at least nk states.*

Proving lower bounds on the size of graph-walking automata is generally not easy. Informally, it has to be proved that the automaton must remember a lot; however, in theory, it can always return to the initial node and recover all the information it has forgotten. In order to eliminate this possibility, the initial node shall be placed in a special subgraph H_{start}, from which the automaton can easily get out, but if it ever needs to reenter this subgraph, finding the initial node would require too many states. This subgraph is constructed in the following lemma; besides H_{start}, there is another subgraph $H_{\text{dead end}}$, which is identical to H_{start} except for not having an initial label; then, it would be hard for an automaton to distinguish between these two subgraphs from the outside, and it would not identify the one in which it has started.

Lemma 1. *For every $k \geqslant 4$ there is a signature S_{start} with k directions, with two pairs of opposite directions $+1$, -1 and $+2$, -2, such that for every $n \geqslant 2$ there are graphs H_{start} and $H_{\text{dead end}}$ over this signature, with the following properties.*

    I. *The subgraph H_{start} contains an initial node, whereas $H_{\text{dead end}}$ does not; both have one external edge in the direction $+1$.*

    II. *There is an n-state automaton, which begins its computation on H_{start} in the initial node, and leaves this subgraph by the external edge.*

    III. *Every automaton with fewer than $2(k-3)(n-1)$ states, having entered H_{start} and $H_{\text{dead end}}$ by the external edge in the same state, either leaves both graphs in the same state, or accepts both, or rejects both, or loops on both.*

The proof reuses a graph constructed by the authors in a recent paper [16]. Originally, it was used to show that there is an n-state graph-walking automaton, such that every automaton that accepts the same graphs and returns to the initial node after acceptance must have at least $2(k-3)(n-1)$ states [16, Thm. 18], cf. upper bound $2nk + n$ [16, Thm. 9]. The adaptation of this argument necessary to match the statement of Lemma 1 is omitted due to space constraints.

Now, using the subgraphs H_{start} and $H_{\text{dead end}}$ as building blocks, the next goal is to construct a subgraph which encodes a number from 0 to $n - 1$, so that this number is easy to calculate along with getting out of this subgraph for the first time, but if it is ever forgotten, then it cannot be recovered without using too many states. For each number $i \in \{0, \ldots, n-1\}$ and for each direction $d \in D$, this is a graph $F_{i,d}$ that contains the initial label and encodes the number i, and a graph F_d with no initial label that encodes no number at all.

Lemma 2. *For every $k \geqslant 4$ there is a signature S_F obtained from S_{start} by adding several new node labels, such that, for every $n \geqslant 2$ there are subgraphs $F_{i,d}$ and F_d, for all $i \in \{0, \ldots, n-1\}$ and $d \in D$, with the following properties.*

    I. *Each subgraph $F_{i,d}$ and F_d has one external edge in the direction d. Subgraphs of the form $F_{i,d}$ have an initial node, and subgraphs F_d do not have one.*

    II. *There is an automaton with states $\{q_0, \ldots, q_{n-1}\}$, which, having started on every subgraph $F_{i,d}$ in the initial node, eventually gets out in the state q_i.*

    III. *Every automaton with fewer than $2(k-3)(n-1)$ states, having entered $F_{i,d}$ and F_d with the same d by the external edge in the same state, either leaves both subgraphs in the same state, or accepts both, or rejects both, or loops on both.*

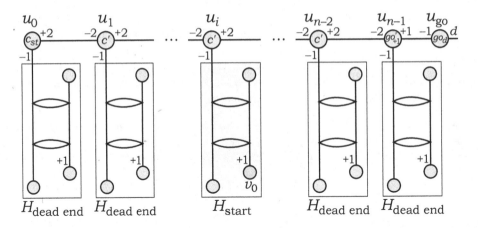

Fig. 1. The subgraph $F_{i,d}$, with $d \neq -1$; for $d = -1$ the subgraph has u_{n-1} labelled with go'_{+2}, and a $(+2, -2)$-edge to u_{go}.

Each subgraph $F_{i,d}$ is a chain of n nodes, with the subgraph H_{start} attached at the i-th position, and with $n-1$ copies of $H_{dead\ end}$ attached at the remaining positions, as illustrated in Fig. 1. The automaton in Part II gets out of H_{start} and then moves along the chain to the left, counting the number of steps, so that it gets out of the final node u_{go} in the state q_i. The proof of Part III relies on Lemma 1 (Part III): if an automaton enters $F_{i,d}$ and F_d from the outside, it ends up walking over the chain and every time it enters any of the attached subgraphs H_{start} and $H_{dead\ end}$, it cannot distinguish between them and continues in the same way on all $F_{i,d}$ and F_d.

Proof (of Theorem 2). The signature S is S_F from Lemma 2, with a few extra node labels: $\{ go_{-d,+1} \mid d \in D \setminus \{-1\} \} \cup \{ go_{+1,+2}, c_-, q_0? \} \cup \{ d? \mid d \in D \} \cup \{ acc_d, rej_d \mid d \in D \}$. Let the directions be cyclically ordered, so that $next(d)$ is the next direction after d and $prev(d)$ is the previous direction. The order is chosen so that, for each direction d, its opposite direction is neither $next(d)$ nor $next(next(d))$.

The new labels have the following sets of directions: $D_{go_{d_1,d_2}} = \{d_1, d_2\}$; $D_{c_-} = \{-1, +1\}$; $D_{q_0?} = \{-1\}$; $D_{d?} = D$ for all $d \in D$; $D_{acc_d} = D_{rej_d} = \{-d, -next(d), next(next(d))\}$ for all $d \in D$, where the directions $-d, -next(d), next(next(d))$ are pairwise distinct by assumption.

The homomorphism h affects only new labels of the form $d?$, with $d \in D$, whereas the rest of the labels are unaffected. Each label $d?$, for $d \in D$, is replaced with a circular subgraph $h(d?)$, as illustrated in Fig. 3. The node entered in the direction d has label acc_d, and every other node is labelled with rej_e, with $e \neq d$. When the automaton enters this subgraph in the image, it knows the direction it came from, whereas in the original graph, it has to remember this direction in its state.

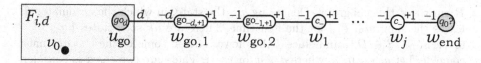

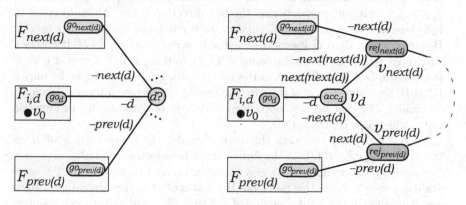

Fig. 2. The graph $G_{i,j,d}$, with $d \neq -1$; for $d = -1$ the graph has $w_{go,1}$ labelled with $go_{+1,+2}$ and $w_{go,2}$ labelled with $go_{-2,+1}$, linked with a $(+2, -2)$-edge.

Fig. 3. The graph $G_{i,d,d}$ and its image $h(G_{i,d,d})$.

The graph $G_{i,j,d}$ is defined by taking $F_{i,d}$ from Lemma 2 and attaching to it a chain of $j + 3$ nodes, as shown in Fig. 2.

The graph $G_{i,d,d'}$ is presented in Fig. 3 for the case $d = d'$. It has a subgraph $F_{i,d}$ with the initial node, and $k - 1$ subgraphs F_e, with $e \in D \setminus \{d\}$. The external edges of these k subgraphs are all linked to a new node v labelled with $d'?$.

Claim 1. There exists an n-state automaton A, which accepts $h(G_{i,j,d})$ if and only if $i = j$, and which accepts $h(G_{i,d,d'})$ if and only if $d = d'$.

The automaton is based on the one defined in Lemma 2 (Part II). On the graph $h(G_{i,j,d})$, it gets out of the subgraph $F_{i,d}$ in the state q_i, and then decrements the counter j times as it continues to the right; if it reaches the end of the chain in q_0, it accepts. On the graph $h(G_{i,d,d'})$, the automaton comes to the ring $h(d'?)$; if $d = d'$, it arrives at the node with label acc_d and accepts; otherwise, the label is rej_d, and it rejects.

Claim 2. Let an automaton B accept a graph G if and only if A accepts $h(G)$. Then B has at least nk states.

The proof is by contradiction. Suppose that B has fewer than nk states. Since $nk \leqslant 2 \cdot \frac{2}{3}k \cdot \frac{3}{4}n \leqslant 2(k-3)(n-1)$, Lemma 2 (Part III) applies, and the automaton B cannot distinguish between the subgraphs $F_{i,d}$ and F_d if it enters them from the outside.

On the graph $G_{i,j,d}$, the automaton must check that i is equal to j, where the latter is the number of labels c_- after the exit from $F_{i,d}$. In order to check this,

B must exit this subgraph. Denote by $q_{i,d}$ the state, in which the automaton B leaves the subgraph $F_{i,d}$ for the first time. There are nk such states $\{\, q_{i,d} \mid i = 0, \ldots, n-1; d \in D \,\}$, and since B has fewer states, some of these states must coincide. Let $q_{i,d} = q_{j,d'}$, where $d \neq d'$ or $i \neq j$. There are two cases to consider.

- Case 1: $d \neq d'$. The automaton B must accept $G_{i,d,d}$ and reject $G_{j,d',d}$. On either graph, it first arrives to the corresponding node v in the same state $q_{i,d} = q_{j,d'}$, without remembering the last direction taken. Then, in order to tell these graphs apart, the automaton must carry out some further checks. However, every time B leaves the node v in any direction $e \in D$, it enters a subgraph, which is either the same in $G_{i,d,d}$ and $G_{j,d',d}$ (if $e \neq d, d'$), or it is a subgraph that is different in the two graphs, but, according to Lemma 2 (Part III), no automaton of this size can distinguish between these subgraphs. Therefore, B either accepts both graphs, or rejects both graphs, or loops on both, which is a contradiction.
- Case 2: $d = d'$ and $i \neq j$. In this case, consider the computations of B on the graphs $G_{i,j,d}$ and $G_{j,j,d}$: the former must be rejected, the latter accepted. However, by the assumption, the automaton leaves $F_{i,d}$ and $F_{j,d}$ in the same state $q_{i,d} = q_{j,d}$. From this point on, the states of B in the two computations are the same while it walks outside of $F_{i,d}$ and $F_{j,d}$, and each time it reenters these subgraphs, by Lemma 2 (Part III), it either accepts both, or rejects both, or loops on both, or leaves both in the same state. Thus, the whole computations have the same outcome, which is a contradiction.

The contradiction obtained shows that B has at least nk states. $\square$

4   A Characterization of Regular Tree Languages

The next question investigated in this paper is whether the family of graph languages recognized by graph-walking automata is closed under homomorphisms. In this section, non-closure is established already for tree-walking automata and for injective homomorphisms.

The proof is based on a seemingly unrelated result. Consider the following known representation of regular string languages.

Theorem A (Latteux and Leguy [15]). *For every regular language $L \subseteq \Sigma^*$ there exist alphabets Ω and Γ, a special symbol $\#$, and homomorhisms $f \colon \Omega^* \to \#^*$, $g \colon \Omega^* \to \Gamma^*$ and $h \colon \Sigma^* \to \Gamma^*$, such that $L = h^{-1}(g(f^{-1}(\#)))$.*

A similar representation shall now be established for regular tree languages, that is, those recognized by deterministic bottom-up tree automata.

For uniformity of notation, tree and tree-walking automata shall be represented in the notation of graph-walking automata, as in Sect. 2, which is somewhat different from the notation used in the tree automata literature. This is only notation, and the trees and the automata are mathematically the same.

Definition 5. *A signature $S = (D, -, \Sigma, \Sigma_0, (D_a)_{a \in \Sigma})$ is a* tree signature*, if: the set of directions is $D = \{+1, -1, \ldots, +k, -k\}$, for some $k \geqslant 1$, where directions $+i$ and $-i$ are opposite to each other; for every label $a \in \Sigma$, the number of its children is denoted by $\operatorname{rank} a$, with $0 \leqslant \operatorname{rank} a \leqslant k$; every initial label $a_0 \in \Sigma_0$ has directions $D_{a_0} = \{+1, \ldots, +\operatorname{rank} a_0\}$; every non-initial label $a \in \Sigma \setminus \Sigma_0$ has the set of directions $D_a = \{-d, +1, \ldots, +\operatorname{rank} a\}$, for some $d \in \{1, \ldots, k\}$.*

A tree *is a connected graph over a tree signature.*

This implements the classical notion of a tree. The initial node is its root. In a node v with label a, the directions $+1, \ldots, +\operatorname{rank} a$ lead to its children, and the child in the direction $+i$ has direction $-i$ to its parent. There is no direction to the parent in the root node. Labels a with $\operatorname{rank} a = 0$ are used in the leaves.

Definition 6. *A (deterministic bottom-up)* tree automaton *over a tree signature $S = (D, -, \Sigma, \Sigma_0, (D_a)_{a \in \Sigma})$ is a triple $A = (Q, q_{acc}, (\delta_a)_{a \in \Sigma})$, where*

- *Q is a finite set of states;*
- *$q_{acc} \in Q$ is the accepting state, effective in the root node;*
- *$\delta_a: Q^{\operatorname{rank} a} \to Q$, for each $a \in \Sigma$, is a function computed at the label a.*

Given a tree T over a signature S, a tree automaton A computes the state in each node, bottom-up. The state in each leaf v labelled with a is set to be the constant $\delta_a()$. Once a node v labelled with a has the states $q_1, \ldots, q_{\operatorname{rank} a}$ in its children, the state in the node v is $\delta_a(q_1, \ldots, q_{\operatorname{rank} a})$. This continues until the value in the root is computed. If it is q_{acc}, then the tree is accepted, and otherwise it is rejected. The tree language recognized by A is the set of all trees over S that A accepts. A tree language recognized by some tree automaton is called *regular*.

The generalization of Theorem A to the case of trees actually uses only two homomorphisms, not three. The inverse homomorphism f^{-1} in Theorem A generates the set of all strings with a marked first symbol out of a single symbol; trees cannot be generated this way. The characterization below starts from the set of all trees over a certain signature, with their roots marked by definition; this has the same effect as $f^{-1}(\{\#\})$ in Theorem A. The remaining two homomorphisms do mostly the same as in the original result, generalized to trees.

Theorem 3. *Let L be a regular tree language over a tree signature S_{reg}. Then there exists tree signatures S_{comp} and S_{mid}, and injective homomorphisms $g: L(S_{comp}) \to L(S_{mid})$ and $h: L(S_{reg}) \to L(S_{mid})$, such that $L = h^{-1}(g(L(S_{comp})))$.*

Proof (a sketch). Let L be a non-empty regular tree language over a signature $S_{reg} = (D, -, \Sigma, \Sigma_0, (D_a)_{a \in \Sigma})$, recognized by a tree automaton $A = (Q, q_{acc}, (\delta_a)_{a \in \Sigma})$. Let $Q = \{1, \ldots, n\}$.

The homomorphism h is defined to effectively replace each $(+i, -i)$-edge with a *fishbone subgraph*, as illustrated in Fig. 4. The original nodes and their labels are not affected. This is formally done by replacing each non-initial node labelled with $a \in \Sigma \setminus \Sigma_0$ with the same node with the edge to the parent replaced with a

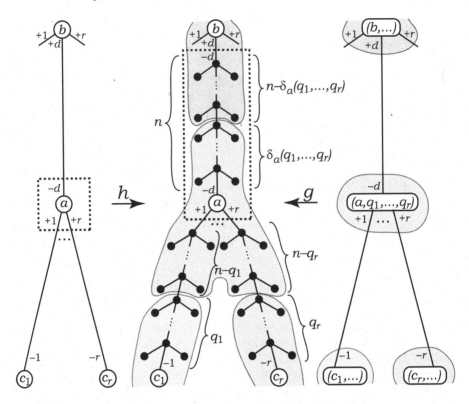

Fig. 4. Homomorphisms h and g mapping the original tree T (left) and the corresponding valid annotated tree T_{comp} (right) to the same tree with fishbones.

fishbone. The initial node is mapped to itself. The signature S_{mid} extends S_{reg} with the labels needed to define the fishbones.

The main idea of the construction is to take a tree accepted by A and annotate node labels with the states in the accepting computation of A on this tree. Another homomorphism g maps such annotated trees to trees over the signature S_{mid}, with fishbones therein. Annotated trees that correctly encode a valid computation are mapped to trees with all fishbones of length exactly n; then, h^{-1} decodes the original tree out of this encoding. On the other hand, any mistakes in the annotation are mapped by g to fishbones of length other than n, and the resulting trees have no pre-images under h.

Trees with annotated computations, defined over the signature S_{comp}, have each node labelled with a pair $(a, (q_1, \ldots, q_{\mathrm{rank}\, a}))$, where $a \in \Sigma$ is its label in the original tree, and $q_1, \ldots, q_{\mathrm{rank}\, a} \in Q$ are meant to be the states computed by A on the children of this node. The homomorphism g replaces such a node with a node labelled a, with attached fragments of fishbones in all directions. The fishbone directed to the i-th child has length $n - q_i$, and the fishbone in the direction upwards is of length $\delta_a(q_1, \ldots, q_{\mathrm{rank}\, a})$. In the root node, only labels $(a_0, (q_1, \ldots, q_{\mathrm{rank}\, a}))$ with $\delta_{a_0}(q_1, \ldots, q_{\mathrm{rank}\, a}) = q_{acc}$ are allowed.

Let T be a tree accepted by A, and let T_{comp} be an annotated tree that encodes the computation of A on T. Then the image $g(T_{comp})$ has each fishbone made of two fragments, one of length q coming from the child, where q is the state in the child, and the other of length $n - q$ coming from the parent. Thus, every fishbone is of length n, and $g(T_{comp})$ has a pre-image under h, which is T.

On the other hand, every annotated tree $\widetilde{T}$ over the signature S_{comp} which encodes something other than a valid accepting computation, has at least one mismatch in the states between a parent and a child, and g maps this mismatch to a fishbone of length other than n. So, $g(\widetilde{T})$ has no pre-images under h. This proves that $h^{-1}(g(L(S_{comp}))) = L$. $\qquad\square$

Theorem 4. *The class of tree languages recognized by tree-walking automata is not closed under injective homomorphisms.*

Proof. Suppose it is closed. It is claimed that then every regular tree language is recognized by a tree-walking automaton. Let L be a regular tree language over some tree signature S_{reg}. Then, by Theorem 3, there exist tree signatures S_{comp} and S_{mid}, and injective homomorphisms $g\colon L(S_{comp}) \to L(S_{mid})$ and $h\colon L(S_{reg}) \to L(S_{mid})$, such that $L = h^{-1}(g(L(S_{comp})))$. The language $L(S_{comp})$ is trivially recognized by a tree-walking automaton that accepts every tree right away. Then, by the assumption on the closure under g, the language $g(L(S_{comp}))$ is recognized by another tree-walking automaton. By Theorem 1, its inverse homomorphic image L is recognized by a tree-walking automaton as well. This contradicts the result by Bojańczyk and Colcombet [2] on the existence of regular tree languages not recognized by any tree-walking automata. $\qquad\square$

5 Future Work

The lower bound on the complexity of inverse homomorphisms is obtained using graphs with cycles, and thus does not apply to tree-walking automata (TWA). On the other hand, in the even more restricted case of 2DFA, the state complexity of inverse homomorphisms is $2n$ [9], which is in line of the kn bound in this paper, as 2DFA have $k = 2$. It would be interesting to fill in the missing case of TWA.

References

1. Bojanczyk, M., Colcombet, T.: Tree-walking automata cannot be determinized. Theor. Comput. Sci. **350**(2–3), 164–173 (2006)
2. Bojanczyk, M., Colcombet, T.: Tree-walking automata do not recognize all regular languages. SIAM J. Comput. **38**(2), 658–701 (2008)
3. Budach, L.: Automata and labyrinths. Mathematische Nachrichten **86**(1), 195–282 (1978)
4. Culík, K., II., Fich, F.E., Salomaa, A.: A homomorphic characterization of regular languages. Discret. Appl. Math. **4**(2), 149–152 (1982)
5. Disser, Y., Hackfeld, J., Klimm, M.: Tight bounds for undirected graph exploration with pebbles and multiple agents. J. ACM **66**(6), 40:1–40:41 (2019)

6. Fraigniaud, P., Ilcinkas, D., Peer, G., Pelc, A., Peleg, D.: Graph exploration by a finite automaton. Theor. Comput. Sci. **345**(2–3), 331–344 (2005)

7. Geffert, V., Mereghetti, C., Pighizzini, G.: Converting two-way nondeterministic unary automata into simpler automata. Theor. Comput. Sci. **295**, 189–203 (2003)

8. Geffert, V., Okhotin, A.: Deterministic one-way simulation of two-way deterministic finite automata over small alphabets. In: Han, Y., Ko, S. (eds.) Descriptional Complexity of Formal Systems - 23rd IFIP WG 1.02 International Conference, DCFS 2021, Virtual Event, 5 September 2021, Proceedings. LNCS, vol. 13037, pp. 26–37. Springer, Cham (2021). https://doi.org/10.1007/978-3-030-93489-7_3

9. Jirásková, G., Okhotin, A.: On the state complexity of operations on two-way finite automata. Inf. Comput. **253**, 36–63 (2017)

10. Kapoutsis, C.: Removing bidirectionality from nondeterministic finite automata. In: Jedrzejowicz, J., Szepietowski, A. (eds.) MFCS 2005. LNCS, vol. 3618, pp. 544–555. Springer, Heidelberg (2005). https://doi.org/10.1007/11549345_47

11. Kapoutsis, C.A., Pighizzini, G.: Two-way automata characterizations of l/poly versus NL. Theory Comput. Syst. **56**(4), 662–685 (2015)

12. Kunc, M., Okhotin, A.: Describing periodicity in two-way deterministic finite automata using transformation semigroups. In: Mauri, G., Leporati, A. (eds.) DLT 2011. LNCS, vol. 6795, pp. 324–336. Springer, Heidelberg (2011). https://doi.org/10.1007/978-3-642-22321-1_28

13. Kunc, M., Okhotin, A.: State complexity of operations on two-way finite automata over a unary alphabet. Theor. Comput. Sci. **449**, 106–118 (2012)

14. Kunc, M., Okhotin, A.: Reversibility of computations in graph-walking automata. Inf. Comput. **275**, 104631 (2020)

15. Latteux, M., Leguy, J.: On the composition of morphisms and inverse morphisms. In: Diaz, J. (ed.) ICALP 1983. LNCS, vol. 154, pp. 420–432. Springer, Heidelberg (1983). https://doi.org/10.1007/BFb0036926

16. Martynova, O., Okhotin, A.: Lower bounds for graph-walking automata. In: Bläser, M., Monmege, B. (eds.) 38th International Symposium on Theoretical Aspects of Computer Science, STACS 2021, 16–1, March 2021, Saarbrücken, Germany (Virtual Conference). LIPIcs, vol. 187, pp. 52:1–52:13. Schloss Dagstuhl - Leibniz-Zentrum für Informatik (2021)

17. Martynova, O., Okhotin, A.: State complexity of union and intersection on graph-walking automata. In: Han, Y., Ko, S. (eds.) Descriptional Complexity of Formal Systems - 23rd IFIP WG 1.02 International Conference, DCFS 2021, Virtual Event, September 5, 2021, Proceedings. LNCS, vol. 13037, pp. 125–136. Springer, Cham (2021). https://doi.org/10.1007/978-3-030-93489-7_11

18. Petrov, S., Okhotin, A.: On the transformation of two-way deterministic finite automata to unambiguous finite automata. In: Leporati, A., Martín-Vide, C., Shapira, D., Zandron, C. (eds.) LATA 2021. LNCS, vol. 12638, pp. 81–93. Springer, Cham (2021). https://doi.org/10.1007/978-3-030-68195-1_7

Nondeterministic State Complexity
of Site-Directed Deletion

Oliver A.S. Lyon[✉] and Kai Salomaa[✉]

School of Computing, Queen's University, Kingston, ON K7L 3N6, Canada
{oliver.lyon,salomaa}@queensu.ca

Abstract. Site-directed deletion is a biologically inspired operation that removes a contiguous substring from the host string guided by a template string. The template string must match the prefix and suffix of a substring. When this occurs the middle section of the substring not contained in the prefix or suffix is removed. We consider the nondeterministic state complexity of the site-directed deletion operation. For regular languages recognized by nondeterministic finite automata with N and M states, respectively, we establish a new upper bound of $2NM + N$ and a new worst case lower bound of $2NM$. The upper bound improves a previously established upper bound, and no non-trivial lower bound was previously known for the nondeterministic state complexity of site-directed deletion.

Keywords: Descriptional complexity · Nondeterministic finite automaton · Fooling set · Bio-inspired operations

1 Introduction

Polymerase Chain Reaction (PCR) is a family of laboratory methods for editing and manipulating DNA [16]. One such method is site-directed mutagenesis, which uses single strands of DNA as a template to guide the insertion or deletion of DNA [3]. In general, insertion and deletion operations are natural complementary operations when working with DNA editing. We consider site-directed deletion mutagenesis, which uses DNA primers to identify complementary substrings in a host strand and remove the contiguous substring between the primers. We can informally describe the site-directed deletion operation as using a target string to identify a non-empty outfix of a substring from the host string. Once a non-empty outfix is identified, the section of substring not contained in the outfix is deleted.

Algorithms and computational models employing PCR have been studied previously [1,8,15,17]. There have been several studies of bio-inspired insertion and deletion systems to assess computational power [13,14,18]. Since biology has a wide variety of methods for editing and manipulating DNA, there have been several definitions developed in formal languages to describe different deletion operations [7,9,12].

© Springer Nature Switzerland AG 2022
P. Caron and L. Mignot (Eds.): CIAA 2022, LNCS 13266, pp. 189–199, 2022.
https://doi.org/10.1007/978-3-031-07469-1_15

Site-directed insertion is, roughly speaking, the operation complementary to site-directed deletion. The language-theoretic properties and state complexity of site-directed insertion have been considered in [5,6]. The language-theoretic definitions of site-directed deletion were originally given by Cho et al. [4]. In this work they also provide an upper bound for the nondeterministic state complexity.

In this paper, we develop new bounds on the nondeterministic state complexity for site-directed deletion. We begin by improving the upper bound on the nondeterministic state complexity of site-directed deletion, and then we provide a nearly matching lower bound for site-directed deletion. Finally, we establish tight bounds on the nondeterministic state complexity of site-directed deletion as it acts over unary languages.

2   Preliminaries

This paper uses much of the notation defined in introductory automata textbooks [11]. In this section, a review of the essentials is provided. We are primarily focused on nondeterministic finite automata (NFA) and their associated state complexity.

In the following Σ is a finite alphabet, Σ^* is the set of all strings over Σ, Σ^+ is the subset of Σ^* where all strings have length greater than zero. We use ε to represent the empty string. The length of a string is denoted by $\mid w \mid$ for a string $w \in \Sigma^*$.

An NFA A is represented with a tuple $(Q, \Sigma, \delta, s, F)$, where Q is the finite set of states of A, Σ is the finite alphabet, δ is the partial transition function defined over $Q \times \Sigma \to 2^Q$, $s \in Q$ is the start state and, $F \subseteq Q$ is the set of final states. A path $\mathcal{P}$ is a sequence of states in A that are connected by transitions. Each path is associated with a string w. We consider a path accepting if it starts at s and ends at $q \in F$. The language $L(A)$ is the set of all strings in Σ^* with accepting paths in A. We also introduce the function $Closure_A$, defined for NFA A as follows, $Closure_A(q) = \{q' \mid \exists \text{ path } \mathcal{P} \text{ from } q \text{ to } q' \text{ in } A\}$

To establish lower bounds on nondeterministic state complexity we recall the fooling set technique.

Proposition 1 (Fooling Set Technique [2]**).** *Let $L \subset \Sigma^*$ be a regular language. Additionally consider a set containing pairs of strings $FS = \{(x_1, y_1), (x_2, y_2), \cdots, (x_n, y_n)\}$ such that $x_i y_i \in L$, for $i = 1, 2, ..., n$ and $x_i y_j \notin L$ or $x_j y_i \notin L$ where $1 \leq i, j \leq n$ and $i \neq j$. Then any NFA recognizing L must contain at least n states.*

We now introduce the definition of site-directed deletion language operation as it was defined by Cho et al. [4].

Definition 1. *For languages L_1 and L_2, the site-directed deletion language of L_2 on L_1 is defined as follows:*

$$L_1 \xleftarrow{SDD} L_2 = \{xy_1 y_2 z \mid xy_1 \bar{y} y_2 z \in L_1, y_1 y_2 \in L_2, y_1 \neq \varepsilon, y_2 \neq \varepsilon\}.$$

Cho et al. [4] showed that for regular languages L_1 and L_2 the language $L_1 \xleftarrow{SDD} L_2$ is regular and their construction implies an upper bound for the nondeterministic state complexity of site-directed deletion.

3 General Alphabet Site-Directed Deletion

We consider the nondeterministic state complexity of site-directed deletion over a general alphabet. We begin by improving the known $2NM + 2N$ upper bound from Cho et al. [4].

Theorem 1. *For NFAs A_1 and A_2 with N and M states, respectively, the language $L(A_1) \xleftarrow{SDD} L(A_2)$ is recognized by an NFA with $2NM + N$ states.*

Proof. For NFAs $A_1 = (Q, \Sigma, \delta, s_1, F_1)$ and $A_2 = (P, \Sigma, \gamma, s_2, F_2)$, we can define the automaton $A_{SDD} = (Q_{SDD}, \Sigma, \Omega, (s_1, s_2)_{\mathcal{X}_1}, F_{SDD})$, which recognizes the language $L(A_1) \xleftarrow{SDD} L(A_2)$. We define the states in Q_{SDD} as follows:

$$Q_{SDD} = (Q \times P)_{\mathcal{X}_1} \cup (Q \times P)_{\mathcal{X}_2} \cup (Q \times \{p_f\}).$$

Subscripts indicate copies of the Cartesian product of the sets Q and P. The set of final states is defined as:

$$F_{SDD} = \{(q, p_f) \mid q \in F_1\}.$$

We define the transition function Ω for $\alpha \in \Sigma$ as follows:

(i) for $(q, s_2)_{\mathcal{X}_1}$ where $q \in Q$:

$$\begin{aligned} \Omega((q, s_2)_{\mathcal{X}_1}, \alpha) = &\{(q', s_2)_{\mathcal{X}_1} \mid q' \in \delta(q, \alpha)\} \\ &\cup \{(q', p')_{\mathcal{X}_1} \mid q' \in \delta(q, \alpha), p' \in \gamma(s_2, \alpha)\} \\ &\cup \{(q'', p')_{\mathcal{X}_2} \mid q'' \in Closure_{A_1}(q'), q' \in \delta(q, \alpha), p' \in \gamma(s_2, \alpha)\}. \end{aligned}$$

(ii) for $(q, p)_{\mathcal{X}_1}$ where $q \in Q$ and $p \in P$:

$$\begin{aligned} \Omega((q, p)_{\mathcal{X}_1}, \alpha) = &\{(q', p')_{\mathcal{X}_1} \mid q' \in \delta(q, \alpha), p' \in \gamma(p, \alpha)\} \\ &\cup \{(q'', p')_{\mathcal{X}_2} \mid q'' \in Closure_{A_1}(q'), q' \in \delta(q, \alpha), p' \in \gamma(p, \alpha)\}. \end{aligned}$$

(iii) for $(q, p)_{\mathcal{X}_2}$ where $q \in Q$ and $p \in P$:

$$\begin{aligned} \Omega((q, p)_{\mathcal{X}_2}, \alpha) = &\{(q', p')_{\mathcal{X}_2} \mid q' \in \delta(q, \alpha) \text{ and } p' \in \gamma(p, \alpha)\} \\ &\cup \{(q', p_f) \mid q' \in \delta(q, \alpha) \text{ and } \gamma(p, \alpha) \cap F_2 \neq \emptyset\}. \end{aligned}$$

(iv) for (q, p_f) where $q \in Q$:

$$\Omega((q, p_f), \alpha) = \{(q', p_f) \mid q' \in \delta(q, \alpha)\}.$$

We first show the inclusion $L(A_1) \xleftarrow{SDD} L(A_2) \subseteq L(A_{SDD})$.

To prove the inclusion we consider a string $xy_1y_2z \in L(A_1)\xleftarrow{SDD} L(A_2)$, where $xy_1\bar{y}y_2z \in L(A_1)$ and $y_1y_2 \in L(A_2)$. To provide insight we can generally say the states $(q, s_2)_{\mathcal{X}_1}$ read the prefix x. The states $(q, p)_{\mathcal{X}_1}$ are used to read the substring y_1 and ensure that it is non-empty. The states $(q, p)_{\mathcal{X}_2}$ read the substring y_2 and also ensure that it is non-empty. Lastly, the states (q, p_f) are used to read any suffix z.

For a string $xy_1y_2z \in L(A_1)\xleftarrow{SDD} L(A_2)$, there exist accepting paths $\mathcal{P}_{A_1} = s_1, \ldots, q_x, \ldots, q_{y_1}, \ldots, q_{\bar{y}}, \ldots, q_{y_2}, \ldots, q_z$ in A_1 recognizing $xy_1\bar{y}y_2z$ and $\mathcal{P}_{A_2} = s_2, \ldots, p_{y_1}, \ldots, p_{y_2}$ in A_2 recognizing y_1y_2.

From the initial state $(s_1, s_2)_{\mathcal{X}_1}$, the prefix x can be read using the transitions defined in (i) to arrive at the state $(q_x, s_2)_{\mathcal{X}_1}$. The substring y_1 can be read using transitions defined in (ii) to arrive at the state $(q_{\bar{y}}, p_{y_1})_{\mathcal{X}_2}$. To follow an accepting path the last symbol of y_1 is read nondeterministically to transition to $(q_{\bar{y}}, p_{y_1})_{\mathcal{X}_2}$ instead of $(q_{y_1}, p_{y_1})_{\mathcal{X}_1}$. This choice of state allows the transition to enforce the non-empty condition on reading y_1. The substring y_2 is read using transitions defined in (iii) to arrive at the state (q_{y_2}, p_f). Once again a nondeterministic choice to move to this state forces the non-empty condition on the substring y_2. Lastly, the suffix z is read using the transitions defined in (iv) to arrive at the final state (q_z, p_f).

We next show the inclusion $L(A_{SDD}) \subseteq L(A_1)\xleftarrow{SDD} L(A_2)$.. Let xy_1y_2z be a string with an accepting path in A_{SDD}. We can decompose the strings accepting path into four paths as follows:

$$\mathcal{P}_1 = (s_1, s_2)_{\mathcal{X}_1}, \ldots, (q_x, s_2)_{\mathcal{X}_1}, \mathcal{P}_2 = (q_x, s_2)_{\mathcal{X}_1}, \ldots, (q_{\bar{y}}, p_{y_1})_{\mathcal{X}_2}$$

$$\mathcal{P}_3 = (q_{\bar{y}}, p_{y_1})_{\mathcal{X}_2}, \ldots, (q_{y_2}, p_f) \text{ and } \mathcal{P}_4 = (q_{y_2}, p_f), \ldots, (q_z, p_f)$$

The path $\mathcal{P}_1$ implies that a path $s_1, \ldots, q_x$ exists in A_1 recognizing x. The path $\mathcal{P}_2$ implies the existence of the paths $q_x, \ldots, q_{y_1}$ in A_1 and $s_2, \ldots, p_{y_1}$ in A_2 recognizing the substring y_1. There is a nondeterministic transition from state $(q_{y_1}, p_{y_1})_{\mathcal{X}_1}$ to $(q_{\bar{y}}, p_{y_1})_{\mathcal{X}_2}$ in A_{SDD}. These transitions exist because there is a path between q_{y_1} and $q_{\bar{y}}$ in A_1 recognizing a substring $\bar{y}$. The path $\mathcal{P}_3$ implies the existence of paths $q_{\bar{y}}, \ldots, q_{y_2}$ in A_2 and $p_{y_1}, \ldots, p_{y_2}$ recognizing the substring y_2 where p_{y_2} is a final state in A_2. Finally, the path $\mathcal{P}_4$ implies that the path $q_{y_2}, \ldots, q_z$ exists in A_1 recognizing the suffix z. These paths allow us to draw the conclusion that $xy_1\bar{y}y_2z \in L(A_1)$ and $y_1y_2 \in L(A_2)$.   □

Figure 1 depicts the automaton A_{SDD}. The different boxes identify states that have different outgoing transitions. The box labeled with $\mathcal{X}_1$ contains a rectangle, which contains states with outgoing transitions defined in (i). The remainder of the states in box $\mathcal{X}_1$ have outgoing transitions defined in (ii). The middle box labeled with an $\mathcal{X}_2$ contains states with outgoing transitions defined in (iii). Lastly, the states labeled with (q, p_f) have outgoing transitions defined in (iv).

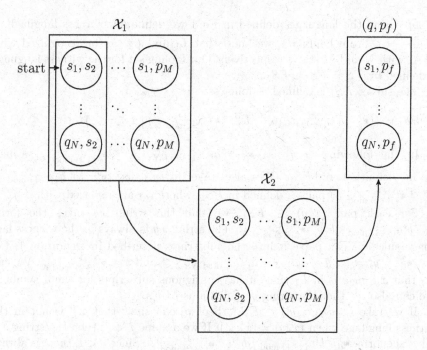

Fig. 1. The construction of the site-directed deletion automaton.

Next we turn to the lower bound. To obtain a lower bound that is reasonably close to the upper bound, we use languages defined over a variable size alphabet, that is, the size of the alphabet depends on the number of states in the automata.

To prove the lower bound on nondeterministic state complexity of site-directed deletion, we introduce notation to simplify the following proof. We use the notation $\bullet_i^j$ for $i \leq j < N$ to be the string $a_i a_{i+1} \ldots a_{j-1} a_j$, where each symbol is unique and contained in the alphabet $\Sigma_a = \{a_0, a_1, \ldots, a_N\}$ For example, $\bullet_1^4 = a_1 a_2 a_3 a_4$.

Let $\Sigma = \Sigma_a \cup \{b\}$. The lower bound construction of Theorem 2 uses the following languages over Σ:

$$L_1 = (b^* a_0 b^* a_1 b^* \cdots b^* a_{N-2} b^* a_{N-1} b^*)^*$$
$$L_2 = \{w \in \{a_0, \cdots, a_{N-1}, b\}^* \mid \#_b(w) \equiv 0 \pmod{M}\} \qquad (1)$$

Lemma 1. *The languages L_1 and L_2 in Eq. 1 can be recognized with NFAs that have N and M states respectively.*

Lemma 1 is self-evident, thus the proof is omitted.

Theorem 2. *For $2 \leq M, N \in \mathbb{N}$, there exist two regular languages L_1 and L_2 over an alphabet of size $N+1$ with NFAs that have N and M states, respectively such that any NFA recognizing the language $L_1 \xleftarrow{SDD} L_2$ needs at least $2NM$ states.*

Proof. Using the languages defined in Eq. 1 we define our witness language as $L_1 \xleftarrow{SDD} L_2$. From Lemma 1, we know that L_1 and L_2 can be recognized with NFAs with N and M states respectively. Our fooling set for the witness language is defined by $FS = FS_1 \cup FS_2$.

The subset FS_1 is defined as follows:

$$FS_1 = \{(\bullet_0^{j-1} b^i a_{(j+1) \bmod N}, \quad b^{M-i} \bullet_{(j+2) \bmod N}^{N-1}) \mid 1 \leq i \leq M, 1 \leq j \leq N\}$$

In the following (x, y) is $(\bullet_0^{j-1} b^i a_{(j+1) \bmod N}, \quad b^{M-i} \bullet_{(j+2) \bmod N}^{N-1})$ a pair as in definition of FS_1. We also take (x', y') as $(\bullet_0^{j'-1} b^{i'} a_{(j'+1) \bmod N},$ $b^{M-i'} \bullet_{(j'+2) \bmod N}^{N-1})$ pair as defined in FS_1, where i, j are replaced with i', j'.

For each pair $(x, y) \in FS_1$, we find the string xy takes the form, $\bullet_0^{j-1} b^i a_{(j+1) \bmod N} b^{M-i} \bullet_{(j+2) \bmod N}^{N-1}$. The string xy is always in the witness language since we can parse it into the substrings described in Definition 1. Let $x = \bullet_0^{j-1}$, $y_1 = b^i$, $\bar{y} = a_j$, $y_2 = a_{(j+1) \bmod N} b^{M-i}$ and $z = \bullet_{(j+2) \bmod N}^{N-1}$. We can see that $xy_1 \bar{y} y_2 z$ is in L_1 since it has contiguous subscripts for the a symbols. We can also see that the string $y_1 y_2$ contains M b's.

If we take $(x, y), (x', y') \in FS_1$, then we can show that xy' is not in the witness language when $(x, y) \neq (x', y')$. If we assume $i < i'$, then the string xy' takes the form, $\bullet_0^{j-1} b^i a_{(j+1) \bmod N} b^{M-i'} \bullet_{(j+2) \bmod N}^{N-1}$. Since $0 < i$, there is always at least one b symbol between a_{j-1} and a_{j+1}, which implies it is either in the substring y_1 or y_2. The string xy' does not contain a multiple of M b symbols, which implies it is not possible to parse the string xy' to meet the criteria set by L_2 in the definition of the operation.

Secondly, in the case where $j < j'$ the string xy' is not in the language. The string xy' takes the form, $\bullet_0^{j-1} b^i a_{(j+1) \bmod N} b^{M-i'} \bullet_{(j'+2) \bmod N}^{N-1}$. The string xy' is not in the language since there must have been two deletions conducted in this string to have the substring $a_{j-1} b^i a_{(j+1) \bmod N} b^{M-i} a_{(j'+2) \bmod N}$. Therefore the properties of a fooling set are upheld by FS_1

The subset FS_2 is defined as follows:

$$FS_2 = \{(\bullet_0^{j-2} b^i, \quad a_{(j-1) \bmod N} b^{M-i} \bullet_{(j+1) \bmod N}^{N-1}) \mid 0 \leq i \leq M-1, 2 \leq j \leq N+1\}$$

Similarly to the pairs of FS_1, each pair $(x, y) \in FS_2$, forms the string xy which is in the witness language. The string xy takes the form, $\bullet_0^{j-2} b^i a_{(j-1) \bmod N} b^{M-i} \bullet_{(j+1) \bmod N}^{N-1}$, and can be parsed with accordance to Definition 1. We can take $x = \bullet_0^{j-2}$, $y_1 = b^i a_{(j-1) \bmod N}$, $\bar{y} = a_{(j) \bmod N}$, $y_2 = b^{M-i}$, and $z = \bullet_{(j+1) \bmod N}^{N-1}$.

If we take $(x, y), (x', y') \in FS_2$, then we can show that $x'y$ is not in the witness language when $(x, y) \neq (x', y')$. Let $i < i'$, then the string $x'y$ takes the form, $\bullet_0^{j-2} b^{i'} a_{(j-1) \bmod N} b^{M-i} \bullet_{(j+1) \bmod N}^{N-1}$. This string is not in the language since there is at least one b symbol in gap between $a_{(j-1) \bmod N}$ and $a_{(j+1) \bmod N}$, which implies that the b's are in the substring y_1 or y_2. Since there are not M b's in the string $x'y$, it is not possible for y_1 and y_2 to form a string in L_2.

Secondly, in the case where $j < j'$ we can show that $x'y$ is not in the witness language. The string $x'y$ takes the form, $\bullet_0^{j'-2} b^i a_{(j-1) \bmod N} b^{M-i} \bullet_{(j+1) \bmod N}^{N-1}$. The string $x'y$ is not in the language since there must have been at least two deletion operations to contain the substring $a_{j'-2} b^i a_{(j-1) \bmod N} b^{M-i} a_{(j+1) \bmod N}$. This can be seen since for $(j-1) \bmod N$ to be sequential after $j'-2$, j would have to equal j'. Thus FS_2 is internally consistent with the properties of a fooling set.

If we take $(x,y) \in FS_1$ and $(x'y') \in FS_2$, then the string xy' is not in the witness language. The string xy' takes the form, $\bullet_0^{j-1} b^i a_{(j+1) \bmod N} a_{(j'-1) \bmod N} b^{M-i'} \bullet_{(j'+1) \bmod N}^{N-1}$. This string is not in the witness language since for any value of j or j', it would appear that two deletions present in the string. Thus, the set FS_2 maintains the fooling set properties. $\square$

4   Unary Alphabet Site-Directed Deletion

In this section we consider the nondeterministic state complexity of site-directed deletion when restricted to languages over a unary alphabet. To prove the upper bounds on nondeterministic state complexity, several properties must be observed.

We first observe that unary concatenation is commutative and this implies that we are able to rewrite the definition of site-directed deletion in the unary case in order to simplify later proofs.

Proposition 2. *For unary languages L_1 and L_2,*

$$L_1 \xleftarrow{SDD} L_2 = \{y_1 y_2 x z \mid x y_1 \bar{y} y_2 z \in L_1, y_1 y_2 \in L_2, y_1 \neq \varepsilon, y_2 \neq \varepsilon\}$$

The second property of interest is that with unary languages L_1 and L_2, the language $L_1 \xleftarrow{SDD} L_2$ is equivalent to the language $L_1 \xleftarrow{SDD} \{w\}$, where w is the shortest string in L_2 that has a length greater than 1.

Lemma 2. *For a unary language L_1 and two strings w and w' where $2 \leq |w| < |w'|$, we have $L_1 \xleftarrow{SDD} \{w'\} \subseteq L_1 \xleftarrow{SDD} \{w\}$.*

Proof. If we consider $w = y_1 y_2$ and $w' = y_1 y_2'$ where $y_2 < y_2'$, then the strings produced by SDD with $y_1 y_2'$ are a subset of those recognized by $y_1 y_2$. If a string $y_1 y_2'$ is in $L_1 \xleftarrow{SDD} \{w'\}$, then it must also be in $L_1 \xleftarrow{SDD} \{w\}$ and can be parsed with respect to Proposition 2 as $y_1 y_2 x z$ with w where $|xz| = |y_1 y_2'| - |y_1 y_2|$. $\square$

The final property we consider is if L_1 has infinite cardinality, the language $L_1 \xleftarrow{SDD} L_2$ contains all strings longer than the shortest string $w_2 \in L_2$. This occurs because a string of arbitrary length from $w_1 \in L_1$ can be selected and strings of length between $|w_2|$ and $|w_1|$ are generated.

Lemma 3. *Let L_1 and L_2 be unary languages and L_1's cardinality be infinite. All strings of length at least k will be in $L_1 \xleftarrow{SDD} L_2$ where k is the length of the shortest string in L_2 of length at least that of the smallest string $w \in L_2$ such that $2 \leq |w|$.*

Proof. Let $y_1 y_2$ be the shortest string in L_2 of length at least 2, where $y_1 \neq \varepsilon$ and $y_2 \neq \varepsilon$. Consider an arbitrary $p \in \mathbb{N}$, $p \geq |y_1 y_2|$.

Choose $w \in L_1$ such that $|w| \geq p$ and write $w = w_1 w_2$ where $|w_1| = p - |y_1 y_2|$.

Now $w_1 y_1 w_2 y_2 \in L_1$, $y_1 y_2 \in L_2$ and, by the definition of site-directed deletion, $w_1 y_1 y_2 \in L_1 \xleftarrow{SDD} L_2$. Thus $L_1 \xleftarrow{SDD} L_2$ contains a string of length p. $\square$

Consider NFAs A_1 and A_2 with N and M states, respectively. Using these properties we can show that an NFA with either N or M states recognizes the language $L(A_1) \xleftarrow{SDD} L(A_2)$, depending on whether or not $L(A_1)$ is a finite language.

Theorem 3. *For unary NFAs A_1 and A_2 with N and M states, respectively, the language $L(A_1) \xleftarrow{SDD} L(A_2)$ is recognized by an NFA with N states, when $L(A_1)$ is finite.*

Proof. Let $A_1 = (Q, \Sigma, \delta, q_0, F_1)$ and $A_2 = (P, \Sigma, \gamma, p_0, F_2)$ be automata recognizing the unary languages L_1 and L_2 with N and M states respectively. Given these NFAs, we can construct the NFA $A_{u-SDD} = (Q_{u-SDD}, \Sigma, \Omega, p_0, F_{u-SDD})$.

If we label the states in Q and P with a subscript i, such that i is the minimal number of steps from the start sate. If we also define k to be the shortest string in L_2 with length greater than 1. We then define the states in Q_{u-SDD} as follows:

$$Q_{u-SDD} = \{p_0, p_1, \ldots, p_{k-1}\} \cup \{q_k, \ldots, q_{N-1}\}$$

A state q_i is in F_{u-SDD} when $q_i \in F_1$ and $k \leq i < N$. The transitions of Ω for $\alpha \in \Sigma$ are defined as follows:

(i) for the state $p \in P$:

$$\Omega(p_i, \alpha) = \{p' \mid p' \in \gamma(p_i, \alpha) \text{ and } p' \notin F_2\}$$
$$\cup \{q_j \mid 1 < i < j < N \text{ and } \gamma(p_i, \alpha) \cap F_2 \neq \emptyset\}.$$

(ii) for the state $q \in Q$:

$$\Omega(q, \alpha) = \{q' \mid q' \in \delta(q, \alpha)\}.$$

First we show the inclusion $L(A_1) \xleftarrow{SDD} L(A_2) \subseteq L(A_{u-SDD})$. Generally speaking, the automaton A_{u-SDD} uses the states $\{p_0, p_1, \ldots, p_{k-1}\}$ to compute the substring $y_1 y_2$, and the states $\{q_k, \ldots, q_{N-1}\}$ to compute xz.

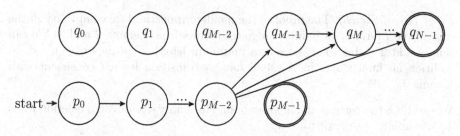

Fig. 2. NFA construction of the case where L_1 is finite for unary SDD. This diagram retains the unused states without transitions to illustrate the state savings visually.

If we take an arbitrary string $y_1 y_2 xz$ from $L(A_1) \xleftarrow{SDD} L(A_2)$, there exists paths, $\mathcal{P}_{A_1} = q_0, \ldots, q_{y_1}, \ldots, q_{y_2}, \ldots, q_{\bar{y}}, \ldots, q_x, \ldots, q_z$ recognizing $y_1 y_2 \bar{y} xz$ in A_1 and $\mathcal{P}_{A_2} = p_0, \ldots, p_{y_1}, \ldots, p_{y_2}$ recognizing $y_1 y_2$ in A_2.

We can construct an accepting path through A_{u-SDD} to read the string $y_1 y_2 xz$. Starting at p_0, we next read the prefix y_1 using the transition defined in (i) to arrive at the state p_{y_1}. Again, using the transitions defined in (i) we read y_2 to arrive at the state $q_{\bar{y}}$. It is important to note that the transition (i) nondeterministically chooses $q_{\bar{y}}$ since $q_{\bar{y}}$ has a subscript larger than $k-1$ by definition. Finally, the suffix xz is read using the transitions defined in (ii) to arrive at the accepting state q_z.

We next show the inclusion $L(A_{u-SDD}) \subseteq L(A_1) \xleftarrow{SDD} L(A_2)$. For a string $y_1 y_2 xz$ recognized by an accepting path $\mathcal{P}_{u-SDD} = p_0, \ldots, q_{\bar{y}}, \ldots, q_z$ in A_{u-SDD}, we can decompose this path into $\mathcal{P}_1 = p_0, \ldots, q_{\bar{y}}$ and $\mathcal{P}_2 = q_{\bar{y}}, \ldots, q_z$.

The path $\mathcal{P}_1$ implies that the prefix $y_1 y_2$ is recognized by A_2. The second path $\mathcal{P}_2$ nondeterministically guesses how long $\bar{y}$ is and implies that a string $y_1 y_2 \bar{y} xz$ is recognized by L_1. □

Figure 2 illustrates the construction of A_{u-SDD} when L_1 is a finite language. We next establish a matching lower bound on state complexity for unary site-directed deletion, when L_1 is a finite language.

Theorem 4. *Let* $M, N \in \mathbb{N}$ *where* $2 \leq M$. *There exists a finite unary language* L_1 *with an NFA with* N *states and* L_2 *with an NFA with* M *states such that any NFA recognizing the language* $L_1 \xleftarrow{SDD} L_2$ *needs at least* N *states.*

Proof (Proof Sketch). From the witness language $a^{N-1} \xleftarrow{SDD} \{a^2, a^{M-1}\} = \{a^2, a^3, \ldots, a^{N-1}\}$, we can produce the fooling set $\{(a^{N-1-i}, a^i) \mid 0 \leq i \leq N-1\}$. □

The second case we consider for unary site-directed deletion is the case when L_1 is an infinite language.

Theorem 5. *For* $M, N \in \mathbb{N}$. *Let* A_1 *and* A_2 *be unary NFAs with* N *and* M *states, respectively, where* $L(A_1)$ *is infinite. Then* $L(A_1) \xleftarrow{SDD} L(A_2)$ *is recognized by an NFA with* $M + 2$ *states.*

Proof (Proof Sketch). The proof of the nondeterministic state complexity in the case where $L(A_1)$ is an infinite language follows from Lemma 2 and 3. We can simply add 2 states to A_2 to add a minimum length of strings recognized. In addition all final states in A_2 shall have a transition its self consistent with Lemma 3.   □

We establish the corresponding lower bound for unary site-directed deletion when L_1 has infinite cardinality.

Theorem 6. *Let* $M, N \in \mathbb{N}$, *where* $3 \leq M$. *There exists an infinite unary language* L_1 *recognized by an NFA with* N *states and* L_2 *with an NFA containing* M *states such that, any NFA recognizing the language* $L_1 \xleftarrow{SDD} L_2$ *needs at least* $M + 2$ *states.*

Proof (Proof Sketch). The lower bound follows from the witness language $(a^N)^* \xleftarrow{SDD} a(a^M)^* = a^{M+1}(a)^*$, this follows from Lemma 3. The accompanying fooling set is as follows: $\{(a^i, a^{M+1-i}) \mid 0 \leq i \leq M + 1\}$.   □

For an N (respectively, M) state unary NFA A_1 (respectively, A_2) we have observed the following concerning the nondeterministic state complexity of $L(A_1) \xleftarrow{SDD} L(A_2)$. When the cardinality of $L(A_1)$ is known, then a tight bound on the nondeterministic state complexity can be found. When $L(A_1)$ has finite cardinality, a tight bound of N states is required. When $L(A_1)$ is an infinite language, a tight bound of $M + 2$ states is required. In the general case of site-directed deletion over unary languages we can conclude that the state complexity is bound between $\min(N, M + 2)$ and $\max(N, M + 2)$.

5   Conclusion

Tight bounds on nondeterministic state complexity over unary languages were obtained when the cardinality of L_1 is known. For site-directed deletion of languages over a general alphabet, tight nondeterministic state complexity bounds were not obtained. An upper bound of $2NM + N$ was shown to be sufficient in Theorem 1. This marks an improvement of N states from the bound $2NM + 2N$, which was previously established by Cho et al. [4]. We were also able to obtain a lower bound of $2NM$ in Theorem 2. The lower bound required alphabets to be of variable size. It remains an open problem to reduce the alphabet size, and to produce a tight bound on nondeterministic state complexity for general alphabet site-directed deletion. Future work could examine the deterministic state complexity of site-directed deletion. Tight bounds for deterministic state complexity of unconstrained deletion have been established by Han et al. [10].

References

1. Adleman, L.: Molecular computation of solutions to combinatorial problems. Science **266**(5187), 1021–1024 (1994)

2. Birget, J.C.: Intersection and union of regular languages and state complexity. Inf. Process. Lett. **43**(4), 185–190 (1992)
3. Carter, P.: Site-directed mutagenesis. Biochem. J. **237**(1), 1–7 (1986)
4. Cho, D.-J., Han, Y.-S., Kim, H., Salomaa, K.: Site-directed deletion. In: Hoshi, M., Seki, S. (eds.) DLT 2018. LNCS, vol. 11088, pp. 219–230. Springer, Cham (2018). https://doi.org/10.1007/978-3-319-98654-8_18
5. Cho, D.J., Han, Y.S., Ng, T., Salomaa, K.: Outfix-guided insertion. Theoret. Comput. Sci. **701**, 70–84 (2017)
6. Cho, D.J., Han, Y.S., Salomaa, K., Smith, T.: Site-directed insertion: language equations and decision problems. Theoret. Comput. Sci. **798**, 40–51 (2019)
7. Domaratzki, M.: Deletion along trajectories. Theoret. Comput. Sci. **320**(2), 293–313 (2004)
8. Franco, G., Manca, V.: Algorithmic applications of XPCR. Nat. Comput. Int. J. **10**(2), 15 (2011)
9. Han, Y.S., Ko, S.K., Ng, T., Salomaa, K.: State complexity of insertion. Int. J. Found. Comput. Sci. **27**(07), 863–878 (2016)
10. Han, Y.-S., Ko, S.-K., Salomaa, K.: State complexity of deletion and bipolar deletion. Acta Informatica **53**(1), 67–85 (2015). https://doi.org/10.1007/s00236-015-0245-y
11. Hopcroft, J.E., Ullman, J.D.: Introduction to Automata Theory, Languages, and Computation. Addison-Wesley Publishing Company, Boston (1979)
12. Ito, M., Kari, L., Thierrin, G.: Insertion and deletion closure of languages. Theoret. Comput. Sci. **183**(1), 3–19 (1997)
13. Kari, L.: On Insertion and Deletion in Formal Languages. Ph.D. thesis, University of Turku (1991)
14. Kari, L., Thierrin, G.: Contextual insertions/deletions and computability. Inf. Comput. **131**(1), 47–61 (1996)
15. Manca, V., Franco, G.: Computing by polymerase chain reaction. Math. Biosci. **211**(2), 282–298 (2008)
16. Mullis, K., Faloona, F., Scharf, S., Saiki, R., Horn, G., Erlich, H.: Specific enzymatic amplification of DNA in vitro: the polymerase chain reaction. Cold Spring Harb. Symp. Quant. Biol. **51**, 263–273 (1986). https://doi.org/10.1101/sqb.1986.051.01.032
17. Paun, G., Rozenberg, G., Salomaa, A.: DNA Computing: New Computing Paradigms (Texts in Theoretical Computer Science. An EATCS Series). Springer, Berlin (2006)
18. Takahara, A., Yokomori, T.: On the computational power of insertion-deletion systems. In: Hagiya, M., Ohuchi, A. (eds.) DNA 2002. LNCS, vol. 2568, pp. 269–280. Springer, Heidelberg (2003). https://doi.org/10.1007/3-540-36440-4_24

Energy Complexity of Regular Language Recognition

Öykü Yılmaz[1], Fırat Kıyak[2], Meriç Üngör[1], and A. C. Cem Say[1(✉)]

[1] Department of Computer Engineering, Boğaziçi University, İstanbul, Turkey
say@boun.edu.tr
[2] Department of Mathematics, Boğaziçi University, İstanbul, Turkey

Abstract. The erasure of each bit of information by a computing device has an intrinsic energy cost. Although any Turing machine can be rewritten to be thermodynamically reversible without changing the recognized language, finite automata that are restricted to scan their input once in "real-time" fashion can only recognize the members of a proper subset of the class of regular languages in this reversible manner. We use a general quantum finite automaton model to study the thermodynamic cost per step associated with the recognition of different regular languages. We show that zero-error quantum finite automata have no energy cost advantage over their classical deterministic counterparts, and prove an upper bound for the cost that holds for all regular languages. We also demonstrate languages for which "error can be traded for energy", i.e. whose zero-error recognition is associated with provably bigger energy cost per step when compared to their bounded-error recognition by real-time finite-memory quantum devices.

Keywords: Quantum finite automata · Reversibility

1 Introduction

The discovery of the relationship between thermodynamics and computation, revealing the links between the concepts of heat, entropy, and information, is a landmark scientific achievement [10]. As shown by Landauer [9], the erasure of each bit of information by a computing device necessitates the dissipation of an amount of heat proportional to the absolute temperature of the device, and therefore has an unavoidable minimum energy cost for any fixed temperature. Turing machine programs [2] (and even finite automata with two-way access to their input strings [7]) can be rewritten to be *reversible*, so that each one of their configurations has a single possible predecessor, and their computational steps can therefore in principle be executed using arbitrarily small amounts of energy, but things change when one limits attention to real-time finite automata.

It is known [13] that reversible real-time finite automata (where each state has at most one incoming transition with each possible symbol of the input alphabet) recognize only a proper subset of the class of regular languages, so some regular languages necessarily have automata with states receiving multiple transitions

© Springer Nature Switzerland AG 2022
P. Caron and L. Mignot (Eds.): CIAA 2022, LNCS 13266, pp. 200–211, 2022.
https://doi.org/10.1007/978-3-031-07469-1_16

with the same symbol. Intuitively, it is impossible to "rewind" computations of such machines, since they "forget" which one of a set of possible predecessor states led them to their present state. It is natural to ask if this energy-related criterion could be used to define a hierarchy whose levels are associated with the minimum values of these "in-degrees" required to recognize the languages in question.

It was precisely because of the reversibility requirement inherent in unitary matrices that early definitions of real-time quantum finite automata (QFAs) [3, 7, 12] were not able to capture all regular languages. Modern definitions of QFAs [5, 14], which recognize all and only the regular languages with bounded error, are able to handle irreversible languages by using not one but many instances of an architectural component (called an *operation element*) that can be seen to correspond to the notion of "incoming transitions" discussed above, so the hierarchy question raised above is relevant for the study of bounded-error QFAs as well.

In this paper, we use the general QFA model of [14] which allows us to model the information loss inherent in the computations of such machines, establishing a clear link with Landauer's principle (Sect. 2) to study the thermodynamic cost per step associated with the recognition of different regular languages. In Sect. 3, we show that zero-error quantum finite automata have no energy cost advantage over their classical deterministic counterparts. That equivalence is used in Sect. 4 to establish an upper bound on the number of bits that have to be "forgotten" per computational step during the recognition of any regular language, namely, any such language on an alphabet with k symbols can be recognized by a zero-error quantum finite automaton that has at most $k + 1$ operation elements for each input symbol, and thus requires no more than $\log_2(k + 1)$ bits to be erased per step. In Sect. 5, we demonstrate languages for which "error can be traded for energy", i.e. whose zero-error recognition is associated with provably bigger energy cost per step when compared to their bounded-error recognition by real-time finite-memory quantum devices. Section 6 lists some open questions.

2   The General QFA Framework and Information Erasure

Although classical physics, on which the intuition underlying deterministic computation models is based, is supposed to be subsumed by quantum physics, early definitions of quantum finite automata (e.g. [7, 12]) resulted in "weak" machines that could only capture a proper subset of the class of regular languages. The cause of this apparent contradiction was identified [5] to be those early definitions' imposition of unnecessarily strict limitations on the interaction of the automata with their environments. Classical finite automata, after all, are not "closed" systems, with loss of information about the preceding configuration and the ensuing transfer of heat to the environment implied by their logical structure. The modern definition of QFAs to be given below [5, 14] allows a sufficiently flexible repertory of unitary transformations and measurements that does not overrule any physically realizable finite-memory computation.[1]

A *quantum finite automaton* (QFA) is a 5-tuple $(Q, \Sigma, \{\mathcal{E}_\sigma | \sigma \in \Sigma_\triangleright\}, q_1, F)$, where

1. $Q = \{q_1, \ldots, q_n\}$ is the finite set of machine states,
2. Σ is the finite input alphabet,
3. $q_1 \in Q$ is the initial state,
4. $F \subseteq Q$ is the set of accepting states, and
5. $\Sigma_\triangleright = \Sigma \cup \{\triangleright\}$, where $\triangleright \notin \Sigma$ is the left end-marker symbol, placed automatically before the input string, and for each $\sigma \in \Sigma_\triangleright$, $\mathcal{E}_\sigma$ is the superoperator describing the transformation on the current configuration of the machine associated with the consumption of the symbol σ. For some $l \geq 1$, each $\mathcal{E}_\sigma$ consists of l operation elements $\{E_{\sigma,1}, \ldots, E_{\sigma,l}\}$, where each operation element is a complex-valued $n \times n$ matrix.

Although it is customary in the literature to analyze these machines using density matrices [1,5], we take the alternative (but equivalent) approach of [14], which makes the thermodynamic cost of computational steps explicit by representing the "periphery" that will support intermediate measurements during the execution of our QFA. For this purpose, consider an *auxiliary system* with the state set $\Omega = \{\omega_1, \ldots, \omega_l\}$, and an additional set of classical states $\{s_1, \ldots, s_l\}$ that will mirror the members of Ω during computation, as will be described below.

Considered together, the auxiliary system and the "main system" of our machine defined above have the state set $\Omega \times Q$. The quantum state space of the overall system is $\mathcal{H}_l \otimes \mathcal{H}_n$, the composite of the corresponding finite-dimensional Hilbert spaces. Initially, this composite system is in the quantum state $|\omega_1\rangle \otimes |q_1\rangle$, and the classical state is s_1. At the beginning of every computational step, it will be ensured that the auxiliary system is again at one of its computational basis states, i.e. $|\omega_j\rangle$ for some j, and the classical state will be s_j.

Let $|\psi_x\rangle = \alpha_1 |q_1\rangle + \ldots + \alpha_n |q_n\rangle$ denote any vector in $\mathcal{H}_n$ that is attained by our QFA with nonzero probability after it has consumed the string $x \in \Sigma^*$. We will examine the evolution of the overall system for a single step starting at a state $|\omega_j\rangle \otimes |\psi_x\rangle$. If the symbol σ is consumed from the input, the composed system first undergoes the unitary operation described by the product $U_\sigma U_{s_j}$, as described below.

U_{s_j} is designed so that its application rotates the auxiliary state from ω_j to ω_1, so that U_σ will act on

$$|\Psi_x\rangle = |\omega_1\rangle \otimes |\psi_x\rangle = (\ \underbrace{\alpha_1, \alpha_2, \ldots, \alpha_n}_{\text{amplitudes of } |\psi_x\rangle}\ , \ \underbrace{0, 0, \ldots, 0}_{(l-1)\times n \text{ times}}\ )^T.$$

Only the leftmost n columns of the matrix U_σ are significant for our purposes, and the remaining ones can be filled in to ensure unitarity. Those first n columns

---

[1] References [1] and [14] provide a more comprehensive introduction to the quantum computation notation and concepts discussed here.

will be provided by the operation elements $E_{\sigma,1}, \ldots, E_{\sigma,l}$, as indicated by the following partitioning of U_σ into $n \times n$ blocks:

$$U_\sigma = \begin{bmatrix} E_{\sigma,1} & * & \cdots & * \\ E_{\sigma,2} & * & \cdots & * \\ \vdots & \vdots & \ddots & \vdots \\ E_{\sigma,l} & * & \cdots & * \end{bmatrix}$$

(Since U_σ is unitary, one sees that the operation elements should satisfy the constraint $\sum_{j=1}^{l} E_{\sigma,j}^\dagger E_{\sigma,j} = I$.)

Consider the n-dimensional vectors $\widetilde{|\psi_{x\sigma,i}\rangle} = E_{\sigma,i}|\psi_x\rangle$ for $i \in \{1, \ldots, l\}$. Clearly, the vector $\widetilde{|\Psi_{x\sigma}\rangle} = U_\sigma|\Psi_x\rangle$ that represents the overall system state obtained after the unitary transformation described above can be written by "stacking" these vectors, each of which corresponds to a different auxiliary state, on top of each other, as seen in Eq. 1.

$$\widetilde{|\Psi_{x\sigma}\rangle} = \begin{bmatrix} \widetilde{|\psi_{x\sigma,1}\rangle} \\ \widetilde{|\psi_{x\sigma,2}\rangle} \\ \vdots \\ \widetilde{|\psi_{x\sigma,l}\rangle} \end{bmatrix} = |\omega_1\rangle \otimes \widetilde{|\psi_{x\sigma,1}\rangle} + |\omega_2\rangle \otimes \widetilde{|\psi_{x\sigma,2}\rangle} + \ldots + |\omega_l\rangle \otimes \widetilde{|\psi_{x\sigma,l}\rangle} \quad (1)$$

At this point in the execution of our QFA, the auxiliary system is measured in its computational basis. The probability p_k of observing outcome "ω_k" out of the l different possibilities is the square of the length of $\widetilde{|\psi_{x\sigma,k}\rangle}$. As a result of this probabilistic branching, the main system collapses to the state $|\psi_{x\sigma,k}\rangle = \frac{\widetilde{|\psi_{x\sigma,k}\rangle}}{\sqrt{p_k}}$ with probability p_k (for k such that $p_k > 0$), and the fact that this observation result is recorded for usage in the next step is represented by setting the classical state to s_k, overwriting its present value. It is this final action of "forgetting" the previous value of the classical state that causes the energy cost associated per step of a QFA: $\log_2 l$ classical bits are required to hold this information, and one needs to expend a minimum of $k_B T \ln 2$ joules to erase each bit, where k_B is Boltzmann's constant, and T is the ambient temperature in kelvins [9]. A machine with $l > 1$ operating elements in its superoperators is therefore faced with an energy cost proportional to $\log_2 l$.

After processing the entire input string symbol by symbol in this manner, the main system, described by some n-dimensional vector $|\psi\rangle$, is measured in its computational basis. The probability of acceptance at this point is the sum of the squares of the lengths of the amplitudes of the accepting states in $|\psi\rangle$. Rejection is similarly defined in terms of the non-accepting states. A language L is said to be recognized by a QFA with *bounded error* if there exists a number $\epsilon < \frac{1}{2}$ such that every string in L is accepted and every string not in L is rejected by that QFA with probability at least $1 - \epsilon$. If $\epsilon = 0$, i.e. the QFA has the property that

it accepts every input string with either probability 0 or 1, it is said to recognize
the set of strings that it does accept with *zero error*.

It is known [11] that "modern" QFAs defined in this manner can recognize
all and only the regular languages with bounded error.[2] Given any deterministic
finite automaton (DFA) with n states, it is straightforward to build a QFA
with n machine states that recognizes the same language M with zero error. An
examination of this construction is useful for understanding the nature of the
information lost when the classical state is overwritten during a computational
step of a QFA.

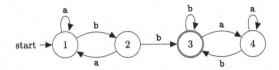

(a) DFA transition diagram

$$E_{a,1} = \begin{bmatrix} 1&0&0&0 \\ 0&0&0&0 \\ 0&0&0&0 \\ 0&0&1&0 \end{bmatrix} \qquad E_{b,1} = \begin{bmatrix} 0&0&0&0 \\ 1&0&0&0 \\ 0&1&0&0 \\ 0&0&0&0 \end{bmatrix}$$

$$E_{a,2} = \begin{bmatrix} 0&1&0&0 \\ 0&0&0&0 \\ 0&0&0&0 \\ 0&0&0&1 \end{bmatrix} \qquad E_{b,2} = \begin{bmatrix} 0&0&0&0 \\ 0&0&0&0 \\ 0&0&1&0 \\ 0&0&0&0 \end{bmatrix}$$

$$E_{a,3} = \begin{bmatrix} 0&0&0&0 \\ 0&0&0&0 \\ 0&0&0&0 \\ 0&0&0&0 \end{bmatrix} \qquad E_{b,3} = \begin{bmatrix} 0&0&0&0 \\ 0&0&0&0 \\ 0&0&0&1 \\ 0&0&0&0 \end{bmatrix}$$

(b) Superoperator for **a**   (c) Superoperator for **b**

Fig. 1. A DFA and superoperators for its QFA implementation

Consider the DFA whose state diagram is shown in Fig. 1a. Figures 1b and 1c
depict the operation elements associated with symbols **a** and **b** in the QFA implementation of this machine.[3] In each square matrix, both the rows and columns
correspond to the states of the QFA, which in turn correspond to the states of
the DFA of Fig. 1a. The entry at row i, column j of the k'th operation element
for symbol **a** represents the transition that the QFA would perform from its j'th

---

[2] "Zero-energy" QFAs with a single operation element in each superoperator correspond to the earliest definition in [3,12], and can recognize all and only the group
languages (a proper subclass of the class of regular languages, whose DFAs have
the property that one again obtains a DFA if one reverses all their transitions) with
bounded error [3,4].

[3] The left end-marker is inconsequential in DFA simulations, and its superoperator is
not shown.

machine state to the combination of its i'th machine state and k'th auxiliary state upon consuming **a**. Starting with the vector $(1, 0, 0, 0)^T$ representing the machine being at the initial state with probability 1, the QFA would trace every step in the execution of the DFA on any input string, and recognize the same language with zero error.

The reader will note in Fig. 1 that the superoperators, which are just adjacency matrices for the DFA, have not one, but three operation elements precisely because state 3 has three incoming transitions labeled with the same symbol in Fig. 1a: We cannot have two 1's in the same row of two different columns of the matrices in Figs. 1b and 1c, since they must be orthonormal. We use the additional operation elements to represent the additional ways in which the machine can switch to state 3 with input **b**. Intuitively, the auxiliary state records which of the three transitions was used to enter state 3, and it is not possible to "trace the computation backwards" from that state when one has forgotten that information.[4] This is why the language recognized by these machines is not "reversible" [8].

We have seen how any DFA with n states and at most l incoming transitions to the same state with the same symbol can be simulated by a zero-error QFA with n machine states and l operation elements (that only contain 0's and 1's) per superoperator. Note that the QFAs that are constructed to imitate DFAs in the fashion exemplified above do not use any "quantumness": At all times, the state vector of the QFA never represents a superposition of more than one classical state, and just tracks the execution of the DFA faithfully. There is no probabilistic "branching" (since only one auxiliary state has nonzero amplitude at any step), and no constructive or destructive interference among amplitudes. It is natural to ask if QFAs with other complex-valued entries in their operation elements can utilize the famous non-classical capabilities of quantum systems to perform the same task in a more energy-efficient manner, i.e. with fewer operation elements. We turn to this question in the next section.

3   Zero-Error QFAs Have No Energy Advantage

For any language L defined over alphabet Σ, the "indistinguishability" relation $\equiv_L$ on the set Σ^* is defined as follows:

$$(x \equiv_L y) \iff (\forall z \in \Sigma^*[xz \in L \iff yz \in L]).$$

Lemma 1. *Let M be a QFA recognizing a language L with zero error. Let x and y be strings such that $x \not\equiv_L y$. If $|\psi_x\rangle, |\psi_y\rangle \in \mathcal{H}_n$ are any two vectors that are attained by M with nonzero probability after it reads x or y, respectively, then $\langle \psi_x | \psi_y \rangle = 0$.*

---

[4] Since none of the three states with **b**-transitions into state 3 is more likely to be the source than the others, this information amounts to $\log_2 3$ bits.

Proof. Let us say that *x and y are distinguishable with respect to L in k steps*
if there exists a string z of length k that distinguishes them, i.e. $xz \in L$ if and
only if $yz \notin L$. We will prove the statement by induction on the number of steps
in which x and y are distinguishable with respect to L.

Basis:

If x and y are distinguishable with respect to L in 0 steps, let us say without loss
of generality that $x \in L$ and $y \notin L$. In this case, all entries of $|\psi_x\rangle$ corresponding
to the non-accepting states in Q must be zero, since M would otherwise reject
x with nonzero probability. Similarly, all entries of $|\psi_y\rangle$ corresponding to the
accepting states in Q must be zero. But this means that $\langle\psi_x|\psi_y\rangle = 0$.

Induction Step:

Assume that the statement is true for all pairs of strings that are distinguishable
with respect to L in k steps, where $k \geq 0$, and consider the case of any x and y
that are distinguishable in $k + 1$ steps. In this context, we will further assume
that $\langle\psi_x|\psi_y\rangle \neq 0$, and reach a contradiction.

Let σ be the leftmost symbol of the string z (of length $k+1$) that distinguishes
x and y. Consider two copies of M at states $|\psi_x\rangle$ and $|\psi_y\rangle$. When these two
machines consume the input symbol σ, the corresponding vectors representing
the composite system of the machine and its environment are both multiplied
by the unitary matrix U_σ to yield two nl-dimensional vectors, say,

$$|\widetilde{\Psi_{x\sigma}}\rangle = \begin{bmatrix} |\widetilde{\psi_{x\sigma,1}}\rangle \\ |\widetilde{\psi_{x\sigma,2}}\rangle \\ \vdots \\ |\widetilde{\psi_{x\sigma,l}}\rangle \end{bmatrix} \text{ and } |\widetilde{\Psi_{y\sigma}}\rangle = \begin{bmatrix} |\widetilde{\psi_{y\sigma,1}}\rangle \\ |\widetilde{\psi_{y\sigma,2}}\rangle \\ \vdots \\ |\widetilde{\psi_{y\sigma,l}}\rangle \end{bmatrix}, \tag{2}$$

where n and l are respectively the numbers of machine and auxiliary states,
as we saw in Eq. 1. Since U_σ preserves inner products and angles, these "tall"
vectors are also not orthogonal by our assumption that $\langle\psi_x|\psi_y\rangle \neq 0$.

As discussed in Sect. 2, the state vectors that M can attain with nonzero
probability after consuming this σ are the normalized versions of the (nonzero) n-
dimensional "slices" of $|\widetilde{\Psi_{x\sigma}}\rangle$ and $|\widetilde{\Psi_{y\sigma}}\rangle$. Note in Eq. 2 that if $\langle\widetilde{\psi_{x\sigma,j}}|\widetilde{\psi_{y\sigma,j}}\rangle = 0$
for all $j \in \{1, \ldots, l\}$, then $|\widetilde{\Psi_{x\sigma}}\rangle$ and $|\widetilde{\Psi_{y\sigma}}\rangle$ must also be orthogonal. This means
that $\langle\psi_{x\sigma,j}|\psi_{y\sigma,j}\rangle \neq 0$ for at least one j, which is a contradiction, since $x\sigma$ and
$y\sigma$ are distinguishable in k steps. $\square$

It follows that the subspace generated by the vectors attainable by M through
reading strings in a particular equivalence class of $\equiv_L$ must be orthogonal to all
the subspaces corresponding to the other classes. This provides a new proof of the
(already known) fact that zero-error QFAs can only recognize regular languages.

Corollary 1. *If a language L is recognized by a zero-error QFA M with n
machine states, each equivalence class C of $\equiv_L$ corresponds to a subspace S_C
of $\mathcal{H}_n$, and any two subspaces corresponding to different classes are orthogonal*

to each other. Since the sum of the dimensions of these subspaces is at most n, $\equiv_L$ can have at most n equivalence classes, and L is regular by the Myhill-Nerode theorem.

We can now demonstrate that every zero-error QFA M has a corresponding DFA M' which recognizes the same language, and is as efficient as M in terms of both memory (number of states) and energy requirement per computational step.[5]

Theorem 1. *For any $n, l > 0$, if a language is recognized with zero error by a QFA with n machine states and l operation elements per superoperator, then the same language is also recognized by a DFA with n states and at most l incoming transitions to the same state with the same symbol.*

Proof. Let M be a zero-error QFA with n machine states and l operation elements per superoperator. By Corollary 1, M recognizes a regular language L. Let k be the number of states of the minimal DFA D recognizing L. Each input string x that carries D to state $i \in \{1, \ldots, k\}$ of D will carry M to a state vector in a corresponding subspace S_i of $\mathcal{H}_n$.[6] Consider the DFA M' that is described by the 5-tuple $(Q, \Sigma, \delta, q_1, F)$, where

1. Q is the finite set of states, containing $\sum_i \dim(S_i)$ elements, with $\dim(S_i)$ equivalent states corresponding to S_i for each $i \in \{1, \ldots, k\}$,
2. Σ is the same as the input alphabet of M,
3. q_1 is the initial state, selected arbitrarily from among the elements of Q that correspond to the subspace containing the vector attained by M after consuming the empty input string,
4. F is the set of accepting states, designated to contain all and only the elements of Q that correspond to any subspace containing vectors attained by M after consuming members of L, and
5. δ is the transition function, which mimics M's action on its state vector, as follows: For each $i \in \{1, \ldots, k\}$, call the subset of $\dim(S_i)$ states corresponding to S_i "the i'th bag". If M maps vectors in S_i to vectors in S_j upon reading a symbol σ, all states in the i'th bag of M' will transition to states in the j'th bag with the symbol σ. For each bag, incoming transitions will be distributed as "evenly" as possible among the members of that bag, so that if M' has a total of T_j incoming σ-transitions to its j'th bag, no state in that bag will have more than $\lceil T_j / \dim(S_j) \rceil$ incoming σ-transitions.

---

[5] The fact that zero-error QFAs have no advantage over equivalent DFAs in terms of the number of machine states was first proven by Klauck [6], using Holevo's theorem and communication complexity arguments.

[6] At this point, one may be tempted to declare that the set of subspaces already provides the state set of the DFA we wish to construct. After all, each matrix of the form U_σ that we saw in Sect. 2 "maps" a vector in S_i to one or more vectors in S_j if and only if D switches from state i to state j upon consuming σ. However, this simple construction does not guarantee our aim of keeping the maximum number of incoming transitions with the same label to any state in the machine to a minimum.

Let us calculate the maximum possible number of incoming σ-transitions that can be received by a state in M'. Let j be some state of D with p incoming σ-transitions from states $\{i_1, i_2, ..., i_p\}$. For any $r \in \{1, 2, ..., p\}$, let x be some string which carries D to state i_r and M to some vector $|\psi_x\rangle \in \mathcal{H}_n$ with nonzero probability. We know that the processing of σ corresponds to the action of the matrix we called U_σ in Sect. 2. Recall from Eq. 1 that

$$U_\sigma(|\omega_1\rangle \otimes |\psi_x\rangle) = |\omega_1\rangle \otimes \widetilde{|\psi_{x\sigma,1}\rangle} + |\omega_2\rangle \otimes \widetilde{|\psi_{x\sigma,2}\rangle} + \ldots + |\omega_l\rangle \otimes \widetilde{|\psi_{x\sigma,l}\rangle}.$$

Since M transitions to a vector in S_j with probability 1 upon receiving σ, all the $\widetilde{|\psi_{x\sigma,k}\rangle}$ must lie in S_j (for $1 \leq k \leq l$). We therefore have $U_\sigma(|\omega_1\rangle \otimes |\psi_x\rangle) \subseteq \mathcal{H}_l \otimes S_j$. This is true for all x and $|\psi_x\rangle$, and S_{i_r} is, by definition, generated by such vectors; therefore, $U_\sigma(\mathbb{C}|\omega_1\rangle \otimes S_{i_r}) \subseteq \mathcal{H}_l \otimes S_j$.

By Corollary 1, the spaces $\mathbb{C}|\omega_1\rangle \otimes S_{i_r}$ are disjoint for all $r \in \{1, 2, ..., p\}$. We have

$$\dim(\mathbb{C}|\omega_1\rangle \otimes S_{i_1}) + \dim(\mathbb{C}|\omega_1\rangle \otimes S_{i_2}) + \ldots + \dim(\mathbb{C}|\omega_1\rangle \otimes S_{i_p}) \leq \dim(\mathcal{H}_l \otimes S_j),$$

since U_σ is an injective linear map. In other words,

$$T_j = \dim(S_{i_1}) + \dim(S_{i_2}) + \ldots + \dim(S_{i_p}) \leq l.\dim(S_j).$$

Therefore, $\frac{T_j}{\dim(S_j)} \leq l$, and no state receives more than l incoming σ-transitions. $\square$

Having seen that the erasure costs associated with zero-error QFAs are precisely representable by DFAs, we will use this link to establish an upper bound for the energy requirement of regular language recognition in the next section.

4   An Upper Bound for Information Erasure Per Step

It is natural to ask if there exists a universal bound on the number of bits that have to be "forgotten" per computational step of any finite automaton. In this section, we provide an answer to this question.

Theorem 2. *Every language on an alphabet Σ can be recognized by a DFA that has at most $|\Sigma| + 1$ incoming transitions labeled with the same symbol to any of its states.*

Proof. See the unabridged version of the paper at arXiv:2204.06025 [cs.CC]. $\square$

We now show that the bound shown in Theorem 2 is tight.

Theorem 3. *For every $j \geq 1$, there exists a language L_j on a j-symbol alphabet with the following property: All DFAs recognizing L_j have a state q such that at least $j + 1$ states transition to q upon receiving the same symbol.*

Proof. For the unary alphabet, it is easy to see that the language L_1 containing all strings except the empty string must have the property. For $j > 1$, define the "successor" function F on $\{1, ..., j\}$ by $F(i) = (i \bmod j) + 1$, and let B be F's inverse. On the alphabet $\Sigma_j = \{\sigma_1, ..., \sigma_j\}$, define

$$L_j = \{w|\ w \text{ ends with } \sigma_i \sigma_{F(i)} \text{ for some } 1 \le i \le j\}.$$

Let M be a DFA recognizing L_j. Assume, without loss of generality, that M does not have unreachable states.

Similarly to the proofs of Theorems 1 and 2, we will be talking about "bags" into which the states of M are partitioned. Each bag contains states that are equivalent to the ones in the same bag, and distinguishable from all states in the other bags. S is the bag that contains the initial state. For each k, A_k is the bag containing the state reached by the input $\sigma_{B(k)}\sigma_k$, and R_k is the bag containing any state reached by inputs of the form $\tau\sigma_k$, where τ is any substring not ending with $\sigma_{B(k)}$. Note that A_i and R_k are distinct bags for any $i, k \le j$, because all states in A_i are accepting states and those in R_k are not. For $X \in \{A, R\}$, X_k and X_l are also distinct when $k \ne l$, since M would reach an accepting state if it consumes the symbol $\sigma_{F(k)}$ when in a member of X_k, whereas it would reach a rejecting state with that symbol from a state in X_l. S is distinct from all the A_i and R_i, because it contains the only state which is two steps away from any accept state. The bags $(A_k)_k$, $(R_k)_k$ and S partition the entire state set.

The definition of L_j dictates that all incoming transitions to states in A_k or R_k are labeled with the symbol σ_k. Let i ($1 \le i \le j$) be the index minimizing $|A_i| + |R_i|$, i.e. the sum of states in A_i and R_i. Note that all states in all bags $(A_k)_k$, $(R_k)_k$ and S transition to either A_i or R_i upon reading the symbol σ_i, so there are

$$\Big(\sum_{1 \le k \le j} |A_k| \Big) + \Big(\sum_{1 \le k \le j} |R_k| \Big) + |S|$$

transitions with the symbol σ_i. Since $|A_i| + |R_i|$ is minimal and $|S| > 0$, this number is strictly larger than $j(|A_i|+|R_i|)$. At least one state in A_i or R_i should thus have at least $j + 1$ incoming σ_i-transitions by the pigeonhole principle. $\square$

Theorems 2 and 3 imply that, for any particular temperature T, given any amount of energy, there exists a regular language (on a suitably large alphabet) whose recognition at T requires a DFA with at least that much energy cost per computational step. When the alphabet is fixed, one can always rewrite any DFA on that alphabet to obtain an "energy-efficient" machine recognizing the same language with each step costing no more than the bound proven in Theorem 2. By Theorem 1, the same energy costs are associated with zero-error QFAs for that language.

Since smaller alphabets are associated with less energy cost per step, one may ask whether encoding a language on a bigger alphabet by replacing each symbol by a binary substring would decrease the overall energy consumption. For any $j > 1$, any machine recognizing language L_{2^j} as defined in the proof of

Theorem 3 needs to forget $n \log_2(2^j + 1)$ bits to process an input of length n. For a machine recognizing a version of L_j encoded in binary, the cost per step would be less, but the encoded input string would be longer, with the total number of erased bits amounting to the greater value $nj \log_2 3$.

5   Trading Energy for Error

It turns out that the minimum energy required for the recognition of some regular languages is reduced if one allows the finite automaton to give erroneous answers with probability not exceeding some bound less than $\frac{1}{2}$.

Recall the language family $\{L_j | j \geq 1\}$ defined in the proof of Theorem 3. Any zero-error QFA recognizing some L_j must have at least $j + 1$ operating elements by Theorem 1. Since L_1 is not a group language, no QFA with a single operating element can recognize it, even with bounded error [4].

Theorem 4. *There exists a QFA with two operating elements per superoperator that recognizes the language L_2 with bounded error.*

Proof. See the unabridged version of the paper at arXiv:2204.06025 [cs.CC].

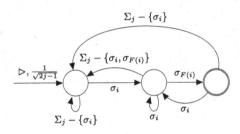

Fig. 2. Submachine $M_{j,i}$ in the construction of Theorem 5

Theorem 5. *For all $j \geq 3$, there exists a QFA M_j with three operating elements per superoperator that recognizes the language L_j with error probability bounded by $\frac{j-1}{2j-1}$.*

Proof. The argument is similar to the one in the proof of Theorem 4. Machine M_j has $j + 1$ submachines. For $i \in \{1, \dots, j\}$, submachine $M_{j,i}$ (depicted in Fig. 2) accepts its input if and only if it ends with $\sigma_i \sigma_{F(i)}$, whereas submachine $M_{j,j+1}$ accepts every input. (In Fig. 2, arrow labels of the form $\Sigma_j - \Gamma$ express that all symbols of the input alphabet except those in set Γ effect a transition with amplitude 1 between the indicated states.) M_j starts by branching with amplitude $\frac{1}{\sqrt{2j-1}}$ to each of $M_{j,i}$ for $i \in \{1, \dots, j\}$, and with amplitude $\frac{\sqrt{j-1}}{\sqrt{2j-1}}$ to $M_{j,j+1}$. Strings in L_j must lead one of the first j submachines to acceptance, and "tip the balance" for the overall machine to accept with probability at least $\frac{j}{2j-1}$. It is easy to see in Fig. 2 that the superoperators would have just three operating elements. □

6   Concluding Remarks

The approach we present for the study of energy complexity can be extended to several other scenarios, like interactive proof systems, involving finite-memory machines. We end with a list of some open questions.

- Is there a regular language whose zero-error recognition requires a QFA with more than two operation elements, whereas no energy savings are possible when one allows some bounded error in the recognition process?
- Is there a regular language whose bounded-error recognition requires a QFA with more than three operation elements?
- Can the construction in the proof of Theorem 5 be improved to reduce the error bounds, the energy requirement, or both?

References

1. Ambainis, A., Yakaryılmaz, A.: Automata and quantum computing (2018). arXiv:1507.01988v2
2. Bennett, C.H.: Logical reversibility of computation. IBM J. Res. Dev. **17**(6), 525–532 (1973)
3. Bertoni, A., Carpentieri, M.: Regular languages accepted by quantum automata. Inf. Comput. **165**(2), 174–182 (2001)
4. Brodsky, A., Pippenger, N.: Characterizations of 1-way quantum finite automata. SIAM J. Comput. **31**, 1456–1478 (2002)
5. Hirvensalo, M.: Quantum automata with open time evolution. Int. J. Nat. Comput. **1**, 70–85 (2010)
6. Klauck, H.: On quantum and probabilistic communication: Las Vegas and one-way protocols. In: 32th ACM Symposium on Theory of Computing, pp. 644–651 (2000)
7. Kondacs, A., Watrous, J.: On the power of quantum finite state automata. In: Proceedings 38th Symposium on Foundations of Computer Science, pp. 66–75 (1997)
8. Kutrib, M.: Aspects of reversibility for classical automata. In: Calude, C.S., Freivalds, R., Kazuo, I. (eds.) Computing with New Resources. LNCS, vol. 8808, pp. 83–98. Springer, Cham (2014). https://doi.org/10.1007/978-3-319-13350-8_7
9. Landauer, R.: Irreversibility and heat generation in the computing process. IBM J. Res. Dev. **5**(3), 183–191 (1961)
10. Leff, H.S., Rex, A.F. (eds.): Maxwell's Demon 2: Entropy, Classical and Quantum Information, Computing. CRC Press, Boca Raton (2002)
11. Li, L., Qiu, D., Zou, X., Li, L., Wu, L., Mateus, P.: Characterizations of one-way general quantum finite automata. Theoret. Comput. Sci. **419**, 73–91 (2012)
12. Moore, C., Crutchfield, J.P.: Quantum automata and quantum grammars. Theoret. Comput. Sci. **237**(1), 275–306 (2000)
13. Pin, J.-E.: On reversible automata. In: Simon, I. (ed.) LATIN 1992. LNCS, vol. 583, pp. 401–416. Springer, Heidelberg (1992). https://doi.org/10.1007/BFb0023844
14. Say, A.C.C., Yakaryılmaz, A.: Quantum finite automata: A modern introduction. In: Calude, C.S., Freivalds, R., Kazuo, I. (eds.) Computing with New Resources. LNCS, vol. 8808, pp. 208–222. Springer, Cham (2014). https://doi.org/10.1007/978-3-319-13350-8_16

Real-Time, Constant-Space, Constant-Randomness Verifiers

Özdeniz Dolu, Nevzat Ersoy, M. Utkan Gezer[(⊠)], and A. C. Cem Say

Department of Computer Engineering, Boğaziçi University,
34342 Bebek, İstanbul, Turkey
{ozdeniz.dolu,nevzat.ersoy,utkan.gezer,say}@boun.edu.tr

Abstract. We study the class of languages that have membership proofs which can be verified by real-time finite-state machines using only a constant number of random bits, regardless of the size of their inputs. Since any further restriction on the verifiers would preclude the verification of nonregular languages, this is the tightest computational budget which allows the checking of externally provided proofs to have meaningful use. We show that all languages that can be recognized by two-head one-way deterministic finite automata have such membership proofs. For any $k > 0$, there exist languages that cannot be recognized by any k-head one-way nondeterministic finite automaton, but that are nonetheless real-time verifiable in this sense. The set of nonpalindromes, which cannot be recognized by any one-way multihead deterministic finite automaton, is also demonstrated to be verifiable within these restrictions.

Keywords: Interactive proof systems · Real-time finite automata · Probabilistic finite automata

1 Introduction

The characterization of problem classes in terms of the computational requirements on machines that are supposed to check purported proofs of membership of their input strings in a language has been an important theme of complexity theory, leading to landmark achievements like the PCP Theorem [2,3] and celebrated open questions like the P vs. NP problem.

As expected, imposing tighter bounds on the computational resources of the verifiers for these proofs of membership seems to restrict the associated language classes: Limiting a polynomial-time deterministic verifier to use only a logarithmic, rather than polynomially bounded amount of working memory "shrinks" the class of verifiable languages to NL from NP, and the same apparent loss of power also occurs when a logarithmic-space, polynomial-time probabilistic verifier is restricted to use only a constant, rather than logarithmically bounded number of random bits for bounded-error verification. [4,12]

In this paper, we focus on the tightest possible "budgetary" restrictions that can be imposed on such verifiers by considering the case where the machine's

© Springer Nature Switzerland AG 2022
P. Caron and L. Mignot (Eds.): CIAA 2022, LNCS 13266, pp. 212–224, 2022.
https://doi.org/10.1007/978-3-031-07469-1_17

working memory *and* the amount of usable random bits are both constants irrespective of the input length, and the runtime is maximally constrained, so that only a real-time scan of the input string is allowed. We examine the class of languages whose membership proofs can be checked under these extreme conditions. Note that decreasing the number of random bits from a positive constant to zero would make such a proof system equivalent to a nondeterministic finite automaton, unable to recognize any nonregular languages. Since membership in any regular language can be decided by a "stand-alone" real-time deterministic finite automaton with no need of an externally provided certificate, the machines we consider are truly the weakest possible verifiers of meaningful use, highlighting the issues involved in the checking of the proofs of extremely long claims.

We build on previous work [12] which showed an equivalence between constant-space, constant-randomness verifiers and multihead nondeterministic finite automata working as language recognizers. This equivalence breaks down when the machines are restricted to consume their inputs in real-time fashion: A real-time multihead automaton is no more powerful than a single-head one, and can only recognize a regular language, whereas Say and Yakaryılmaz were able to demonstrate a nonregular language [12] which has membership proofs that can be checked by a real-time finite-state verifier with a fixed number of coin tosses.

In this paper, we prove the following facts about these very weak verifiers: All languages that can be recognized by two-head one-way deterministic finite automata have membership proofs that can be verified by these machines. For any $k > 0$, there exist languages that cannot be recognized by any k-head one-way nondeterministic finite automaton, but that are nonetheless real-time verifiable in this sense. The set of nonpalindromes, which cannot be recognized by any one-way multihead deterministic finite automaton, is also demonstrated to be verifiable in this setup. We conjecture that the real-time requirement truly decreases the verification power, i.e. that there exist languages that can be verified only when the definition of these machines is relaxed to allow them the ability to pause on the input tape.

The rest of the paper is structured as follows: Sect. 2 provides the necessary definitions and previous results regarding the relation between multihead finite automata and constant-randomness finite-state verifiers. Our results are presented in Sect. 3. Section 4 is a conclusion.

2 Preliminaries

2.1 One-Way Multihead Finite Automata

A *one-way k-head nondeterministic finite automaton* ($1\mathrm{nfa}(k)$) is a nondeterministic finite-state machine with k read-only heads that it can direct on an input string flanked by two end-marker symbols. Each head can be made to stay put or move one symbol to the right in each computational step. Formally, a $1\mathrm{nfa}(k)$ is a 6-tuple $(Q, \Sigma, \delta, q_0, q_{\mathrm{acc}}, q_{\mathrm{rej}})$, where

1. Q is the finite set of internal states,
2. Σ is the finite input alphabet,
3. $\delta \colon Q \times \Sigma_{\bowtie}^{k} \to \mathcal{P}(Q \times \Delta^k)$ is the transition function describing the sets of alternative moves the machine may perform at each execution step, where each move is associated with a state to enter and whether or not to move each head, given the machine's current state and the list of symbols that are currently being scanned by the k input heads:
   - $\Delta = \{\, 0, +1 \,\}$ is the set of possible head movements, where 0 means "stay put" and $+1$ means "move right",
   - $\Sigma_{\bowtie} = \Sigma \cup \{\, \triangleright, \triangleleft \,\}$, where $\triangleright, \triangleleft \notin \Sigma$ are respectively the left and right end-markers, placed automatically to mark the boundaries of the input,
4. $q_0 \in Q$ is the initial state,
5. $q_{\mathrm{acc}} \in Q$ is the final state at which the machine halts and accepts, and
6. $q_{\mathrm{rej}} \in Q$ is the final state at which the machine halts and rejects.

Given an input string $w \in \Sigma^*$, a 1nfa(k) $M = (Q, \Sigma, \delta, q_0, q_{\mathrm{acc}}, q_{\mathrm{rej}})$ begins execution from the state q_0, with $\triangleright w \triangleleft$ written on its tape, and all k of its heads on the left end-marker. At each timestep, M nondeterministically updates its state and head positions according to the choices dictated by its transition function. Computation halts if one of the states q_{acc} or q_{rej} has been reached, or a head has moved beyond the right end-marker.

Each different sequence of choices M may take corresponds to a different *computation history*, i.e. a sequence of tuples describing all the state and head positions that M goes through in that particular eventuality.

M is said to *accept* w if there exists a computation history where it reaches the state q_{acc}, given w as the input. M is said to *reject* w if every computation history of M on w either reaches q_{rej}, ends with a transition whose associated set of choices is $\emptyset$, or a head has moved beyond the right end-marker without a final state being entered. M might also loop on the input w, neither accepting nor rejecting it.

The *language recognized by* M is the set of strings that it accepts.

A *one-way k-head deterministic finite automaton*, denoted 1dfa(k), is a special case of 1nfa(k) $(Q, \Sigma, \delta, q_0, q_{\mathrm{acc}}, q_{\mathrm{rej}})$ whose transition function presents exactly one "choice" of move for every input ($|\delta(q, x_1, \ldots, x_k)| = 1$ for all $q \in Q$ and $x_1, \ldots, x_k \in \Sigma_{\bowtie}$).

1nfa(1) and 1dfa(1) are simply called *one-way nondeterministic* and *deterministic finite automata*, respectively. The "real-time" versions of these single-head machines are obtained by forcing the head to move to the right at each step (by setting $\Delta = \{\, +1 \,\}$). Real-time nondeterministic and deterministic finite automata have runtimes of at most $n + 2$ on input strings of length n.

The classes of languages recognized by each of the machine models defined above will be denoted by the uppercase versions of the associated machine denotations. For example, 1NFA(6) denotes the class of languages recognizable by 1nfa(6)'s. The following facts [7] about these language classes will be useful:

For any $k \geq 1$,

$$\text{1DFA(k)} \subsetneq \text{1DFA(k} + 1).$$
$$\text{1NFA(k)} \subsetneq \text{1NFA(k} + 1).$$

L_{nonpal} is the language which contains every string except palindromes on the alphabet $\{0, 1\}$. This language can be recognized by a 1nfa(2). Since its complement cannot be recognized by any 1dfa(k) for any k [9], there exists no deterministic one-way multihead automaton that recognizes L_{nonpal} either, by the fact [11] that the class of languages recognized by 1dfa(k)'s is closed under complementation. This proves the inequality $\text{1NFA(2)} \setminus \bigcup_k \text{1DFA(k)} \neq \emptyset$.

2.2 Verifiers

There exist several elegant characterizations of language classes in terms of bounds imposed on the resources available to probabilistic Turing machines ("verifiers") tasked with checking purported proofs ("certificates") of membership of their input strings in a language.

Formally, a *verifier* is a 6-tuple $(Q, \Sigma, \Phi, \Gamma, \delta, q_0)$, where

1. Q is the finite set of states, such that $Q = P \cup D \cup \{q_{\text{acc}}, q_{\text{rej}}\}$ where
   - P is the set of coin-tossing states,
   - D is the set of deterministic states, such that $P \cap D = \emptyset$, and
   - q_{acc} and q_{rej} are the accept and reject states, respectively.
2. Σ is the input alphabet, not containing the end-markers $\rhd$ and $\lhd$,
3. Φ is the work tape alphabet,
4. Γ is the certificate alphabet, not containing $\lhd$,
5. δ is the transition function, described below, and
6. q_0 is the initial state, $q_0 \in Q$.

As in Sect. 2.1, $\Sigma_{\bowtie}$ will be used to denote the union $\Sigma \cup \{\rhd, \lhd\}$.

The transition function δ is constructed in two parts, as follows: For $q \in P$, $q' \in Q$, $\sigma \in \Sigma_{\bowtie}$, $\phi, \phi' \in \Phi$, $\gamma \in \Gamma \cup \{\lhd\}$, $b \in \{0, 1\}$, $d_i, d_w \in \{-1, 0, +1\}$, and $d_c \in \{0, +1\}$, $\delta(q, \sigma, \phi, \gamma, b) = (q', \phi', d_i, d_w, d_c)$ dictates that the machine will switch to state q', write ϕ' on the work tape, and move the input, work tape and certificate heads in directions d_i, d_w, and d_c, respectively, if it is originally in state q, scanning σ, ϕ, and γ on the three respective tapes, and has obtained the random bit b as the result of a fair coin toss. For $q \in D$, $\delta(q, \sigma, \phi, \gamma) = (q', \phi', d_i, d_w, d_c)$ dictates a similar, but deterministic transition.

A verifier halts with acceptance (rejection) when it executes a transition entering q_{acc} (q_{rej}). Any transition that moves the input or certificate head beyond an end-marker delimiting the string written on the associated read-only tape leads to a rejection, unless that last move enters q_{acc}. The head on the certificate tape is defined to be one-way, since it is known [1] that allowing two-way access to that tape can lead to "unfair" accounting of the space usage. The input and work tape heads are two-way in the general definition above, although we will be considering restricting the movement types of the input tape head (and completely removing the work tape) in most of the following.

We say that such a machine V verifies a language L with error ϵ if there exists a number $\epsilon < 1$ where

- for all input strings $w \in L$, there exists a certificate string c_w such that V halts by accepting with probability 1 when started on w and c_w, and,
- for all input strings $w \notin L$ and for all certificates c, V halts by rejecting with probability at least $1 - \epsilon$ when started on w and c.

We will be using the notation VER(restriction₁,restriction₂,...,restrictionₖ) to denote the class of languages that can be verified by machines that operate within the added restrictions indicated in the parentheses. These may represent bounds for runtime, working memory usage, and number of random bits to be used as a function of the length of their input strings. The terms 0, con, log, and poly will be used to represent the well-known types of functions to be considered as resource bounds, with "con" standing for constant functions of the input length, the others being self evident, to form arguments like "poly-time" or "log-space". The "one-way" mode, where the input head is not allowed to move left, will be indicated by the parameter "1way-input", whereas the further restriction to real-time movement, where the head is not allowed to pause at any step during its left-to-right scan, will be indicated by "rt-input".

The following characterizations in terms of zero-error verifiers are well known.

$$\text{VER}\big(\text{poly-time,poly-space,0-random-bits}\big) = \text{NP}$$
$$\text{VER}\big(\text{poly-time,log-space,0-random-bits}\big) = \text{NL}$$

When one allows nonzero error, significant gains in space usage seem to be achievable:

$$\text{VER}\big(\text{poly-time,log-space,log-random-bits}\big) = \text{NP} \qquad [4]$$
$$\text{VER}\big(\text{con-space,con-random-bits}\big) = \text{NL} \qquad [12]$$

For verifiers using at least logarithmic space, the magnitude of the one-sided error can be reduced without significant increase in the runtime, whereas the constant-space verifiers of [12] (all of which have correct certificates that can be checked in polynomial time) do not seem [6] to have this property in general.[1]

Say and Yakarıylmaz [12] also considered the case where a constant-space, constant-randomness verifier is forbidden to move its input head to the left. Using their techniques, one can obtain the following characterization:

Theorem 1.

$$\text{VER}\big(\text{con-space,con-random-bits,1way-input}\big) = \bigcup_k \text{1NFA}(k).$$

---

[1] Note that a constant-space machine is equivalent to a finite-state automaton with no work tape, since the bounded amount of information in the work tape of a constant-space verifier can also be kept using a suitably large set of internal states.

Proof. Given a 1nfa(k) M recognizing a language L_M, one can construct a one-way, constant-space, constant-randomness verifier V_M for L_M as follows: V_M expects the certificate to contain a proof of the existence of an accepting computation history (in the form of a sequence of tuples representing the nondeterministic branch taken and list of symbols scanned by the heads at each step) of M working on the input string. V_M uses its random bits to select a head of M and simulates its execution on the input, relying on the certificate for information on what symbols would be scanned by the other heads of M at every step. If V_M ever sees the certificate reporting that the head it is tracking is currently scanning a symbol other than the correct value, it rejects. If the input is in L_M, a correct certificate that carries V_M to acceptance with probability 1 exists. Otherwise, in order to trick V_M to reach an accept state, the certificate would have to "lie" about what is being seen by at least one of the heads of M in at least one step, and V_M has a constant probability of having selected that head, and therefore rejecting the input. Since M can be assumed to run in linear time in all its nondeterministic branches without loss of generality, any attempt by an overly long certificate to trick V_M to loop without accepting will also be caught by nonzero probability.

In the reverse direction, given a finite-state verifier V with one-way input that uses at most r random bits, one can build a 1nfa(2^r) M_V for the verified language L_V as follows: V's behavior on each different random bit sequence can be represented by a deterministic verifier obtained by "hardwiring" that particular sequence into V's transition function. M_V is designed to nondeterministically guess a certificate and use its heads to simulate all these 2^r deterministic verifiers operating on the input string and the common certificate. For each newly guessed certificate symbol, M_V goes through all the deterministic verifiers, tracing each one's execution (by changing its state and possibly moving the corresponding head) until that deterministic verifier accepts, rejects, or performs a transition consuming that new certificate symbol by moving its certificate tape head. (Since the collection of deterministic verifiers has only a fixed number of possible tuples of states, M_V can detect when the deterministic verifiers run for more than that number of steps without moving any input heads, and reject on such nondeterministic branches corresponding to unnecessarily long certificates.) This procedure continues until either a deterministic verifier rejects, or all the 2^r deterministic verifiers are seen to accept. M_V accepts if it arrives in a state representing all the deterministic verifiers having accepted.   □

This link between finite-state constant-randomness verifiers and multihead automata is broken when one further restricts the input heads to be real-time: A multihead finite automaton operating all its heads in real time is easily seen to be no stronger than a single-head finite automaton, and therefore cannot recognize a nonregular language. Say and Yakaryılmaz, however, were able to demonstrate [12] a finite-state constant-randomness verifier with real-time input that verifies the nonregular language $L_{\text{twin}} = \{\, w\#w \mid w \in \{0,1\}^* \,\}$ on the alphabet $\{\,0,1,\#\,\}$:[2] The certificate is expected to consist of the string w, which is supposed to appear on both sides of the symbol $\#$ in the input. The machine tosses a coin to decide whether it should compare the substring appearing to the left or to the right of the $\#$ with the certificate as it is consuming the input in real time, and accepts only if this comparison is successful. Acceptance with probability 1 is only possible for members of the language associated with well-formed certificates.

Note that such a machine must use its capability to pause the *certificate* tape head for some steps. This is easy to see when one considers the computational power of a verifier with real-time heads on both the input and certificate tapes: All the "deterministic" verifiers that can be obtained from the probabilistic verifier by hardwiring the possible random sequences (as we saw in the proof of Theorem 1) would then be running both their heads on exactly the same strings in perfect synchrony, and it would be possible to build a single real-time one-head finite automaton simulating this collection. This machine would be equivalent to a one-head nondeterministic finite automaton, with no power of recognizing nonregular languages.

In a very real sense, VER(con-space,con-random-bits,rt-input) corresponds to the weakest computational setup where externally provided proofs are meaningful. In the next section, we will examine this interesting class and its relationship with VER(con-space,con-random-bits,1way-input) in detail.

3   Real-Time, Finite-State, Constant-Randomness Verification

3.1   1DFA(2) is Real-Time Verifiable

We start by demonstrating that every language that is recognizable by a 1dfa(2) is verifiable by a constant-space, constant-randomness verifier that scans its input in real time. The technique employed in the proof of Theorem 1 for constructing verifiers is not useful here, since it requires the verifier to pause its input head occasionally when processing certain portions of the certificate. We will show that all languages in 1DFA(2) have more concise proofs of membership that can be checked by our restricted machines. Some examples of languages on the alphabet $\{\,0,1,\#\,\}$ in 1DFA(2) are L_{twin}, the set of all strings containing equal numbers of 0's and 1's, the set of all odd-length binary strings with the symbol $\#$ at the middle position, the language $\{\,w \mid w \in (x\#)^{+}, x \in (0 \cup 1)^{+}\,\}$, and their complements.

Theorem 2. $1\mathrm{DFA}(2) \subseteq \mathrm{VER}(\text{con-space,con-random-bits,rt-input})$.

---

[2] Note that the construction in the proof of Theorem 1 produces a multihead automaton with heads that can pause on the input, even when it is fed a verifier with real-time input.

Proof. Let $M = (Q_M, \Sigma, \delta_M, q_0, q_{acc}, q_{rej})$ be a 1dfa(2) recognizing some language A. At any given step of its execution, M might be moving none, one, or both of its heads. We start by modifying M to obtain a 1dfa(2) $M' = (Q_{M'}, \Sigma, \delta_{M'}, q_0, q_{acc}, q_{rej})$ that recognizes the same language while moving exactly one of its heads at every step, starting with the first head. The details of this construction procedure are as follows:

The state set of the machine M' is defined as $Q_{M'} = Q_M \cup \{ q' \mid q \in Q_M \}$. Each transition of M that moves both heads at once is simulated by two transitions that move the heads one after another in M'. Formally, for all $q, s \in Q_M$, $x, y \in \Sigma_{\bowtie}$, if $\delta_M(q, x, y) = (s, +1, +1)$, we set $\delta_{M'}(q, x, y) = (s', +1, 0)$. Furthermore, for all $s \in Q_M$, $x, y \in \Sigma_{\bowtie}$, we set $\delta_{M'}(s', x, y) = (s, 0, +1)$.

If a transition of M is stationary, i.e., is of the form $\delta_M(q, x, y) = (s, 0, 0)$, it is a member of either an infinite sequence representing a loop (of length at most $|Q_M|$) in which M scans the symbols x and y without changing the head positions, or a finite sequence ending with acceptance, rejection, or the moving of some head. In the infinite-loop case, we set the corresponding transition in M' to $\delta_{M'}(q, x, y) = (q_{rej}, +1, 0)$. In the finite-sequence case, the value of $\delta_{M'}(q, x, y)$ will be set to $(q_{acc}, +1, 0)$ or $(q_{rej}, +1, 0)$ if the sequence is ending with acceptance or rejection, respectively, and to the value of the final transition in the sequence otherwise.

Any transition of M that moves a single head is inherited without modification by M'.

It may be the case that the new machine built according to these specifications moves its second head first. This problem can be handled easily by just rearranging the transition function to effectively "swap" the names of the two heads. (Such a simple swap is possible, because the fact that both heads scan the left end-marker symbol at the beginning means that it is only the transition function, and not the particular input string, that determines which head moves first.)

Consider the computation history of M' running on an input string w: Keeping in mind that exactly one head moves at every step, the computation history can be split into sub-histories $H_1, H_2, H_3, H_4, \ldots$, where only the first head moves during the odd-numbered sub-histories, and the second head moves during the even-numbered ones. Let us call $H_1 H_3 H_5 \cdots$ (i.e. the concatenation of the odd-numbered sub-histories) the *odd part* of the history, and $H_2 H_4 H_6 \cdots$ the *even part*.

Note that, if one visualizes the odd part of the history, one sees the first head moving in real time. Furthermore, the state sequence traversed during these moves is easy to trace step by step employing knowledge of M''s transition function, except at the "joints" between sub-histories, where the machine's state and the position of the second head make "leaps" corresponding to (possibly long) sequences of moves made by the second head while the first head was pausing. A similar observation can be made for the even part. Intuitively, both parts of the history can be thought of as describing the execution of a real-time automaton that momentarily "blacks out" as it switches from any H_i to H_{i+2}, finding the machine's state and the other head's position updated to new values when it wakes up. Our strategy for real-time verification will follow directly from this observation, and the certificate will supply the necessary information to deal with the blackouts.

We will construct a real-time, finite-state verifier V that uses a single random bit to verify the language A. The certificate alphabet of V is $Q_{M'} \times \Sigma_{\bowtie} \times Q_{M'} \times \Sigma_{\bowtie}$, with each symbol corresponding to a tuple of two states and two input symbols (including end-markers) of M'.

The certificate c_w for a string $w \in A$ will be a concise description of the state and head position values required by the two probabilistic paths of V that will be assigned (as will be described shortly) to trace the odd and even parts of the computation history of M' on w to recover from the blackouts mentioned above:

$$c_w = (s_1, z_1, s_2, z_2)(s_3, z_3, s_4, z_4)(s_5, z_5, s_6, z_6) \cdots$$

The sequence above is to be interpreted as follows: For each i, the certificate "claims" that M' will be in state s_i at the end of H_i. For odd i, it claims that the first head will be scanning the input symbol z_i at the end of H_i. Finally, for even i, the certificate claims that the second head will be scanning the symbol z_i at the end of H_i.

Given an input and a certificate, V starts by tossing a coin to choose which head of M' to trace. If the first head is chosen, V initiates a simulation of M' from q_0 using its knowledge that the second head is paused on the symbol $\triangleright$ to determine the next state to transition to at each step. V traces the first head of M' with its own real-time head until it reaches a point during the simulation where M' pauses the first head. (Recall that pausing its own head is impossible for V.) At that point, V performs the following two operations at once: It verifies that it has just transitioned out of the state s_1 and that its input head is indeed scanning the symbol z_1, consistently so with the claims of the first certificate symbol (s_1, z_1, s_2, z_2) (rejecting immediately if it discovers an inconsistency). It also advances its certificate head, and continues its simulation from the "wake-up" state s_2 with the transition $\delta_{M'}(s_2, z_1, z_2)$, assuming that the second head is now paused on the symbol z_2 as claimed by the certificate.[3]

The procedure to be followed by V if it chooses the second head at the beginning is similar, with some minor differences: In this case, V moves the certificate head at its first step, leaving the first certificate symbol (s_1, z_1, s_2, z_2) behind. (It stores s_2 and z_2 in its memory for later use.) V starts simulating M' from the state s_1, trusting the certificate's claim that M''s first head is paused on the symbol z_1, and using its own real-time head to mimic M''s second head.[4] This simulation proceeds until the point where M' pauses its second head. V checks whether the certificate's claims about s_2 and z_2 were indeed consistent with its current information about the simulation state and head reading, consumes the next certificate symbol, and proceeds simulation from the new "wake-up" setting as described above if it has not discovered a lie of the certificate.

---

[3] If $\delta_{M'}(s_2, z_1, z_2)$ happens to be a transition that moves the second head, V rejects.

[4] If the first simulated step from state s_1 does not move the second head, V rejects.

Each probabilistic branch of V accepts if and only if the simulation reaches the accept state of M'. All $w \in A$ are accepted by V with probability 1 when coupled with a proper certificate c_w describing the sub-history transitions correctly. Whenever $w \notin A$, a c_w that describes the history faithfully will lead both branches of V to rejection. Any dishonest certificate trying to divert a branch to acceptance by giving false wake-up values will be caught out by the other branch that has direct access to the relevant state and head information, so all nonmembers of A will be rejected with probability at least $\frac{1}{2}$.   □

3.2   Real-Time Verification Beyond 1DFA(2)

Consider the language $L_{IK} = \{ a^i b^j c^k \mid i = j \text{ or } i = k \text{ or } j = k \}$, which is in 1DFA(3), but not in 1DFA(2) [8]. A real-time, finite-state verifier using a single random bit can verify L_{IK} by checking certificates of the form σx^l, where σ is a ternary symbol that indicates which two of the three "segments" of the input string are claimed to be of the same length l. Depending on the values of σ and the random bit, the verifier decides which segment to attempt to match with the certificate postfix x^l, and accepts only if this match succeeds.

More generally, for any $k > 0$, there exists a language of the form

$$L_n = \{ y_1 \# y_2 \# \cdots \# y_{2n} \mid y_i \in \{ a, b \}^* \text{ and } y_i = y_{2n+1-i}, \text{ for } 1 \leq i \leq n \}$$

which can be recognized by a 1dfa($k+1$), but not by any 1nfa(k) [13]. Such a language L_n can be verified by a real-time, constant-space machine using $\lceil \log(n+1) \rceil$ random bits to split into $n+1$ paths that would compare the relevant segments of a certificate of the form $y_1 \# y_2 \# \cdots \# y_n$ with the corresponding input segments. So we have VER(con-space,con-random-bits,rt-input) \ 1NFA(k) $\neq \emptyset$ for all $k \geq 1$.

We now exhibit a language that is verifiable in real time by constant-randomness finite-state machines, but is unrecognizable by any deterministic multihead automaton.

Theorem 3. VER(con-space,con-random-bits,rt-input) \ $\bigcup_k$ 1DFA(k) $\neq \emptyset$.

Proof. We will construct a verifier V for the language L_{nonpal}, which was noted to be outside $\bigcup_k$ 1DFA(k) in Sect. 2.

Every string w in L_{nonpal} matches the pattern $x\sigma y\sigma' z$, where $x, y, z \in \{ 0, 1 \}^*$ and $\sigma, \sigma' \in \{ 0, 1 \}$, such that $|x| = |z|$ and $\sigma \neq \sigma'$. The correct certificate c_w for such an input will encode the positions of the "unmatching" symbols σ and σ' as follows:

$$c_w = 0^{|x|} 1 0^{|y|}$$

V tosses a single coin at the beginning of the computation to probabilistically "branch" to one of two "deterministic verifiers" V_0 and V_1, each of which checks the certificate $0^i 1 0^j$ in a different way, as described below.

Note that, if $0^i 1 0^j$ is indeed a correct certificate for the input, claiming that the two unmatching symbols are at positions $i + 1$ and $i + j + 2$, then the input string must be exactly $i + 1$ symbols longer than this certificate. V_0 checks this by moving the certificate head only once for every two moves of the input head over the input string until it passes over the 1 in the certificate. At that point, it switches to moving the certificate head at every step as well. If the certificate is of the correct length, the two heads will consume their right end-markers simultaneously, in which case V_0 will accept.

The task of V_1 is to assume that the certificate is well-formed in the sense described above, and accept if the two symbols at positions $i + 1$ and $i + j + 2$ really are unequal. This can be done by moving the certificate head at the same speed as the input head, recording the symbol at position $(i + 1)$ in memory, and comparing it with the input symbol scanned at the step where the certificate string has been consumed completely.

If the input is a member of L_{nonpal}, both V_0 and V_1 accept with the correct certificate. Otherwise, the input is a palindrome, and the certificate will either be malformed (and therefore be rejected by V_0), or the two symbols it points out will be equal, in which case it will be rejected by V_1.   □

4   Concluding Remarks

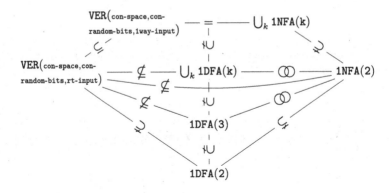

Fig. 1. An inclusion diagram of our results.

Figure 1 summarizes the landscape of complexity classes covered in this paper. The ⊕ symbol denotes that the two related sets are neither disjoint, nor a subset of one another.

We conjecture that

$$\text{VER}(\text{con-space,con-random-bits,rt-input}) \subsetneq \text{VER}(\text{con-space,con-random-bits,1way-input}),$$

that is, restricting the input head to move in real-time yields machines which are not capable of verifying some languages that can be handled by verifiers with one-way input. The reasoning behind this conjecture is based on considerations of the following languages:

$$L_{\text{match}} = \left\{ \left. x \# y_1 \# y_2 \# \cdots \# y_k \; \right| \; \begin{array}{l} x, y_i \in \{0,1\}^+ \text{ for all } i, k > 0, \\ \text{and } y_i = x \text{ for some } i \end{array} \right\}$$

$$L_{\frac{1}{2}} = \{ ww \mid w \in \{0,1\}^* \}$$

$$L_{\frac{2}{3}} = \{ xwx \mid x, w \in \{0,1\}^* \text{ and } |x| = |w| \}$$

These languages, which are in VER(con-space,con-random-bits,1way-input), seem to be beyond the capabilities of real-time verifiers. Verification of membership in these languages requires two input substrings (whose lengths are not bounded, and which cannot therefore fit in a fixed amount of memory) to be "matched" in a certain sense. Furthermore, the start position of the second substring cannot be determined in a one-way pass without external help. Therefore, membership certificates have to contain information about both the position of the second substring and the content of these substrings. We suspect that it is impossible to design certificates from which real-time input machines can acquire these two pieces of information without getting tricked into accepting some illegal inputs.

For further study, it would be interesting to examine the power of real-time finite-state verifiers with less severe bounds on the amount of randomness that can be used, as well as real-time verification of debates [5] between two opposing "provers" by similarly restricted machines. Restricting the verifiers further by imposing other conditions like reversibility [10] is another possible direction.

Acknowledgment. The authors thank Martin Kutrib for his helpful answers to several questions. This work is supported by the Turkish Directorate of Strategy and Budget under the TAM Project number 2007K12-873.

References

1. Arora, S., Barak, B.: Computational Complexity: A Modern Approach. Cambridge University Press, USA (2009)
2. Arora, S., Lund, C., Motwani, R., Sudan, M., Szegedy, M.: Proof verification and the hardness of approximation problems. J. ACM **45**(3), 501–555 (1998)
3. Arora, S., Safra, S.: Probabilistic checking of proofs: a new characterization of NP. J. ACM **45**(1), 70–122 (1998)
4. Condon, A., Ladner, R.: Interactive proof systems with polynomially bounded strategies. J. Comput. Syst. Sci. **50**(3), 506–518 (1995)
5. Demirci, H.G., Say, A.C.C., Yakaryılmaz, A.: The complexity of debate checking. Theor. Comput. Syst. **57**(1), 36–80 (2015)
6. Gezer, M.U., Say, A.C.C.: Constant-space, constant-randomness verifiers with arbitrarily small error. Inf. Comput. 104744 (2021, in press)
7. Holzer, M., Kutrib, M., Malcher, A.: Complexity of multi-head finite automata: origins and directions. Theor. Comput. Sci. **412**(1–2), 83–96 (2011)
8. Ibarra, O.H., Kim, C.E.: On 3-head versus 2-head finite automata. Acta Informatica **4**(2), 193–200 (1975)

9. Kutrib, M., Malcher, A., Wendlandt, M.: Set automata. Int. J. Found. Comput. Sci. **27**(02), 187–214 (2016)
10. Pin, J.-E.: On reversible automata. In: Simon, I. (ed.) LATIN 1992. LNCS, vol. 583, pp. 401–416. Springer, Heidelberg (1992). https://doi.org/10.1007/BFb0023844
11. Rosenberg, A.L.: On multi-head finite automata. IBM J. Res. Dev. **10**(5), 388–394 (1966)
12. Say, A.C.C., Yakaryılmaz, A.: Finite state verifiers with constant randomness, Logical Methods Comput. Sci. **10**(3) (2014). https://lmcs.episciences.org/724
13. Yao, A.C., Rivest, R.L.: k + 1 heads are better than k. J. ACM **25**(2), 337–340 (1978)

Constrained Synchronization for Monotonic and Solvable Automata and Automata with Simple Idempotents

Stefan Hoffmann[✉] [ID]

Fachbereich 4 - Abteilung Informatikwissenschaften, Universität Trier,
Trier, Germany
hoffmanns@informatik.uni-trier.de

Abstract. For general input automata, there exist regular constraint languages such that asking if a given input automaton admits a synchronizing word in the constraint language is PSPACE-complete or NP-complete. Here, we investigate this problem for the following classes of input automata: monotonic automata, solvable automata and automata with simple idempotents over a binary alphabet. The latter class contains, for example, the Černý family of automata, an infinite family of n-state automata whose shortest synchronizing words have length $(n-1)^2$. Solvable automata generalize both commutative automata and weakly acyclic automata. We find that for monotonic automata, the problem is solvable in nondeterministic logarithmic space, for every regular constraint language. We identify a subclass of solvable automata for which the problem is in NP. This subclass strictly contains the weakly acyclic automata. In the course of our investigation we derive a sharp linear upper bound for the length of a shortest synchronizing word in a given constraint language, improving previous quadratic bounds for weakly acyclic and commutative automata. We also give structural characterizations of solvable automata and their recognized languages that imply that they recognize languages for which partial commutation closures give regular languages. Lastly, we show that for input automata with simple idempotents over a binary alphabet and with a constraint language given by a partial automaton with up to three states, the constrained synchronization problem is in P.

Keywords: Constrained synchronization · Monotonic automata · Solvabe automata · Automata with simple idempotents

1 Introduction

A deterministic semi-automaton (which is an automaton without a distinguished start state and without a set of final states) is *synchronizing* if it admits a reset word, i.e., a word which leads to a definite state, regardless of the starting state. This notion has a wide range of applications, from software testing, circuit synthesis, communication engineering and the like, see [15,18].

© Springer Nature Switzerland AG 2022
P. Caron and L. Mignot (Eds.): CIAA 2022, LNCS 13266, pp. 225–237, 2022.
https://doi.org/10.1007/978-3-031-07469-1_18

The famous Černý conjecture [2] states that a minimal synchronizing word, for an n-state automaton, has length at most $(n-1)^2$. The best general upper bound known so far is cubic [16].

The sharp upper bound of $n-1$ was shown for n-state commutative automata [12] and for monotonic automata [1]. For automata with simple idempotents, the bound $2(n-1)^2$ is known [13].

In [4] the *constrained synchronization problem* was introduced, where we ask for a synchronizing word contained in a given (fixed) contraint language. It was shown that we can realize PSPACE-complete, NP-complete or polynomial time solvable constrained problems by appropriately choosing a constraint language. Investigating the reductions from [4], we see that most reductions yield automata with a sink state, which then must be the unique synchronizing state. Hence, we can conclude that we can realize these complexities with this type of input automaton. Contrary, for example, unary automata are synchronizing only if they admit no non-trivial cycle, i.e., only a single self-loop. In this case, we can easily decide synchronizability for any constraint language in polynomial time (even determinstic logarithmic time). Hence, for these simple types of automata, the complexity drops considerably. So, a natural question is, if we restrict the class of input automata, what complexities are realizable? Or more precisely:

What features in the input automata do we need to realize certain complexities?

In [7] this question was investigated for weakly acyclic, or partially ordered, input automata. These are automata where all cycles are trivial, i.e., the only loops are self-loops. It was shown that in this case, the constrained synchronization problem is always in NP and, for suitable constraint languages, NP-complete problems are realizable.

Contribution. Here, we investigate the constrained synchronization when the input is restricted to the class of monotonic automata, the class of solvable automata and to automata with simple idempotents. Solvable automata generalize weakly acyclic automata, previously investigated in [7], and commutative automata [7]. We state that for monotonic input automata, the constrained synchronization problem is solvable in nondeterministic logarithmic space for every constraint automaton. For a subclass of solvable automata we show containment in NP. This subclass properly contains the weakly acyclic automata. Furthermore, we give a sharp linear upper bound for the length of a shortest synchronizing word with respect to a given constraint. This improves previously given quadratic bounds [6,7]. Furthermore, we show that languages recognized by solvable automata are in the unambiguous polynomial closure of commutative 0-group[1] languages. This implies that partial commutation closures on these languages give regular languages.

---

[1] A 0-group language $L \subseteq \Sigma^*$ is a language recognized by a 0-group (a group with zero), i.e. there exists a morphism $\varphi : \Sigma^* \to G$ into a 0-group, a group G with a zero symbol, such that $L = \varphi^{-1}(\varphi(L))$.

Lastly, we show that for input automata with simple idempotents over a binary alphabet and small constraint automata, the constrained synchronization problem is in P.

2 Preliminaries and Some Known Results

We assume the reader to have some basic knowledge in computational complexity theory and formal language theory, as contained, e.g., in [9]. For instance, we make use of regular expressions to describe languages. By Σ we denote the *alphabet*, a finite set. For a word $w \in \Sigma^*$ we denote by $|w|$ its *length*, and, for a symbol $x \in \Sigma$, we write $|w|_x$ to denote the *number of occurrences of x* in the word. We denote the empty word, i.e., the word of length zero, by ε. We call $u \in \Sigma^*$ a *prefix* of a word $v \in \Sigma^*$ if there exists $w \in \Sigma^*$ such that $v = uw$. For $U, V \subseteq \Sigma^*$, we set $U \cdot V = UV = \{uv \mid u \in U, v \in V\}$ and $U^0 = \{\varepsilon\}$, $U^{i+1} = U^i U$, and $U^* = \bigcup_{i \geq 0} U^i$ and $U^+ = \bigcup_{i > 0} U^i$. We also make use of complexity classes like NL, P, NP, or PSPACE.

A tuple $\mathcal{A} = (\Sigma, Q, \delta, q_0, F)$ is a *partial deterministic finite automaton (PDFA)*, where Σ is a finite set of *input symbols*, Q is the finite *state set*, $q_0 \in Q$ the *start state*, $F \subseteq Q$ the *final state set* and $\delta \colon Q \times \Sigma \rightharpoonup Q$ the *partial transition function*. The *partial transition function* $\delta \colon Q \times \Sigma \rightharpoonup Q$ extends to words from Σ^* in the usual way. Furthermore, for $S \subseteq Q$ and $w \in \Sigma^*$, we set $\delta(S, w) = \{\delta(q, w) \mid \delta(q, w)$ is defined and $q \in S\}$. We call $\mathcal{A}$ a *complete (deterministic finite) automaton* if δ is defined for every $(q, a) \in Q \times \Sigma$. If $|\Sigma| = 1$, we call $\mathcal{A}$ a *unary automaton* and $L \subseteq \Sigma^*$ is also called a *unary language*. The set $L(\mathcal{A}) = \{w \in \Sigma^* \mid \delta(q_0, w) \in F\}$ denotes the language *recognized* (or *accepted*) by $\mathcal{A}$.

A *deterministic and complete semi-automaton (semi-DFA)* $\mathcal{A} = (\Sigma, Q, \delta)$ is a deterministic and complete finite automaton without a specified start state and with no specified set of final states. When the context is clear, we call both deterministic finite automata and semi-automata simply *automata*. Here, when talking about semi-automata, we always mean complete and deterministic semi-automata, as we do not consider other models of semi-automata. Concepts and notions that only rely on the transition structure carry over from complete automata to semi-automata and vice versa and we assume, for example, that every notion defined for semi-automata has also the same meaning for complete automata with a start state and a set of final states.

Let $\mathcal{A} = (\Sigma, Q, \delta)$ be a semi-automaton. A maximal subset $S \subseteq Q$ with the property that for every $s, t \in S$ there exists $u \in \Sigma^*$ such that $\delta(s, u) = t$ is called a *strongly connected component* of $\mathcal{A}$. We also say that a state $s \in Q$ is *connected* to a state $t \in Q$ (or t is *reachable* from s) if there exists $u \in \Sigma^*$ such that $\delta(s, u) = t$.

A complete automaton $\mathcal{A}$ is called *synchronizing* if there exists a word $w \in \Sigma^*$ with $|\delta(Q, w)| = 1$. In this case, we call w a *synchronizing word* for $\mathcal{A}$. We call a state $q \in Q$ with $\delta(Q, w) = \{q\}$ for some $w \in \Sigma^*$ a *synchronizing state*. For a semi-automaton (or PDFA) with state set Q and transition function

$\delta : Q \times \Sigma \rightharpoonup Q$, a state q is called a *sink state*, if for all $x \in \Sigma$ we have $\delta(q, x) = q$. Note that, if a synchronizing automaton has a sink state, then the synchronizing state is unique and must equal the sink state.

Let $\mathcal{A} = (\Sigma, Q, \delta)$ be a semi-automaton. Then, $\mathcal{A}$ is called an *automaton with simple idempotents*, if every $a \in \Sigma$ either permutes the states or maps precisely two states to a single state and every other state to itself. More formally, every $a \in \Sigma$ either (1) permutes the states, i.e., $\delta(Q, a) = Q$, or (2) it is a *simple idempotent*, i.e., we have $|\delta(Q, a)| = |Q| - 1$ and $\delta(q, aa) = \delta(q, a)$ for every $q \in Q$. Letters fulfilling condition (1) are also called *permutational letters*, and letters fulfilling (2) are called *simple idempotent letters*.

The automaton $\mathcal{A}$ is a *permutation-reset automaton* if every letter is a permutational letter (or *permutation symbol*) or a *reset symbol*, i.a. a symbol $a \in \Sigma$ mapping every state to a single state (the letter induces a constant mapping on the states). A permutation-reset automaton without a reset symbol is called a *permutation automaton*.

An automaton $\mathcal{A} = (\Sigma, Q, \delta)$ with $Q = \{1, \ldots, n\}$ is *monotonic*, if $i \le j$ implies $\delta(i, x) \le \delta(j, x)$ for each $x \in \Sigma$. We assume that for a given monotonic automaton, the linear order is encoded into the states (by representing them by numbers) and hence can be read off readily.

The semi-automaton $\mathcal{A}$ is called *commutative*, if for all $a, b \in \Sigma$ and $q \in Q$ we have $\delta(q, ab) = \delta(q, ba)$. The semi-automaton $\mathcal{A}$ is called *weakly acyclic*, if there exists an ordering $q_1, q_2, \ldots, q_n$ of its states such that if $\delta(q_i, a) = q_j$ for some letter $a \in \Sigma$, then $i \le j$ (such an ordering is called a *topological sorting*). An automaton is weakly acyclic, if $\delta(q, uxv) = q$ for $u, v \in \Sigma^*$ and $x \in \Sigma$ implies $\delta(q, x) = q$, i.e., the only loops in the automaton graph are self-loops. This is also equivalent to the fact that the reachability relation between the states is a partial order.

The class of *solvable automata* was introduced in [12] as a generalization of commutative automata. It was shown that for a synchronizable solvable n-state automaton the length of a shortest synchronizing word is at most $n - 1$.

Originally, in [12] this class was introduced only for so called 0-automata, i.e., automata having a sink state. However, the notions transfer without difficulty to general automata. Let $\mathcal{A} = (\Sigma, Q, \delta)$ be a semi-DFA and $S \subseteq Q$. Then this subset of states defines a *subautomaton* $\mathcal{B} = (\Sigma, S, \delta)$ if $\delta(S, a) \subseteq S$ for each $a \in \Sigma$. Note that the subautomaton has the same transition function, but restricted to the subset S. Having a subautomaton $\mathcal{B} = (\Sigma, S, \delta)$, we can define the *factor automaton* $\mathcal{A}/\mathcal{B} = (\Sigma, T, \mu)$ with state set $T = Q \setminus S \cup \{S\}$ and, for each $a \in \Sigma$ and $q \in Q \setminus S$, transition function $\mu(q, a) = \delta(q, a)$ if $\delta(q, a) \notin S$, $\mu(q, a) = S$ if $\delta(q, a) \in S$ and $\mu(S, a) = S$, i.e., we collapse S to a single sink state.

Let $\mathcal{A} = (\Sigma, Q, \delta)$ be a semi-DFA. A *composition series* is a maximal sequence of subautomata $\mathcal{A}_i = (\Sigma, S_i, \delta)$, $i \in \{0, \ldots, m\}$ with $\mathcal{A}_m = \mathcal{A}$, such that

$$S_0 \subseteq S_1 \subseteq \ldots \subseteq S_m = Q. \tag{1}$$

A maximal such sequence is called a *composition series* in [12].

The semi-DFA $\mathcal{A}$ is called *solvable* if there exists a composition series as in Eq. (1) such that the factor automata $\mathcal{A}_i/\mathcal{A}_{i-1}$ for $i \in \{1, \ldots, m\}$ and $\mathcal{A}_0$ are commutative. In fact, the requirement of maximality can be dropped and only the existence of a series as in Eq. (1) with commutative factor automata and $\mathcal{A}_0$ commutative equivalently characterizes solvability.

Remark 1. Our notion of solvability generalizes the notion of solvability introduced in [12] for synchronizable automata with a sink state. In [12] another notion of solvability is introduced that only applies to synchronizable automata. Our definition allows non-synchronizable but solvable automata.

In [4] the *constrained synchronization problem* was defined for a fixed PDFA $\mathcal{B} = (\Sigma, P, \mu, p_0, F)$.

Decision Problem 1: [4] $L(\mathcal{B})$-Constr-Sync
Input: semi-DFA $\mathcal{A} = (\Sigma, Q, \delta)$.
Question: Is there a synchronizing word $w \in \Sigma^*$ for $\mathcal{A}$ with $w \in L(\mathcal{B})$?

The automaton $\mathcal{B}$ will be called the *constraint automaton*. If an automaton $\mathcal{A}$ is a yes-instance of $L(\mathcal{B})$-Constr-Sync we call $\mathcal{A}$ *synchronizing with respect to* $\mathcal{B}$. Occasionally, we do not specify $\mathcal{B}$ and rather talk about L-Constr-Sync.

Previous results have shown that unconstrained synchronization is solvable in polynomial time, and constrained synchronization in polynomial space.

Theorem 2.1 ([18]). *We can decide Σ^*-Constr-Sync in time $O(|\Sigma||Q|^2)$.*

Theorem 2.2 ([4]). *For any constraint automaton $\mathcal{B} = (\Sigma, P, \mu, p_0, F)$ the problem $L(\mathcal{B})$-Constr-Sync is in PSPACE.*

In [4], a complete analysis of the complexity landscape when the constraint language is given by small partial automata was done.

Theorem 2.3 ([4]). *Let $\mathcal{B} = (\Sigma, P, \mu, p_0, F)$ be a PDFA. If $|P| \leq 1$ or $|P| = 2$ and $|\Sigma| \leq 2$, then $L(\mathcal{B})$-Constr-Sync $\in$ P. For $|P| = 2$ with $\Sigma = \{a, b, c\}$, up to symmetry by renaming of the letters, $L(\mathcal{B})$-Constr-Sync is either in P or is PSPACE-complete precisely in the following cases for $L(\mathcal{B})$:*

$$
\begin{array}{llll}
a(b+c)^* & (a+b+c)(a+b)^* & (a+b)(a+c)^* & (a+b)^*c \\
(a+b)^*ca^* & (a+b)^*c(a+b)^* & (a+b)^*cc^* & a^*b(a+c)^* \\
a^*(b+c)(a+b)^* & a^*b(b+c)^* & (a+b)^*c(b+c)^* & a^*(b+c)(b+c)^*.
\end{array}
$$

For $|P| = 3$ and $|\Sigma| = 2$, the following is known: In [4] it has been shown that (ab^*a)-Constr-Sync is NP-complete for general input automata. In [4, Theorem 33] it was shown that $(b(aa+ba)^*)$-Constr-Sync is PSPACE-complete for general input automata. Further, it was shown [8] that for the following constraint languages the constrained problem is PSPACE-complete: $b^*a(a+ba)^*$, $a(b+ab)^* + b(bb^*a)^*$, which are all accepted by a 3-state PDFA over a binary alphabet. So, with Theorem 2.3, at least three states are necessary and sufficient over a binary alphabet to realize PSPACE-complete problems.

For an overview of the results for different classes of input automata, see Table 1.

Table 1. Overview of known result of the complexity landscape of $L(\mathcal{B})$-CONSTR-SYNC with $\mathcal{B} = (\Sigma, P, \mu, p_0, F)$ when restricted to certain input automata. Constraint languages giving intractable problems are written next to the hardness claim. For a binary alphabet, the 3-state PDFA language $b(aa + ba)^*$ gives an PSPACE-complete problem for general input automata.

Input Aut. type	Complexity class	Hardness	Reference
General automata	PSPACE	PSPACE-hard for $a(b + c)^*$	[4]
With sink state	PSPACE	PSPACE-hard for $a(b + c)^*$	[4]
Weakly acyclic	NP	NP-hard for $a(b + c)^*$	[7]
Monotonic	NL	–	Theorem 3.1
Solvable with cycle restriction	NP	contains weakly acyclic, hence NP-hard by [7]	Theorem 4.6
Simple idempotents	P for $|\Sigma| = 2, |P| \leq 3$	–	Theorem 5.3

3   Monotonic Automata

Monotonic automata[2] were introduced by Ananichev & Volkov [1]. In [14], further problems related to (subset) synchronization problems on monotonic automata were investigated. Checking if a given automaton is monotonic is NP-complete [17].

Theorem 3.1. *Let $\mathcal{B} = (\Sigma, P, \mu, p_0, F)$ be a constraint automaton. For monotonic input automata it is in NL to decide whether there exists a synchronizing word of this automaton in $L(\mathcal{B})$ when the minimal and maximal states are known. Furthermore, a shortest synchronizing word in $L(\mathcal{B})$ for an n-state monotonic automaton has length at most $n \cdot |P|$ and this bound is sharp.*

4   Solvable Automata

Beside the rather algebraic treatment by Rystsov [12] himself, the following properties equivalently characterize solvable automata.

Theorem 4.1. *Let $\mathcal{A} = (\Sigma, Q, \delta)$ be a complete and determinstic semi-DFA. Then the following are equivalent:*

1. *$\mathcal{A}$ is solvable,*
2. *There exists a composition series $Q = S_m \supset S_{m-1} \supset \ldots \supset S_0$ where the factor automata $\mathcal{A}_i/\mathcal{A}_{i-1}$, $i \in \{1, \ldots, m\}$, are commutative permutation-reset automata and $\mathcal{A}_0$ is a commutative permutation automaton,*
3. *For every strongly connected component $S \subseteq Q$, the following two conditions hold true:*
   (a) for all $a \in \Sigma$, we either have $\delta(S, a) \cap S = \emptyset$ or $\delta(S, a) = S$,

---

[2] Note that the monotonic automata as introduced earlier by Eppstein [3] are more general, as they are only required to respect a cyclic order (they were called *oriented* automata by Ananichev & Volkov in [1]).

(b) if $a, b \in \Sigma$ are such that $\delta(S, a) = \delta(S, b) = S$, then[3] $\delta(q, ab) = \delta(q, ba)$ for all $q \in S$.

Given a class of language $\mathcal{C}$, the *polynomial closure* are all finite unions of *marked products*, i.e., languages of the form $L_0 a_1 L_1 \cdots a_n L_n$ with L_i being languages from the class with $L_i \subseteq \Sigma^*$ and $a_i \in \Sigma$ for $i \in \{1, \ldots, n\}$.

The *unambiguous polynomial closure* is the same construction but with the additional requirements that (1) we are taking the finite union over disjoint languages and (2) instead of marked products, we have *unambiguous marked products*, where a marked product $L_0 a_1 L_1 \cdots a_n L_n$ is unambiguous if for each $u \in L_0 a_1 L_1 \cdots a_n L_n$ the factorization $u = u_0 a_1 u_1 \cdots a_n u_n$ with the $u_i \in L_i$, $i \in \{0, 1, \ldots, n\}$, is unique.

Proposition 4.2. *The languages accepted by solvable automata are in the unambiguous polynomial closure of commutative 0-group languages.*

Partial commutation closures arises in model-checking and verification. In general, this operation does not preserve regularity. In [5, Corollary 2.4] it was shown that when a class of regular languages has the property that partial commutation closures give regular languages, then the polynomial closure has this property as well. Hence, with the previous result, we can deduce that partial commutation closures of languages accepted by solvable automata give regular languages.

The solvable automata generalize commutative and weakly acyclic automata. For commutative automata this is clear by definition.

By Theorem 4.1, the factor automata are permutation-reset automata.

That every weakly acyclic automaton is a solvable automaton follows with Theorem 4.1 as the only strongly connected components are singleton sets in a weakly acyclic automaton and so the factor automata are two-state automata with a sink state, hence commutative. Property 3a from Theorem 4.1 is clearly satisfied.

Proposition 4.3. *Every commutative DFA is solvable and every weakly acyclic DFA is solvable.*

Next, we state an upper bound for the length of a shortest synchronizing word in a given constraint language.

Proposition 4.4. *Let $\mathcal{B} = (\Sigma, P, \mu, p_0, F)$ and $\mathcal{A} = (\Sigma, Q, \delta)$ be a solvable and synchronizable semi-DFA with n states. Then a shortest synchronizing word for $\mathcal{A}$ in $L(\mathcal{B})$ has length at most $n \cdot |\Sigma| \cdot L \cdot |P| - 1$, where L denotes the least common multiple of the cycle lengths for the letters, i.e.,*

$$L = \mathrm{lcm}\{p \mid \exists q \in Q \ \exists a \in \Sigma : \delta(q, a^p) = q \wedge p > 0 \wedge p \text{ minimal}\}.$$

Furthermore, there exist constraint automata and solvable input automata attaining the bound.

---

[3] If the images are not in S, then $\delta(q, ab) \neq \delta(q, ba)$ is possible.

Proof (sketch). We only sketch the argument for the upper bound. It follows by inductively showing the following statement: Given a composition series $Q = S_m \supset S_{m-1} \supset \ldots \supset S_0$, let $i \in \{1, \ldots, m\}$ and $u \in \Sigma^*$ be such that $|\delta(T, u)| = 1$ with $T \subseteq S_i$ non-empty and $\mu(p, u) \in F$ for some $p \in P$. Then we claim that there exists $u' \in \Sigma^*$ with $|u'| \leq (i + 1) \cdot |\Sigma| \cdot L \cdot |P| - 1$, $|\delta(T, u')| = 1$ and $\mu(p, u') \in F$.

In the induction step, we can, by commutativity, rearrange u into $|\Sigma|$ blocks of single letters. When one block has length at least $(i + 1) \cdot L \cdot |P|$, then there exists a shorter word that ends at the same states (for this we need L) in $\mathcal{A}$ and at the same state in $\mathcal{B}$ (for this we need $|P|$).

That the bound is sharp is easily seen by considering a constraint automaton with a single state recognizing Σ^* and a unary input semi-DFA $\mathcal{A} = (\{a\}, Q, \delta)$ with n states $Q = \{q_0, q_1, \ldots, q_{n-1}\}$ such that $\delta(q_i, a) = q_{\min\{i+1, n-1\}}$. $\square$

For weakly acyclic automata, we can improve the stated bound.

Proposition 4.5. *Let $\mathcal{B} = (\Sigma, P, \mu, p_0, F)$ and $\mathcal{A} = (\Sigma, Q, \delta)$ be a weakly acyclic and synchronizable automaton with n states. Then a shortest synchronizing word for $\mathcal{A}$ in $L(\mathcal{B})$ has length at most $n \cdot |P| - 1$ and there exists input automata and constraint automata such that this bound is attained.*

The constraint automaton and input automata attaining the bound in the proof sketch of Proposition 4.4 also works for Proposition 4.5.

Landau's function $g(n)$ equals the largest order of a permutation on n points or the least common multiple of any partition of n. As we can have arbitrary cycles in the strongly connected components, we find that in general L from Proposition 4.4 grows asymptotically like $g(n)$, which asymptotically equals $\exp(1 + o(1))\sqrt{n \ln n}$ [10].

However, for input automata where L is bounded by a polynomial, we can guess and check a given synchronizing word in non-deterministic polynomial time.

Theorem 4.6. *Let $\mathcal{B} = (\Sigma, P, \mu, p_0, F)$. For solvable input automata $\mathcal{A} = (\Sigma, Q, \delta)$ with n states the constrained synchronization problem with constraint language $L(\mathcal{B})$ is in NP for the following classes of solvable input automata:*

1. *when the shortest cycles in $\mathcal{A}$ have the same length,*
2. *when the lengths of the shortest cycles divide n,*
3. *when there exists a polynomial p such that the least common multiple of the lengths of the shortest cycles with the property that every transition in the cycle is labeled by the same letter (where distinct letters for different such cycles are allowed) is bounded by $p(n)$.*

Note that the previous statement properly extends the result for weakly acyclic input semi-automata [7].

By the results from [7] and Proposition 4.3, there exist constraint automata such that the problem is NP-complete, as it is already NP-hard for weakly acyclic automata.

5 Synchronizing Automata with Simple Idempotents over a Binary Alphabet

Here, we show that for input automata with simple idempotents over a binary alphabet and a constraint given by a PDFA with at most three states, the constrained synchronization problem is always solvable in polynomial time. Note that, as written at the end of Sect. 2, the smallest constraint languages giving PSPACE-complete problems are given by 3-state automata over a binary alphabet. But, as shown here, if we only allow automata with simple idempotents as input, the problem remains tractable in these cases.

Intuitively, by applying an idempotent letter, we can map at most two states to a single state. Hence, to synchronize an n-state automaton with simple idempotents, we have to apply at least $n-1$ times an idempotent letter. This is the content of the next lemma.

Lemma 5.1. Let $\mathcal{A} = (\Sigma, Q, \delta)$ be an n-state semi-automaton with simple idempotents and let $\Gamma \subseteq \Sigma$ be the set of all simple idempotent letters (that are not permutational letters). Suppose $w \in \Sigma^*$ is a synchronizing word for $\mathcal{A}$. Then, $\sum_{a \in \Gamma} |w|_a \geq n-1$.

In [11, Proposition 6.2] it was shown that the possible synchronizing automata with simple idempotents over a binary alphabet fall into two classes, depicted in Fig. 1 (note our parameter p has a different meaning as in [11, Proposition 6.2], where it denotes $p+1$ in our notation).

A more formal statement of this fact is given next.

Proposition 5.2. Let $\Sigma = \{a, b\}$ be a binary alphabet and $\mathcal{A} = (\Sigma, Q, \delta)$ be an n-state automaton with simple idempotents. Suppose $\mathcal{A}$ is synchronizing and $n > 3$. Then, up to renaming of the letters, we have only two cases for $\mathcal{A}$:

1. There exists a sink state $t \in Q$, the letter b permutes the states in $Q \setminus \{t\}$ in a single cycle and $|\delta(Q, a)| = n-1$ with $t \in \delta(Q \setminus \{t\}, a)$, i.e., $t = \delta(t, a) = \delta(s, a)$ for two distinct states $s, t \in Q$.
2. The letter b permutes the states in Q in a single cycle and there exists $0 < p < n$ coprime to n and two distinct states $s, t \in Q$ such that $t = \delta(s, a) = \delta(s, b^p)$.

Recall that as a is a simple idempotent letter, we have $\delta(q, a) = q$ for each $q \in Q \setminus \{s\}$ in both cases.

Note that the set of synchronizing words can be rather complicated in both cases. For example, the language $\Sigma^* a^+ (b((ba^*)^{n-1})^*) a^+)^{n-2} \Sigma^*$ contains[4] only synchronizing words for automata of the first type in Proposition 5.2, and, similarly, $\Sigma^* a^+ ((ba^*)^{n-p}(ba^*)^n a^+)^{n-2} \Sigma^*$ in the second case. However, for example,

---

[4] Note that there might be other synchronizing words not in the stated language. For example if $n = 6$, the word $abbabbabbabba$ synchronizes the automaton of the first type from Proposition 5.2.

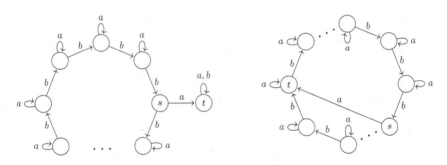

Fig. 1. The two cases from Prop. 5.2. In the second case, for $p = 1$ with the notation from the statement, we get Černy family [2], a family of automata giving the lower bound $(n-1)^2$ for the length of a shortest synchronizing word.

the language $(bbba)^*bb(bbba)^*bb(bbba)^*$ contains synchronizing words and non-synchronizing words for automata of the first type.

Finally, for binary automata with simple idempotents and an at most 3-state constraint PDFA, the constrained synchronization problem is always solvable in polynomial time. The proof works by case analysis on the possible sequences of words in the constraint language and if it is possible to synchronize the two automata types listed in Proposition 5.2 with those sequences.

Theorem 5.3. *Let $\mathcal{B} = (\Sigma, P, \mu, p_0, F)$ be a constraint automaton with $|P| \leq 3$ and $|\Sigma| \leq 2$. Let $\mathcal{A} = (\Sigma, Q, \delta)$ be an input semi-automaton with simple idempotents. Then, deciding if $\mathcal{A}$ has a synchronizing word in $L(\mathcal{B})$ can be done in polynomial time.*

Proof (sketch). The cases $|\Sigma| \leq 1$ or $|P| \leq 2$ and $|\Sigma| = 2$ are polynomial time decidable in general as shown in [4, Corollary 9 & Theorem 24]. So, we can suppose $\Sigma = \{a, b\}$ and $P = \{1, 2, 3\}$ with $p_0 = 1$. As in [4], we set $\Sigma_{i,j} = \{x \in \Sigma : \mu(i, x) = j\}$. If the cases in Proposition 5.2 apply, and if so, which case, can be checked in polynomial time, as we only have to check that one letter is a simple idempotent and the other letter permutes the states in a single cycle or two cycles with the restrictions as written in Proposition 5.2.

So, we can assume $\mathcal{A}$ has one of the two forms as written in Proposition 5.2. Without loss of generality, we assume a is the simple idempotent letter and b the permutational letter. Set $n = |Q|$. We also assume $n > 4$. If $n \leq 4$, then we have to compare $\mathcal{A}$ to finitely many automata that are synchronizing for a given (fixed) constraint language $L(\mathcal{B})$. This can be done in constant time.

Next, we only handle the first case of Proposition 5.2 by case analysis. The other case can be handled similarly. Further, let $t \in Q$ be the state as written in the first case of Proposition 5.2.

Further, in this sketch, we only handle the case that the strongly connected components of $\mathcal{B}$ are $\{1\}$ and $\{2, 3\}$ and the subautomaton between the states $\{2, 3\}$ is one of the automata listed in Table 2. These are the most difficult cases, for the remaining cases of $\mathcal{B}$ we refer to the full proof in the appendix.

Table 2. Cases for a partial subautomaton between the states $\{2,3\}$ that is not complete. See the proof of Theorem 5.3 for details.

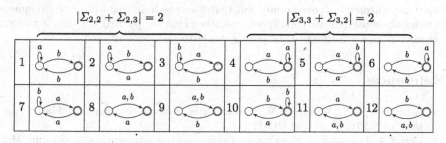

For $p \in P$ and $E \subseteq P$, we write $\mathcal{B}_{p,E} = (\Sigma, P, \mu, p, E)$ for the PDFA that results from $\mathcal{B}$ by changing the start state to p and the set of final states to E.

We present the arguments for Case 1 and 4.

<u>Case 1</u> In this case $L(\mathcal{B}_{2,\{2\}}) = (a + bb)^*$. We show that in the case under consideration, if $\mathcal{A}$ has the form stated in case one of Proposition 5.2, $\mathcal{A}$ is synchronizing if and only if n is even. Let $s \in Q \setminus \{t\}$ be the state with $\delta(s, a) = \delta(t, a) = t$. If n is odd, then $|Q \setminus \{t\}|$ is even and the single cycle induced by b on the states in $Q \setminus \{t\}$ splits into two cycles for the word bb, i.e., we have precisely two disjoint subsets $A, B \subseteq Q \setminus \{t\}$ of equal size such that the states in one subset can be mapped onto each other by a word in $(bb)^*$ but we cannot map states between those subset by a word from $(bb)^*$. Suppose, without loss of generality, that $s \in B$. For each $q \in A$ we have $\delta(q, a) = q$ and $\delta(q, bb) \in A$. Hence, we cannot map a state from A to s, and so not to t, the unique synchronizing state. As $n \geq 5$, which implies $|A| = |B| \geq 2$, and for every $w \in \Sigma_{1,1}^* \Sigma_{1,2}$ we have $|\delta(Q, w)| \geq n - 1$ (recall $\Sigma_{1,1} \cup \Sigma_{1,2} \subseteq \{a, b\}$ and $\Sigma_{1,1} \cap \Sigma_{1,2} = \emptyset$ as $\mathcal{B}$ is a deterministic automaton), we must have $\delta(Q, w) \cap A \neq \emptyset$ for every $w \in \Sigma_{1,1}^* \Sigma_{1,2}$. So, $\mathcal{A}$ cannot be synchronized by a word from $L(\mathcal{B}_{1,\{2\}}) = \Sigma_{1,1}^* \Sigma_{1,2}(a + bb)^*$. If n is even, than bb also permutes the states in $Q \setminus \{t\}$ in a single cycle and the word $a(bba)^{n-2}$ synchronizes $\mathcal{A}$. So, picking any $u \in \{a, b\}^*$ with $\mu(1, u) = 2$, the word $u(bba)^{n-1} \in L(\mathcal{B})$ synchronizes $\mathcal{A}$.

<u>Case 4</u> In this case $L(\mathcal{B}_{2,\{2\}}) = (aa^*b)^*$. The word $(ab)^{n-1}$ synchronizes $\mathcal{A}$. Pick any $u \in L(\mathcal{B}_{1,\{2\}})$, then $u(ab)^{n-1} \in L(\mathcal{B})$ synchronizes $\mathcal{A}$. Hence, if $\mathcal{A}$ has the form as assumed, then there always exists a synchronizing word for it in the constraint language. $\square$

6   Conclusion

It is still an open problem if the constrained synchronization problem is in NP for arbitrary solvable input automata and if it is always polynomial time solvable for arbitrary automata with simple idempotents as input. Furthermore, with respect to Theorem 3.1, we conjecture that there exist constraint automata for which the problem NL-hard when restricted to monotonic input automata.

Acknowledgement. I thank the anonymous reviewers for careful reading, spotting typos and unclear formulations. Furthermore, I thank two reviewers for helping me in improving Theorem 3.1: one pointed out that it can be improved to show containment in nondeterministic logarithmic space, the other reviewer pointed out that it yields a polynomial time algorithm to compute a shortest synchronizing word.

References

1. Ananichev, D.S., Volkov, M.V.: Synchronizing monotonic automata. Theor. Comput. Sci. **327**(3), 225–239 (2004)
2. Černý, J.: Poznámka k. homogénnym experimentom s konecnými automatmi. Mat. fyz. čas SAV **14**, 208–215 (1964)
3. Eppstein, D.: Reset sequences for monotonic automata. SIAM J. Comput. **19**(3), 500–510 (1990)
4. Fernau, H., Gusev, V.V., Hoffmann, S., Holzer, M., Volkov, M.V., Wolf, P.: Computational complexity of synchronization under regular constraints. In: Rossmanith, P., Heggernes, P., Katoen, J. (eds.) MFCS 2019. LIPIcs, vol. 138, pp. 63:1–63:14. Schloss Dagstuhl - Leibniz-Zentrum für Informatik (2019)
5. Gómez, A.C., Guaiana, G., Pin, J.: Regular languages and partial commutations. Inf. Comput. **230**, 76–96 (2013)
6. Hoffmann, S.: Constrained synchronization and commutativity. Theor. Comput. Sci. **890**, 147–170 (2021)
7. Hoffmann, S.: Constrained synchronization and subset synchronization problems for weakly acyclic automata. In: Moreira, N., Reis, R. (eds.) DLT 2021. LNCS, vol. 12811, pp. 204–216. Springer, Cham (2021). https://doi.org/10.1007/978-3-030-81508-0_17
8. Hoffmann, S.: Ideal separation and general theorems for constrained synchronization and their application to small constraint automata. In: Chen, C.-Y., Hon, W.-K., Hung, L.-J., Lee, C.-W. (eds.) COCOON 2021. LNCS, vol. 13025, pp. 176–188. Springer, Cham (2021). https://doi.org/10.1007/978-3-030-89543-3_15
9. Hopcroft, J.E., Ullman, J.D.: Introduction to Automata Theory, Languages, and Computation. Addison-Wesley Publishing Company, Boston (1979)
10. Landau, E.: über die Maximalordnung der Permutationen gegebenen Grades. Archiv der Mathematik und Physik **5**(3), 92–103 (1903)
11. Martyugin, P.: Complexity of problems concerning reset words for some partial cases of automata. Acta Cybernetica **19**(2), 517–536 (2009)
12. Rystsov, I.: Reset words for commutative and solvable automata. Theor. Comput. Sci. **172**(1–2), 273–279 (1997)
13. Rystsov, I.: Estimation of the length of reset words for automata with simple idempotents. Cybern. Syst. Anal. **36**(3), 339–344 (2000)
14. Ryzhikov, A., Shemyakov, A.: Subset synchronization in monotonic automata. Fundamenta Informaticae **162**(2–3), 205–221 (2018)
15. Sandberg, S.: 1 homing and synchronizing sequences. In: Broy, M., Jonsson, B., Katoen, J.-P., Leucker, M., Pretschner, A. (eds.) Model-Based Testing of Reactive Systems. LNCS, vol. 3472, pp. 5–33. Springer, Heidelberg (2005). https://doi.org/10.1007/11498490_2
16. Shitov, Y.: An improvement to a recent upper bound for synchronizing words of finite automata. J. Autom. Lang. Comb. **24**(2–4), 367–373 (2019)

17. Szykuła, M.: Checking whether an automaton is monotonic is NP-complete. In: Drewes, F. (ed.) CIAA 2015. LNCS, vol. 9223, pp. 279–291. Springer, Cham (2015). https://doi.org/10.1007/978-3-319-22360-5_23
18. Volkov, M.V., Kari, J.: Černý's conjecture and the road colouring problem. In: Éric Pin, J. (ed.) Handbook of Automata Theory, vol. I, pp. 525–565. European Mathematical Society Publishing House (2021)

An Ambiguity Hierarchy of Weighted Context-Free Grammars

Yusuke Inoue$^{(\boxtimes)}$, Kenji Hashimoto, and Hiroyuki Seki

Graduate School of Informatics, Nagoya University, Nagoya, Japan
{y-inoue,seki}@sqlab.jp, k-hasimt@i.nagoya-u.ac.jp

Abstract. Weighted context-free grammar (WCFG) is a quantitative extension of context-free grammar (CFG). It is known that unambiguous weighted automata (WA), finitely-ambiguous WA, polynomially-ambiguous WA and general WA over the tropical semiring have different expressive powers. We prove that there exists a similar ambiguity hierarchy of WCFG over the tropical semiring, using an extended Ogden's lemma. Furthermore, we show that the hierarchy we proved is different from the known ambiguity hierarchy of unweighted CFG.

Keywords: Weighted context-free grammar · Ambiguity · Pumping lemma

1 Introduction

Weighted context-free grammar (WCFG) is a quantitative extension of context-free grammar (CFG). WCFG originates from the study of algebraic formal series by Chomsky and Schützenberger [2]. Since then, mathematical properties of WCFG and the formal series (or functions) defined by WCFG have been extensively studied. There are various applications of WCFG to real-world problems such as parsing natural language sentences and biological sequence analysis [4]. In some applications, weights correspond to probabilities, which are useful for selecting better estimations of the hidden structure from experimental or observable data. However, it is not yet very clear whether and how a hierarchy in terms of the expressive power is induced in the class of context-free languages by introducing weights to CFG.

In general, a weighted model (automaton, grammar, etc.) is defined with a semiring, and each model defines a function that maps a word to an element of the semiring, instead of a language. When the semiring is positive, the support of the function defined by a weighted model naturally corresponds to the language generated by the unweighted counterpart of the model, where the support is a homomorphism from the semiring to Boolean semiring $\{0, 1\}$.

The expressive power of weighted automata (WA) has been studied in the literature. In particular, it is known that unambiguous WA, finitely-ambiguous WA, polynomially-ambiguous WA and general WA over the tropical semiring have different expressive powers [1,7]. Unambiguous WA (resp. finitely-ambiguous WA, polynomially-ambiguous WA) are WA such that the number

© Springer Nature Switzerland AG 2022
P. Caron and L. Mignot (Eds.): CIAA 2022, LNCS 13266, pp. 238–250, 2022.
https://doi.org/10.1007/978-3-031-07469-1_19

of accepting runs is bounded by one (resp. by a constant, by a polynomial in the size of an input) for any input. Similar results are known for weighted tree automata over the tropical semiring [6] although the tree languages proved to be in the gaps between the adjacent two layers are essentially the same as those in [1,7]. For an (unweighted) finite automaton (FA), the ambiguity does not affect the expressive power since the determinization is possible for nondeterministic FA and a deterministic FA is apparently unambiguous. Therefore, the above mentioned results on WA indicate that the strict ambiguity hierarchy is caused by introducing weights. On the other hand, the ambiguity already increases the expressive power for unweighted CFG because there exist inherently ambiguous CFG [8]. In fact, it is shown that unambiguous CFG, finitely-ambiguous CFG, polynomially-ambiguous CFG and general CFG have different expressive powers [9].

In this paper, we study an ambiguity hierarchy of WCFG over the tropical semiring where the ambiguity of a word w in a WCFG G means the number of distinct parse trees of w in G. We show that there is a strict ambiguity hierarchy of WCFG over the tropical semiring caused by introducing weights. Specifically, we prove that there exist functions $f_{EX2}, f_{EX3}, f_{EX4} \in$ U-CF such that $f_{EX2} \in$ FA-WCF \ U-WCF, $f_{EX3} \in$ PA-WCF \ FA-WCF and $f_{EX4} \in$ WCF \ PA-WCF. U-CF is the class of functions defined by WCFG over the tropical semiring whose supports coincide with the languages defined by unambiguous CFG, i.e., U-CF corresponds to the class of unambiguous context-free languages. U-WCF, FA-WCF, PA-WCF and WCF are the classes of functions defined by unambiguous WCFG, finitely-ambiguous WCFG, polynomially-ambiguous WCFG and general WCFG over the tropical semiring, respectively. That is, functions f_{EX2}, f_{EX3} and f_{EX4} exist in the gaps caused by introducing weights (see Fig. 1).

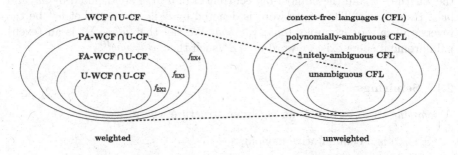

Fig. 1. The ambiguity hierarchy caused by introducing weights

Deciding the expressive power of weighted models is more difficult than that of unweighted ones. For unweighted automata (resp. grammars), we only need to check the existence of an accepting run (resp. a parse tree). For weighted automata (resp. grammars), we have to consider all accepting runs (resp. parse trees) to compute the weight of a given word because the weight of a word is defined by the semiring sum of the weights of all accepting runs (resp. parse trees) of the word. For example, we have to find the minimum weight among all accepting runs when we compute the function value defined by WA over the tropical semiring. (Note that the sum in the tropical semiring means the minimum.) This difficulty is more remarkable for WCFG than for WA. This is because, the ambiguity for WA is caused by only the choice of a state, while the ambiguity for WCFG is also caused by the shape of a parse tree. Therefore, the expressive power of WCFG cannot be determined by a simple iteration property. For these reasons, we cannot show a strict ambiguity hierarchy of WCFG by a straightforward extension of the discussion on the ambiguity hierarchy for WA. To overcome this problem, we focus on the functions defined by WCFG that assign non-zero weights only to the words having specific form such as palindromes and well-nested parentheses (Dyck words).

In Sect. 2, we introduce semiring, weighted context-free grammar and weight function. Furthermore, we show some examples of functions defined by WCFG (Examples 1 to 5). These functions will be used to prove the strict hierarchy in Sect. 4. In Sect. 3, we show a pumping lemma for CFG, which is helpful for proving the hierarchy (Lemma 3). The lemma is an extension of the theorem for CFG known as Ogden's lemma. In Sect. 4, we prove that functions f_{EX2}, f_{EX3} and f_{EX4} defined in Sect. 2 lie in the gaps caused by introducing weights (Theorems 1, 2 and 3), and as a corollary of them, we show the strict ambiguity hierarchy of WCFG (Corollary 1).

2   Preliminaries

Let $\mathbb{N}$ be the set of all non-negative integers. The cardinality of a set X is denoted by $|X|$. Let Σ be a (finite) alphabet. For a word $w \in \Sigma^*$ and a letter $a \in \Sigma$, the length of w and the number of occurrences of a in w are denoted by $|w|$ and $|w|_a$, respectively. The empty word is denoted by ε, i.e., $|\varepsilon| = 0$. Let w^R be the reversal of w. For example, $(aab)^R = baa$. We say that $w' \in \Sigma^*$ is an (even) palindrome if there exists a word $w \in \Sigma^*$ such that $w' = ww^R$.

2.1   Semirings

A *semiring* $(\mathbb{S}, \oplus, \odot, \mathbb{0}, \mathbb{1})$ is an algebraic structure where

- $(\mathbb{S}, \oplus, \mathbb{0})$ is a commutative monoid,
- $(\mathbb{S}, \odot, \mathbb{1})$ is a monoid,
- $\odot$ distributes over $\oplus$,
- $\mathbb{0}$ is the zero element of $\odot$.

A semiring $(\mathbb{S}, \oplus, \odot, \mathbb{0}, \mathbb{1})$ is called a commutative semiring if $(\mathbb{S}, \odot, \mathbb{1})$ is also a commutative monoid. We abbreviate $(\mathbb{S}, \oplus, \odot, \mathbb{0}, \mathbb{1})$ as $\mathbb{S}$.

In this paper, we mainly consider the following two semirings : the *tropical semiring* $\mathbb{N}_{\min,+} = (\mathbb{N} \cup \{\infty\}, \min, +, \infty, 0)$ and *Boolean semiring* $\mathbb{B} = (\{0, 1\}, \vee, \wedge, 0, 1)$.

For a commutative semiring S, we define the mapping $h_S : S \to \mathbb{B}$ as follows: $h_S(x) = 0$ if $x = 0$, and $h_S(x) = 1$ otherwise. A semiring S is said to be *positive* if $h_S : S \to \mathbb{B}$ is a semiring homomorphism, i.e., $h_S(0) = 0$, $h_S(1) = 1$, $h_S(a \oplus b) = h_S(a) \vee h_S(b)$ and $h_S(a \odot b) = h_S(a) \wedge h_S(b)$ for all $a, b \in S$ [3]. Note that $\mathbb{N}_{\min,+}$ is a positive semiring.

2.2 Weighted Context-Free Grammars

Let S be a commutative semiring. A *weighted context-free grammar* (WCFG) over S is a tuple $G = (V, \Sigma, P, I, \mathrm{wt})$, where

- V is a finite set of *nonterminals*, and $I \in V$ is the *initial* symbol,
- Σ is a finite set of *terminals*, disjoint from V,
- P is a set of *productions* of the form: $A \to \gamma$ where $A \in V$ and $\gamma \in (V \cup \Sigma)^*$,
- $\mathrm{wt} : P \to S \setminus \{0\}$ is a *weight function*.

We say that $(\alpha A \beta, \alpha \gamma \beta) \in ((V \cup \Sigma)^*)^2$ is a *direct derivation* if there exists a production $p = A \to \gamma \in P$, and we write $\alpha A \beta \Rightarrow \alpha \gamma \beta$ or $\alpha A \beta \overset{c}{\Rightarrow} \alpha \gamma \beta$ where $c = \mathrm{wt}(p)$. For a sequence of direct derivations $\rho : \alpha_0 \overset{c_1}{\Rightarrow} \alpha_1 \overset{c_2}{\Rightarrow} \cdots \overset{c_n}{\Rightarrow} \alpha_n$ $(n \geq 0)$, the weight of ρ is defined by $\mathrm{wt}(\rho) = c_1 \odot c_2 \odot \cdots \odot c_n$. We say that ρ is a *derivation*, and we write $\alpha_0 A_0 \beta_0 \Rightarrow^* \alpha_n A_n \beta_n$ or $\alpha_0 A_0 \beta_0 \overset{c}{\Rightarrow}^* \alpha_n A_n \beta_n$ where $c = \mathrm{wt}(\rho)$. If a derivation ρ_1 can be written as $\alpha \Rightarrow^* \alpha_1 \gamma \beta_1 \Rightarrow^* \alpha_1 \delta \beta_1 \Rightarrow^* \eta$ where $\rho_2 : \gamma \Rightarrow^* \delta$ is also a derivation, we say that ρ_2 is a *subderivation* of ρ_1. A derivation $\rho : \alpha_0 A_0 \beta_0 \overset{c_1}{\Rightarrow} \cdots \overset{c_n}{\Rightarrow} \alpha_n A_n \beta_n$ $(n \geq 0)$ is said to be a *leftmost derivation* if $\alpha_0, \cdots, \alpha_n \in \Sigma^*$. A leftmost derivation $\rho : I \overset{c}{\Rightarrow}^* w$ is said to be a *complete leftmost derivation* of w if $c \neq 0$ and $w \in \Sigma^*$. Note that for each word $w \in \Sigma^*$, complete leftmost derivations of w have a one-to-one correspondence with parse trees of w in the usual sense [5]. Therefore, we will call a complete leftmost derivation $\rho : I \Rightarrow^* w$ a parse tree of w. For a word $w \in \Sigma^*$, the weight of w is defined by $[\![G]\!](w) = \bigoplus_{T \in \mathrm{parse}(w)} \mathrm{wt}(T)$ where $\mathrm{parse}(w)$ is the set of parse trees of w. We say that $[\![G]\!] : \Sigma^* \to S$ is the function defined by WCFG G over S.

For a WCFG $G = (V, \Sigma, P, I, \mathrm{wt})$, we say that CFG $G'' = (V, \Sigma, P, I)$ is the underlying CFG of G. If $[\![G]\!](w) \neq 0$, then $w \in L(G'')$ where $L(G'')$ is the language generated by G'' in the standard definition. However, the converse direction does not always hold. For example, if there are two derivations T_1 and T_2 of w in G where $\mathrm{wt}(T_1) = 1$ and $\mathrm{wt}(T_2) = -1$, then $[\![G]\!](w) = 0$ over $(\mathbb{Z}, +, \times, 0, 1)$ while $w \in L(G'')$.

Assume that S is positive (see Sect. 2.1). For the function $f = [\![G]\!]$ defined by a WCFG $G = (V, \Sigma, P, I, \mathrm{wt})$ over S, the *support* of f is defined by $\mathrm{supp}(f) = h_S \circ f$. Then, $\mathrm{supp}(f)$ coincides with the function defined by WCFG $G' = (V, \Sigma, P, I, \mathrm{wt}')$ over $\mathbb{B}$ where $\mathrm{wt}'(p) = h_S(\mathrm{wt}(p))$. Let $G'' = (V, \Sigma, P, I)$ be the underlying CFG of G. Since S is positive,

$$[\![G]\!](w) \neq 0 \iff \mathrm{supp}([\![G]\!])(w) = 1 \iff w \in L(G'').$$

A WCFG G over S is *unambiguous* (U-WCFG) if $|\text{parse}(w)| \leq 1$ for all $w \in \Sigma^*$. G is *finitely-ambiguous* (FA-WCFG) if there exists $m \in \mathbb{N}$ such that $|\text{parse}(w)| \leq m$ for all $w \in \Sigma^*$. G is *polynomially-ambiguous* (PA-WCFG) if there exists a polynomial $p(\cdot)$ such that $|\text{parse}(w)| \leq p(|w|)$ for all $w \in \Sigma^*$.

Fix a semiring S and assume that S is positive. We define U-WCF, FA-WCF, PA-WCF and WCF as the classes of functions defined by U-WCFG, FA-WCFG, PA-WCFG and WCFG over S, respectively. Clearly, U-WCF $\subseteq$ FA-WCF $\subseteq$ PA-WCF $\subseteq$ WCF. Furthermore, we define U-CF $= \{f \mid \exists$ U-WCFG G over $\mathbb{B}. \text{supp}(f) = [\![G]\!]\}$. That is, U-CF is the class of functions whose supports are defined by some U-WCFG over $\mathbb{B}$. In this paper, we fix the semiring S to $\mathbb{N}_{\min,+}$ when we refer to these classes of functions.

Example 1. Let $G_1 = (\{I\}, \{a, b\}, P, I, \text{wt})$ where $P = \{$

$$I \rightarrow aIa \mid bIb \quad \text{(weight : 1)},$$
$$I \rightarrow \varepsilon \quad \text{(weight : 0)} \quad \}.$$

G_1 is a WCFG over $\mathbb{N}_{\min,+}$ and the function f_{EX1} defined by G_1 is

$$f_{\text{EX1}}(w') = \begin{cases} |w| & w' = ww^R, \\ \infty & \text{otherwise}. \end{cases}$$

Clearly G_1 is unambiguous, and hence $f_{\text{EX1}} \in$ U-WCF.

Example 2. Let $G_2 = (\{I, A, B\}, \{a, b\}, P, I, \text{wt})$ where $P = \{$

$$I \rightarrow A \mid B \quad \text{(weight : 0)},$$
$$A \rightarrow aAa \quad \text{(weight : 1)}, \quad A \rightarrow bAb \mid \varepsilon \quad \text{(weight : 0)},$$
$$B \rightarrow bBb \quad \text{(weight : 1)}, \quad B \rightarrow aBa \mid \varepsilon \quad \text{(weight : 0)} \quad \}.$$

G_2 is a WCFG over $\mathbb{N}_{\min,+}$, and the function f_{EX2} defined by G_2 is

$$f_{\text{EX2}}(w') = \begin{cases} \min\{|w|_a, |w|_b\} & w' = ww^R, \\ \infty & \text{otherwise}. \end{cases}$$

G_2 is finitely-ambiguous because there are two parse trees of w' if w' is a palindrome. One of them counts the number of letter a using nonterminal A, and the other counts the number of letter b using nonterminal B. Hence, $f_{\text{EX2}} \in$ FA-WCF.

Example 3. Let $G_3 = (\{A, B\}, \{a, b, \$\}, P, B, \text{wt})$ where $P = \{$

$$B \rightarrow aBa \mid A \mid \$\$ \quad \text{(weight : 0)}, \quad B \rightarrow bBb \quad \text{(weight : 1)},$$
$$A \rightarrow bAb \mid \$\$ \quad \text{(weight : 0)}, \quad A \rightarrow aAa \quad \text{(weight : 1)} \quad \}.$$

G_3 is a WCFG over $\mathbb{N}_{\min,+}$, and the function f_{EX3} defined by G_3 is

$$f_{\text{EX3}}(w') = \begin{cases} \min_{0 \leq i \leq n}\{|a_1 \cdots a_i|_b + |a_{i+1} \cdots a_n|_a\} & w' = ww^R, w = a_1 a_2 \cdots a_n\$, \\ \infty & \text{otherwise}. \end{cases}$$

For a palindrome $w' = ww^R$, G_3 counts the number of letter b using nonterminal B, and counts the number of letter a using nonterminal A. G_3 has a choice when to start counting a. Hence, G_3 is polynomially-ambiguous and $f_{\text{EX3}} \in$ PA-WCF.

Example 4. Let $G_4 = (\{I, A, B\}, \{a, b, \#, \$\}, P, I, \mathrm{wt})$ where $P = \{$

$$
\begin{array}{llll}
I \to A \mid B \mid \$\$ & \text{(weight : 0)}, & & \\
A \to aAa & \text{(weight : 1)}, & A \to bAb \mid \#I\# & \text{(weight : 0)}, \\
B \to bBb & \text{(weight : 1)}, & B \to aBa \mid \#I\# & \text{(weight : 0)} \quad \}.
\end{array}
$$

G_4 is a WCFG over $\mathbb{N}_{\min,+}$ and the function f_{EX4} defined by G_4 is

$$
f_{\mathrm{EX4}}(w') = \begin{cases} \sum_{1 \le i \le n} \min\{|w_i|_a, |w_i|_b\} & w' = ww^R,\ w = w_1\#w_2\#\cdots w_n\#\$, \\ \infty & \text{otherwise} . \end{cases}
$$

For a palindrome $w' = ww^R$, G_4 counts the number of letter a or letter b in w_i. For each i $(1 \le i \le n)$, G_4 has a choice whether to count the number of a in w_i using nonterminal A or to count the number of b in w_i using nonterminal B. Hence, G_4 is not polynomially-ambiguous.

Example 5. Let $G_5 = (\{I\}, \{a, b\}, P, I, \mathrm{wt})$ where $P = \{I \to aIa \mid bIb \mid \varepsilon\}$ and $\mathrm{wt}(p) = 1$ for all $p \in P$. G_5 is a WCFG over $\mathbb{B}$ and the underlying CFG of G_5 is $G_5' = (\{I\}, \{a, b\}, P, I)$. The function f_{EX5} defined by G_5 satisfies $f_{\mathrm{EX5}}(w') = 1$ iff $w' = ww^R$. Furthermore, $\mathrm{supp}(f_{\mathrm{EX1}}) = \mathrm{supp}(f_{\mathrm{EX2}}) = f_{\mathrm{EX5}}$. Clearly G_5 is unambiguous, and hence $f_{\mathrm{EX1}}, f_{\mathrm{EX2}}, f_{\mathrm{EX5}} \in$ U-CF. We can also show that $f_{\mathrm{EX3}}, f_{\mathrm{EX4}} \in$ U-CF by considering variants of G_5.

3   An Extended Ogden's Lemma

In this section, we give an extension of Ogden's lemma, which is useful for proving the main results of this paper. We first review Ogden's lemma. The original Ogden's lemma in [8] is a statement for a word w, but we slightly extend it to a statement for a word w and a parse tree T of w. It is clear from the proof of Ogden's lemma in [8] that this extension also holds.

Lemma 1 (Ogden's Lemma [8]). *For each CFG $G = (V, \Sigma, P, I)$, there exists a constant $N \in \mathbb{N}$ that satisfies the following condition :*

Let w be any word in $L(G)$ and T be any parse tree of w in G. For any way to mark at least N positions in w as distinguished, there exist $A \in V$ and $u, v, x, y, z \in \Sigma^*$ such that
- *T can be represented as $I \Rightarrow^* uAz \Rightarrow^* uvAyz \Rightarrow^* uvxyz = w$,*
- *x has at least one of the distinguished positions,*
- *Either u and v both have distinguished positions, or y and z both have distinguished positions, and*
- *vxy has at most N distinguished positions.*

$\square$

We define the relation $\sqsubseteq_w \subseteq (\Sigma^*)^3 \times (\Sigma^*)^3$ as follows: for a word $w = uvx = \lambda\mu\nu \in \Sigma^*$, $(u, v, x) \sqsubseteq_w (\lambda, \mu, \nu)$ if there exist words $\lambda', \nu' \in \Sigma^*$ such that $\mu = \lambda'v\nu'$, $\lambda\lambda' = u$, $\nu'\nu = x$. If $(u, v, x) \sqsubseteq_w (\lambda, \mu, \nu)$ where the word w and the partitions $w = uvx = \lambda\mu\nu$ are clear or not relevant, we say that μ *contains* v.

Lemma 2. *Let $G = (V, \Sigma, P, I)$ be a CFG and L be the language defined by G. There exists a constant $N \in \mathbb{N}$ that satisfies the following condition :*

Let $w = \lambda\mu\nu \in \Sigma^*$ be any word such that $w \in L$ and $|\mu| \geq N$. For every parse tree T of w, there exist $A \in V$ and $u, v, x, y, z \in \Sigma^*$ such that T can be represented as

$$I \Rightarrow^* uAz \Rightarrow^* uvAyz \Rightarrow^* uvxyz = w \ ,$$

and the following (i) or (ii) holds.
(i) $1 \leq |v| < N$ and μ contains v, i.e., $(u, v, xyz) \sqsubseteq_w (\lambda, \mu, \nu)$.
(ii) $1 \leq |y| < N$ and μ contains y, i.e., $(uvx, y, z) \sqsubseteq_w (\lambda, \mu, \nu)$.

Proof. The above property can be obtained by applying Lemma 1, by letting all letters in μ be distinguished positions. □

Lemma 2 states that every word $w \in L$ having a sufficiently long subword μ can be divided as $w = uvxyz$ such that μ contains one of v and y. We call such a pair (v, y) a pump in w.

As stated in the next theorem, Lemma 2 can be generalized in such a way that if a word $w \in L$ has $2n$ long subwords $\mu_1, \ldots, \mu_{2n}$, then w has n pumps (v_i, y_i) $(1 \leq i \leq n)$ such that some n subwords out of $\mu_1, \ldots, \mu_{2n}$ either contains the left subwords v_i $(1 \leq i \leq n)$ or the right subwords y_i $(1 \leq i \leq n)$. This generalization is essential for proving the existence of a function not in FA-WCF (Theorem 2) and a function not in PA-WCF (Theorem 3).

Lemma 3. *Let $G = (V, \Sigma, P, I)$ be a CFG and L be the language generated by G. There exists a constant $N \in \mathbb{N}$ that satisfies the following condition :*

Let $w = \lambda_1 \cdot \mu_1 \cdot \lambda_2 \cdot \mu_2 \cdot \cdots \cdot \lambda_{2n} \cdot \mu_{2n} \cdot \lambda_{2n+1} \in \Sigma^*$ be any word such that $w \in L$ and $|\mu_1|, \ldots, |\mu_{2n}| \geq N$. For every parse tree T of w, there are subderivations $A_i \Rightarrow^* v_i A_i y_i$ of T where $A_i \in V$, $v_i, y_i \in \Sigma^*$ for each i $(1 \leq i \leq n)$ such that there exists a monotone injection $g : \{1, \ldots, n\} \to \{1, \ldots, 2n\}$ and the following (i) or (ii) holds.
(i) For each i $(1 \leq i \leq n)$, $1 \leq |v_i| < N$ and $\mu_{g(i)}$ contains v_i.
(ii) For each i $(1 \leq i \leq n)$, $1 \leq |y_i| < N$ and $\mu_{g(i)}$ contains y_i.

Proof. Let N be a constant in Lemma 2 and λ'_j, ν'_j be $\lambda'_j = \lambda_1\mu_1 \cdots \lambda_j$, $\nu'_j = \lambda_{j+1}\mu_{j+1} \cdots \lambda_{2n+1}$ for each j $(1 \leq j \leq 2n)$ (see Fig. 2). By applying Lemma 2 to $w = \lambda'_j\mu_j\nu'_j$ (note that $|\mu_j| \geq N$) and a parse tree of w, we obtain that there is a subderivation $A_j \Rightarrow^* v_j A_j y_j$ of T, and (i') μ_j contains v_j such that $1 \leq |v_j| < N$ or (ii') μ_j contains y_j such that $1 \leq |y_j| < N$. Since we have $2n$ subwords $\mu_1, \ldots, \mu_{2n}$ that do not pairwise overlap in w, there exist $j_1, j_2, \cdots, j_n$ $(1 \leq j_1 < j_2 < \cdots < j_n \leq 2n)$ such that the following (i) or (ii) holds.

(i) For each j_i $(1 \leq i \leq n)$, μ_{j_i} contains v_{j_i}.
(ii) For each j_i $(1 \leq i \leq n)$, μ_{j_i} contains y_{j_i}.

Let $A_i = A_{j_i}$, $v_i = v_{j_i}$, $y_i = y_{j_i}$ and define the injection g as $g(i) = j_i$, then the claim of the theorem holds. □

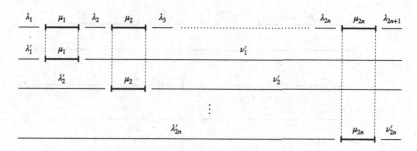

Fig. 2. Illustration for the proof of Lemma 3

4 An Ambiguity Hierarchy of WCFG over $\mathbb{N}_{\min,+}$

The purpose of this paper is to prove a strict ambiguity hierarchy caused by introducing weights. Namely, we would like to prove that there exists a function in (U-CF∩FA-WCF)\U-WCF (resp. a function in (U-CF∩PA-WCF)\FA-WCF, a function in (U-CF∩WCF)\PA-WCF). We use f_{EX2} (resp. f_{EX3}, f_{EX4}) as such a function that exists in the gap. We already know that $f_{\text{EX2}} \in$ U-CF $\cap$ FA-WCF (resp. $f_{\text{EX3}} \in$ U-CF $\cap$ PA-WCF, $f_{\text{EX4}} \in$ U-CF $\cap$ WCF) by Example 2 (resp. Example 3, Example 4) and Example 5. Therefore, we just need to prove $f_{\text{EX2}} \notin$ U-WCF (resp. $f_{\text{EX3}} \notin$ FA-WCF, $f_{\text{EX4}} \notin$ PA-WCF).

To prove them, we use Lemma 3. Note that $\mathbb{N}_{\min,+}$ is a positive semiring (see Sect. 2.1), and hence $[\![G]\!](w) \neq \infty$ iff $w \in L(G'')$ where G is a WCFG over $\mathbb{N}_{\min,+}$ and G'' is the underlying CFG of G. Therefore, Lemma 3 can be applied to WCFG over $\mathbb{N}_{\min,+}$, by regarding "Let $G = (V, \Sigma, P, I)$ be a CFG and L be the language generated by G" as "Let $G = (V, \Sigma, P, I, \text{wt})$ be a WCFG over $\mathbb{N}_{\min,+}$ and f be the function defined by G" and "$w \in L$" as "$f(w) \neq \infty$".

Theorem 1. $f_{\text{EX2}} \notin$ *U-WCF.*

Proof. We suppose that f_{EX2} can be defined by an unambiguous WCFG $G = (V, \Sigma, P, I, \text{wt})$ and let N be a constant in Lemma 3. Consider the word $w = b^N a^{N+1} a^{N+1} b^N$. Clearly, w is a palindrome and $f_{\text{EX2}}(w) = N$. Let T be a parse tree of w such that $\text{wt}(T) = N$.

Let us apply Lemma 3 to w and T by letting $n = 1$ and $w = \lambda_1 \mu_1 \lambda_2 \mu_2 \lambda_3$ where $\lambda_1 = \lambda_3 = \varepsilon$, $\mu_1 = \mu_2 = b^N$ and $\lambda_2 = a^{N+1} a^{N+1}$. Then, T can be written as $I \Rightarrow^* uAz \overset{c}{\Rightarrow}^* uvAyz \Rightarrow^* uvxyz = w$ for some $A \in V$ and $u, v, x, y, z \in \Sigma^*$, and one of the following four conditions holds: (i-1) μ_1 contains v, or (i-2) μ_2 contains v, or (ii-1) μ_1 contains y, or (ii-2) μ_2 contains y (see Fig. 3). We examine these four cases.

The case (i-2) contradicts the definition of f_{EX2}. This is because $w_2 = uvvxyyz = b^N a^{N+1} a^{N+1} b^{N'}$ $(N' > N)$ has a parse tree whose weight is $N + c$ but $f_{\text{EX2}}(uvvxyyz) = \infty$ since w_2 is not a palindrome. The case (ii-1) is not possible by a similar reason to (i-2).

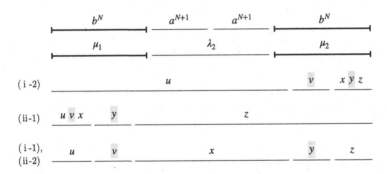

Fig. 3. Case analysis for the proof of Theorem 1

If (i-1) holds, it follows that $v = y = b^k$ $(1 \le k < N)$ and μ_2 contains y because, by the definition of f_{EX2}, $f_{\text{EX2}}(w) \ne \infty$ iff w is a palindrome. If (ii-2) holds, $v = y = b^k$ $(1 \le k < N)$ and μ_1 contains v by the same reason as in the case (i-1). For these subcases (i-1) and (ii-2), consider the parse tree T' of $w' = uv^3xy^3z = b^{N+2k}a^{N+1}a^{N+1}b^{N+2k}$, which is constructed by pumping the subderivation $A \overset{c}{\Rightarrow}^* vAy$ in T twice. Apparently, $\text{wt}(T') = N + 2c$. Because $k \ge 1$, $N + 1 = f_{\text{EX2}}(w') \ne \text{wt}(T')$ for any $c \in \mathbb{N}$. Hence, there exists a parse tree of w' whose weight is $N + 1$. Therefore, $|\text{parse}(w')| \ge 2$, but it contradicts the assumption that G is unambiguous. □

Remark 1. We used a WCFG that generates palindromes to prove Theorem 1, but the technique can be applied to other WCFG. For example, we consider the following function f'_{EX2} defined by FA-WCFG :

$$f'_{\text{EX2}}(w) = \begin{cases} \min\{|w|_{[}, |w|_{\langle}\} & w \in \text{Dyck}([\,], \langle\rangle) \\ \infty & \text{otherwise} \end{cases}$$

where $\text{Dyck}([\,], \langle\rangle)$ is Dyck language consisting of two types of brackets $[\,]$ and $\langle\rangle$. We can prove that f'_{EX2} is not in U-WCF using the word $\langle^N[^{N+1}]^{N+1}\rangle^N$ as well. For Theorems 2 and 3 below, we also use palindromes for simplicity.

Every non-empty (even) palindrome can be written as ww^R where $w = a_1^{n_1}a_2^{n_2}\cdots a_k^{n_k}$, $n_j \ge 1$ for each j $(1 \le j \le k)$ and $a_j \ne a_{j+1}$ for each j $(1 \le j < k)$. We call each $a_j^{n_j}$ a *block* in w. We say that $a_j^{n_j}$ in w and $a_j^{n_j}$ in w^R forms a *symmetrical block pair* of ww^R.

To prove Theorems 2 and 3 below, we show a pumping lemma for CFL that contain only palindromes. Lemma 4 states that if a parse tree T of a palindrome with distinct central positions such as $w\$\$w^R$ where $w \in (\Sigma - \{\$\})^*$ has pumps (v_i, y_i), T must consist of only linear recursions of nonterminals and v_i, y_i are contained in a symmetrical block pair, respectively. This is a generalization of the case analysis in the proof of Theorem 1.

Lemma 4. *Let $G = (V, \Sigma, P, I)$ be a CFG that generates only palindromes, and Σ is divided as $\Sigma = \Gamma \cup \Delta \cup \Omega$ with Γ, Δ, Ω pairwise disjoint. There exists a constant $N \in \mathbb{N}$ that satisfies the following condition :*

Let $ww^R = \lambda_1 \cdot \mu_1 \cdot \lambda_2 \cdot \mu_2 \cdots \lambda_{2n} \cdot \mu_{2n} \cdot \lambda_{2n+1} \in L(G)$ where $|\mu_i| \geq N$, $\mu_i = \mu_{2n+1-i} \in a^*$ with some $a \in \Gamma$, $\lambda_{2n-i+2} = (\lambda_i)^R \in \Delta^*$ for every i $(1 \leq i \leq n)$ and $\lambda_{n+1} \in \Omega^+$ is a palindrome. For every parse tree T of ww^R, there are subderivations $A_i \Rightarrow^* v_i A_i y_i$ of T where $A_i \in V$, $v_i, y_i \in \Sigma^*$ for each i $(1 \leq i \leq n)$ such that

(1) $1 \leq |v_i| < N$ and μ_i contains v_i.
(2) $v_i = y_i$, and
(3) v_i and y_i are contained in a symmetrical block pair of ww^R.

Proof. Let N be a constant in Lemma 2. By applying Lemma 2 to the assumed CFG G in the same way as the proof in Lemma 3, there are subderivations $A_i \Rightarrow^* v_i A_i y_i$ of T where (i') μ_i contains v_i such that $1 \leq |v_i| < N$ or (ii') μ_i contains y_i such that $1 \leq |y_i| < N$, for each i $(1 \leq i \leq 2n)$.

If (ii') holds for some $i \leq n$, then T can be represented as $I \Rightarrow^* uA_i z\lambda_{n+1} z' \Rightarrow^* uv_i A_i y_i z\lambda_{n+1} z' \Rightarrow^* uv_i xy_i z\lambda_{n+1} z' = ww^R$ for some $u, x, z, z' \in \Sigma^*$. Note that $\lambda_{n+1} \in \Omega^*$, $uv_i xy_i z, z' \in (\Gamma \cup \Delta)^*$ and $y_i \neq \varepsilon$, contradicting the assumption that G generates only palindromes. Therefore, (i') holds for every i $(1 \leq i \leq n)$. That is, (1) $1 \leq |v_i| < N$ and μ_i contains v_i for every i $(1 \leq i \leq n)$. Furthermore, we can show the following in the same way as the proof of Theorem 1. Subderivations $A_i \Rightarrow^* v_i A_i y_i$ satisfy the conditions (2) and (3) for each i $(1 \leq i \leq n)$, otherwise, G can generate non palindromes by pumping (v_i, y_i). $\qquad\square$

Theorem 2. $f_{\mathrm{EX3}} \notin FA\text{-}WCF$.

Proof. We suppose that f_{EX3} can be defined by a WCFG $G = (V, \Sigma, P, I, \mathrm{wt})$ such that there exists $m \in \mathbb{N}$ and $|\mathrm{parse}(w)| \leq m - 1$ for all $w \in \Sigma^*$. Let N be a constant in Lemma 4. For each ℓ $(1 \leq \ell \leq m)$, consider the word

$$w_\ell = \alpha_1 \beta_1 \alpha_2 \beta_2 \cdots \alpha_m \beta_m \$\$ \beta_{m+1} \alpha_{m+1} \cdots \beta_{2m-1} \alpha_{2m-1} \beta_{2m} \alpha_{2m}$$

where

$$(\alpha_j, \beta_j) = \begin{cases} (a^{N(m \cdot N! + 1)}, b^{N(m \cdot N! + 1)}) & j = \ell, 2m - \ell + 1, \\ (a^N, b^N) & \text{otherwise}, \end{cases}$$

for each j $(1 \leq j \leq 2m)$. Note that w_ℓ is a palindrome. We include long subwords $a^{N(m \cdot N! + 1)}$ in w_ℓ by the following reason. Below we will show that there are pumps (a^{k_i}, a^{k_i}) and (b^{k_i}, b^{k_i}) where $k_i < N$ $(1 \leq i \leq 2m(1 + N!))$. We would like to obtain an identical word of the form (*3) below from multiple w_ℓ for different ℓ by repeating some of the above pumps depending on ℓ.

By the definition of f_{EX3}, the value $f_{\mathrm{EX3}}(w_\ell)$ is obtained when we divide w_ℓ into $\alpha_1 \beta_1 \alpha_2 \beta_2 \cdots \beta_{\ell-1} \alpha_\ell$ and $\beta_\ell \alpha_{\ell+1} \beta_{\ell+1} \alpha_{\ell+2} \cdots \alpha_m \beta_m \$$. Hence, $f_{\mathrm{EX3}}(w_\ell) = |\alpha_1 \beta_1 \alpha_2 \beta_2 \cdots \beta_{\ell-1} \alpha_\ell|_b + |\beta_\ell \alpha_{\ell+1} \beta_{\ell+1} \alpha_{\ell+2} \cdots \alpha_m \beta_m|_a = (\ell - 1)N + (m - \ell)N = (m - 1)N$. Let T_ℓ be a parse tree of w_ℓ such that $\mathrm{wt}(T_\ell) = (m - 1)N$.

Let us apply Lemma 4 to w_ℓ and T_ℓ by letting $n = 2m(1 + N!)$, $\Gamma = \{a, b\}$, $\Delta = \emptyset$, $\Omega = \{\$\}$ and $\mu_1, \cdots, \mu_{2n} \in \{a^N, b^N\}$, $\lambda_1 = \cdots = \lambda_n = \varepsilon$, $\lambda_{n+2} = \cdots = \lambda_{2n+1} = \varepsilon$, $\lambda_{n+1} = \$\$$ (*1). Then, there are subderivations $A_i \Rightarrow^* v_i A_i y_i$ of T_ℓ where $A_i \in V$, $v_i, y_i \in \Sigma^*$ for each i $(1 \leq i \leq n)$ (*2) such that $1 \leq |v_i| \leq N$, μ_i contains v_i, $v_i = y_i = a^{k_i}$ (or b^{k_i}), and α_{2m-j+1} (or β_{2m-j+1}) contains y_i if α_j (or β_j) contains v_i.

Consider $A_i \overset{c_i}{\Rightarrow^*} v_i A_i y_i$ such that v_i is contained in α_ℓ among the subderivations mentioned in (*2). There are exactly $m \cdot N! + 1$ of such subderivations by the following reason. We have $\alpha_\ell = a^{N(m \cdot N!+1)}$ and by the assumption (*1), α_ℓ is the concatenation of some μ_i of length N and hence the number of such μ_i is exactly $m \cdot N! + 1$. Since $\mathrm{wt}(T_\ell) = (m-1)N < m \cdot N! + 1$ and $c_i \in \mathbb{N}$, there is at least one i such that $c_i = 0$. (Otherwise, $\mathrm{wt}(T_\ell)$ would be greater than or equal to $m \cdot N! + 1$.) For any i such that $c_i = 0$, $v_i = y_i = a^{k_i}$ in α_ℓ can be pumped with weight 0. The same property holds for $v_i = b^{k_i}$ contained in β_ℓ.

Next, we consider $v_i = y_i = a^{k_i}$ (resp. $v_i = y_i = b^{k_i}$) that is not contained in $\alpha_\ell, \alpha_{2n-\ell+1}$ (resp. $\beta_\ell, \beta_{2n-\ell+1}$). Note that $k_i (< N)$ must be a devisor of $m \cdot N!$ and all pumps (v_i, y_i) are nested each other on T_ℓ. Hence we can construct a parse tree T'_ℓ of $w' =$

$$\underbrace{a^{N(m \cdot N!+1)} b^{N(m \cdot N!+1)} \cdots b^{N(m \cdot N!+1)}}_{m} \$\$ \underbrace{b^{N(m \cdot N!+1)} \cdots b^{N(m \cdot N!+1)} a^{N(m \cdot N!+1)}}_{m}$$

$$(*3)$$

by pumping subderivations in T_l.

We now consider two parse trees T'_{ℓ_1}, T'_{ℓ_2} of w' $(1 \leq \ell_1 < \ell_2 \leq m)$. Note that T'_{ℓ_1} can pump subwords a^{k_1} contained in ℓ_1-th $a^{N(m \cdot N!+1)}$ and $b^{k'_1}$ contained in ℓ_1-th $b^{N(m \cdot N!+1)}$ with weight 0, while T'_{ℓ_2} can pump subwords a^{k_2} contained in ℓ_2-th $a^{N(m \cdot N!+1)}$ and $b^{k'_2}$ contained in ℓ_2-th $b^{N(m \cdot N!+1)}$ with weight 0. By the definition of f_{EX3}, the value of f_{EX3} increases if subwords $a^{k_1}, b^{k'_1}, a^{k_2}, b^{k'_2}$ can be all pumped simultaneously. If $T'_{\ell_1} = T'_{\ell_2}$, then this simultaneous pump does not increase the weight, which is a contradiction. Hence, T'_{ℓ_1} and T'_{ℓ_2} are different trees. Thus, $T_1, T_2, \cdots, T_m$ are pairwise different and $|\mathrm{parse}(w')| \geq m$. However, this contradicts the assumption that the ambiguity of G is at most $m - 1$. $\square$

Remark 2. In the proof of Theorem 2, we said that some $v_i = a^{k_i}$ contained in α_ℓ can be pumped with weight 0, but we can also say that every v_i contained in α_ℓ can be pumped with weight 0. That is because, if a subword of α_ℓ is generated by a derivation $A_i \overset{c_i}{\Rightarrow^*} a^{k_i} A_i a^{k_i} \Rightarrow^* a^{k_i} a^k A_j a^k a^{k_i} \overset{c_j}{\Rightarrow^*} a^{k_i} a^k a^{k_j} A_j a^{k_j} a^k a^{k_i}$ (with pairwise different subderivations $A_i \overset{c_i}{\Rightarrow^*} a^{k_i} A_i a^{k_i}$ and $A_j \overset{c_j}{\Rightarrow^*} a^{k_j} A_j a^{k_j}$), there are 2^n ways to derive $a^{(k_i+k_j)n+k}$. This contradicts the assumption that G is finitely-ambiguous. Therefore, all $v_i = a^{k_i}$ contained in α_ℓ are generated by the same subderivation. This remark also holds for the proof in Theorem 3.

We can prove that $f_{\mathrm{EX4}} \notin$ PA-WCF in a similar way to the proof of Theorem 2.

Theorem 3. $f_{EX4} \notin PA\text{-}WCF$.

Corollary 1. $U\text{-}WCF \subsetneq FA\text{-}WCF \subsetneq PA\text{-}WCF \subsetneq WCF$. Furthermore, $(U\text{-}WCF \cap U\text{-}CF) \subsetneq (FA\text{-}WCF \cap U\text{-}CF) \subsetneq (PA\text{-}WCF \cap U\text{-}CF) \subsetneq (WCF \cap U\text{-}CF)$.

5 Conclusion

We proved a pumping lemma for CFG, which is helpful for demonstrating an iteration without increasing weights, and showed the strict ambiguity hierarchy of WCFG. Since the functions proved to exist in the gaps are all in U-CF, this hierarchy is different from the ambiguity hierarchy of CFG known as inherent ambiguity. In other words, the hierarchy shown to exist in this paper is caused by introducing weights.

We defined U-CF as the class of functions whose supports are defined by some U-WCFG over $\mathbb{B}$. Similarly, we can define FA-CF and PA-CF as the classes of functions whose supports are defined by some FA-WCFG over $\mathbb{B}$ and some PA-WCFG over $\mathbb{B}$, respectively. For these classes, we expect to prove the inclusion $(FA\text{-}WCF \cap FA\text{-}CF) \subsetneq (PA\text{-}WCF \cap FA\text{-}CF) \subsetneq (WCF \cap FA\text{-}CF)$ and $(PA\text{-}WCF \cap PA\text{-}CF) \subsetneq (WCF \cap PA\text{-}CF)$ in the same way.

The discussion on the ambiguity hierarchy of WA in [1,7] is generalized by using pumping lemmas that correspond to each hierarchy level. Showing similar pumping lemmas for U-WCFG, FA-WCFG and PA-WCFG is left as future work. However, showing them seems difficult because the expressive power of WCFG cannot be determined by a simple iteration property, as explained in Sect. 1.

The techniques in Theorems 1, 2 and 3 could be applied to other weighted models and other semirings. In particular, Remark 2 is useful. For example, if there are n of the same subderivations $A \overset{c}{\Rightarrow}{}^* vAy$ and $f(w) = W$, then c must be smaller than or equal to $W^{1/n}$ for WCFG over the semiring $(\mathbb{N} \cup \{\infty\}, +, \times, 0, 1)$ of natural numbers.

References

1. Chattopadhyay, A., Mazowiecki, F., Muscholl, A., Riveros, C.: Pumping Lemmas for Weighted Automata, CoRR abs/2001.06272 (2020)
2. Chomsky, N., Schützenberger, M.P.: The algebraic theory of context-free languages. Stud. Logic Found. Math. **26**, 118–161 (1959)
3. M. Droste, W. Kuich and H. Vogler, Handbook of Weighted Automata, Springer Science & Business Media, Berlin (2009). https://doi.org/10.1007/978-3-642-01492-5
4. Durbin, R., Eddy, S.R., Krogh, A., Mitchison, G.: Biological Sequence Analysis: Probabilistic Models of Proteins and Nucleic Acids, Cambridge University Press, Cambridge (1998)
5. Hopcroft, J.E., Ullman, J.D.: Introduction to Automata Theory, Languages, and Computation, Addison-Wesley, Boston (1979)
6. Maletti, A., Nasz, T., Stier, K., Ulbricht, M.: Ambiguity hierarchies for weighted tree automata. In: Maneth, S. (ed.) CIAA 2021. LNCS, vol. 12803, pp. 140–151. Springer, Cham (2021). https://doi.org/10.1007/978-3-030-79121-6_12

7. Mazowiecki, F., Riveros, C.: Pumping lemmas for weighted automata. STACS **50**(1–50), 14 (2018)
8. Ogden, W.: A helpful result for proving inherent ambiguity. Math. Syst. Theor. **2**(3), 191–194 (1968)
9. Wich, K.: Exponential Ambiguity of Context-free Grammars, DLT 1999, pp. 125–138 (1999)

Author Index

Printed in the United States
by Baker & Taylor Publisher Services